Managing
Organizational
DEVIANCE

Managing
Organizational
DEVIANCE

EDITORS

Roland E. Kidwell, Jr.
Niagara University

Christopher L. Martin
Centenary College of Louisiana

SAGE Publications
Thousand Oaks ▪ London ▪ New Delhi

For information:

Sage Publications, Inc.
2455 Teller Road
Thousand Oaks, California 91320
E-mail: order@sagepub.com

Sage Publications Ltd.
1 Oliver's Yard
55 City Road
London EC1Y 1SP
United Kingdom

Sage Publications India Pvt. Ltd.
B-42, Panchsheel Enclave
Post Box 4109
New Delhi 110 017 India

Printed in the United States of America

Library of Congress Cataloging-in-Publication Data

Managing organizational deviance / edited by Roland E. Kidwell Jr. and Christopher L. Martin.
     p. cm.
Includes bibliographical references and index.
ISBN 0-7619-3013-2 (cloth) — ISBN 0-7619-3014-0 (pbk.)
  1. Organizational behavior. 2. Deviant behavior. 3. Personnel management.
I. Kidwell, Roland E. II. Martin, Christopher L.
HD58.7.M363 2005
658.3'14—dc22

                       2004018460

This book is printed on acid-free paper.

04   05   06   10 9 8 7 6 5 4 3 2 1

Acquisitions Editor:	Al Bruckner
Editorial Assistant:	MaryAnn Vail
Copy Editor:	D. J. Peck
Production Editor:	Diane S. Foster
Typesetter:	C&M Digitals (P) Ltd.
Proofreader:	Libby Larson
Indexer:	Jeanne R. Busemeyer
Cover Designer:	Janet Foulger

Contents

Tables and Figures   vii

Preface   ix

Acknowledgments   xvii

1. The Prevalence (and Ambiguity) of   1
    Deviant Behavior at Work: An Overview
    Roland E. Kidwell, Jr., and Christopher L. Martin

        Case 1.1. Columbia/HCA Health Care   23
        Case 1.2. The Undercover Operator   31
        Anita Mancuso and Timothy O. Ireland

2. Why Good Employees Make   39
    Unethical Decisions: The Role of Reward Systems,
    Organizational Culture, and Managerial Oversight
    Jennifer Dunn and Maurice E. Schweitzer

        Case 2. Sears Automotive   61

3. The Role of Leaders in Influencing   69
    Unethical Behavior in the Workplace
    Linda Klebe Treviño and Michael E. Brown

        Case 3. Bernard Ebbers: Innovative   89
                 Leader or Reckless Risk Taker

4. Badmouthing the Company: Bitter   97
    Employee or Concerned Corporate Citizen?
    Robert J. Bies and Thomas M. Tripp

        Case 4. Web Revenge on HealthSouth Corporation   109

5. Withholding Effort at Work: 113
    Understanding and Preventing Shirking,
    Job Neglect, Social Loafing, and Free Riding
    Nathan Bennett and Stefanie E. Naumann

        Case 5. The Low-Quality Loafers   127

6. **Managing Noncompliance in the Workplace**   **131**
    Danielle E. Warren

    Case 6. Noncompliance at Dow Chemical   151

7. **The Difficulties of Telling the Truth at Work**   **157**
    Steven L. Grover

    Case 7.1. George O'Leary's Résumé   173
    Case 7.2. Janet Cooke and the *Washington Post*   178

8. **Bullying and Harassment in the Workplace**   **183**
    Gina Vega and Debra R. Comer

    Case 8. Nurse Cassidy's Dilemma   205
    Julie Ann Cogin

9. **Discouraging Employee Theft by Managing**   **211**
    Social Norms and Promoting Organizational Justice
    Edward C. Tomlinson and Jerald Greenberg

    Case 9. The Purloined Passwords   233

10. **Managing Organizational Aggression**   **237**
    Mark J. Martinko, Scott C. Douglas, Paul Harvey,
    and Charles Joseph

    Case 10. Disney or Bust   261

11. **Addictive Behavior in the Workplace**   **265**
    Paul M. Roman

    Case 11. Gambling at Amyfixe: Reality and Fantasy   281

12. **"I Deserve More Because My Name**   **287**
    Is on the Door": Entitlement, Embeddedness,
    and Employee Deviance in the Family Business
    Rebecca J. Bennett, Stefan Thau, and Jay Scouten

    Case 12. Adelphia Communications and the Rigas Family   301

13. **Organizational Deviance and**   **309**
    Culture: Oversights and Intentions
    Linda Thorne and Joanne Jones

    Case 13. The Bob Smith Affair   329
    Skye Susans and Alan J. Fish

Name Index   **335**

Subject Index   **343**

About the Editors   **351**

About the Contributors   **353**

Tables and Figures

Table 1.1   Terms and Definitions Used When Discussing
Undesirable Workplace Behavior   6

Table 1.2   Examples of the Ambiguity of "Deviant" Behavior   10

Figure 2.1 Theory of Planned Behavior   42

Figure 2.2 Managerial Influence on Ethical Decision Making
(based on theory of planned behavior)   44

Table 4.1   The Stakeholder Framework for Analyzing Revenge   102

Table 6.1   Types of Noncompliance   145

Figure 9.1 Theft Rates as a Function of Conditions in the
Field Experiment by Greenberg (1990)   221

Figure 10.1 A Model of Organizational Aggression   241

Table 12.1 Social Context and Employee Deviance   290

Table 12.2 Organizational Policies to Prevent Deviance in Family Business 295

Table 13.1 Integrated Framework of the Dimensions of National Culture 312

Preface

From a scuffle in a factory break room, to the abuse of an employee by a bullying boss, to a company's financial officers cooking the books, deviant behavior in organizations has created headaches, crises, and ethical challenges for executives, shareholders, employees, and society. Reading the popular press and studying the proliferation of academic research on the topic during the past decade or so, one might conclude that an epidemic of destructive acts committed by employees who intend to harm other individuals or their organizations has taken root in many workplaces. Certainly, the negative impact of deviant behavior at work is considered to be one of the most serious problems facing organizations today (e.g., Bennett & Robinson, 2003; Griffin & O'Leary-Kelly, 2004; Vardi & Weitz, 2004).

It is clear that managers at all organizational levels must confront the reasons why deviant behavior occurs with such alarming frequency and must develop strategies to deal with it. To assist students and teachers of management, as well as practicing managers, we have asked leading scholars in the fields of organizational behavior, organization theory, human resources management, and business ethics to offer their informed views on a variety of topics that relate to the general theme of managing organizational deviance effectively and ethically.

This book is designed to address several needs. Although current books of academic- and practitioner-oriented readings concerning deviance and related topics are excellent, they do not include a collection of cases that specifically relate conceptual material to the practice of management and applied ethics. Current works, with some exceptions, generally focus on deviant behavior primarily from either a macro-organizational perspective or a micro-group/individual perspective. Finally, other books on the topic either limit a focus on ethical considerations of deviance or operate under an overriding assumption that deviant behavior is unethical per se.

The approach taken in this book is intended to assist students, teachers, and managers by providing academic grounding and practical guidance to those who face ambiguous manifestations of deviant behavior at work. In examining the causes and types of deviant behavior, deviance is considered in its moral and ethical implications by focusing on organizational contexts, as well as on individual and group behavior, throughout the book's 13 chapters and 15 cases. Contributors also consider specific contexts for examining aberrant behavior—deviance in the family business and deviance viewed across cultural boundaries. A cross-cultural perspective recognizes that classification of a behavior as deviant may depend on the norms of the culture in which it takes place.

Mechanisms, structures, and values practiced within organizations can lead employees to perform some of the unwanted deviant acts discussed throughout this volume. Just as important, some organizational efforts to eliminate deviant behavior and encourage conformity can lead to unwanted consequences—lack of innovation, absence of principled dissent (Graham, 1986), large doses of group-think (Janis, 1982), and organizational silence (which occurs when employees withhold important information about potential problems) (Morrison & Milliken, 2000). Whereas some manifestations of deviant behavior reflect dangerous and potentially destructive acts—workplace violence, theft, fraud, substance abuse, and so forth—other types of deviance can be constructive in that they stimulate change and innovation or are at most unclear in terms of their positive or negative potential (cf. Warren, 2003).

The spate of deviance and its often adverse consequences challenges organizational leaders to act as an ethical force in discouraging inappropriate deviant behavior and encouraging behavior that helps organizations to face changes demanded by increasingly challenging environmental conditions. In dealing with deviance, leaders and managers would do well to consider the roles that structure, values, and processes play in creating deviant behavior and how these organizational features could be used to effectively channel potential deviance into positive outcomes for organizations.

Guide to the Chapters in This Book

Chapter 1, contributed by the editors, provides readers with an overview of deviant behavior in the workplace. The chapter summarizes the pervasive nature of organizational deviance and its destructive impact. Definitions of deviance from previous research are offered and refined, different manifestations of deviance are discussed, and some of the varying academic approaches that have been taken in classifying deviant behavior are reviewed. Then, the potential ambiguity of organizational deviance is considered. Antecedents of unethical and deviant workplace behavior are briefly summarized. In conclusion, a general approach that can be used to manage organizational deviance effectively and ethically is suggested.

Chapters 2 and 3 provide more in-depth theoretical examinations of the causes of deviant behavior in the workplace. Chapter 2, contributed by Jennifer Dunn and Maurice Schweitzer, focuses on relationships of culture, reward systems, and managerial oversight to unethical behavior. The discussion centers on an ethical decision-making model based on the theory of planned behavior. Dunn and Schweitzer describe how three macro-organizational management tools—incentives, culture, and monitoring—operate within this framework and often lead good employees to make bad (unethical) decisions.

The importance of the leader as a moral influence in establishing culture and transmitting ethical values throughout the organization cannot be overestimated. In Chapter 3, Linda Treviño and Michael Brown stress the important role that leaders play in influencing ethical and unethical behavior among their followers. Treviño and Brown examine ethical relationships between leaders and followers from perspectives that include cognitive moral development, social learning, and social exchange and then present the relationships of various leadership styles to ethical behavior and incidents of misconduct in organizations. They then discuss their research into the characteristics of an ethical leader.

Chapters 4 to 11 focus on specific types of deviance, what can lead to such behaviors, and what managers can do to cope with them in the workplace. Viewing some types of deviance, such as theft, violence, and drug abuse, as having anything but negative results for organizations is difficult if not impossible. Although chapter authors and the case studies that accompany each chapter may address issues of underlying workplace norms, perceptual differences in interpreting the same types of behavior, and the ambiguity of deviance, in the main they focus on how to effectively identify, limit, and manage destructive unethical forms of deviant behavior.

We can group specific types of deviance into three general areas based on who is targeted by the behavior (cf. Robinson & Bennett, 1995; Vardi & Weitz, 2004): intrapersonal (within the individual), interpersonal (targeting individuals within the organization), and organizational (targeting the company in terms of production, politics, and/or property deviance). However, these targets often overlap based on the type of deviance that is involved.

One example of this overlap occurs in Chapter 4, where Robert Bies and Thomas Tripp write about organizational revenge in the form of badmouthing, which can be aimed at individuals or at the organization. In providing an overview of revenge theory and related research findings, Bies and Tripp offer a stakeholder perspective on revenge, arguing that the characterization of revenge as a negative deviant act depends largely on the point of view of those involved and the outcomes of the focal behavior.

In Chapter 5, Nathan Bennett and Stefanie Naumann focus on the phenomenon of withholding job effort, a form of production deviance that targets the company. Bennett and Naumann identify various types of withholding effort (shirking, job neglect, social loafing, and free riding), discuss the antecedents and consequences of these behaviors, and provide strategies for preventing such conduct from occurring in the workplace.

Chapter 6 deals with noncompliance, a form of production and (potentially) political deviance aimed at the organization. Danielle Warren distinguishes among four types of noncompliance—ignorance about rules, ignorance about rule application, opportunistic noncompliance, and principled noncompliance—and discusses the potentially destructive and constructive organizational and individual outcomes associated with each. She then provides strategies that enable organizations to encourage the benefits of constructive deviance while limiting the negative impact of destructive deviance.

Chapter 7 explores political deviance involving other individuals and the organization—lying and dishonesty. Steven Grover reviews the psychological and business ethics literature on lying and addresses questions regarding motivations for lying, whether some people lie more than others, distinctions between lying and impression management, and what (if anything) organizations can do about lying.

In Chapter 8, Gina Vega and Debra Comer distinguish between bullying and harassment in organizations, both of which are types of deviant behavior that are aimed at other people. The chapter's major emphasis is on bullying—types of bullying, the impact of bullying, and the means by which organizations can keep bullying under control. Vega and Comer also discuss situations where bullying might be considered a positive occurrence for the organization.

In Chapter 9, Edward Tomlinson and Jerald Greenberg focus on employee theft, a form of property deviance that targets the organization. Their extensive review of research on the topic highlights traditional and interpersonally oriented approaches to employee theft and differing explanations for why employees steal. Tomlinson and Greenberg suggest that incidences of employee theft can be discouraged, if not eliminated, by effectively managing social norms and promoting justice and fairness within the organization.

Chapter 10 discusses aggression and violence, two forms of interpersonal deviance. Mark Martinko, Scott Douglas, Paul Harvey, and Charles Joseph integrate the most recent theoretical and empirical research on workplace aggression and explain how various warning signs of impending danger can be detected to help prevent future incidents of aggression and violence in organizations.

Finally, in Chapter 11, Paul Roman's look at addictive behavior in organizations considers the dilemmas and contradictions associated with this type of intrapersonal deviance in the workplace. Roman examines the notion of addiction and discusses the loose application of the term to a broad variety of workplace behaviors. The chapter examines reasons why addictive behavior has become such a prominent concept in American culture and describes the impact of addictive behavior, such as drug or alcohol abuse, on the workplace. The chapter places views on alcohol, drugs, and gambling in historical perspective and reviews organizational responses to addictive behavior.

The final two chapters deal with the occurrence of deviant behavior in different venues. Family businesses make up a huge chunk of all U.S. businesses, yet they fail at an alarming rate, sometimes no doubt due to the destructive effects of deviant behavior. In Chapter 12, Rebecca Bennett, Stefan Thau, and Jay Scouten write about deviance within the family business, exploring theories that suggest why family members should be more loyal and committed to their own organizations but proposing conditions in which family bonds might lead to greater deviance and, in so doing, result in harm against the collective good of the family and the business.

Chapter 13, contributed by Linda Thorne and Joanne Jones, focuses on deviant behavior across cultures. In many cases, it is difficult to clearly categorize deviant acts when national cultures enter the mix. For example, in Western cultures, uniqueness is seen as a positive reflection of an important value—individuality. In Eastern cultures, conformity reflects loyalty to the collective interests, again a positive reflection of an important value (Kim & Markus, 1999). Thus, it is evident the same act could have different interpretations as to both its deviance and its acceptability based on the culture in which it takes place. This chapter features an in-depth application of 10 cultural dimensions to examples of deviant workplace behavior.

Analyzing the Chapter Cases

A unique element of this book is the inclusion of case studies that are designed to provide varying perspectives on deviant acts so as to allow teachers, students, and managers to connect theory and practice and to discuss ethical implications of workplace deviance. The cases focus on several well-known executives and companies that have been in the headlines during recent months and years, such as Columbia/HCA Health Care, Adelphia Communications and the Rigas family, and Bernard Ebbers, as well as on rank-and-file employees and mid-level managers of actual organizations whose identities are disguised. Some of the cases take a macro approach by placing the deviant behavior in an organization's strategic context, whereas others are focused at the work group or individual level of analysis.

To assist students in examining the chapter cases, we offer the following model as a general outline for a case analysis that can be performed in conjunction with answering the more specific discussion questions that follow each case and attempting to relate it to the preceding chapter. This model is based on overarching themes that run throughout the book and can be applied to all of the cases.

First, while reading the case, it is important to pinpoint examples of deviant behavior that occur. Group, organizational, and societal norms that are being broken or challenged should be identified along with the individuals and/or other forces that have set the norms and their motivations for establishing such standards of behavior. This identification of norms and deviations from them is helpful in evaluating the nature of the deviant behavior and how these acts fit into the situational context of the organization.

The next step is to determine potentially different interpretations of the behavior based on the point of view of the people involved—employees, managers, stockholders, society, and other stakeholders. The stakeholder model for analyzing revenge, advanced by Bies and Tripp in Chapter 4, and the noncompliance framework, discussed by Warren in Chapter 6, are among the potential tools that could be used in such an analysis.

Once the behavior has been identified and different interpretations of the behavior have been discussed, the consequences of the deviance can be diagnosed through a series of open-ended questions. Who or what is being targeted by the behavior? What elements of the behavior have adverse consequences for the organization, and what are the potentially negative outcomes? Alternatively, are there are any positive, or functional, outcomes for the organization? How might the situation have been managed to allow those positive outcomes to be realized?

We then move on to corrective and/or preventive actions that might be suitable for the dysfunctional elements that have arisen. What remedial action is appropriate for the organization or others to take in dealing with the perpetrator and the dysfunctional consequences that have occurred? More important, what are the underlying causes of the behavior? What can the organization learn from studying the reasons for the behavior? Can changes to organizational processes, structures, leadership, and norms prevent undesired deviant behavior from occurring in the future? What types of macro-organizational changes and micro-organizational applications should be considered to enable positive outcomes to the situation? Discussions of the organizational issues that lead to unethical behavior in Chapters 2 and 3 are relevant to this analysis, as are the prescriptions suggested for preventing employee theft in Chapter 9 and workplace aggression and violence in Chapter 10.

Let us apply a brief example to this model and suggest how an instance of deviant behavior could potentially be constructive or destructive to the organization. The application provides some insights into how deviance can be managed effectively and ethically.

Consider a worker who receives a performance appraisal that she believes is based on a biased appraisal instrument and faulty interpretation by the supervisor. The worker responds by badmouthing the supervisor and management to coworkers, and this act of insubordination gets back to management. Although badmouthing is generally considered a form of destructive deviance, this case may have constructive or destructive outcomes depending on how it is handled.

In this scenario, the employee broke an organizational norm by badmouthing the supervisor. The norm was set by organizational leaders to enable the effective functioning and management of the organization. Based on management's view that the employee deviated from proper conduct, the prescriptive response typically would be to discipline the employee for insubordination, which could lead to increased alienation and further deviance on the part of the employee. Taking a different point of view, the employee reacted the way she did due to perceived unfairness in the appraisal process and believes that her criticism of the organization is justified.

If discipline does not occur, the negative results of the deviant behavior include the cultivation of disrespect for management, which could lead to ineffective operations within the organization. On the surface, a positive outcome might be the employee's opportunity to blow off steam by expressing dissatisfaction with management.

Yet a more constructive outcome would be realized by examining reasons why the deviant behavior may have occurred, that is, an appraisal instrument that is perceived to be biased and a faulty interpretation of the instrument by the supervisor. If the root causes of the deviant act are examined, the poor appraisal instrument may be identified. If management, in its handling of the unkind remarks by the worker, looks into the justice issue involving the appraisal as well as the appraisal process, the employee may be brought back into a positive frame of reference rather than continue on a path of bitterness and perhaps more serious and destructive deviant acts.

Conclusion

In this preface, we have offered a summary of the book's plan and goals, a brief synopsis of chapters, and a model for analyzing cases. The study of organizational deviance has become a common topic in several fields of study and a familiar problem in the workplace. Focusing on and successfully managing such conduct is vital to an effectively functioning organization. Negative acts that employees commit at work have implications for overall organizational performance and for the financial and physical health of the people around them. The role of organizations and their leaders in creating the conditions in which deviant behavior might be more likely to occur is also a key issue.

Organizational deviance is widespread and expensive, and disgrace is often attached to perpetrators once their conduct is revealed. However, deviant behavior often carries a level of ambiguity in some organizational contexts. Thus, not only is it important to consider how to manage and control such behavior, but it is also essential to consider deviant behavior as ethical or unethical conduct. Students of ethics and business who later enter the workplace as employees and managers should become familiar with the ethical implications of deviant behavior as well as its effective management. We now examine these ideas in more detail.

—Roland E. Kidwell, Jr.

—Christopher L. Martin

References

Bennett, R. J., & Robinson, S. L. (2003). The past, present, and future of workplace deviance research. In J. Greenberg (Ed.), *Organizational behavior: The state of the science* (2nd ed., pp. 247–281). Mahwah, NJ: Lawrence Erlbaum.

Graham, J. W. (1986). Principled organizational dissent: A theoretical essay. In B. M. Staw & L. L. Cummings (Eds.), *Research in organizational behavior* (Vol. 8, pp. 1–52). Greenwich, CT: JAI.

Griffin, R. W., & O'Leary-Kelly, A. M. (2004). *The dark side of organizational behavior.* San Francisco: Jossey–Bass.

Janis, I. L. (1982). *Groupthink: Psychological studies of policy decisions and fiascoes.* Boston: Houghton Mifflin.

Kim, H., & Markus, H. R. (1999). Deviance or uniqueness, harmony or conformity? A cultural analysis. *Journal of Personality and Social Psychology, 77,* 785–800.

Morrison, E. W., & Milliken, F. J. (2000). Organizational silence: A barrier to change and development in a pluralistic world. *Academy of Management Review, 25,* 706–725.

Robinson, S., & Bennett, R. (1995). A typology of deviant workplace behaviors: A multi-dimensional scaling study. *Academy of Management Journal, 38,* 555–572.

Vardi, Y., & Weitz, E. (2004). *Misbehavior in organizations: Theory, research, and management.* Mahwah, NJ: Lawrence Erlbaum.

Warren, D. E. (2003). Constructive and destructive deviance in organizations. *Academy of Management Review, 28,* 622–632.

Acknowledgments

We thank the 29 contributors who provided their time and expertise on researching and writing the chapters and cases that are included in this book. These scholars answered our initial call to participate in the project during the spring of 2003 and responded to our comments, feedback, and requests enthusiastically throughout the process. We extend our appreciation to Marilynn Fleckenstein (Niagara University) and Jonathon R. B. Halbesleben (University of Oklahoma), who reviewed earlier versions of the manuscript and made many helpful comments and observations. We also thank Al Bruckner, MaryAnn Vail, D. J. Peck, and Diane Foster (Sage Publications) for their assistance in seeing this project through to its completion.

In addition, Roland Kidwell acknowledges and appreciates support and assistance from the Niagara University Sabbatical Leave Committee and the Niagara University Research Council; David Schoen, director of the Niagara University library; and the reference library staff. At Charles Sturt University in Australia, where Kidwell spent much of the 2003–2004 school year as a visiting research fellow working on this book, he offers special thanks to Alan Fish, Auli O'Donnell, and Andrew Smith of the School of Management; John Williams of the School of Financial Studies; and John Hicks, dean of the Faculty of Commerce. At the University of Queensland School of Business, where Kidwell spent a month as a visiting research fellow in January 2004, he extends his appreciation to Tim Brailsford, Victor Callan, Amanda Roan, and John Gardner. Finally, he wishes to thank Linda Achey Kidwell for her love and support in the completion of this project and many others.

CHAPTER 1

The Prevalence (and Ambiguity) of Deviant Behavior at Work

An Overview

Roland E. Kidwell, Jr.

Christopher L. Martin

J ake LaFrentz, human resources (HR) manager at Fistra, a company of approximately 100 employees, sought to increase the level of employee involvement in the organization. To do so, LaFrentz and Fistra's president, Barbara Maggio, began a series of town hall meetings with the employees to answer their questions and concerns about company operations. The employees were told to come to the meetings with questions and to say what was on their minds.

Just 15 minutes into the very first meeting, an employee named Joe stood up and started berating the president and complaining that an employee had received a big raise not to leave Fistra, whereas another employee—a friend of Joe's—was not given any more money to stay. LaFrentz attempted to interject that the complaint was inaccurate, but Joe refused to yield the floor.

AUTHORS' NOTE: Parts of this chapter are based on Kidwell, R. E., Jr., & Martin, C. L. (2004, August). *Managing the ambiguity of workplace deviance: Lessons from the study of conflict.* Paper presented at the meeting of the Academy of Management, New Orleans, LA.

"He told me not to interrupt until he was finished," LaFrentz said. "Joe went on for about 15 minutes saying that management could not be trusted and calling me and the president liars even after we explained his allegations about the pay raises were not true. Basically, after he had finished, the time set aside for the meeting was over."

LaFrentz's first reaction was to start proceedings to discipline Joe due to his aggressive attacks and insults directed at the company president and personnel director. "He embarrassed us in front of several employees," LaFrentz said. "I don't think it was appropriate for him to bring up pay issues involving specific employees, and I certainly think he was insubordinate for attacking us the way he did. This sort of behavior just doesn't happen at Fistra."

But Maggio suggested that it would not be a good idea to take action against Joe for what he said at the meeting even though he had been so insulting and cantankerous. After all, she said, LaFrentz and she had asked the employees to come to the meeting and say what was on their minds—and that is what Joe did.

This incident, related to the authors by the HR manager of an actual organization whose name has been disguised, illustrates a dilemma that often arises when the subject of deviant behavior in the workplace is raised. Joe apparently broke an established organizational norm by questioning company officials in what they perceived to be a belligerent manner. Thus, company officials identified Joe as a deviant. That raised the question: What should the company do about it? Was Joe engaging in insubordination and spiteful behavior as the HR director believed, or was he exercising an invitation to sincerely voice concerns to those in power at the company? His behavior broke a norm, but did it damage the organization? Would the HR manager's proposed use of discipline have had a more damaging effect?

These types of questions, related workplace behavior, and the theoretical underpinnings of organizational deviance are examined throughout this book. This chapter provides an overview of deviance and its negative impact on the workplace, reviews different types of and approaches to deviance, discusses the potential ambiguity of deviant behavior, and then briefly considers some of the psychological and sociological processes that underlie unethical and deviant workplace behavior. Drawing on organizational conflict research, the chapter concludes by suggesting a general approach that can be used to manage organizational deviance both effectively and ethically.

The Pervasive Nature of Organizational Deviance

Deviance in the workplace has been defined broadly as acts committed by organizational members that have, or are intended to have, the effect of damaging coworkers, managers, or the organization itself (Bennett & Robinson, 2003; Robinson & Bennett, 1995; Robinson & Greenberg, 1998; Vardi & Weitz, 2004). Such behavior at work has received much broadcast play and media ink over the past several years. This notoriety is often due to the sensational negative consequences associated with improper behavior in organizations: financial ruin of many rank-and-file workers due to illegal actions by corporate managers, multiple murders and other violence committed by employees in the workplace, and expensive sexual harassment verdicts. It would be difficult, if not impossible, to produce a truly accurate estimate of the cost of deviant behavior in the workplace, particularly when one includes its many forms—corporate fraud, employee theft, bullying and harassment, revenge, withholding job effort, drug and alcohol abuse, and violence—and the measures taken to prevent and correct them. Yet total estimates in the billions of dollars are routine (Bennett & Robinson, 2003).

To illustrate the pervasive problem of workplace deviance and its negative consequences, consider the sobering statistics in just one survey of 600 hourly restaurant industry workers in Texas and Florida, as reported by Berta (2003). More than a quarter of survey respondents admitted to touching coworkers in a sexually inappropriate way, and 21% of respondents observed coworkers stealing cash but did not report the incidents to management. In addition, 22% reported calling coworkers insulting names, 37% made fun of coworkers' or customers' accents, and 12% prepared or served intentionally contaminated food to customers. Finally, 24% of respondents admitted taking illegal drugs just before coming to work.

During recent years, employees have developed clever and creative means to engage in negative activity. Some of these include using the Internet to play online games and download pornography, transmit harassing and/or threatening e-mail messages, and set up rogue websites to trash their companies to the world (Ackroyd & Thompson, 1999; Armour, 1999; Bennett & Robinson, 2003; Leonard, 1999). And the more traditional and deadly manifestations of workplace deviance continue. In August 2003, after a gunman killed six workers at an auto parts warehouse in Chicago, a wire service provided a record of major workplace shootings in the United States since the mid-1980s. The report listed 23 cases of multiple murders that resulted in the deaths of more than 130 people, not including the perpetrators who killed themselves or were killed by police ("A Record of Workplace Shootings," 2003).

Specific cases of deviant behavior are not hard to find in major newspapers, on television, or in Internet accounts. Optimists can only hope that the reason these incidents receive so much publicity is that the journalism community considers them rare, following the adage that news occurs only when a man bites a dog rather than vice versa. Consider the following examples.

Elyse Glickman got along well with her new boss at first, but that changed very suddenly. He began to insult her on the job, and then he regularly undermined her performance and started comparing her to a coworker who had recently been terminated from the public relations firm where they worked. Glickman was anxious to keep her job, so she put up with the bullying harassing boss until she was fired. It was not the first time Glickman had been bullied at work (Maher, 2003).

Such bullying is not restricted to North America. In Australia, Constantine Aroney, a leading cardiologist, said that he was tormented by a health bureaucrat after it was publicly revealed that he had written a letter to the Queensland premier complaining about proposed cutbacks at a public hospital and that several patients had died due to delays in surgery. In a meeting with the general manager of Queensland Health, the public agency overseeing the hospital system, Aroney said that he had been told, "You come after us with your cheap shots and we will come after you" (O'Malley, 2004).

The *New York Times'* top editors believed that young reporter Jayson Blair had the potential to become a journalistic superstar. Blair rose to a coveted national reporting position in less than 5 years, writing about the Washington, D.C., sniper shootings of 2002, the U.S.–Iraq war, and other prominent stories. But a complaint from a Texas newspaper about a Blair story led to revelations that the young reporter had lied in print, plagiarized other reporters, and pretended to be at the scenes of breaking stories when in fact he had never left New York City (Barry, Barstow, Glater, Liptak, & Steinberg, 2003). The discoveries rocked the reputation of what is considered by many to be the most prominent U.S. newspaper. Within weeks, the paper's two highest ranking editors resigned.

The same day that it devoted four pages to expound on the activities of its own miscreant Blair, the *New York Times* published a scorecard of corporate financial scandals in the United States, highlighting five companies and their executives, including Adelphia Communications Chairman John Rigas, who had been indicted for various manifestations of fraud (see Case 12). The "user's guide" described malfeasance at Enron, HealthSouth, WorldCom, Adelphia, and Tyco International along with the numbers of company officials indicted and those who had pleaded guilty ("Corporate Scandals," 2003).

Less than a week after George O'Leary was hired for his dream job as head football coach at the University of Notre Dame, he was forced to resign when word broke that he had inaccurately enhanced his résumé years earlier. As he progressed through his career as a high school coach, a college assistant, and then a head coach, O'Leary falsely claimed to be a 3-year football letter winner at the University of New Hampshire and to have completed his master's degree. The false information was added to his biographical record at various jobs he had held over two decades, and he never bothered to correct it (Haugh, 2001; Smith, 2002; see also Case 7.1).

These instances of deviant behavior raise serious ethical questions about the causes of deviance, the potential for deviant behavior to create serious harm to organizations and society, and management's role in effectively handling deviance. First, it is important to discuss what academics and managers mean when they refer to deviant behavior and then to examine the difficulty in interpreting some types of "deviant" behavior as clearly negative, unethical, and/or destructive.

Deviant Behavior: Definitions and Terms

The fourth edition of the *American Heritage Dictionary* (American Heritage, 2000) defined deviate (verb) as "to depart, as from a norm, purpose, or subject," whereas a deviant (noun) is "one that differs from a norm, especially a person whose behavior and attitudes differ from accepted social standards" (p. 496). More than 30 years earlier, an edition of the same dictionary identified a "deviate" as a person whose behavior and attitudes differed from moral as well as social standards. Perhaps shedding light on the continuing negative connotations of deviant behavior, the 1969 secondary definition of deviate was that of a "sexual pervert."

Academic researchers originally defined workplace deviance as employee behaviors that break important organizational norms and threaten to damage the organization and/or members of the organization (Robinson & Bennett, 1995), but more recent work in the area has led to a lack of consensus on an appropriate single definition (Bennett & Robinson, 2003). Definitional agreement is particularly complex when anywhere from 8 (Robinson & Greenberg, 1998), to 12 (Bennett & Robinson, 2003), to 19 (Vardi & Weitz, 2004, Appendix 3) terms, definitions, and/or manifestations have been used to refer to the same general realm that represents the "dark side" of organizational behaviors (Griffin & O'Leary-Kelly, 2004).

The amount of research into deviance and discussion of the topic has grown substantially during the past 10 years. Among the most prominent areas of study that relate to deviant behavior are antisocial behavior, counterproductive behavior, dysfunctional behavior, and organizational misbehavior. Table 1.1 provides definitions and examples of these types of undesirable behavior as they relate to the workplace.

Deviant behavior is said to consist of voluntary acts that break major organizational norms and threaten the welfare of the organization and/or its members. Robinson and Bennett (1995) identified the following types of deviant behavior: production (damaging quantity and quality of work), property (abusing or stealing company property), political (badmouthing others or spreading rumors), and personal aggression (being hostile or violent toward others).

Antisocial behavior brings harm or is intended to bring harm to an organization, its employees, or organizational stakeholders. It includes aggression, discrimination, theft, interpersonal violence, sabotage, harassment, lying, revenge, and whistle-blowing. Antisocial behavior focuses more on personal, political, and property interactions and less so on production, with the exception of sabotage (Giacalone & Greenberg, 1997).

Counterproductive behavior is defined as "any intentional behavior on the part of an organization member viewed by the organization as contrary to its legitimate interests" (Sackett, 2002, p. 5). Counterproductive behavior is seen as an element of job performance and includes phenomena such as theft, property destruction, misuse of information, unsafe behavior, poor attendance, and poor quality work.

Dysfunctional behavior occurs when employees commit acts that have negative consequences for an individual within an organization, a group of individuals, and/or the organization itself. There are two general types: violent and deviant (e.g., aggression, physical and verbal assault, terrorism) and nonviolent dysfunctional (e.g., alcohol and drug use, revenge, absence, theft) (Griffin, O'Leary-Kelly, & Collins, 1998).

Organizational misbehavior is a deliberate act by organizational members that violates basic organizational and/or societal norms. Such misbehavior can intend to benefit an individual or the organization and generally includes an objective to inflict damage (Vardi & Weitz, 2004; Vardi & Wiener, 1996). Some writers consider misbehavior in a broad sense (e.g., time wasting, absence, turnover, crime, sexual harassment) and view it as an inevitable result of class tension and conflict between managers and workers (Ackroyd & Thompson, 1999).

Attempting to provide conceptual clarity regarding deviance and its close cousins, Robinson and Greenberg (1998) identified five primary steps in the workplace

Table 1.1 Terms and Definitions Used When Discussing Undesirable Workplace Behavior

	Deviant Behavior	Antisocial Behavior	Counterproductive Behavior	Dysfunctional Behavior	Organizational Misbehavior
Definition	Voluntary behaviors that break significant organizational norms and threaten the well-being of the organization and/or its members	Actions that bring harm, or are intended to bring harm, to an organization, its employees, and/or the organization's stakeholders	Any intentional behavior on the part of an organization member that is viewed by the organization as contrary to its legitimate interests	Actions by employees or groups of employees that have negative consequences for an individual, a group, and/or the organization itself	Acts that violate core organizational and/or societal norms; intentional workplace acts that violate workplace rules pertaining to such behaviors
Examples and/or types	Production deviance (damaging quantity and quality of work), property deviance (abusing or stealing company property), political deviance (bad-mouthing others, spreading rumors), and personal aggression (being hostile or violent toward others)	Aggression, theft, discrimination, interpersonal violence, sabotage, harassment, lying, revenge, and whistle-blowing; focused mainly on personal and property interactions	Refers to elements of job performance such as theft, destruction of property, misuse of information, unsafe behavior, poor attendance, and poor-quality work	Violent and deviant (aggression, physical, verbal assault, terrorism) and nonviolent and dysfunctional (alcohol and drug use, revenge, absence, theft)	Intending to benefit the self and the organization and intending to inflict damage, wasting time, absenteeism, turnover, crime, and sexual harassment
Source	Robinson & Bennett (1995)	Giacalone & Greenberg (1997)	Sackett (2002)	Griffin, O'Leary-Kelly, & Collins (1998)	Vardi & Weitz (2004) and Vardi & Wiener (1996)

deviance process and major dimensions that are associated with each step. The process starts with a perpetrator who can be from inside or outside the organization; most related concepts focus on an inside perpetrator. The second step involves whether the act is intentional or unintentional; most manifestations involve intentional behavior. Robinson and Greenberg's third step considers whether the target of the act is an insider or an outsider; an inside target is generally the focus in each approach. The fourth step focuses on the type of action that has occurred (e.g., indirect–direct, active–passive, verbal–physical), and the final step considers the act's consequences. Some approaches view the act in terms of a violation of norms, whereas others focus on the behavior's outcomes. Finally, most approaches consider only the harmful results of the act, whereas a few regard its potentially beneficial consequences.

Considering this outline of the deviance process, related terms, and definitions, deviance can be exemplified by behaviors such as employee theft, withholding job effort, violence, insubordination, sabotage, lying and deceit, whistle-blowing, poor attendance, misuse of information, addictive behaviors (e.g., drug/alcohol use and abuse, gambling, workaholism), and various types of bullying and harassment.

From the standpoint of managers, as well as that of most researchers, such behavior is considered negative and unethical without a great deal of debate. Indeed, those who engage in deviant activities at work seem to demonstrate a lack of moral strength and character and clearly violate ethical standards (Seabright & Schminke, 2002). Some might be "organizational charlatans" who can manipulate their surroundings through impression management and who receive high subjective evaluations even though their objective performance is not desirable (Parnell & Singer, 2001). Thus, a clear assumption in much deviance research and its practical application has been that deviant individuals, by violating established norms and creating negative consequences, engage in wrongful and unethical activity.

As noted earlier, the frequency and severity of deviant behavior have had a significant impact on the workplace, with the costs of deviant acts such as employee theft, violence, and other forms of aggression, drug/alcohol use and abuse, and even time lost to Web surfing and other forms of withholding job effort totaling in the billions of dollars. Based on its pervasive and costly nature, deviant behavior is clearly categorized by many as a workplace evil that must be stamped out through effective supervision and organizational systems, electronic surveillance, discipline, and (in some instances) use of employee assistance programs. Attempts to establish conformity to rules, regulations, policies, and procedures appear to be well justified when acts such as violence, harassment, fraud, and theft are considered. These types of behavior can clearly lead to destructive outcomes.

Another View: The Ethical Ambiguity of Deviance

Despite long-standing convention that deviance per se is a negative and destructive force in organizations, it is clear that the nature of deviance and its ethical evaluation depends on the characteristics of the behavior, the conditions in which it takes place, and the norms that are employed to define behavior as deviant. As Locke

(2003) noted, "Deviance can be good or bad, beneficial or harmful, depending on the nature of the norms and the nature of the deviance" (p. 426). Thus, in certain circumstances, deviant behavior takes on a level of ambiguity, that is, doubt or uncertainty as to how it should be interpreted. The same behavior can be open to different ethical interpretations based on point of view and motivations of the stakeholders who are involved, the intended and actual results of the behavior, and the level of norms (e.g., group, organizational, societal) that is being considered.

There are alternative ways in which to consider deviant actions based on a more traditional definition of the term *deviance* as a violation of reference group norms and the proposition that some deviant actions can be beneficial, or at least neutral, to the organization (e.g., Bies & Tripp, 1998; Kidwell & Kochanowski, in press; Vardi & Wiener, 1996; Warren, 2003). Such consideration raises several questions. Are there gray areas of ethical behavior where employees deviate from the norm in the pursuit of uniqueness and the rejection of conformity to accepted standards? Are there instances where the deviant acts of employees could lead to positive results for the organization? Can managers create conditions where deviant behavior can be channeled into an ingredient for organizational success? Do organizational leaders and processes contribute to conditions in which destructive deviant and unethical behavior is encouraged? Academic research and the practical experience of managers indicate that the answer to all of these questions is a qualified *yes.*

As others have noted, it is difficult to categorize deviance objectively because norms within organizations are constructed by those who have the authority and/or power to do so (Bennett & Robinson, 2003; Vardi & Wiener, 1996). The breaking of an accepted standard of behavior (i.e., a norm) is generally perceived as a threatening and negative act. This is particularly so to organizational leaders and employees who are heavily involved in setting norms and, thus, are highly invested in seeking compliance to rules, policies, and procedures. Despite the threats implied by deviance, some forms of deviant behavior have the potential for positive, or at least neutral, results for the organization. Conformity to some norms found at various organizational levels does not result in desired performance. Strong group norms that punished rate busters—as well as chiselers and squealers—at the Hawthorne Western Electric plant is a classic example, as is a norm of bullying coworkers that exists in various organizational settings.

Violating organizational rules and standards by disobeying supervisors and other actions can fall under the classification of deviance yet might not have destructive results. Whistle-blowing, innovative thinking related to organizational change, and organizational dissent are among these forms of deviance. These actions may "deviate from the prevailing views or beliefs of an established majority" and thus be considered deviant, but they may also be the source of positive results for the organization (Elmes, 1990, p. 141). Despite their individual and organizational costs, even some forms of "negative" deviance may have positive, or at least ambiguous, consequences for an organization.

The ambiguity of deviance can be illustrated in part by reflecting on an action that violates an organizational norm yet could have varying interpretations based on motive and outcome. Consider an organization, perhaps a public sector agency or a university, where it is very rare to terminate an individual under any circumstances, even poor performance. A manager within that organization fires a longtime employee for incompetence. A year later, another manager fires an otherwise competent employee for personal, arbitrary, or erratic reasons. Both managers have violated a norm by dismissing an employee and, thus, have behaved in a deviant manner. However, the first instance gains the organization a positive outcome, whereas the second results in a negative outcome for the organization. In each instance, there may be a threatening result for the organization, that is, the potential for a lawsuit. But organizational performance might be improved in the first case but not in the second. And one might deem the manager in the first example as ethical and the manager in the second example as unethical (cf. Griffin et al., 1998, p. xx; Kidwell & Kochanowski, 2004).

It is clear from such scenarios that individual motive and circumstance moderate the potential effects of employee behavior in terms of deviance and appropriateness, as could variables such as organizational structure, culture, politics, and national culture. A problem with putting deviant behavior within ethical frameworks is the issue of who decides which behavior is deviant and in what situation—individual workers, work groups, company managers, other stakeholders, or society at large. Table 1.2 illustrates the ambiguity of deviance by listing a sample behavior, its negative interpretation, and its dysfunctional consequences. This is followed by an alternative interpretation of the same behavior and the potentially functional consequences that may be realized depending on how the behavior is perceived and/or managed.

Similar to the examples reviewed in the previous section and in Table 1.2, Warren (2003) discussed several negative deviant behaviors that have been investigated in workplace research, including aggression, lying, theft, misbehavior, sabotage, political activity, and noncompliance to rules or norms. She balanced that list with some examples of positive, yet deviant, behavior from management research, including tempered radicalism, whistle-blowing, exercising voice, and counter-role behavior. She argued that the two research streams—positive and negative deviance—should be integrated into a typology of deviant behavior examining both globally held beliefs and values (i.e., hypernorms) and reference group norms (e.g., organizational standards) in determining the constructive or destructive nature of behavior in organizations. On the one hand, destructive deviance violates both reference group norms and hypernorms, whereas constructive deviance violates reference group norms but not hypernorms. On the other hand, constructive conformity violates neither set of norms, whereas destructive conformity violates hypernorms but not reference group norms (Warren, 2003).

In addition to a potentially neutral act that, although deviant, could be considered ethical or unethical when motive, reference point or national culture is taken into account, let us briefly consider examples of behaviors classified by Warren (2003) and others as deviant yet constructive, perhaps not for norm setters and enforcers but rather for organizations and society. These instances of deviance may actually be appropriate actions for the individual, organization, or society in terms of both outcomes and ethical considerations. Whether deviance is a positive or a

Table 1.2 Examples of the Ambiguity of "Deviant" Behavior

Label	Sample Behavior	Negative Interpretation	Potential Dysfunctional Outcomes	Alternative Interpretation	Potential Functional Outcomes
Risk taking	Chief executive makes bold strategic moves	Recklessness	Threatens financial well-being of organization and employees	Innovation	Achieves organizational growth/success
Expression of voice	Employee complains about management actions	Bad-mouthing	Damage to organization's reputation	Employee participation/appeal, whistle-blowing	Corrects or stops workplace injustice and inefficiency
Noncompliance	Workers refuse to obey manager's directives	Insubordination, rule breaking, loafing	Organizational instability, unmet goals	Counter-role behavior/task revision	Effort diverted from activities that do not meet organizational goals
Withholding information, providing misleading information	Optimism and enthusiasm in the face of failure	Deceit, hubris	Atmosphere of dishonesty, lack of trust, divisive climate in workplace	Commitment to the cause, envisioning uplifting future, "positive leadership"	Keeps morale high, reduces anxiety
Aggressive behavior	Leader berates employee team, verbally abuses and attacks abilities	Harassment, bullying	Unpleasant and dangerous psychological and physical effects	Stern leadership, "aligning the troops"	Desensitizes employees to criticism, motivates toward goal achievement
Conflict	Managers question and dispute chief executive's planned actions	Carping, complaining, selfishness	Damaged relationships	Devil's advocacy, healthy discussion	Improved quality of decisions

negative sometimes lies in the eye of the beholder. In this light, whistle-blowing, innovation, organizational dissent, and resistance to conformity are potentially forms of what can be called positive or constructive deviance.

The positive aspects of whistle-blowing—employees' disclosure of illegitimate or illegal acts by their employers to others who may be able to take corrective action—are frequently recognized (Miceli & Near, 1997). Whistle-blowing may threaten an organization's managers but may be viewed as proper and ethical by other stakeholders and society, who may benefit from the whistle-blower's actions. Workers who have reported their firms for financial or environmental abuses may be attacked by their organizations, but such "deviance" wins high praise for its ethical standards by the media, politicians, customers, and perhaps fellow employees.

It also may be ethical, proper, and ultimately effective for employees to deviate from the norm by taking innovative approaches to problem solving in organizations where such activities are not encouraged. This sort of deviance can be an important element of organizational innovation and the leadership of change. The basic idea is that one way to successfully change an organization is to identify where in the organization norms are being broken in a way that solves problems that the organization is currently facing (Crom & Bertels, 1999). Of course, the success of change leadership and positive deviance appears to require a leader who enables the organization to turn such normative challenges into shared values.

Without such a leader, employees and managers who raise issues that are traditionally not discussed or debated in a particular organization are engaging in deviant conduct that could ultimately benefit the organization. The actions of such radical principled dissenters can lead members of an organization to question underlying assumptions and values and, thus, to be more open to positive change (Elmes, 1990; Graham, 1986). Such disagreement can be compared to employees who exercise voice, deviating from organizational norms by speaking out in pursuit of change. Van Dyne and LePine (1998) defined voice as a means to challenge the status quo and to suggest changes in ways that are intended to improve conditions at work rather than to be critical of standard procedures. Voice can be another form of positive deviance and might be contrasted with badmouthing the organization in the same way that carping has been distinguished from devil's advocacy (Valacich & Schwenk, 1995). Whereas dissenters face the risk of permanently damaging their careers if their actions offend powerful interests within the organization, their behavior would not even be considered deviant in workplaces that encourage lively debate about future actions or establish devil's advocacy as part of the organizational decision-making structure.

Another form of deviance with potentially positive organizational effects is workplace activity in which tempered radicals engage. These people are committed to their organizations but also follow a cause, community, or ideology quite different from, or in opposition to, their organizations' cultures (Meyerson & Scully, 1995). A conservationist who works in an organization that has little concern about the environment may deviate from organizational culture and norms to work for positive changes in the organization's environmental stance, doing so from within the organization. The same might be true of a devout Christian employed by an organization that is focused solely on secular pursuits to the aggressive exclusion of spiritual ones.

Resistance to organizational norms and job requirements may also be viewed as task revision, a form of counter-role behavior that involves actions taken to correct flawed procedures, inaccurate job descriptions, or job role expectations that would potentially result in negative effects on the organization (Staw & Boettger, 1990). When expectations of employee behavior have been incorrectly specified by the organization, an employee engaging in task revision is considered to be an innovator who is behaving in a way that results in excellent performance despite taking actions that are outside approved organizational norms.

Thus, it might be ethical and effective for an individual to fail to carry out established procedures, declining to engage in activities that, although required by the organization, do not really get the job done. Examples include failure to engage in prescribed sales or operational techniques within an organization that, in the judgment of the salesperson, do not result in higher sales volume or potentially have the effect of irritating customers or intruding on their privacy. A few years ago, a prominent national retail chain required employees to collect addresses and phone numbers from customers. Employees who declined to ask for these details were engaging in deviant behavior, weighing the organization's goal of obtaining marketing information against some customers' perceptions that their privacy was being invaded. Customers' problems with this chain's practice became evident when the organization stopped attempting to collect this information and advertised prominently that it no longer did so.

Following on the idea that deviance sometimes can be interpreted differently depending on perspective, consider an organization whose members traditionally do not welcome change. A new management system is introduced, but several workers fail to accept it. On the one hand, the workers who refuse to accept the change and continue to work in the old way may perceive themselves as simply living up to their contracts (and established norms of their organization). On the other hand, the new management system heralds the adoption of a new set of norms by the organization or at least by management. The recalcitrant workers' behavior may be considered unproductive by organizational managers and even deviant when compared with the behavior of their fellow employees. However, the recalcitrant workers receive the same level of wages and are expending no less task-related effort than when they were not considered deviants.

A second factor that is relevant to understanding the so-called deviant behavior in this example is the perception of group norms regarding its acceptability. The norms of one's reference group in the work setting provide guidance as to whether to pursue a particular behavior (Mikulay, Neuman, & Finkelstein, 2001). The norms of the older group of employees suggest staying with the status quo, whereas the norms of the employees who accept the changes reflect positive adjustment, again from the effectiveness and efficiency orientation of management. (For an additional illustration, see Case 5.)

Furthermore, the culture of an organization and its climate can be favorable or unfavorable toward deviant behavior, be it positive or negative (Kamp & Brooks, 1991). Thus, in some organizations, a certain amount of shrinkage, on-the-job drug use, personal surfing of the Internet, bullying, and/or workaholism may be tolerated as norms of organizational life. But "deviants" who break norms by not practicing these sorts of activities may be viewed as performing quite reasonably from an external perspective.

Bob Newburgh: Strong Leader or Workplace Bully?

Bob Newburgh took over the top job at East Sleepy State College after the tenure of a president who retired after 20 years in that post. During discussions with some faculty and staff members in the interview process, Newburgh came to believe that the university needed a significant shake-up in several of its colleges and divisions. Within days of arriving on campus, Newburgh put an organizational change plan into action.

Unfortunately for the administrators and other staff members at Sleepy State, Newburgh brought an aggressive and, some would say, intemperate management style into the mix. Others saw the new president as a micromanager who wanted to be involved in aspects of key departmental operations to an extent that was unknown in the previous administration.

East Sleepy State's former president, A. T. "Happy" Duval, delegated most of the administrative work to vice presidents, deans, and department heads. The university faculty members retained a fair amount of power to block new initiatives and maintain the status quo. The university effectively delivered its teaching and other services to the East Sleepy State area, but it had little regional or national reputation, had few new programs, and was considered to be a low priority when it came to state funding.

Newburgh's road map for change brought the college to a higher level of quality with new regional, national, and even global initiatives; an increase in state and private sector funding; and administrative shake-ups in several key areas. Younger faculty members applauded the plan, and new scholars were attracted to the school due to the programs that began during the Newburgh regime.

As these positive developments took place, Newburgh dismissed a couple of key administrators and alienated some others to the point where they sought positions at other universities. He cut back on traditional sources of faculty input by going around the Faculty Council and Senate of Department Chairs when they interfered with his plans. The Faculty Council, long a center of power within the university under Happy Duval, was rendered rather ineffective, at least from the standpoint of formerly powerful faculty members. Adding insult to injury, Newburgh personally badmouthed some longtime faculty members, questioning their usefulness to a successful university.

As the new initiatives took place, Newburgh began to micromanage their formulation and implementation. Faculty members and administrators indicated that Newburgh had a strong strategic vision for the school but was very poor at planning and interpersonal skills. In meetings, he was known to yell at administrators and humiliate staff members when problems occurred, reports were not complete, or solutions were not to his satisfaction. Many older faculty members were alienated by Newburgh's initiatives and management style, and early retirements began to occur with increased regularity.

After several years at the helm, Newburgh had a falling out with the Board of Trustees over the direction of his programs and university funding levels. These factors and some internal sabotage from enemies who still remained with the university led to his eventual departure to another school, where he became its president. East Sleepy State, however, thrived under his replacement, who carried out a variety of Newburgh's programs during the first years of her administration and advanced new programs under administrators and faculty members who were eager to change with the times.

Antecedents of Deviant Behavior at Work

To most individuals, verbal attacks, yelling, use of profanity, threats of retaliation, and the "silent treatment" would seem to be prime examples of negative forms of organizational deviance. Surprisingly, in many organizations, employees and management often view top-producing, successful bosses as bullies who exhibit one or more of these behaviors (Dumaine, 1993). We witnessed one manager publicly berating an employee in the workplace. He later apologized—*to us*. Yet he defended his actions, stating that he had to "put the fear of God into some of these people or they'd walk all over [him]. . . . I've got to get their attention."

This manager's acts, and those of Bob Newburgh to some degree, were effective in getting results (i.e., a constructive consequence of deviance). However, there are serious risks involved in condoning such behavior, including turnover of valuable employees, absenteeism, potential for legal exposure, and (in Newburgh's case) eventual sabotage of one's change efforts. Furthermore, in this case and others we have witnessed, when the bottom-line results turn negative, behavior such as Newburgh's might no longer be tolerated by the organization. And obviously, there are effective and more ethical management styles that can gain favorable results and, at the same time, maintain the dignity of people.

One can also raise the issue that Newburgh's actions are a prime example of what can lead to deviant and unethical behavior among employees within an organization. Previous research has examined a variety of psychological and sociological processes related to the individual, the job, the work group, and the organization that are considered to be among the general antecedents of deviant behavior (Bennett & Robinson, 2003; Vardi & Weitz, 2004).

Factors examined as precursors to deviant behavior include reactions to frustration, perceived threats and perceived injustice, personality traits (e.g., dispositional aggressiveness), and cues suggested by the social context (Bennett & Robinson, 2003; Robinson & Greenberg, 1998). Job and work group factors may include design and conditions of particular tasks and various types of pressures that come from a work group's current and past circumstances. Organizational factors may include work experiences that are perceived as unfair, pressure to pursue established goals, an organization's control and reward systems, organizational culture, and the actions (or inactions) of leaders. Subsequent chapters in this volume expand on such psychological and sociological processes in detail and summarize theoretical approaches and empirical findings related to various types of deviance and the contexts in which deviant behavior occurs.

In brief, acts of deviant behavior by employees, including aggression, violence, theft, and revenge, have been linked with variables such as high stress levels, feelings of powerlessness, arbitrary and unjust actions by the organization and its managers, and antagonistic labor relations (Bennett, 1998; Bies & Tripp, 1998; Greenberg & Alge, 1998; Mack, Shannon, Quick, & Quick, 1998). For example, a stressful work environment can trigger a process that eventually leads to aggression and violence (Martinko, Douglas, Harvey, & Joseph, this volume) or to occasions of employee alcohol use and possibly abuse (Matano, Futa, Wanat, Mussman, & Leung, 2000). An employee reacting to a perceived management injustice might also consider revenge (Bies & Tripp, 1998) or theft (Greenberg, 1997).

The influences of leadership, organizational structure, and organizational culture on the presence of negative deviance and the benefits of establishing an ethical culture are clear (e.g., Boye & Jones, 1997; Schein, 1985; Sims & Brinkmann, 2002), and their theoretical and empirical relationships to employee behavior are discussed extensively in Chapters 2 and 3 of this volume. Shared values, decision-making capabilities, and a leader's vision and motivational techniques are seen as positive ethical forces in organizational success, variables that lead to the elimination of destructive deviant behavior and the pursuit of positive results within an ethical framework. However, shared values and the behavior of the leader can create conditions for unethical behavior and destructive deviance. Employees might engage in deviant and unethical behavior because they perceive an incentive to do so due to organizational structure and culture, the organization's reward system, and/or the leadership of the organization. Newburgh's attempts to change the school's culture could well have led otherwise good employees to engage in unethical activity.

Strong leaders are often praised for maintaining optimism during serious organizational adversity. Problems with such a stance in the face of impending failure are obvious. On the one hand, the leader who is excessively confident or optimistic in a situation where catastrophe is the clear outcome is misleading followers and creating conditions that could breed deviant behavior among employees due to the eventual realization of injustice or betrayal. On the other hand, the leader who establishes a record of lies, deceit, and unjust acts is encouraging followers to do the same. Such a leader is also breeding whistle-blowers within the firm. In these circumstances, deviance may be less an example of unethical behavior than a result of such behavior.

But as organizational leaders attempt to establish or modify an organizational culture, what was once considered deviant behavior could become ingrained within the organization with positive results. Shared values of innovation, principled dissent, integrity, and willingness to accept failure can sow the seeds that result in expressions of deviance that could ultimately affect the organization in a positive way as compared with industry competitors that seek to eliminate all acts of deviance.

Deviance, Conflict, and Effective Management

Where deviance is seen as one of the most critical issues facing organizations, conflict is regarded as one of the workplace's most frequent phenomena (Dirks & McLean Parks, 2003). Conflict in the workplace was traditionally considered—and still is in some quarters—to be a type of destructive deviance because it violated norms of harmony sought in many organizations and often led to dysfunctional consequences. In contrast to contemporary views, managers traditionally assumed that conflict itself was detrimental to the efficient functioning of their organizations and that those who caused conflict were deviants who should be admonished, with disputes being eliminated or at least minimized.

As detailed by Rahim (2001), classical organizational theorists tried to eliminate conflict by designing bureaucratic or mechanistic structures that prescribed proper behavior and an organizational command hierarchy that would keep friction and disagreement to a minimum. Neoclassical or human relations theorists tried to eliminate conflict by improving operations of the organization's social system.

Mayo (1933) and Parsons (1949) emphasized a need for cooperation and for eliminating conflict so that greater organizational and societal effectiveness could be pursued. Child (1995) concluded that Mayo had a

> deep abhorrence of conflict in any form. . . . Mayo and his colleagues . . . assumed that ordinary employees were largely governed by a "logic of sentiment," which was of a different order from managers' rational appraisal of the situation in terms of costs and efficiency. Conflict with management was thus an aberration that threatened the effectiveness of organizations. (pp. 88–89)

Parsons (1949) viewed society as inherently stable, integrated and functional, therefore conflict was seen as an abnormal and dysfunctional phenomenon.

Many of those involved in conflict situations over organizational resources traditionally took a win–lose stance, failing to consider that opposing sides in an organizational conflict could enjoy positive gains from the resulting tension (Dirks & McLean Parks, 2003). This perception of conflict often had negative consequences for the organization in the form of suboptimal decision making and poor employee morale. The functional benefits of conflict were not truly realized until the second half of the 20th century. For example, when substantive conflict is encouraged within organizations or teams, various parties to a dispute or decision have the opportunity to air their differences and concerns. This activity positively affects the quality of decision making (Janis, 1982) and may prevent unethical behavior that can result from groupthink (Sims, 1992).

We would suggest that some forms of deviant organizational behavior should be considered in a similar vein as today's views on conflict. That is, like conflict, other forms of deviance (e.g., risk taking, expression of voice, noncompliance, aggressive behavior) can have both positive and negative implications for organizations, depending on how they are managed.

Many instances of deviance are clearly wrong, destructive, and/or unethical. However, before ethical judgments can be made, some deviant behavior would be better viewed in a neutral way, depending on the norms that exist and the type of deviance (Locke, 2003). Robinson and Bennett (1995) pointed out, "Although a particular behavior can be both deviant and unethical, the two qualities are not inevitably linked" (p. 556). Recognizing the potential ambiguity discussed earlier, we now offer ideas about putting a general plan of deviance management into effect.

As noted, much can be accomplished by an organization's leadership—formal as well as informal—to encourage positive forms of deviating from the norm and to discourage negative acts by the way that shared values, decision-making methods, and justice in the organization are managed. Negative deviance in the form of workplace violence, fraud, theft, and lying can be addressed by determining and working on the causes of the behavior as well as by building a positive ethical climate.

However, an ongoing deviance management approach that might encourage constructive forms of handling deviance would be well informed by considering evolving views toward organizational conflict, which occurs as people, teams, departments, and organizations that perceive opposition in goals, aims, and values interact with other parties they perceive as potentially interfering with the realization of their goals (Dirks & McLean Parks, 2003, p. 285).

Managers who handle conflict and academics who research it developed the premise that conflict is not necessarily bad. A confrontational (integrative) approach to conflict might result in a win–win situation where both parties achieved their crucial goals and preserved personal relationships, the two dimensions that underlie responses to conflict (Moberg, 2001). Although an integrative approach may tend to bring conflict to a positive conclusion, organizational reactions to conflict traditionally included the view that all conflict is dysfunctional and should be avoided or stamped out.

Similar responses have been applied to various forms of deviance. Deviant people are generally perceived as interfering with the realization of organizational goals. Deviance is considered to be bad behavior because it breaks norms. If possible, it should be ignored and the deviant person should be isolated. Compromises regarding relatively milder forms of deviance (e.g., withholding effort) might be made, whereas the more serious negative forms should be eliminated. However, just as with conflict, an effort to surface deviant behavior at earlier stages and confront it might lessen the occurrence of more serious forms of deviance and their consequences in the future.

The traditional view of conflict avoided the idea that individuals faced with conflict situations engage in defensive reasoning to prevent embarrassment and personal threat that might result from the conflict (Rahim, 2001). These individual defense mechanisms were complemented by organizational defensive routines that included policies and rules to help employees avoid threat or embarrassment. The old conflict paradigm, unlike more enlightened approaches to handling conflict, did not see these defensive routines as barriers to the organization's ability to deal with the conflict and actually made it impossible to design effective conflict management systems.

According to Rahim (2001), "Traditional conflict resolution does not question whether the structure and processes of an organization are deficient [and] are causing dysfunctional conflict. It tries to resolve or reduce conflict at the microlevel within the existing system" (p. 72). Defensive routines limit the ability of organizational leaders and managers to see much positive in deviant acts by employees and to ignore faulty organizational processes. Defensive routines and rules, policies, and procedures lead to a quick judgment that deviant behavior is a negative unethical act that should be handled on an incident-by-incident basis.

Organizations should consider a new deviance model similar to that suggested in handling organizational conflict, that is, one that involves changes at the group and organizational levels. This approach sees the major issue as organizational learning about processes and systems, not as elimination of isolated acts. If justice issues that lead to arguably less severe forms of deviance—badmouthing, insubordination, withholding effort, and the like—are brought to the surface and dealt with effectively, more severe forms of deviance—violence, addictive behavior, harassment, and the like—might be avoided. Chapter 9 in this volume expands on this idea regarding the topic of employee theft.

Returning to the opening vignette of Fistra's employee involvement program, a growing body of research links deviant behaviors, such as workplace violence, theft, workplace slowdowns, and sabotage, with perpetrators' perceptions of being unfairly treated by their supervisors and their organizations (e.g., Neuman & Baron, 1998). This perception of unfairness is particularly high under conditions where procedural fairness has been violated or ignored. Providing the opportunity for employee voice to "right a wrong" or simply to be heard is one means to enhance the perception of procedural fairness and, in turn, to lessen the likelihood of retaliatory deviant behavior. However, at Fistra, the HR manager viewed the employee's expression of frustration, reactions to management decisions, and challenges to management practices *as the negative and deviant behaviors*. The employee's comments were viewed as inappropriate and unfounded attacks on management that should be punished.

As we stated earlier in this chapter, we find it increasingly common for managers to take just such a defensive stance in regard to their employees voicing workplace concerns and frustrations. This can have negative consequences for the organization in that employee voice may communicate needed change that might not be heard elsewhere. Furthermore, providing mechanisms for voice implies that employee comments, concerns, and opinions are worthy of being heard by someone in authority. Ignoring employee concerns, or attempting to squelch opinions that attack or embarrass management, will likely lead to heightened employee frustration, unethical behavior, and other forms of destructive deviance.

Conclusion

As managers and academics have begun to realize, it is time to get beyond the formulation of all deviance as unethical negative acts. Although organizational leaders should not abandon the view that many deviant acts are clearly wrong and unethical, these leaders should be encouraged to better learn how to manage deviance and, when possible, make productive lemonade from deviant lemons.

Others have made the point that organizations that are able to reap the benefits of positive deviance will find themselves in a superior competitive position (Bennett & Robinson, 2003). Encouraging employees to think and act outside the constraints of organizational norms, to dissent vociferously from dubious courses of action, to turn in offenders who are placing the company in a bad light by behaving unethically or illegally, and to break rules that stand in the way of effective, yet ethical, performance all are ways in which organizations can be more successful through managing deviance. Examining organizational processes and systems in handling other forms of deviance and having the willingness to change faulty processes that spawn deviant behavior are other means to enhance organizational performance through the ethical management of deviant behavior.

References

A record of workplace shootings in United States since mid-1980s. (2003, August 27). *Associated Press.* Retrieved January 15, 2004, from LexisNexis database.

Ackroyd, S., & Thompson, P. (1999). *Organizational misbehaviour.* London: Sage.

American Heritage. (2000). *American Heritage dictionary of the English language* (4th ed.). Boston: Houghton Mifflin.

Armour, S. (1999, July 12). Web locales become whine country: Employees turning to sites to air their workplace gripes. *USA Today,* p. B3.

Barry, D., Barstow, D., Glater, J. D., Liptak, A., & Steinberg, J. (2003, May 11). Times reporter who resigned leaves long trail of deception. *The New York Times,* pp. 1, 20–23.

Bennett, R. J. (1998). Perceived powerlessness as a cause of employee deviance. In R. W. Griffin, A. O'Leary-Kelly, & J. M. Collins (Eds.), *Dysfunctional behavior in organizations: Violent and deviant behavior* (Vol. 23, Part A, pp. 221–239). Stamford, CT: JAI.

Bennett, R. J., & Robinson, S. L. (2003). The past, present, and future of workplace deviance research. In J. Greenberg (Ed.), *Organizational behavior: The state of the science* (2nd ed., pp. 247–281). Mahwah, NJ: Lawrence Erlbaum.

Berta, D. (2003, August 4). Employee behavior study alarms operators. *Nation's Restaurant News,* pp. 1, 16, 99.

Bies, R. J., & Tripp, T. M. (1998). Revenge in organizations: The good, the bad, and the ugly. In R. W. Griffin, A. O'Leary-Kelly, & J. M. Collins (Eds.), *Dysfunctional behavior in organizations: Violent and deviant behavior* (Vol. 23, Part B, pp. 49–67). Stamford, CT: JAI.

Boye, M. W., & Jones, J. W. (1997). Organizational culture and employee counterproductivity. In R. A. Giacalone & J. Greenberg (Eds.), *Antisocial behavior in organizations* (pp. 172–184). Thousand Oaks, CA: Sage.

Child, J. (1995). Constructive conflict. In P. Graham (Ed.), *Mary Parker Follett: Prophet of management—A celebration of writings from the 1920s* (pp. 67–95). Boston: Harvard Business School Press.

Corporate scandals: A user's guide. (2003, May 11). *The New York Times,* sec. 4, p. 2.

Crom, S., & Bertels, T. (1999). Change leadership: The virtues of deviance. *Leadership & Organization Development Journal, 20,* 162–167.

Dirks, K. T., & McLean Parks, J. (2003). Conflicting stories: The state of the science of conflict. In J. Greenberg (Ed.), *Organizational behavior: The state of the science* (2nd ed., pp. 283–324). Mahwah, NJ: Lawrence Erlbaum.

Dumaine, B. (1993, October 18). America's toughest bosses. *Fortune,* pp. 128–129, 138. Retrieved May 23, 2003, from http://proquest.umi.com/pqdweb

Elmes M. (1990). Radical dissent and learning in human systems. *Consultation, 9,* 141–151.

Giacalone, R. A., & Greenberg, J. (1997). *Antisocial behavior in organizations.* Thousand Oaks, CA: Sage.

Graham, J. W. (1986). Principled organizational dissent: A theoretical essay. In B. M. Staw & L. L. Cummings (Eds.), *Research in organizational behavior* (Vol. 8, pp. 1–52). Greenwich, CT: JAI.

Greenberg, J. (1997). The STEAL motive: Managing the social determinants of employee theft. In R. Giacalone & J. Greenberg (Eds.), *Antisocial behavior in organizations* (pp. 85–108). Thousand Oaks, CA: Sage.

Greenberg, J., & Alge, B. J. (1998). Aggressive reactions to workplace injustice. In R. W. Griffin, A. O'Leary-Kelly, & J. M. Collins (Eds.), *Dysfunctional behavior in organizations: Violent and deviant behavior* (Vol. 23, Part A, pp. 83–117). Stamford, CT: JAI.

Griffin, R. W., & O'Leary-Kelly, A. M. (2004). *The dark side of organizational behavior.* San Francisco: Jossey–Bass.

Griffin, R. W., O'Leary-Kelly, A., & Collins, J. M. (Eds.), (1998). *Dysfunctional behavior in organizations: Violent and deviant behavior* (Vol. 23, Part A). Stamford, CT: JAI.

Haugh, D. (2001, December 15). O'Leary resigns: "Breach of trust," "Puff piece" unearth bio inaccuracies. *www.southbendtribune.com.* Retrieved May 15, 2002, from http://proquest.umi.com/pqdweb

Janis, I. L. (1982). *Groupthink: Psychological studies of policy decisions and fiascoes.* Boston: Houghton Mifflin.

Kamp, J., & Brooks, P. (1991). Perceived organizational climate and employee counterproductivity. *Journal of Business and Psychology, 5,* 447–458.

Kidwell, R. E., Jr., & Kochanowski, S. M. (in press). The morality of employee theft: Teaching about ethics and deviant behavior in the workplace. *Journal of Management Education.*

Leonard, B. (1999, November). Cyberventing. *HR Magazine,* pp. 34–39.

Locke, E. A. (2003). Good definitions: The epistemological foundation of scientific progress. In J. Greenberg (Ed.), *Organizational behavior: The state of the science* (2nd ed., pp. 415–444). Mahwah, NJ: Lawrence Erlbaum.

Mack, D. A., Shannon, C., Quick, J. D., & Quick, J. C. (1998). Stress and the preventative management of workplace violence. In R. W. Griffin, A. O'Leary-Kelly, & J. M. Collins (Eds.), *Dysfunctional behavior in organizations: Violent and deviant behavior* (Vol. 23, Part A, pp. 119–141). Stamford, CT: JAI.

Maher, K. (2003, April 15). Career journal: The jungle. *The Wall Street Journal,* p. B8. Retrieved May 23, 2003, from http://proquest.umi.com/pqdweb

Martinko, M. J., Douglas, S. C., Harvey, P., & Joseph, C. (2005). Managing organizational aggression. In R. E. Kidwell, Jr., & C. L. Martin (Eds.), *Managing organizational deviance* (pp. 237–259). Thousand Oaks, CA: Sage.

Matano, R. A., Futa, K. T., Wanat, S. F., Mussman, L. M., & Leung, C. W. (2000). The Employees Stress and Alcohol Project: The development of a computer-based alcohol abuse prevention program for employees. *Journal of Behavioral Health Services & Research, 27,* 152–165.

Mayo, E. (1933). *The human problems of industrial civilization.* New York: Macmillan.

Meyerson, D., & Scully, M. (1995). Tempered radicalism and the politics of ambivalence and change. *Organization Science, 6,* 585–600.

Miceli, M. P., & Near, J. P. (1997). Whistle-blowing as anti-social behavior. In R. A. Giacalone & J. Greenberg (Eds.), *Antisocial behavior in organizations* (pp. 130–149). Thousand Oaks, CA: Sage.

Mikulay, S., Neuman, G., & Finkelstein, L. (2001). Counterproductive workplace behaviors. *Genetic, Social, and General Psychology Monographs, 127,* 279–300.

Moberg, P. J. (2001). Linking conflict strategy to the Five-Factor Model: Theoretical and empirical foundations. *International Journal of Conflict Management, 12,* 47–68.

Neuman, J. H., & Baron, R. A. (1998). Workplace violence and workplace aggression: Evidence concerning specific forms, potential causes, and preferred targets. *Journal of Management, 24,* 391–420.

O'Malley, B. (2004, January 10). Bullying claim by top heart surgeon. *The Courier Mail,* p. 1. (Brisbane, Australia)

Parnell, J. A., & Singer, M. G. (2001). The Organizational Charlatan Scale: Developing an instrument to measure false performance. *Journal of Management Development, 20,* 441–455.

Parsons, T. (1949). *Essays in sociological theory: Pure and applied.* Glenco, IL: Free Press.

Rahim, M. A. (2001). *Managing conflict in organizations* (3rd ed.). Westport, CT: Quorum Books.

Robinson, S., & Bennett, R. (1995). A typology of deviant workplace behaviors: A multi-dimensional scaling study. *Academy of Management Journal, 38,* 555–572.

Robinson, S. L., & Greenberg, J. (1998). Employees behaving badly: Dimensions, determinants, and dilemmas in the study of workplace deviance. In C. L. Cooper & D. M. Rousseau (Eds.), *Trends in organizational behavior* (Vol. 5, pp. 1–30). New York: John Wiley.

Sackett, P. R. (2002). The structure of counterproductive work behaviors: Dimensionality and relationships with facets of job performance. *International Journal of Selection and Assessment, 10*(1/2), 5–11.

Schein, E. (1985). *Organizational culture and leadership.* San Francisco: Jossey–Bass.

Seabright, M. A., & Schminke, M. (2002). Immoral imagination and revenge in organizations. *Journal of Business Ethics, 38*(1/2), 19–31.

Sims, R. R. (1992). Linking groupthink to unethical behavior in organizations. *Journal of Business Ethics, 11,* 651–662.

Sims, R. R., & Brinkmann, J. (2002). Leaders as moral role models: The case of John Gutfreund at Salomon Brothers. *Journal of Business Ethics, 35,* 327–339.

Smith, G. (2002, April 8). Lying in wait. *Sports Illustrated,* pp. 70–87.

Staw, B. M., & Boettger, R. D. (1990). Task revision: A neglected form of work performance. *Academy of Management Journal, 33,* 534–559.

Valacich, J. S., & Schwenk, C. (1995). Structuring conflict in individual, face-to-face, and computer mediated group decision making: Carping versus objective devil's advocacy. *Decision Sciences, 26,* 369–393.

Van Dyne, L., & LePine, J. A. (1998). Helping and voice extra-role behaviors: Evidence of construct and predictive validity. *Academy of Management Journal, 41,* 108–119.

Vardi, Y., & Weitz, E. (2004). *Misbehavior in organizations: Theory, research, and management.* Mahwah, NJ: Lawrence Erlbaum.

Vardi, Y., & Wiener, Y. (1996). Misbehavior in organizations: A motivational framework. *Organization Science, 7,* 151–165.

Warren, D. E. (2003). Constructive and destructive deviance in organizations. *Academy of Management Review, 28,* 622–632.

Columbia/HCA
Health Care

T he U.S. government clearly stated its position on Columbia/HCA
Healthcare in 74 pages of court affidavits reported by the *Wall Street
Journal* on October 7, 1997.

A Federal Bureau of Investigation (FBI) and Defense Criminal Investigative
Service probe had "uncovered a systemic corporate scheme perpetrated by
corporate officers and managers of Columbia's hospitals, home health agencies, and other facilities in the states of Tennessee, Florida, Georgia, Texas,
and elsewhere to defraud Medicare, Medicaid, and the [Civilian Health and
Medical Program of the Uniformed Services]."

One of the government's largest Medicare fraud investigations in history,
focusing on the biggest for-profit hospital chain in the United States, had
begun several years earlier. Investigators alleged that Columbia/HCA, one of
the nation's top 10 employers and the largest buyer of medical supplies in the
world, improperly overstated the yearly reimbursements it received from
Medicare, Medicaid, and the military health care program. The company
was also charged with attempting to hide internal documents that may have
disclosed the alleged fraud and was accused of softening the language in its
internal audits that were critical of company practices.

Other allegations included false billing for laboratory blood tests, providing financial kickbacks to physicians for admitting patients into Columbia
hospitals, allowing doctors to invest in hospitals where they worked, and
charging the government for costlier care than what was provided by the
company's medical facilities.

AUTHOR'S NOTE: This case was prepared by Roland Kidwell (Niagara University) as
the basis for classroom discussion. It was developed from accounts listed in the bibliography at the end of the case. All names of individuals and the organization are real.

The probe had come to light during the summer of 1997, leading to the quick exit of Chief Executive Officer Richard Scott, the founder and prime mover in the speedy growth of Columbia/HCA. His successor as chief executive, Thomas Frist, Jr., was a Nashville, Tennessee, cardiologist who had been serving as the company's president. Frist was highly respected in the local community and the hospital industry. "We have the responsibility as caregivers to avoid even the appearance of conflicts of interest," Frist said. "Put simply, this is a new day at Columbia/HCA."

Frist initiated an independent audit of the corporation, ended physician investment in hospitals, and dropped plans for Columbia to buy hospitals in places where it faced local opposition. As the government probe of Columbia continued and spread into other segments of the U.S. health care industry, the company's reputation and stock performance spiraled downward. Frist gave himself 100 days to propose ways for the company to improve its standing among investors and other stakeholders. He stated that one element of the plan must be "a world-class ethics and compliance program."

Strategies for Rapid Growth

Scott had significant and, some believed, controversial ideas for health care. In less than 10 years, he turned two small hospitals in Texas into a 68,000-bed health care giant. Scott, a lawyer who specialized in mergers and acquisitions, established Columbia with the help of $125,000 and financier Richard Rainwater. He quickly grew the company to 600 subsidiaries and affiliates.

In 1990, Columbia became a publicly traded company. Three years later, it acquired the Galen group, adding 71 hospitals. In 1994, Columbia became the world's biggest hospital chain when it merged with HCA, a for-profit, 100-facility company founded in 1968 by Frist and his father. When Columbia/HCA was termed the "Wal-Mart of the hospital business," it was meant as a compliment.

The organization's speedy growth came during a period when the U.S. government was significantly cutting reimbursements to hospitals for Medicare, the federal government's health care program for the nation's elderly. The Medicare cutbacks led to financial crises for many for-profit and nonprofit hospitals. Columbia/HCA purchased and rescued many small hospitals from closure, but some of those purchases met with strong resistance in local communities. Critics charged that Scott was too forceful in purchasing nonprofit community hospitals and then keeping details of the transactions secret. This lack of disclosure led opponents to believe that the small hospitals were making poor deals in selling to Columbia/HCA.

By 1997, Columbia/HCA owned and operated more than 340 hospitals, 150 outpatient surgery centers, and 570 home health care locations and spas. Through the mid-1990s, the company grew by double digits nearly every year and held assets worth more than $21.3 billion. In 1996, it employed more than 285,000 people (more than General Motors) and generated $19.9 billion in revenue.

Scott, a demanding executive who scheduled weekly meetings on Mondays at 6 am, pursued a strategy of high-volume, low-cost health care. The approach included—yet went beyond—traditional means of gaining operating efficiencies such as bulk buying of medical supplies, cutting staff, and driving hard bargains with providers. Columbia/HCA engaged in what critics called the practice of corporate medicine, involving maneuvers that were viewed with disdain by some industry observers.

"For not-for-profits and for-profits, all the [operating] costs are about the same," Gerard Anderson, a health care finance expert at Johns Hopkins University, told *U.S. News and World Report.* "After you've cut costs, one way you boost revenue is by taking liberties."

Doctors were encouraged to invest in the Columbia/HCA hospitals where they were on the staffs. These investments gave the physicians financial incentives to improve quality and keep the hospitals' beds full. But the American Medical Association questioned the ethics of the practice, claiming that it hurt doctor–patient trust. Other detractors suggested that doctors would be more likely to admit insured patients to their own hospitals and send patients who could not pay to charity hospitals due to the doctors' personal financial incentives. This system was sometimes called patient skimming.

Columbia/HCA was also accused of luring high-quality doctors to work in its facilities by buying them overseas trips, providing half-priced office rent, and offering the prospect of high financial returns on investments in the hospitals.

Finally, Columbia/HCA's opponents viewed as unseemly the company's forceful competition for patients in places where its hundreds of subsidiaries and affiliates operated as well as its target of 20% profit goals, well above industry averages. To help achieve its goals, Columbia/HCA sent consultants to its hospitals to work on ensuring that maximum reimbursement for programs such as Medicare would be paid by the government. The company's goals for financial return led to suspicions that patient care was being sacrificed, but little evidence existed that the goals led to a decline in care at Columbia facilities.

Federal investigators were most interested in allegations involving fraud, kickbacks, improper referrals, laboratory billing, and a cover-up. The investigation relied heavily on company documents and more than two dozen whistle-blowers inside Columbia. The results included indictments of company subsidiaries and a handful of mid-level managers. Investigators served search warrants on company facilities in six states as part of the multiyear probe. More than 10 states began their own inquiries of Medicaid billing by the company. During the federal investigation, FBI agents moved Columbia/HCA records from company offices. One set of documents was found in a trash bin outside a gas station in El Paso, Texas.

Less than 3 months after Frist became chief executive, and a few days after the federal indictments were unsealed, Columbia/HCA hired an individual to give it an ethics makeover. Alan Yuspeh became senior vice president of ethics, compliance, and corporate responsibility.

Arrival of the Ethics Czar

When Yuspeh was introduced as Columbia/HCA's new executive devoted to ethics and compliance, he quickly stated a clear mission. He vowed to work toward establishing "the finest compliance program in the country."

Yuspeh had spent nearly two decades in Washington, D.C., as a lawyer and public servant. He served as general counsel to the Senate Armed Services Committee and as chief of staff to a U.S. senator. During the 1980s, he had been lauded for his work as executive director of the Defense Industry Initiative on Business Ethics and Conduct.

Yuspeh's voluntary compliance efforts in the defense industry began after several highly publicized scandals involving alleged private sector abuse of Pentagon contracts. Stories of $9,000 wrenches and $600 toilet seats, allegations of overcharges and fraudulent billings, and criminal investigations led to a forum in which contractors and compliance officers could discuss how to do business legally and ethically. As a result of the initiative, major defense contractors vowed to strictly enforce individual codes of ethics and promised to alert the government to any improprieties.

Only a few weeks after his arrival at Columbia/HCA, Yuspeh had written the draft of a wide-ranging new ethics code and sent it to company managers. He announced plans to send audit teams of employees to hospitals to review documents related to coding of patients' illnesses to see whether the code matched the one sent to the government for reimbursement. The audit teams were charged with ensuring that the company was not taking advantage of any gray areas in Medicare reimbursement rules.

To emphasize a culture change, Yuspeh called an ethics summit of 200 company executives in February 1998. Michael Chertoff, who led the company's defense team against federal criminal charges, warned the executives not to take risky and dubious actions in pursuing revenue for the organization. "There is a tremendous temptation to shift" costs onto Medicare reports to inflate reimbursements, Chertoff said. "But that is a real no-no."

Under Yuspeh's guidance, the company went to work on policies to make sure that overbilling was disclosed to the government on discovery rather than waiting for an investigation. Within 6 months, all of the Columbia/HCA hospitals had special ethics and compliance officers on-site to oversee and enforce operations that complied with the letter and spirit of the law. Compliance involved obeying more than 130,000 pages of Medicare rules.

The Columbia/HCA ethics and compliance plan contained basic components that Yuspeh and his ethics colleagues suggested, in a 1999 article, could serve as best practices in the health care industry: (a) structures in the organization that support the program, (b) documents such as codes of conduct that set standards of what is acceptable behavior, (c) methods to create awareness of the program among staff members, (d) a means by which violations of the standards can be reported, and (e) a way in which to monitor and audit ethical performance. In the article, Yuspeh and his colleagues wrote that establishing these elements enables an ethics and compliance program to achieve its two main purposes: (a) to make sure that everyone in the organization obeys laws and regulations and (b) to communicate ethical standards so that members of the organization have practical guidelines in making decisions that involve potentially ambiguous areas. But such a program would not work without top management leadership and commitment to change organizational culture.

Yuspeh said that the company was successful in turning around its misfortune due to values-based, principled leadership. Writing in *Executive Excellence* in 2002, Yuspeh identified three elements of principled leadership: (a) communicating principles and values such as compassion, honesty, fairness, loyalty, and respect; (b) demonstrating those principles and values in decisions made by leaders; and (c) reflecting those principles and values when dealing with others.

From those three elements, Yuspeh suggested that a person who practices principled leadership articulates primary values, principles, and goals—and sticks to them—is proactive and innovative, confronts problems directly and honestly, cares about people inside and outside the organization, listens to others and includes them in making decisions, is humble and honest, gives as much responsibility to others as possible, builds a team, and celebrates organizational achievements. Yuspeh wrote that Frist and his father, who had founded HCA many years earlier, had laid the foundation for principled leadership in the company.

A Settlement Is Reached

More than 3 years after Yuspeh and his colleagues began putting the company's ethical house in order, judgment day arrived with the federal government. By that time, the company had been renamed HCA to further diminish the taint of scandal associated with the Columbia label.

The company pleaded guilty to unlawful billing practices and was assessed more than $840 million in criminal fines, damages, and civil penalties. The company admitted to overstating expenses for reimbursement to the government, embellishing patient diagnoses to get higher reimbursements, improperly structuring its business deals to shift costs to Medicare, and giving doctors kickbacks in exchange for patient referrals. Two middle managers who had been convicted in connection with the investigation had their convictions overturned on appeal. No senior executives were criminally charged.

Along with the fines, HCA agreed to an 8-year corporate integrity agreement with the U.S. Department of Health and Human Services, requiring the company to increase its reviews of inpatient coding, laboratory billing, outpatient billing, and financial relationships with physicians and to report its activities to the government.

The settlement helps to "allow us to move forward, maintaining our focus on providing quality patient care," Frist said.

The New HCA: An Ethical and Effective Organization?

We are committed to an environment in which compliance with rules, regulations, and sound business practices is woven into the corporate culture. We accept responsibility to aggressively self-govern and monitor adherence to the requirements of law and to our Code of Conduct. (HCA Code of Conduct, April 2003, http://ec.hcahealthcare.com)

HCA's corporate integrity accord, agreed to on January 25, 2001, is to stay in effect until 2009. As part of its compliance program, the company handles hundreds of ethics-related complaints each year. To assist in enforcing its program, the HCA board has established an ethics and compliance committee of independent directors and two separate corporate committees to draft ethics policy and monitor ethical behavior. HCA spends approximately $4 million a year on its ethics department in addition to the costs of ethics monitors in its hospitals and ethics training for all of its employees, according to *Forbes* magazine.

In 2004, HCA employees numbered around 190,000 due to the restructuring and sale of more than 160 HCA hospitals over several years. Industry observers cited the restructuring as one reason why HCA stock rose nearly 15% over 2 years to $41 in May 2003. (The S&P 500 lost approximately a third of its value during the same period.) The company's net income for 2002 rose 35%, and revenues were up 10%. (In 1998, a few months after the scandal surfaced, the stock price had dipped below $20 a share and profits experienced a substantial decline.)

As part of its compliance plan, all HCA locations display posters that urge employees to report various violations to supervisors or to call a 24-hour ethics hotline. The code of conduct also includes limits on invitations to social events worth more than $100 per event, sets limits on gifts from business associates ($50 or less per year from the same person), and restricts employees making gifts to Medicare or Medicaid beneficiaries to $10 per gift and $50 per year per recipient.

"Internal controls can always be corrupted," Jack O. Bovender, HCA's chief executive, said in an interview with *Forbes* magazine in 2003. "We've tried to come up with a system that would require a lot of people to conspire."

Another view came from a rank-and-file employee. "The [ethics] training is a waste of time and money," a nurse at a Florida hospital told *Forbes*.

"Anyone with two brain cells could figure out the stuff they're teaching us, and besides, the fraud that supposedly happened was high up in the company."

Discussion Questions

1. List and analyze some examples of deviant and destructive behavior discovered in Columbia/HCA. Why did this behavior occur, and how might it have been prevented?

2. Explain the process used to discourage improper behavior and encourage ethical behavior within the organization. What key steps were involved?

3. Access the HCA Code of Conduct (http://hcahealthcare.com). What are the significant elements of the HCA code, and how are they designed to limit illegal and unethical behavior within the organization? If you were a colleague (employee) of HCA, how would you feel about working at this company?

4. Was HCA's emphasis on ethics useful in helping the company to achieve its goals? Is it a more effective company due to its ethics and compliance emphasis? Why or why not?

Bibliography

Charatan, F. (2001). U.S. settles biggest ever healthcare fraud case. *British Medical Journal, 322,* 10. Retrieved August 7, 2003, from http://proquest.umi.com/pqdweb

Headden, S. (1997, August 11). Code blue at Columbia/HCA. *U.S. News & World Report,* pp. 20–22. Retrieved August 7, 2003, from http://proquest.umi.com/pqdweb

HCA Healthcare. (2003). HCA Code of Conduct (effective April 15, 2003). Retrieved November 12, 2003, from http://ec.hcahealthcare.com

Lagnado, L. (1997, October 14). Columbia taps lawyer for ethics post: Yuspeh led defense initiative of 1980s. *The Wall Street Journal,* p. B6. Retrieved August 7, 2003, from http://proquest.umi.com/pqdweb

Lagnado, L. (1998, February 13). Lawyer tells Columbia/HCA officials not to "push the envelope" for profits. *The Wall Street Journal,* p. B7. Retrieved November 11, 2003, from http://proquest.umi.com/pqdweb

Lagnado, L. (1999, November 24). Columbia/HCA whistle-blowers to fight for gold: Lawyers and clients maneuver as settlement talks heat up in probe of Medicare fraud. *The Wall Street Journal,* pp. B1–B2. Retrieved August 7, 2003, from http://proquest.umi.com/pqdweb

Pasztor, A., & Lagnado, L. (1997, November 26). Health care: Ethics czar aims to heal Columbia. *The Wall Street Journal,* p. B1. Retrieved August 7, 2003, from http://proquest.umi.com/pqdweb

Rodriguez, E. M., & Lagnado, L. (1997, October 7). U.S. claims deep fraud at Columbia. *The Wall Street Journal,* p. A3. Retrieved August 7, 2003, from http://proquest.umi.com/pqdweb

Roslokken, D. W. (1997, December). Columbia/HCA under siege. *Managed Healthcare,* pp. 34–36. Retrieved August 7, 2003, from http://proquest.umi. com/pqdweb

Taylor, M. (2000, December 18–25). The dust finally clears. *Modern Healthcare,* pp. 3, 14. Retrieved August 7, 2003, from http://proquest.umi.com/pqdweb

Weinberg, N. (2003, March 17). Healing thyself. *Forbes,* pp. 64–68. Retrieved August 7, 2003, from http://proquest.umi.com/pqdweb

Yuspeh, A. (2002, January). Principled leadership. *Executive Excellence, 19*(1), 3–4. Retrieved November 11, 2003, from http://proquest.umi.com/pqdweb

Yuspeh, A., Whalen, K., Cecelic, J., Clifton, S., et al. (1999, Winter). Above reproach: Developing a comprehensive ethics and compliance program [electronic version]. *Frontiers of Health Services Management,* pp. 3–38.

The Undercover Operator

Anita Mancuso

Timothy O. Ireland

T he use of undercover police work is a source of debate, not only among criminal justice scholars but also in society at large.

Some argue that the police must—in all situations, including undercover actions—obey the law. Any erosion of the rule of law has long-term negative consequences that arguably work to unravel the very fabric of organized society and outweigh any short-term benefits. Others argue that undercover operations are a "necessary evil." For example, there is no better way to catch a drug dealer than to buy drugs from him or her or to investigate public corruption than to bribe a government official.

Undercover operations, by definition, take place outside the regular scrutiny of departmental supervisors, uniformed colleagues, and the general public. As a result, concerns about the discretion and conduct of undercover operators come to the forefront and their actions are often called into question. Also, research on undercover operations has not consistently shown benefits in terms of arrests and/or prosecutions that exceed the monetary costs of the operations or the personal costs to the undercover operators. In fact, some research suggests that undercover police actions can entice the average person, who might not have otherwise committed an illegal act, to do so.

When most people think of undercover operations, what comes to mind is something along the lines of infiltration by an undercover operator into an organization systematically engaged in crime such as the Mafia or a motorcycle gang. In theory, these operations target career criminals. Undercover operations also can be set up as integrity tests for those who might be tempted to commit a crime given a certain set of circumstances. Finally, undercover operations may use informants to assist undercover operators in building a case against a particular individual or organization. Some informants conduct their own criminal ventures behind the protective cloak of "working for the police," and this is problematic.

This case is designed to provide a context for exploring some of the complexities of undercover operations and to address the ambiguous nature of deviant behavior. In the case, a fictional police officer discusses various issues involved in undercover operations. The officer is a composite of numerous contacts, discussions, and experiences of the authors, and his narrative highlights some of the ethical challenges of working undercover.

Undercover Work

I've been a police officer in a major metropolitan city in North America for the past 15 years. After about a year on road patrol, I began making repeated requests to join the drug squad, the street crime unit, or the vice unit. I finally got a call to assist the street crime unit. I knew this was a temporary thing; they just needed a fresh face for a short term of "sting" play. But I also recognized that this was the opportunity I had been waiting for and that it could open the door to a permanent position. I knew that to do well as an undercover officer, I had to make arrests. So, my first time with the street crime unit, I was hungry to make arrests.

I had a strange feeling that first night. I had never reported for duty without wearing my uniform. The uniform always reminded me of who I was; it governed my actions, what I said, and how I acted. Also, because of the uniform, everyone else was quick to tell me what I couldn't do and what I couldn't say. Without a uniform, I could blend in with the street life and disappear for hours. It didn't seem like I was accountable to either my supervisor or, for that matter, the public.

Anyway, I was assigned to a detail with two other undercover officers, and our job was to focus on robberies and larcenies in the subway system. I told them that I needed an arrest to increase my chances of getting a permanent assignment to an undercover squad. They both agreed to "work" and described a decoy strategy that was sure to land a quick and easy arrest.

Following their directions, I poured booze on my clothes and pretended to be passed out on a bench on the subway platform waiting for the train. My props were a flashy gold watch and a money clip partially hanging out of my front pocket. I was supposed to portray a possible victim—an easy mark—waiting for someone to rip me off. As the time ticked by, I had to remain in the "role" of a drunk. I couldn't shift my position, I couldn't get up and stretch, and I couldn't open my eyes and look around. I had to remain "passed out." Sometime later, a few people came into the tunnel. As the cover team waited and watched, I heard a group of guys arguing. Then I heard footsteps heading toward me, and I felt one of the guys kick my feet—I guess to see whether I was asleep. I groaned but pretended not to wake up. I was nervous—anything could happen. I couldn't tell if they were armed, and I couldn't tell how many of them there were or even where they were or what they were doing. In fact, I realized that I had no idea what any of them even looked like.

As the train pulled into the station, I felt a hand go into my pocket and another tug at my wrist. I had never done this before, but my partners had told me not to react, and I fought my instincts and training. I was dying to jump up and grab whoever it was, but I didn't. I continued to lay there as though I was too drunk to feel anything. My partners appeared, and they arrested three young males. I made sure I didn't blow my cover, and my team "woke me up" to inform me that the suspects had attempted to rob me. I guess that was to ensure that I could repeat my performance on the next night without anyone knowing that I was a decoy.

All three arrestees claimed to be college students who had never been in trouble with the police before. This didn't seem to matter to my partners, who called for a wagon to transport them to the precinct where the arrests were processed. In fact, all three had told the truth; none of the thieves had been arrested before, and the night court judge released them without bail.

I couldn't believe that this was my "job" and I was getting paid for doing it. Over the next few months, I acted as a decoy on occasion. Each time we went out, we were able to make an arrest, and I began to develop a reputation as a good undercover cop. However, of all the people arrested while I was acting as a decoy, only one had a criminal history. For all of the others, it was their first arrest.

I continued to pester the sergeants heading up the undercover units, and after about 3 years on the job, I was transferred to the drug squad. Although I had received some on-the-job training as a decoy, the permanent assignment to the drug squad was a whole new experience and I had to learn a new "game" basically through trial and error. My first detail was to work in a drug-infested area of the city with an open-air drug market. Through conversations with some of the more senior undercover operators in the drug squad, I tried to learn the language of the streets. I listened to hours of war stories. I watched how they walked and talked, how they dressed, and how they wore their hair. I studied their mannerisms. Of course, as the rookie, I said nothing. I knew that this was the only way I was going to become a successful undercover operator. I also learned that it was all a game, that the rules were defined by deception, and that the only winners had to be us.

Drug dealers are always watching out for signs that the buyer is not a legitimate user but instead a police officer. The dealers will look for a variety of cues to determine whether a prospective buyer is legitimate—are the clothes too nice, are the shoes too new, is the hair too clean, and how about the hands and under the fingernails? The dealer constantly asks himself how the buyer was introduced and by whom—does the buyer speak too properly, does he or she smell too good, is there nervousness in the body language or the voice, is there desperation in the eyes? All of these cues let the seller know whether the buyer is legitimate or a narc. I realized that there was no school for this kind of training, that there were no formalized rules, and that you simply learned what works and what doesn't through trial and error as well as vicariously through other cops' experiences.

The first time I did a buy and bust, I was nervous as hell, but it worked. I walked away with a package of heroin, and my cover team observed the transaction and then executed an arrest as I walked away with the drugs. The next day, I did the exact same play, except this time the dealer gave me his cell phone number. He told me to call him anytime I wanted to score. I wasn't sure exactly what to do with the number, but this guy just didn't seem to be your average everyday street user/dealer. He was slick, and everyone around seemed to be showing him respect. So, I made the decision not to signal for his arrest.

I met with the members of my cover team instead and told them what had happened. I guess it was the right thing to do. They were ecstatic and advised our boss of the situation. One member of the cover team recognized the dealer as a small-time criminal from the projects, but based on the seller's behavior, the cop figured he had become a big-time heroin supplier in the neighborhood.

Our supervisor approved the launch of a project revolving around this key player, and it became my full-time job, that is, 24/7. All of a sudden, I didn't have days off, and the fictional person I created to make a simple street buy took on his own three-dimensional life. I befriended the dealer, and we became "business associates." Besides several long meetings to plan and buy heroin, I socialized with him and became his friend. As time went on, I met his wife and kids, his brother, and some of his other business associates. As I bought more and more heroin and spent more money, it seemed as though the dealer's trust in me grew. In fact, he didn't seem to be such a bad guy after I got to know him, and he always seemed to want to please me.

The department higher-ups began to get nervous and wanted arrests and seizures, but what they really wanted was for us to get to the dealer's suppliers. That day finally came when I ordered more heroin than my dealer could be trusted to deliver. The plan worked, and his supplier had to meet me to complete the deal. My dealer introduced me as his best customer from way back, although in reality I'd known him for only a few months. At that very moment, I knew my dealer had signed his own death warrant, not with the police but with those he feared more—the suppliers.

The deal went through without a hitch, and at the end of a very long 36-hour shift, 18 search warrants were executed, 27 people were placed under arrest, 254 charges were filed, and 10 semiautomatic handguns, 14 kilos (more than 30 pounds) of heroin, and $1.5 million were seized.

Eventually, most of the players got bail. The next time I saw all of the arrested parties was at the courthouse several months later. They all looked at me as though I was the bad guy. Everyone was there except my dealer. A warrant is still out for his arrest. Some say he was killed by the suppliers for bringing me into the organization, and others say he left the country. I prefer to believe the latter, although other guys on the crew say he got what he deserved. You know, "What goes around comes around, and when you play with fire you get burned. Besides, he was a drug dealer."

After months on the streets working as an undercover operator in the drug squad, I developed relationships with several informants who helped me to make cases. Each of the informants was involved in the criminal lifestyle in one way or another, and many had drug problems. Some were "small fish" who I had arrested in the past and who wanted to trade information for consideration on their charges. Other informants were "cop wannabes" who probably watched too many cop shows on television. These informants tended to live on the periphery of the criminal world for the sole purpose of working with police. Still others decided to become informants to make money off the system. These "informants for profit" often had the best information, but they were also the most dangerous because they would sell information to the highest bidder—cop or criminal.

Shortly after finishing the heroin project, a call came into the office from an informant. The informant was a "proven and reliable" source, which basically meant that in the past he had given information that turned out to be accurate and could withstand the scrutiny of the judicial system. This informant claimed that he knew the location of a large stash of cocaine and a handgun. All that we had to do in return for the information was to help him out of a bit of trouble with uniformed officers first. This informant, like the majority of informants I met over the years, was drug addicted. As a result, he periodically had problems with paranoia, trust, reliability, clarity of thinking, and recall. After checking out his information, we agreed that the target had a lot of potential. The informant agreed to take me in an undercover capacity and introduce me to the target. So, I was launched into another full-scale illicit drug project. I ended up buying several pounds of cocaine over a span of 6 months. My relationship with the dealer developed into a routine business partnership grounded in mutual respect and trust. The deals went smoothly, and I eventually became a recognized element of the organization's hierarchy. But after several months, the project was finally slated to end.

The supervisors and project leaders decided on one last big buy to draw out the major players and the main supplier/importer. As I did on every occasion, I called my connection and we made our usual plan to meet and talk face-to-face about my order. But I knew something was wrong; it was in his voice, and I felt it again when he told me where to meet him. I tried to convince my boss and crew that something was up, but the higher-ups decided that I had to make this final deal happen. The department had spent too much time and money to pull out and not arrest the supplier. I took all the extra precautions that I usually didn't bother with; I hid a small gun in my boot, and I wore a transmitter so that my cover team could monitor the meeting.

When I arrived at the meeting location, my informant was sitting in the corner just looking at me; he didn't say a word. I hadn't seen or heard from him in a couple of months, and by the looks of things, he had fallen on desperate times. Obviously, to feed his addiction, he had given me up to the target. My connection began the meeting by calling me by my real name, telling me my address, and listing off the names of my girlfriend and her kids. I could see the gun, a semiautomatic, sitting in his waistband, and I also could see that the target had brought friends. I tried my best to buy time by discrediting the "junkie" informant. I knew that the dealer was weighing his options; if the informant was telling the truth, he was looking at a long prison sentence, but if the informant was lying, he didn't want to blow such a profitable deal.

My crew, listening outside, picked up on the problem and decided to execute the arrests before I lost the dance and got shot. The arrests didn't go down easily, and the informant was shot in the leg; I'm not sure whether it was by us or them. One of my crew members was shot in the shoulder while he was covering me, and two of the dealer's crew members were shot and killed. A shipment of cocaine and millions of dollars and assets were seized. In all, 14 members of the drug organization were arrested and 167 charges were filed. All of those arrested were convicted, even the informant.

I guess that the operation was a success because the department put out a major press release. However, what it meant to me didn't make the news. After the arrests, I received a number of death threats directed at me and my family. The department considered the threats to be authentic and feared for my family's safety. So, they set up uniformed police cars outside my house until the defendants were convicted and sentenced. I continued to work undercover for several more years, always looking over my shoulder and worrying about the well-being of my family.

Conclusion

In the end, after years in the drug squad, I requested a transfer back to patrol. Had I done any good? Were crime rates lower in the city? What had I accomplished with all of the risks I had taken? I know now what I lost—my personal life was in shambles. My girlfriend decided that seeing me once every 2 or 3 weeks just was not a relationship, and all of my civilian friends no longer called me. I also experienced types of stress that patrol officers typically do not face, for example, the risk of saying the wrong thing at the wrong time and compromising my cover, the constant moral ambiguity of using questionable means to bring about desired ends, and the possibility of running into a mark when I was not "on the job."

Working undercover is not a promotion in most police departments. Instead, it is an assignment. At the end of the assignment, most undercover operators return to traditional road patrol, but because they have been outside the traditional command-and-control structure, they have missed out on opportunities for additional training and promotion. That is exactly what happened to me.

Finally, there was quite a disconnect between the criteria used to hire me as a police officer and the skill set required to be a successful undercover operator. During the initial hiring process, significant resources were expended to make sure that I was of good moral character and that I exemplified honor, integrity, and courage. However, on entering undercover police work, I was required to leave much of my moral character at the precinct. Out on the streets, what worked was deceiving, cheating, establishing false friendships, developing false trust, and manipulating people, all in the name of fighting crime. However, this skill set cannot be used when dealing with supervisors, it certainly cannot be used in the courts, and it is not supposed to spill over into an officer's personal life. Reflecting back on my experiences, it truly was a strange experience for a young rookie cop, and it significantly affected both my personal and professional lives.

Discussion Questions

1. Of the three undercover scenarios described in the case, which is the most morally questionable? Which is the least questionable? Why? Explain the functional and dysfunctional aspects of the undercover officer's behavior in the case.

2. Consider the points of view regarding deviance that are expressed in Chapter 1. Is the undercover operator in this case engaging in deviant behavior? Is the operator's behavior positive or negative? Why or why not?

3. Should the police be involved in integrity tests using decoys designed to entice generally law-abiding citizens and/or other police officers into criminal activity? What ethical standards should be required of undercover operators?

4. What is the level of training that this undercover officer received? Should there be more training of undercover officers? Is it unethical to demand results (e.g., more arrests, reduced crime, higher sales, high-quality work) from people in high-stress jobs with minimal training or support services? Explain.

5. In many undercover operations, achieved ends are said to justify questionable means. What can happen in business when such an ethos is practiced?

CHAPTER 2

Why Good Employees Make Unethical Decisions

The Role of Reward Systems, Organizational Culture, and Managerial Oversight

Jennifer Dunn

Maurice E. Schweitzer

> *It was just something we hoped would go away.*
>
> —Anonymous Beech-Nut employee

On November 5, 1986, Neils Hoyvald, the president of Beech-Nut, and five others were indicted for knowingly selling sugar water as apple juice concentrate. The evidence was overwhelming, and in 1987 Beech-Nut and its supplier, Universal Juice Company, pleaded guilty and agreed to pay a record $2 million fine and an additional $7.5 million to settle a class-action lawsuit ($2.5 million to retailers and $5 million to customers). Beech-Nut's market share fell by 20%, and overall the company lost $25 million in fines, legal fees, and lost

AUTHORS' NOTE: We thank Michael Darer for research assistance.

sales. In addition, two Beech-Nut executives were found guilty, fined $100,000, and sentenced to a year and a day in jail (Welles, 1988).

Beech-Nut's problems started in 1977 when the company agreed to purchase apple juice concentrate from Interjuice Trading Corporation. The wholesaler charged Beech-Nut prices that were 20% below market. The research and development department was suspicious at the time, and initial tests conducted by a company-hired laboratory indicated that the apple juice concentrate might be adulterated. Despite these concerns, senior management decided to purchase and market the concentrate. The concentrate, which was actually sugar water, was labeled as 100% apple juice and was sold in 20 states and five foreign countries.

As the U.S. government began to conduct laboratory tests on the concentrate in September 1982, Beech-Nut had it shipped to a different warehouse and then to Puerto Rico to avoid detection. (Notably, even this concentrate was sold, apparently so that Beech-Nut would not lose the $3.5 million it had spent to purchase the concentrate.) An anonymous letter sent to the Food and Drug Administration in 1983 revealed Beech-Nut's early knowledge of the adulteration and led to the subsequent criminal and civil charges.

The story of Beech-Nut holds several important lessons. The Beech-Nut employees involved in this conduct were not hardened miscreants, yet the problems at Beech-Nut were pervasive. In this chapter, we consider the important question of why otherwise good employees engage in unethical actions, and we identify specific steps that managers can take to guide ethical behavior within their organization.

Why Focus on Ethics?

Unethical behavior represents a serious organizational challenge. Although recent scandals have uncovered serious misconduct by top executives at companies such as Enron, WorldCom, and Tyco, unethical behavior pervades all levels of organizational life. According to the 2000 KPMG Organizational Integrity Survey, 76% of surveyed employees had observed illegal or unethical conduct at work, and 49% had observed serious misconduct (KPMG, 2000). Unethical acts can cause serious harm to an organization as well as to the broader community. Donaldson (2001) argued that nations as a whole benefit from a strong commitment to ethics and that a commitment to moral principles offers a competitive economic advantage.

Even small ethical failures matter. Small lapses may be more frequent as people find them easier to justify (Schweitzer & Hsee, 2002). As the Beech-Nut example illustrates, however, small unethical actions can easily grow into larger problems. Beech-Nut employees first purchased suspicious concentrate, then knowingly sold mislabeled concentrate, and finally worked to conceal their actions.

Fortunately, managerial action can have a significant impact on ethical behavior within an organization. We discuss actions that managers at all levels can take to influence ethical behavior within their organizations.

The Manager's Tool Kit

Managers strive to maximize the productivity of their employees. At the same time, however, managers need to care not only about *what* their employees produce but also about *how* the employees achieve their outcomes.

In motivating performance and guiding ethical behavior, managers need to balance a number of competing concerns. We consider three specific tools that managers can use to influence their employees: (a) reward systems, (b) organizational culture, and (c) monitoring systems. Reward systems reflect the incentives that employees face. Within an organization, what actions are rewarded? What actions are punished? And, importantly, what gets measured? Organizational culture represents the set of workplace norms. These norms include unstated rules regarding expected behavior. Monitoring represents the amount of oversight that managers use to examine organizational processes. We describe how each of these tools affects employee attitudes and perceptions about ethics that ultimately influence employees' ethical behavior.

A Model of Ethical Decision Making

In this section, we describe a basic model of ethical decision making based on the theory of planned behavior (Ajzen, 1985, 1987). First we describe the model, and then we describe how the three tools—incentives, organizational culture, and monitoring—operate within this theoretical framework.

Theory of Planned Behavior

We depict the theory of planned behavior in Figure 2.1. This theory assumes that an individual's behavior is influenced by a number of factors, including judgments of expected costs and benefits, group norms, and self-efficacy. We use this framework for several reasons. First, the theory of planned behavior framework offers insight into how reward systems, organizational culture, and monitoring affect ethical decision making. Second, the model successfully explains many human behaviors (Madden, Ellen, & Ajzen, 1992; Sheppard, Hartwick, & Warshaw, 1988) and has been applied to ethical decision making involving software piracy (Chang, 1998), overselling (Kurland, 1995), and reporting misconduct (Randall & Gibson, 1991). Third, this theory is consistent with a number of other theoretical models of decision making (e.g., Lewicki, 1983).

According to the theory of planned behavior, three key factors influence intentions and thereby influence behavior: *attitudes* toward the behavior, *subjective norms,* and *perceived control.* These three factors are influenced by *behavioral, normative,* and *control* beliefs, respectively. The theory of planned behavior is an extension of the theory of reasoned action (Ajzen & Fishbein, 1980), with the chief modification being the addition of perceived behavioral control and beliefs that influence perceived control.

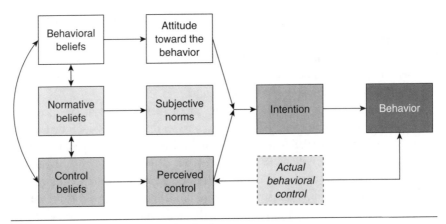

Figure 2.1   Theory of Planned Behavior

SOURCE: Ajzen (1985).

Behavioral Beliefs and Attitudes

Before taking an action, people assess the consequences of different alternatives. These assessments include judgments of the likelihood of different outcomes and the costs and benefits associated with those outcomes. For example, consider a potential seller who contemplates misrepresenting the condition of her used car. This seller might judge potential outcomes of the unethical act (misrepresenting the condition of the car) in the following way: an 80% chance of receiving an additional $500 from the potential buyer and a 20% chance of losing the sale. In this model, *behavioral beliefs* (a decision maker's expectations for a particular ethical behavior) influence *attitudes* (general feelings of favorableness for the behavior). In our example, the more money the seller believes that she might get by misrepresenting the condition of the car, the more favorable her attitude will be for engaging in this unethical act. Importantly, behavioral beliefs are grounded in *perceptions* of the costs, benefits, and likelihoods of different outcomes. Factors that influence these perceptions will influence both behavioral beliefs and attitudes and subsequently will influence ethical behavior. For example, if the buyer announces that he plans to take the car to a mechanic before he makes an offer, the seller might lower her perceived likelihood of making additional money from a misrepresentation (to a probability less than 80%).

Normative Beliefs and Subjective Norms

People's ethical decisions are also heavily influenced by the ethical views held by those around them. More formally, decision makers develop *subjective norms* by considering the *normative beliefs* of salient peers. For example, employees are more likely to think that padding an expense report is acceptable (a subjective norm) if the coworkers they respect (their salient peers) think that padding an expense report is acceptable (their coworkers' normative beliefs). The views of some peers are more influential than the views of other peers. For example, some coworkers, such as managers, will exert more influence (i.e., have a greater impact on an individual's subjective norms) than will other coworkers. In addition, the relative importance of different peer views can change across contexts. For example, an employee may value a coworker's ethical opinion regarding how honestly to complete an expense report but might not value that same coworker's ethical opinion regarding how ethical it is to illegally download copyrighted music.

Control Beliefs and Perceived Control

Ethical decision making is also influenced by *control beliefs*, that is, an individual's beliefs about his or her power to engage in a particular behavior. These beliefs are informed by perceived opportunities to commit an unethical act, resources to commit the act, and the decision maker's self-efficacy (belief in his or her own ability) for a particular behavior. For example, an employee may consider lying to his boss to attend an afternoon baseball game. The employee may want to do so (a behavioral belief) and may have coworkers urging him to do so (with these coworkers informing his normative beliefs), but he may perceive himself to be a poor and unconvincing liar and, thus, is unable to do so (his control belief). Even if the employee has confidence in his deceptive ability and intends to lie to his boss, he might find that his boss is unreachable for the rest of the day, precluding him from engaging in this particular unethical act. Both perceived control over behavior and actual control over behavior influence ethical actions.

Applications to Ethical Behavior

We depict the relationship between the managerial tools of reward systems, organizational culture, and monitoring and ethical behavior in Figure 2.2. The thick arrows between tools and beliefs represent the primary influence that we expect each tool to have on beliefs that drive ethical behavior. The dashed lines represent secondary effects that each tool may have on other beliefs.

A number of factors not included in this model are also important to ethical decision making (e.g., gender, personality, religiosity). In this chapter, however, we focus on the specific tools of reward systems, organizational culture, and monitoring for two reasons. First, the tools we identify are particularly important drivers of ethical behavior within organizations. For example, as the Sears case that follows this chapter (Case 2) illustrates, managers who change incentive systems can dramatically affect ethical decision making within their organization. Second, these tools are readily available to most managers. That is, managers can influence incentives, culture, and monitoring within their organization more easily than they can influence other factors such as the personalities of their employees.

In the next three sections, we describe the relationship between each of these tools and ethical behavior. We conclude the chapter by discussing the interdependence of

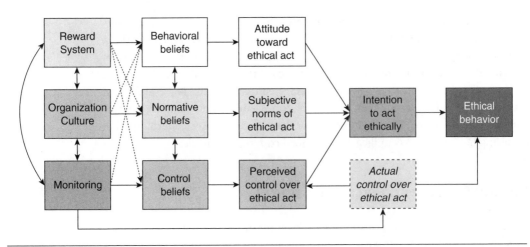

Figure 2.2   Managerial Influence on Ethical Decision Making (based on theory of planned behavior)

SOURCE: Ajzen (1985).

the three tools and by describing specific actions that managers can take to promote ethical behavior within their organization.

Reward Systems

Reward systems represent a direct managerial lever for influencing behavior. Reward systems include both positive and negative incentives and can take a number of different forms such as salary, promotions, bonuses, and sanctions.

Reward systems are typically designed to motivate work performance, but they can have important and unintended consequences for unethical behavior. For example, the owner of a car dealership might pay her employees a large bonus for selling 30 cars during a month. This incentive system communicates clear goals and identifies desirable organizational behavior, that is, to work hard to sell cars. Unfortunately, this incentive system might also encourage employees to engage in unethical behavior. Employees may perceive that unethical practices (e.g., using high-pressure sales tactics, recording fake sales) will lead to outcomes (sales) that are rewarded by the organization. As a result, employees' attitudes toward some unethical behaviors may become more favorable and may ultimately increase their likelihood of engaging in unethical acts.

The challenge of structuring an incentive system that motivates constructive effort without motivating unethical behavior is ubiquitous. Take, for example, law and consulting firms that offer a bonus for billing a specific number of hours. On the one hand, this incentive system leads employees to work long hours when they might otherwise leave work early. On the other hand, this system sometimes leads employees to work inefficiently or to misrepresent the number of hours they actually worked.

The case of L&H Korea offers an illustrative example of how incentive systems can contribute to ethical lapses ("L&H Korea Probe Reports," 2001). L&H Korea, a South Korean software company, offered employees large financial incentives for reaching ambitious sales targets. In fact, the head of the company, Joo Chul Seo, earned a $25 million bonus for reaching specific sales targets. These incentive systems encouraged L&H employees to work very hard to sell software. Unfortunately, these same incentives also encouraged L&H employees to misrepresent their sales.

In fact, L&H Korea employees routinely falsified accounting books to hit sales targets. Of the $160 million in sales booked from September 1999 through June 2000, 70% were fictitious. L&H had misrepresented factoring arrangements with South Korean banks to convince the company's auditor, KPMG, that customers had paid when in fact they had not.

The deception even went a step further. When KPMG accountants sought to verify that the payments did in fact come from customers, L&H Korea employees would pose as clients. When this deception was uncovered, L&H's share price dropped from $70 a share to approximately $1 a share, the company's stock was removed from the NASDAQ exchange, and the South Korea operations were shut down.

As the L&H Korea example suggests, reward systems need to be carefully designed and, as we discuss later in this chapter, performance needs to be carefully monitored. In many cases, employees face significant performance pressure that drives unethical behavior. The 2000 KPMG Organizational Integrity Survey found that three of the top four causes of unethical behavior were related to performance pressure and the desire to succeed (KPMG, 2000). In fact, at Beech-Nut, management was under great financial pressure, and the use of inexpensive (nonjuice) concentrate offered a way in which to "save" millions of dollars.

These findings are consistent with academic work that has consistently found that incentives influence unethical decision making (Flannery & May, 2000; Hegarty & Sims, 1978; Tenbrunsel, 1998). In a negotiation exercise, Tenbrunsel (1998) found that 41% of participants in the "low-incentive" condition misrepresented information, whereas 70% of participants in the "high-incentive" condition misrepresented information. In a business simulation, Hegarty and Sims (1978) informed participants that some of their salesmen were providing kickbacks to purchasing agents. They varied participants' expected consequences for stopping the kickbacks. These authors found that participants were less likely to stop kickbacks when they expected sales to decline than when they did not know whether or not they would lose sales. In a study of metal-finishing managers, Flannery and May (2000) found that intentions to pollute the environment were positively related to the perceived costs of more ethical alternatives.

Goal Setting and Unethical Behavior

A large goal-setting literature (for a review, see Locke & Latham, 1990) describes the role of goals in motivating effort. Relatively few studies, however, have examined the role of these same incentive systems in motivating unethical behavior (for an exception, see Schweitzer, Ordonez, & Douma, 2004). As Schweitzer and colleagues (2004) demonstrated, just as goal setting motivates constructive effort, goal setting also motivates unethical behavior. Just as employees of L&H Korea were motivated to work harder, they were also motivated to act unethically. More broadly, Jensen (2001) suggested that corporate budgeting systems that offer executives performance-based incentives create incentives to "game the system." Ultimately, to reach specific goals, executives may take actions that decrease the value of the company.

The vast majority of studies investigating goal setting have found that goals motivate people to work more persistently. In addition to monetary awards for reaching goals, the goal-setting process creates psychological rewards that motivate both constructive and unethical behaviors. When employees reach their goals, they derive psychological rewards (e.g., satisfaction). However, people may derive psychological rewards for merely *claiming* to have reached a goal even when in fact they have not. Work by Schweitzer and colleagues (2004) found that people with a goal were more likely to claim that they had completed work, when in fact they had not, than were people without a goal. In fact, people who fell just short of their goal were those who were most likely to lie about having met the goal when in fact they had not.

Sanctions

Just as the perceived benefits of unethical behavior can encourage unethical acts, so too can the perceived costs of unethical behavior curtail unethical acts. This is particularly true for strong sanctions. In their business simulation, Hegarty and Sims (1978) found that participants who were informed that retaining kickbacks put them at risk for legal liability were more likely to stop retaining kickbacks than were participants who did not receive a liability threat. For the metal-finishing managers in Flannery and May's (2000) research, when the environmental consequences of unethical behavior were extreme, managers were less likely to make unethical decisions even when ethical behavior was costly.

There is also evidence that the use of sanctions can have adverse effects. Tenbrunsel and Messick (1999) found that weak sanctions can harm cooperation and ethical behavior. In fact, the mere presence of a sanction system can influence the way in which people perceive the nature of the decision they face. Specifically, when faced with possible sanctions, employees are more likely to perceive a decision as a "business" decision than as an ethical decision. By changing the nature of the decision, sanctions may exacerbate an individual's focus on financial costs and benefits at the expense of focus on psychological outcomes (e.g., moral beliefs about the behavior).

Prescriptions for Managing Incentives

Managers need to consider a number of factors in designing appropriate incentive systems. In some cases, such as with goal setting and sanctions, managers will need to make trade-offs with respect to motivating performance and, perhaps unintentionally, motivating unethical behavior.

An important and related issue is that of measurement. That is, what is it that managers measure when rewarding employees? Is it hours worked, cars sold, or phone calls answered? For example, employees in a call center who are rewarded for the number of calls they complete may deliver bad service and hang up prematurely to "complete" calls as quickly as they can. People respond to the incentive system in place and often ignore other stated goals (Kerr, 1995). In the case of the phone operators, employees who face an incentive system that measures the number of calls they complete might focus on the reward system (e.g., calls completed) and ignore other stated goals (e.g., high-quality service). By focusing on the broader objectives of the organization, a manager can design incentives to reflect the organization's goals.

Ethical decision making itself should be rewarded in the organization. For example, employees should be rewarded for whistle-blowing. Unethical behavior should be punished, but as Tenbrunsel and Messick (1999) and Treviño, Weaver, Gibson, and Toffler (1999) found, it is more important for ethical behavior to be rewarded than for unethical behavior to be punished.

In addition to identifying appropriate measurement standards, managers should identify appropriate measurement time horizons. For example, are the reward systems designed to reward short-term or long-term performance? In general, a short-term focus will promote more unethical behavior than will a long-term focus. In working toward short-term rewards, individuals may reap the immediate rewards of unethical behavior long before their unethical actions are discovered (this may be after the employees have left the organization). In addition, individuals under time pressure may view unethical "quick fixes" as a way to avoid, at least in the short term, the costs of underperformance. Some employees may plan to repair their unethical actions "once the pressure is off," but a sequence of short-term fixes may exacerbate the underlying condition. Ultimately, a series of small unethical actions by well-intentioned but misguided employees can create serious long-term consequences.

Incentive systems can influence factors in addition to the perceived costs and benefits of unethical behavior. As we depict in Figure 2.2, reward systems can also affect perceptions of control and subjective norms related to unethical behavior. For example, group rewards may alter an individual's perceived control and normative beliefs about behavior. Accountability to group members will lower the resources and opportunities available for an individual to act in a manner opposed by the group, and this will lower the perceived (and actual) control that the individual has over that behavior. Furthermore, group rewards will make these group members more salient referents, thereby increasing the likelihood that their opinions will influence the individual's subjective norms. When a group is composed primarily of highly ethical individuals, group rewards should increase ethical behavior by lowering opportunities for unethical behavior and increasing the ethicality of subjective norms. However, the converse is also true for unethical groups. When a group is composed of fewer ethical employees, an individual may feel less control to act ethically and may be influenced by subjective norms that encourage unethical behavior.

The perceived fairness of a reward system may also influence an individual's subjective norms. Individuals are less likely to comply with the norms of their manager and organization if they perceive their manager or institution to be unfair. Instead, they are likely to consider more general norms of fairness (e.g., "equal pay for equal work," "an eye for an eye") that extend beyond organizational values. If the reward system seems unfair, employees may act unethically to make up for lost rewards that they believe they deserve (Treviño & Weaver, 2001). In an experiment, individuals who were treated unfairly (i.e., paid less than they were originally told they would be paid) were more likely to steal from the experimenter than were individuals who were paid the amount they were expecting (Greenberg, 1990). An important way in which to increase perceptions of fairness is to involve employees in the reward-setting process.

Changing an Incentive System to Improve Ethical Decision Making

In some cases, major changes to incentive systems can inadvertently promote unethical behavior. A case involving Sears automotive centers illustrates this point ("Avoiding the Shaft," 1992; see also Case 2). The incentive problems started with a shift to commission-based pay during the 1990s. Mechanics were required to meet sales quotas or risk being transferred to another department or having their work hours cut. In this change, base salaries were cut by as much as 50% and workers were forced to sell more to make up for the lower pay. Service advisers earned commissions for reaching specific goals: product-specific sales per shift and dollar volume quotas per hour.

The primary problem with this incentive system is that it promoted overselling. Sears employees performed unnecessary work and cut corners by not performing needed repairs. The California Department of Consumer Affairs conducted an undercover investigation and found that Sears recommended and performed unnecessary service 90% of the time, with an average oversell of $200. Even worse, the investigation revealed that the vehicles sometimes were returned to their owners in unsafe conditions.

Following the investigation, Sears auto service sales fell 15%. Sears ultimately paid $15 million in refunds and other costs to settle charges in 41 states and 19 related class-action lawsuits. In announcing changes to their reward systems, Sears Chairman Edward Brennan admitted, "The policies for compensation and goal setting, created by management for our service advisers in the auto centers, were mistakes." With that, Sears discontinued its policy of setting sales goals for service advisers.

Organizational Culture

Organizational culture is "a pattern of basic assumptions, invented, discovered, or developed by a given group, as it learns to cope with its problems of external adaptation and internal integration, that has worked well enough to be considered valid and, therefore, is to be taught to new members as the correct way to perceive, think, and feel in relation to those problems" (Schein, 1990, p. 111).

The socialization of employees' perceptions, thoughts and feelings suggests that culture can have a strong impact on an individual's normative beliefs.

Organizational culture influences behavior at all levels of organizational life. This is particularly true for ethical behavior. Managers set the moral tone within an organization, and the belief systems they endorse have significant consequences for ethical decision making (Messick & Bazerman, 1996). Stated in terms of the theory of planned behavior, managers who create an organizational culture with a strong ethical climate influence employee behavior by affecting normative beliefs and subsequent subjective norms. That is, organizational culture creates social pressure for employees to act in specific ways. Ethical organizational cultures promote ethical decision making, whereas unethical organizational cultures promote unethical decision making. The following example illustrates the consequences of creating an unethical organizational culture.

HJ Meyers was a brokerage firm where fear and intimidation ruled the office ("State Aims to Oust Brokerage," 1997). In a civil complaint, the Massachusetts Securities Division alleged that Meyers ran a "boiler room" where salespeople employed "dishonest, unethical, and other fraudulent high-pressure sales tactics" to hawk stocks by phone. As one former Meyers employee commented, "The Meyers tactics are strictly the tactics of the '70s—fear and intimidation."

Senior management applied daily pressure on HJ Meyers managers and brokers to sell stocks with little regard for whether or not the stocks were appropriate for the targeted investors. In many cases, brokers at Meyers used high-pressure sales tactics to push Meyers stocks without disclosing their risks. The national sales manager, William Massuci, would scold brokers for not selling enough Meyers stocks and would charge brokers with $50 or $100 fines for letting customers sell Meyers stocks. The Boston sales manager, Tobin Senefeld, allegedly even wielded a baseball bat. Brokers were forced to stand at their desks until they met sales quotas and to work some nights until 9 o'clock making cold calls. In addition, brokers were ordered to call customers who had already bought stock and to badger them to buy more. Furthermore, brokers in Boston were tempted by offers of 10% commissions, twice the amount normally permitted by the National Association of Securities Dealers (NASD).

Following customer complaints and employee defections, the State Security Division launched an investigation. The results of the investigation led the division to revoke HJ Meyers's Bay State license, alleging fraudulent sales practices, and in June 1997 Meyers shut down its Boston stockbrokers office. By July 1997, the NASD had ordered Meyers to pay a $250,000 fine and to repay customers more than $1 million for alleged unfair pricing of stocks (restitution to 3,000 customers).

Organizational Culture and Ethics

Prior work has explored the influence of organizational culture in a number of different areas. This work has consistently identified organizational culture as a key driver of employee behavior and the broader employee experience. Organizational culture influences job satisfaction (Johnson & McIntye, 1998), turnover (O'Reilly, Chatman, & Caldwell, 1991; Vandenberghe, 1999), cooperation at work (Chatman & Barsade, 1995), distribution of resources (Mannix, Neale, & Northcraft, 1995), and organizational performance (Petty, Beadles, Lowery, Chapman, & Connell, 1995). In addition to these outcomes, organizational culture significantly influences ethical behavior.

Data from the National Business Ethics Survey (Ethics Resource Center, 2003) links organizational culture to ethical decision making. In the survey, 25% of employees who believed that honesty was applied frequently in their organizations reported that they had observed misconduct within the past year. Notably, observed misconduct was much higher among those who believed that honesty was applied only occasionally (52%) or rarely/never (71%). Similarly, the pressure to commit misconduct was higher among employees who believed that honesty was applied occasionally (25%) or rarely/never (44%) than among employees who believed that honesty was applied frequently in their organizations (9%). Those who believed that honesty was applied frequently would consider ethical behavior to be the subjective norm in their workplaces.

Through their actions and inactions, senior managers set the ethical tone for an organization. Leaders create an ethical organization by the way in which they behave, allocate rewards, hire and fire people, focus their attention (Sims & Brinkmann, 2002), and set standards (Tenbrunsel, Wade-Benzoni, Messick, & Bazerman, 2000). As the case of HJ Meyers demonstrates, the ethical climate created by senior management affects employee behavior throughout the organization (Wimbush & Shepard, 1994). Employees often view leaders within their organization as role models and attempt to emulate their behavior (Sims & Brinkmann, 2002). In fact, some studies have found that the primary determinant of a subordinate's ethical conduct is the ethical behavior of his or her supervisor (Posner & Schmidt, 1984; see also Treviño & Brown, this volume, pp. 69–87). When developing normative beliefs about ethical behavior at work, individuals look to their leaders and coworkers. Individuals will be particularly motivated to comply with the norms of those who evaluate and pay them (e.g., supervisors, company leaders). In other words, as employees develop subjective norms for ethical behaviors, they are likely to be significantly influenced by their managers.

The influence of managerial actions in shaping employee normative beliefs is epitomized by the following case involving an employee who was caught embezzling $20,000 over a 15-year period (Carroll, 1992). The employee explained that she thought her behavior was acceptable because of the way in which the president of the organization acted. The president had company personnel rake the leaves in his yard, he took cash out of the company's petty cash box, he took coins out of the soft drink machine, and he took stamps from the company stamp box for his personal letters. In this context, the president had blurred the lines between company and personal business and had inadvertently created an unethical organizational culture.

In addition to altering subjective norms for behavior, an ethical climate can change perceived costs and benefits of ethical behavior. Deshpande (1996) found that people who believed that their organization had a "caring" climate perceived strong positive links between ethical behavior and success in their organization. In contrast, employees who believed that their organization had an "instrumental" climate perceived a negative link between ethical behavior and success. In some cases, even unconscious biases may lead people to make unethical decisions (Banaji, Bazerman, & Chugh, 2003). For example, people may be unaware of the important role that conflicts of interest or favoritism (Messick, 1996) play in their ethical decision making. Ultimately, it is organizational cultural factors, such as stereotype cues in an organization and the mind-set used to make certain decisions, that can enable people to overcome these biases.

Prescriptions for Creating an Ethical Organizational Culture

Organizational culture involves three levels: artifacts, values, and assumptions (Schein, 1990). *Artifacts* represent the physical evidence regarding the way in which the company operates. For example, artifacts include dress codes and signs hung within the organization. *Values* are what drive decision making. For example, is the organization customer focused or profit driven? *Assumptions* are the lens through which employees evaluate their environment. Assumptions derive from employee experiences and tend to be deeply embedded within the organization. In some cases, assumptions can even limit the set of possible solutions that employees consider in solving a problem. For example, employees who have a basic assumption that the organization makes ethical decisions will not consider solutions to a problem that involve unethical actions.

To create an ethical organizational culture, managers need to embed ethics within all three levels of culture: artifacts, values, and assumptions. Each of these factors can influence the normative beliefs of employees, and the importance of these factors may depend on employee tenure. For example, a new employee may immediately recognize the culture's artifacts, whereas values and assumptions will become more familiar to the employee through training and experience in the organization.

Artifacts fostering an ethical culture include a company code of ethics and an emphasis on ethics in routine employee materials. Ethical values are fostered through ethics training, incentives to motivate ethical behavior, systems to provide advice on ethical dilemmas (e.g., an anonymous company hotline to field ethics questions), and procedures for whistle-blowing. For example, managers should create a reporting system for whistle-blowing, such as a telephone hotline, so that employees can readily report unethical behavior.

To create ethical assumptions, managers need to demonstrate ethical behavior through their actions and create norms for ethical behavior. This process takes time as a company develops a history for respecting ethical decision making. Another key issue for managers in this process is accessibility. When managers are accessible, employees can get good advice earlier in their ethical decision-making processes. Ideally, accessible managers will also be able to learn of problems as they are developing rather than after the problems have grown. Importantly, an organization with accessible managers should be one in which employees are able to deliver bad news without fear of reprisals (Treviño et al., 1999).

This attention to all three levels of culture is important. Whereas prior work has demonstrated that codes of ethics and ethics training alone can make a significant difference in organizational behavior (Delaney & Sockell, 1992; Treviño & Youngblood, 1990; Weaver, Treviño, & Cochran, 1999), it is the broader integration of ethical issues that has the greatest impact on behavior. In addition to ethics programs, managers should work to make ethical issues a part of the performance review process and not just an isolated segment within an orientation program. Notably, most companies that have ethics programs do not make ethics an integral part of the organizational fabric (Meyer & Rowan, 1977; Weaver et al., 1999).

As illustrated by the case of HJ Meyers, some managers foster unethical organizational cultures. In many cases, managers create an unethical organizational culture unintentionally. The following cultural traits have been linked with unethical behavior:

1. Focus on profits (Sims, 2000)

2. Focus on short-term gains (Cooke, 1991)

3. Focus on self-interests

4. Culture of unquestioning obedience to leadership

5. Perception that ethical programs are designed to shield top management from lawsuits (Treviño et al., 1999)

The experience of Texas Instruments (TI) offers an example of how managers can create a positive ethical climate (TI, 2003). To create this ethical climate, managers at TI infused ethics throughout the organization. First, TI introduced an ethics code of conduct in 1961. Since that time, much of the company's written material has focused on ethical considerations (e.g., "TI Standard Policies and Procedures," "The TI Commitment," "Values and Ethics of TI"). In fact, all employees are given a business card-sized pamphlet with the "Ethics Quick Test." The pamphlet states, "Is the action legal? Does it comply with our values? If you do it, will you feel bad? How will it look in the newspaper? If you know it's wrong, don't do it! If you're not sure, ask. Keep asking until you get an answer."

Second, TI established an ethics committee in 1987. This committee is composed of high-level TI managers, including a senior vice president who reports to the audit committee of the board of directors. This committee communicates ethical expectations to TI employees and provides channels of communication so that employees can ask questions, voice concerns, and seek help for resolving ethical issues.

TI's efforts have won the company numerous ethics awards, including the Lincoln Award for Ethics and Excellence in Business (in 1991), the American Business Ethics Award (in 1994), and the Bentley College Center for Business Ethics Award (in 1994). TI was also recognized as one of the "100 Best Corporate Citizens" in 2000 (when it ranked No. 1), 2001, 2002, and 2004.

Cross-Cultural Concerns

Many managers will need to work across cultures. For example, many U.S. managers must navigate cultural divides with partners and employees who may be accustomed to different normative beliefs about ethical behaviors. In these cases, U.S. managers must take particular care. First, ethical standards differ markedly across cultures in ways that may surprise U.S. managers (Puffer & McCarthy, 1995; Vogel, 1992). Second, the rules that govern U.S. managers are different from those that govern their foreign counterparts. For example, U.S. managers must comply with the U.S. Foreign Corrupt Practices Act.

Preparation is an essential first step. For example, managers should anticipate different norms for gift giving and bribes. Although managers might be able to adapt to some local norms (e.g., by bringing a large number of gifts bearing the company logo), there are broader ethical standards that constrain U.S. managers (e.g., the inability to give bribes). First, managers should develop their understanding of the norms and ethical standards of their business partners. Second, managers should articulate the standards of their own companies early in their interactions with others to avoid potentially harmful misunderstandings. For example, company rules that limit the value of gifts that managers can give or receive should be clearly stated to avoid potential slights when managers give inexpensive gifts or attempt to return expensive gifts.

Managerial Oversight

The third tool we consider is managerial oversight or monitoring. The use of monitoring systems is the most direct way for managers to control the process of how employees complete their work. Monitoring systems can take a number of different forms, including direct observation, surveillance (e.g., with cameras or recordings), and audits. Monitoring systems influence individuals' perceived and actual control over their ethical behavior. Individuals operating in a highly monitored system may believe that they cannot successfully commit an unethical act (and, as a result, do not attempt to commit an unethical act), or they may attempt to commit an unethical act but be detected and prevented from actually completing the act.

We begin with an example from Prudential that illustrates how the lack of managerial oversight, coupled with an unethical organizational culture, can influence behavior. During the early 1990s, a multistate task force found that deceptive sales practices were common in Prudential offices around the country. From their findings, investigators claimed that senior executives should have exerted greater oversight to discover and prevent the wrongdoing. Ultimately, state regulators forced a restitution package estimated at between $280 million and $1 billion in addition to a $35 million fine ("Prudential Insurance to Change," 1996).

The focus of the regulatory probe involved "churning," a practice under which agents persuade customers to use the cash value of older policies to finance new, more expensive policies. Prudential customers were often deceived about the cost of these transactions and the extent to which they harmed the values of their older policies.

When a new chairman took over in 1994, he fired nearly 1,000 agents and managers, revamped the sales program, and installed new senior managers in the company's life insurance unit. One of the key goals of the reorganization was to give company officials better oversight. The reorganization also placed salaried underwriters, who were not motivated by commissions, in personal contact with applicants. These underwriters were instructed to go through a lengthy checklist of questions to establish that customers were really knowledgeable about what they were buying. The reorganization made it much more difficult for agents to churn customers.

In addition to restricting opportunities to act unethically, monitoring systems influence ethical decision making by changing a decision maker's attitudes about outcomes. For example, by changing perceptions of the likelihood that an unethical behavior will be detected, monitoring systems change an employee's expected value (reward and punishment expectations) for engaging in the unethical act.

Naturally, monitoring systems need to match the workplace setting. Monitoring systems will curtail unethical behavior only when employees believe that the system restricts their opportunities, resources, and/or efficacy for conducting unethical behavior. In general, the more complex the work, the more difficult it is to monitor. Simple monitoring systems might not be effective for professionals working on multifaceted projects. In these cases, managers need more sophisticated monitoring solutions such as random audits of project records and anonymous group/client evaluations of ethical behavior.

Even when employee outcomes are easy to measure, managers still need to exert care in the way in which they structure a monitoring system. For example, managers might need to check *reporting* accuracy (e.g., were 50 cases of apple juice actually sold?) as well as *process* accuracy (e.g., was it really apple juice that was sold?). In some cases, there are many process steps to check (e.g., were the 50 cases shipped to the right place, and were they actually paid for?). Furthermore, employees working on different processes might need different levels of monitoring.

Costs of Oversight

In implementing monitoring systems, managers need to balance the costs and benefits of monitoring. The costs of monitoring include the obvious financial costs for personnel and monitoring equipment as well as the less obvious psychological costs of increased monitoring.

The psychological costs of monitoring include reduced morale. Surveys of employees indicate that monitoring systems in general, and intrusive monitoring systems in particular, are not welcomed by employees. In addition, monitoring systems communicate to employees that they are not trusted. When employees perceive that they are not trusted, this can lead to *psychological reactance* (Cialdini, 1998). That is, the monitoring system can change what employees believe is expected behavior in that people who are monitored might begin to believe that they are expected to behave unethically. As a result, in cases where they are not monitored, they might be more likely to behave dishonestly than they would without the monitoring system.

A number of recent experiments have demonstrated this principle. When individuals interact with a high level of monitoring, they are likely to attribute trustworthy behavior to the monitoring system (Malhotra & Murnighan, 2002). Once monitoring is removed, individuals may be more likely to attribute their past ethical behavior to the monitoring system and act unethically. Perhaps ironically, people need opportunities for unethical behavior to build trust. That is, managers might need to take some risks and make themselves vulnerable to create an ethical environment. On the other hand, if managers employ *very* infrequent monitoring, they might inadvertently convey indifference to the process by which outcomes are produced. If unethical behaviors go undetected, unethical acts are likely to be rewarded and employees may come to view unethical behavior more favorably. That is, monitoring systems can influence attitudes by altering employee perceptions of the likelihood that their unethical actions will be rewarded.

Prescriptions for Managerial Oversight

Prescriptively, managers need to find a balance between monitoring and trusting their employees. Managerial attention is limited and the psychological costs of monitoring can be high. As a result, managers need to allocate their attention judiciously. There are certain times when managers should focus their attention very carefully on what employees are doing.

First, managers should focus their attention on employee behavior when they use goal setting and employees are very close to a goal or deadline. For example, when employees with a specific goal (e.g., selling 30 cars during a month) are very close to attaining the goal (e.g., have sold 29 cars with 1 day left in the month), managers should devote particular attention to how employees complete their work. Second, managers should be particularly vigilant when employees perceive themselves to be in a loss domain. For example, when Beech-Nut employees had already spent money on fake juice, they may have been particularly tempted to act unethically to avoid "losing money" on the product they purchased. Similar logic may have influenced Sears employees when they had their salaries cut and were then given incentives to "make up the losses" in their salaries through additional sales. That is, when operating in the domain of losses, employees may increase their value for improved financial outcomes and generate more favorable attitudes toward unethical acts. Monitoring in these situations can deter unethical behavior by (a) reducing employees' perceived power to engage in unethical acts and (b) detecting and impeding attempts to act unethically.

In deciding when to monitor employees, managers should consider results from prior research that found that random unanticipated monitoring is more effective than routine and predictable monitoring (Ho & Schweitzer, 2003). On average, people are more responsive to unanticipated monitoring schemes than to anticipated monitoring schemes. However, for specific events, such as an anticipated annual inspection, anticipated monitoring can focus attention and improve ethical behavior for that specific period of time.

In designing monitoring systems, managers must take care to tailor the systems they develop to the nature of their organization. For example, some environments (e.g., those that pay employees an hourly wage) might need oversight for shirking, whereas others (e.g., those that pay their employees commissions) might need oversight for overselling. A related issue involves the balance between the monitoring frequency and the magnitude of sanctions when unethical actions are detected (e.g., zero-tolerance policies). Because attitudes toward unethical behavior are influenced by the expected costs of engaging in the act (Expected Cost = Cost of Detection × Probability of Detection), high sanctions that increase the cost of being caught can be substituted for frequent monitoring that increases the likelihood of being caught.

An additional consideration in designing a monitoring system is the issue of who should do the monitoring. Potential monitors include supervisors, coworkers, and auditors. Of course, the choice of who does the monitoring depends on the nature of the work being monitored and who the employees perceive as credible actors that would block their ability to act unethically. The key issues to consider include how easy it is to recognize unethical behavior, how easy it is to attribute the behavior to a specific perpetrator, how common the behavior is, how costly the behavior is to the organization, and how much privacy is breached in monitoring (e.g., by accessing an employee's e-mail records). A final issue that managers should consider in selecting monitors is the impact that monitoring has on those who do the monitoring. Prior work has found that people who conduct surveillance become less trusting (Kruglanski, 1970).

In some cases, groups may merit close monitoring (Banaji et al., 2003). Prior work has documented a number of phenomena that influence groups that might lead to unethical behavior. These include a risky shift (as groups favor risky decisions relative to individual decisions), groupthink (as group members become less critical of ideas discussed in a group decision), and group dominance (as ideas that come from people in positions of power are challenged less often in group settings).

Conclusion

Managers can influence employee ethical behavior in a number of different ways. In this chapter, we have considered three specific tools: incentives, organizational culture, and oversight. Importantly, managers should not think of these three factors as being independent of one another. Instead, managers should choose incentive and oversight systems that reflect the culture they aim to develop. For example, incentive systems codify what the organization values, whereas oversight policies are evidence of what the organization is concerned about with respect to employee behavior. Additionally, monitoring is related to the organizational culture dimension of autonomy. Within an organization, employees can be either closely monitored or largely autonomous.

One factor that is crucial to creating an ethical organization is communication. As managers institute changes to these incentive, cultural, and monitoring systems, they should pay particular attention to how they communicate these changes to their employees. Specifically, it is very important that employees understand the reasons for any changes. Employees who believe that changes are motivated by an underlying desire to reward ethical behavior are much more likely to act ethically than are employees who believe that the organization distrusts its employees or that senior management is merely trying to protect itself from future lawsuits.

The most durable change that managers can make to influence ethical behavior is to establish a culture of high ethical norms. This is a difficult task that also requires clear communication. The creation of an ethical workplace involves more than a single workshop, poster, or checklist. Although all of these tools can help, the key to fostering an ethical workplace is communication. When managers communicate, they must be clear, consistent, and open. The values of ethical decision making must be clearly stated. The messages must be consistent, and all levels of management must communicate the same message about the value of ethical decision making. In addition, managerial actions must match the message.

Managerial communication also needs to be open. In particular, managers need to listen to their employees, and they need to be available to employees to help guide the latter's ethical choices. Just as employees feel pressure to produce results, they should also feel empowered to seek ethical guidance when they need it. In one study, employees reported that they received insufficient help from their supervisors in navigating ethical issues (Badaracco & Webb, 1995). The authors of the study reported that employees found their supervisors to be "out of touch" on ethical issues. These results suggest that open communication represents an important challenge, that is, that current managers might not be adequately trained or sufficiently accessible to their employees. This challenge, however, also represents a set of opportunities to create a more ethical organization. Specifically, managers can take the following steps. First, through training, managers can develop their ability to identify and make ethical decisions. Second, managers can create an open-door policy or set aside specific times during the week to increase their accessibility to their employees. Third, managers can devote greater attention to the communication process.

Managers have a responsibility to guide the ethical decisions that their employees make. This responsibility cannot be absolved with the addition of an ethics training seminar. Instead, ethical practices must be consistently communicated through a variety of channels and a commitment to professional integrity (Donaldson, 2000). When managers fail to recognize, or actively ignore, the ethical breaches of their employees, they fail as managers. As Beech-Nut's managers learned, this approach to management is both unacceptable and illegal.

References

Ajzen, I. (1985). From intentions to actions: A theory of planned behavior. In J. Kuhl & J. Beckman (Eds.), *Action-control: From cognition to behavior* (pp. 11–39). Heidelberg, Germany: Springer.

Ajzen, I. (1987). Attitudes, traits, and actions: Dispositional prediction of behavior in personality and social psychology. In L. Berkowitz (Ed.), *Advances in experimental social psychology* (Vol. 20, pp. 1–63). San Diego: Academic Press.

Ajzen, I., & Fishbein, M. (1980). *Understanding the attitudes and predicting social behavior.* Englewood Cliffs, NJ: Prentice Hall.

Avoiding the shaft: Sears auto repair scandal fallout. (1992, June 22). *The Washington Post,* p. B5.

Badaracco, J., & Webb, A. (1995). Business ethics: A view from the trenches. *California Management Review, 37,* 8–28.

Banaji, M. R., Bazerman, M. H., & Chugh, D. (2003). How (un)ethical are you? *Harvard Business Review, 81*(12), 56.

Carroll, A. (1992). *Business and society* (2nd ed.). Cincinnati, OH: South-Western.

Chang, M. K. (1998). Predicting unethical behavior: A comparison of the theory of reasoned action and the theory of planned behavior. *Journal of Business Ethics, 17,* 1825–1834.

Chatman, J. A., & Barsade, S. G. (1995). Personality, organizational culture, and cooperation: Evidence from a business simulation. *Administrative Science Quarterly, 40,* 423–443.

Cialdini, R. (1998). *Influence: Science and practice* (4th ed.). New York: HarperCollins.

Cooke, R. (1991). Danger signs of unethical behavior: How to determine if your firm is at ethical risk. *Journal of Business Ethics, 10,* 249–253.

Delaney J. T., & Sockell, D. (1992). Do company ethics training programs make a difference? An empirical analysis. *Journal of Business Ethics, 11,* 719–727.

Deshpande, S. P. (1996). The impact of ethical climate types on facets of job satisfaction: An empirical investigation. *Journal of Business Ethics, 15,* 655–660.

Donaldson, T. (2000). Are business managers "professionals"? *Business Ethics Quarterly, 10,* 83–94.

Donaldson, T. (2001). The ethical wealth of nations. *Journal of Business Ethics, 31,* 25–37.

Ethics Resource Center. (2003). *National Business Ethics Survey.* Washington, DC: Author.

Flannery, B. L., & May, D. R. (2000). Environmental ethical decision making in the U.S. metal-finishing industry. *Academy of Management Journal, 43,* 642–662.

Greenberg, J. (1990). Employee theft as a reaction to underpayment inequity: The hidden cost of pay cuts. *Journal of Applied Psychology, 75,* 561–568.

Hegarty, W. H., & Sims, H. P. (1978). Some determinants of unethical decision behavior: An experiment. *Journal of Applied Psychology, 63,* 451–457.

Ho, T., & Schweitzer, M. (2003). *Transparency and trust: What you see is what you get.* Working paper, Wharton School, University of Pennsylvania.

Jensen, M. C. (2001). Corporate budgeting is broken: Let's fix it. *Harvard Business Review, 79*(10), 94–101.

Johnson, J. J., & McIntye, C. L. (1998). Organizational culture and climate correlates of job satisfaction. *Psychological Reports, 82,* 843–850.

Kerr, S. (1995). On the folly of rewarding A while hoping for B. *Academy of Management Executive, 9*(1), 7–14.

KPMG. (2000). *Organizational Integrity Survey.* Washington, DC: Author.

Kruglanski, A. (1970). Attributing trustworthiness in supervisor–worker relations. *Journal of Experimental Social Psychology, 6,* 214–232.

Kurland, N. B. (1995). Ethical intentions and the theories of reasoned action and planned behavior. *Journal of Applied Social Psychology, 25,* 297–313.

L&H Korea probe reports 70% of sales were fictitious: Managers fooled auditors with fancy fraud schemes; CEO suggests schools use ploys as case studies. (2001, April 10). *The Asian Wall Street Journal,* p. N8.

Lewicki, R. J. (1983). Lying and deception: A behavioral model. In M. H. Bazerman & R. J. Lewicki (Eds.), *Negotiating in organizations* (pp. 68–90). Beverly Hills, CA: Sage.

Locke, E. A., & Latham, G. P. (1990). Work motivation and satisfaction: Light at the end of the tunnel. *Psychological Science, 1,* 240–246.

Madden, T. J., Ellen, P. S., & Ajzen, I. (1992). A comparison of the theory of planned behavior and the theory of reasoned action. *Personality and Social Psychology Bulletin, 18,* 3–9.

Malhotra, D., & Murnighan, J. K. (2002). The effects of contracts on interpersonal trust. *Administrative Science Quarterly, 47,* 534–559.

Mannix, E. A., Neale, M. A., & Northcraft, G. B. (1995). Equity, equality, or need: The effects of organizational culture on the allocation of benefits and burdens. *Organizational Behavior and Human Decision Processes, 63,* 276–286.

Messick, D. M. (1996). Why ethics is not the only thing that matters. *Business Ethics Quarterly, 6,* 223–236.

Messick, D. M., & Bazerman, M. H. (1996). Ethical leadership and the psychology of decision making. *MIT Sloan Management Review, 37,* 9–23.

Meyer, J. W., & Rowan, B. (1977). Institutionalized organizations: Formal structure as myth and ceremony. *American Journal of Sociology, 83,* 340–363.

O'Reilly, C. A., Chatman, J., & Caldwell, D. F. (1991). People and organizational culture: A profile comparison approach to assessing person–organization fit. *Academy of Management Journal, 34,* 487–516.

Petty, M. M., Beadles, N. A., Lowery, C. M., Chapman, D. F., & Connell, D. W. (1995). Relationships between organizational culture and organizational performance. *Psychological Reports, 76,* 483–492.

Posner, B., & Schmidt, W. (1984). Values and the American manager: An update. *California Management Review, 26,* 202–216.

Prudential insurance to change way it sells policies in wake of criticism. (1996, June 17). *The Wall Street Journal,* p. B5.

Puffer, S., & McCarthy, D. (1995). Finding the common ground in Russian and American business ethics. *California Management Review, 37,* 29–46.

Randall, D. M., & Gibson, A. M. (1991). Ethical decision-making in the medical profession: An application of the theory of planned behavior. *Journal of Business Ethics, 10,* 111–122.

Schein, E. H. (1990). Organizational culture. *American Psychologist, 45,* 109–119.

Schweitzer, M. E., & Hsee, C. (2002). Stretching the truth: Elastic justification and motivated communication of uncertain information. *Journal of Risk and Uncertainty, 25,* 185–201.

Schweitzer, M. E., Ordonez, L., & Douma, B. (2004). Goal setting as a motivator of unethical behavior. *Academy of Management Journal, 47,* 422–432.

Sheppard, B. H., Hartwick, J., & Warshaw, P. R. (1988). The theory of reasoned action: A meta-analysis of past research with recommendations for modifications and future research. *Journal of Consumer Research, 15,* 325–343.

Sims, R. (2000). Changing an organization's culture under new leadership. *Journal of Business Ethics, 25,* 65–78.

Sims, R. R., & Brinkmann, J. (2002). Enron ethics (or: Culture matters more than codes). *Journal of Business Ethics, 45,* 243–256.

State aims to oust brokerage for alleged unethical tactics. (1997, August 22). *Boston Herald,* p. 1.

Tenbrunsel, A. (1998). Misrepresentation and expectations of misrepresentation in an ethical dilemma: The role of incentives and temptation. *Academy of Management Journal, 41,* 330–339.

Tenbrunsel, A., & Messick, D. (1999). Sanctioning systems, decision frames, and cooperation. *Administrative Science Quarterly, 44,* 684–707.

Tenbrunsel, A., Wade-Benzoni, K., Messick, D., & Bazerman, M. (2000). Understanding the influence of environmental standards on judgments and choices. *Academy of Management Journal, 43,* 854–866.

Texas Instruments. (2003). *Ethics at TI.* Retrieved July 18, 2003, from www.ti.com/corp/docs/company/citizen/ethics/index.shtml

Treviño, L. K., & Brown, M. A. (2005). The role of leaders in influencing unethical behavior in the workplace. In R. E. Kidwell, Jr., & C. L. Martin (Eds.), *Managing organizational deviance* (chap. 3). Thousand Oaks, CA: Sage.

Treviño, L, Weaver, G., Gibson, D., & Toffler, B. (1999). Managing ethics and legal compliance: What works and what hurts. *California Management Review, 41,* 131–151.

Treviño, L. K., & Weaver, G. R. (2001). Organizational justice and ethics program "follow-through": Influences on employees' harmful and helpful behavior. *Business Ethics Quarterly, 11,* 651–671.

Treviño, L. K., & Youngblood, S. A. (1990). Bad apples in bad barrels: A causal analysis of ethical decision-making behavior. *Journal of Applied Psychology, 75,* 378–385.

Vandenberghe, C. (1999). Organizational culture, person–culture fit, and turnover: A replication in the health care industry. *Journal of Organizational Behavior, 20,* 175–184.

Vogel, D. (1992). The globalization of business ethics: Why America remains distinctive. *California Management Review, 35,* 30–49.

Weaver, G. R., Treviño, L. K., & Cochran, P. L. (1999). Integrated and decoupled corporate social performance: Management commitments, external pressures, and corporate ethics practices. *Academy of Management Journal, 42,* 539–552.

Welles, C. (1988, February). What led Beech-Nut down the road to disgrace? Under financial pressure, the company ignored warnings of adulterated juice. *BusinessWeek,* p. 124.

Wimbush, J., & Shepard, J. (1994). Toward an understanding of ethical climate: Its relationship to ethical behavior and supervisory influence. *Journal of Business Ethics, 13,* 637–647.

Sears Automotive

S am Thompson was worried. As a Sears automotive center manager in California for the previous 6 years, Thompson had become increasingly concerned about the retail giant's new incentive system for its sales advisers and mechanics. Under the plan, sales advisers were compensated based on how many parts were sold and how much work was completed on each repair job. Mechanics' hourly pay had been cut, and mechanics were rewarded based on how many procedures (e.g., front-end wheel alignments) they completed per shift. Pressure was up to sell higher numbers of brakes, struts, and shock absorbers and to perform more oil changes and brake work during each shift.

Thompson's unease was apparently justified by an upswing in the number of customer complaints about overcharging that he had received during recent months. A fellow manager at a nearby store privately expressed his feelings to Thompson. The incentive structure was out of control, the other manager said. Meeting sales goals had become a condition for continuing employment with the company. One way in which those targets were achieved, the manager suggested, was for mechanics to perform unnecessary repairs on the cars of unsuspecting customers.

Rumor had it that some Sears employees had been dismissed either for failing to meet sales targets or for refusing to authorize unneeded repairs so that goals could be met. Thompson also heard that dissatisfied customers had flooded the office of the California Department of Consumer Affairs with complaints about repair work rip-offs. Finally, managers had been discussing

AUTHOR'S NOTE: This case was prepared by Roland Kidwell (Niagara University) as the basis for classroom discussion. It was developed from accounts listed in the bibliography at the end of the case. Sam Thompson is a fictional character whose experiences represent those of some actual Sears auto center managers. All other names of individuals and companies are real.

the possibility that state authorities were conducting some sort of sting operation at Sears auto centers.

The Cost of "Unnecessary" Repairs: An Undercover Investigation

The managers' fears were justified. In December 1991, California authorities provided Sears with the results of an undercover investigation conducted over the previous year. Investigators claimed that 27 of the 72 Sears auto centers in California had engaged in methodical overselling of repairs and replacement parts under the guise of preventative maintenance. The investigation, focused chiefly on 33 Sears auto centers, found that unnecessary repairs were recommended at those centers 90% of the time. Sears quickly denied that its commission structure and sales goals were to blame for the abuses, but sales at its auto centers nationwide, which had averaged $1 billion per year, quickly dropped 15%.

That was just the start of the costs incurred by the nation's largest independent auto repair business. In 1992, the company shelled out $8 million to settle class-action lawsuits brought on behalf of former auto customers, and it eventually agreed to award $50 vouchers to customers in more than 40 states who had been overcharged over a 2-year period. Sears disbursed $1.5 million for auto repair training programs at California's community colleges, and it settled a similar investigation in New Jersey by paying $200,000 to set up an Auto Repair Industry Reform Fund in that state. The company also made a nationwide public apology.

The California investigation occurred in two parts. First, undercover agents took approximately 40 cars with worn brakes but no other mechanical problems to Sears auto centers throughout the state. Nearly 90% of the time, the agents were told that additional, more expensive repairs were needed, overcharging an average of more than $200 per case. At one store outside San Francisco, an investigator was charged nearly $600 too much to have a variety of unneeded work performed. In addition, agents claimed that in some cases cars were returned with damages or in unsafe operating order.

After the authorities had informed Sears of the investigation, the department conducted 10 more undercover tests, and 7 of these resulted in unneeded repairs. Although the center employees stopped selling unneeded parts during the second phase of the investigation, the government claimed that the employees still fleeced the agents by $100 on average.

"There was a deliberate decision by Sears management to set up a structure that made it totally inevitable that the consumer would be oversold," Roy Liebman, deputy attorney general of California, told the media.

How could this happen at a company that had built a reputation for trustworthiness in its auto service business over many years?

Sears Auto's Incentive Plan

For much of the 20th century and into the 21st century, Sears has been a household word in American commerce. A vast department store chain that had its beginnings as a mail-order concern during the 1880s, the company grew rapidly, surpassing $1 billion in sales in 1945 and establishing a strong reputation in general merchandise retailing, insurance, and financial services. The company's success attracted imitators and, eventually, strong competitors.

During the late 1980s, just after its 100th anniversary, Sears faced trouble on several fronts. An economy starting to weaken, coupled with the rise of retailers such as J.C. Penney and Wal-Mart, led to sagging profits for the company. Sears's merchandise group profits were falling as profits of other retailers were seeing slight increases. The auto centers were dependable performers for the company. Analysts believe that as gains shrank in other areas, the auto centers became the focus of an effort to maintain and grow profitability. The division, a reliable profit center, produced approximately 10% of Sears's merchandise group's revenue and had been among its fastest-growing, most lucrative units, servicing 20 million vehicles a year before the investigation came to light.

Industry observers believe that Sears, in attempting to solidify gains from its auto repair sector and help maintain the company's total earnings levels, began a new incentive system for the 1990s. Service advisers traditionally had been paid by the hour rather than by the amount of work done on their shifts. But that system ended in February 1990 when a new standardized commission policy, which sought to increase revenues and cut costs, took effect across all stores.

In California, state officials claimed that the number of customer complaints about Sears to the state Department of Consumer Affairs began to increase not long after Sears began a daily quota for parts, services, and repair sales by its employees. Jim Conran, the state consumer affairs director, said that employees were told to sell a minimum quantity of shock absorbers or struts on each shift and that those who failed to meet these targets either were transferred to another department or had their hours cut.

Within months of the alleged quota system, mechanics' hourly wages were reduced and mechanics went on piecework incentives as well. According to one former Sears auto center manager, mechanics who had been paid $15 per hour were cut to $12 an hour and received additional compensation based on the type of job performed and the time budgeted to do it. For example, mechanics who were paid $3 for each front-end wheel alignment, which should have taken an hour or so, could make more money by completing the job quickly and doing another one, critics charged. One former Sears employee claimed that he was pressured to complete 16 oil changes per day. When he said that he could not keep up, managers told him to fill the oil halfway and move to the next job, the former employee claimed.

At the same time that mechanics were paid per job, service advisers were attempting to meet sales goals. Both sets of employees were earning commissions—one for selling parts and the other for making repairs. Service advisers had no incentive to check on whether the mechanics' work was of high quality. Service advisers were busy striving for sales goals, which were constantly being revised upward, according to one of the center's former managers.

The ex-manager told *Incentive* magazine that he could not effectively check on workers' activities because he and other managers "were so busy with charts and graphs that we couldn't supervise this highly competitive sales environment. Then consumers would come in and complain, and we had to respond to that. It was basically a case of chasing your tail."

Commissions at Pep Boys:
A Contemporary Alternative to Sears

In April 1992, just before the employee incentive problems at Sears became public, rival Pep Boys, under the guidance of President and Chief Executive Officer Mitchell Leibovitz, announced that all of its technicians and mechanics would go on commission. However, Pep Boys, an auto parts supply/repair chain that then boasted $1.2 billion in annual sales and 3,200 auto service bays, experienced few of the problems that tarnished the image of one of its chief competitors.

The Pep Boys incentive plan for its repair shops, outlined in *Financial World* magazine, had the following characteristics:

- Only highly skilled technicians and mechanics (who were considered less skilled than technicians) received payment in a true commission system.
- Problem diagnosis and repair were separated. Service managers, who recommend repairs, were paid a small commission based on the number of problems diagnosed, not on revenues that resulted from fixing those problems.
- The commission structure was designed to maximize productivity. The system provided incentives for technicians and mechanics to finish jobs more quickly, allowing them to complete more work if they wanted to make more money.
- As a check on quality, employees agreed that their commissions would be reduced if it turned out their work needed to be redone.
- The company had no sales quotas and paid no commissions on the sales of parts.
- The company ethics policy stated that charging for unnecessary repairs could lead to dismissal.
- Customers could complain in various ways, including a toll-free number posted in every service bay and a stack of postage-paid feedback cards—addressed to the chief executive—beside the cash registers.
- A corporate response team monitored customer feedback. Complaints were entered into a computer system to determine whether complaints were centered on a particular store. Regional sales managers, empowered to solve problems, contacted anyone who made a complaint.

- Any employee who received a customer compliment got a congratulatory note from Leibovitz and membership in the President's Club for Customer Service Excellence.

After the Pep Boys commission system was established, same-store retail sales grew faster than repair work and related parts sales, indicating to Leibovitz that Pep Boys managers and technicians were not pushing products and repairs to increase commissions. The system enabled the company to attract a talented group of technicians and mechanics with a variety of advanced skills. At the time, analyst Dana Telsey of CJ Lawrence told *Financial World* magazine, "This company is living proof that a commission program can work terrifically if it's done right."

Sears Responds to the Scandal

We have concluded that our incentive compensation and goal-setting program inadvertently created an environment in which mistakes have occurred. We are moving quickly and aggressively to eliminate that environment. We have eliminated incentive compensation and goal-setting systems for automotive service advisors. (Edward Brennan, then Sears chairman and chief executive officer, in a full-page ad in the *Wall Street Journal,* June 25, 1992)

Full-page advertisements in various newspapers marked the first time that Brennan's signature had been used in company advertising. Despite denying that the commission system and goal-setting policies were directly responsible for its woes, Sears announced that it would eliminate them. "When trust is at stake, we can't merely react, we must overreact," Brennan said. "Sears wants you to know that we would never intentionally violate the trust customers have shown in our company for 105 years."

The company suggested that some of its problems in California stemmed not from its incentive system but rather from its emphasis on preventative maintenance, which was not accepted in California as justification for repairs to parts that still work, even if they work poorly. Brennan wrote,

Our policy of preventative maintenance—recommending replacement of worn parts before they fail—has been criticized by the California Bureau of Automotive Repair as constituting unneeded repairs. We don't see it that way. We recommend preventative maintenance because that's what our customers want and because it makes for safer cars on the road. In fact, 75 percent of the consumers we talked to in a nationwide survey last weekend [June 23–24, 1992] told us auto repair centers should recommend replacement parts for preventative maintenance.

Sears spokesman Greg Rossiter commented to *Incentive* magazine that the commission structure was changed because Sears was unable to determine whether its employees were overselling products and wanted to avoid an appearance that they were. He denied that Sears employees had engaged in any systematic fraud and pointed out that Sears auto centers had performed 1.8 million repair jobs in California during 1991 and received fewer than 60 customer complaints. In addition, Sears's policy of "Satisfaction Guaranteed or Your Money Back" should have given recourse to customers who had complaints about repair work.

Sears officials defended the incentive structure as an extremely valuable way in which to determine how employees are performing and as a superb motivational tool. There were no problems with mechanics remaining on an incentive system, Rossiter said. The company's goals were to get the mechanics to do the required work in the right amount of time as a means to keep the company competitive with other auto centers.

Yet Rossiter confirmed that emphasizing customer service rather than sales would be the company's main focus to rebound from its difficulties. Not long after the problems in California, officials in New York and Illinois announced their own undercover investigations of Sears similar to those in California and New Jersey. To the company's relief, investigators in those states did not detect overcharging at Sears auto service centers.

The Years That Followed: Lessons Learned?

In 1994, the *Wall Street Journal* reported that Sears had partly reestablished elements of the sales practices that led to the charges in California and had plans to bring back the practice on a large scale. Although Sears had stated it would stop using the commission system in favor of a full-salary plan, the former plan never went away entirely.

When the company restructured operations a few months after the scandal, it eliminated the position of service adviser, who had been paid on commission, and created a new position called service consultant. Service consultants, some of whom were former service advisers, were put on a partial commission plan that expected them to earn at least 40% of their total pay on the commission sale and installation of tires, batteries, shock absorbers, and struts. But the new plan did not include sale of brakes and front-end wheel alignment work, products and services that were a focus of the overcharging allegations.

Two years later, Sears was hit with a civil lawsuit in Alabama contending that the company cleaned up and put back on the shelf DieHard batteries that had been used in cars and returned by customers. At the time, DieHard batteries, a popular brand, held the largest share of the U.S. retail battery market at 8%.

The plaintiff's lawyers hired an investigator who said that he had purchased 100 batteries from Sears stores in 32 states and that 78 of the batteries showed previous signs of use. The investigator allegedly bought back from three Sears stores batteries that he had used, drained of power, and returned. Before he had taken them back, the investigator recorded the batteries' case numbers so that he could identify them when he purchased them a second time. Two of the stores were in Birmingham, Alabama, and the other was in Atlanta, Georgia.

Sears and its lawyers vehemently denied they had a policy to sell used batteries. The company noted that many of the bad batteries were found in or close to Birmingham, indicating that the problem was not company wide. Sears also pointed out that a great deal of the testimony in the case came from former employees, implying perhaps that they might have dubious motives in coming forward.

Several years after the auto center scandal, E. Ronald Culp, senior vice president of public relations and government affairs with Sears, participated in a roundtable discussion regarding business ethics that was later published in a 2002–2003 issue of *Communication World*. Culp indicated that the auto center incidents had resulted in significant changes within the company. He said that the problems had greatly disturbed Sears managers and employees and that the results led to new enthusiasm about ethics policies. Damage to the company and the employees' own compensation levels provided a "wake-up call" to everyone. A toll-free ethics hotline was created for employees who needed guidance about decisions. Culp said that corporate officials would attempt to find answers if employees were confused about whether their actions were considered to be improper.

Discussion Questions

1. How did elements of organizational culture, reward systems, and monitoring systems at Sears lead to unethical behavior among automotive sales advisers and mechanics?

2. Compare the Pep Boys incentive system with the Sears incentive plan. Why did the Pep Boys incentive structure appear to succeed, whereas the Sears incentive plan had problems?

3. Use the theory of planned behavior discussed in Chapter 2 to explain the reasons why the "good" employees at Sears who overcharged customers may have believed that their actions were ethical and proper.

4. Research an organization that has recently implemented a continuous improvement program and a reward system that may include pay for performance and/or goal setting as motivational tools. Based on information contained in Chapter 2, how can reward systems, organizational culture, and monitoring systems be structured effectively to avoid overzealous and potentially deviant behavior on the part of employees?

Bibliography

Berner, R. (1997, August 26). Legal beat: Sears faces another controversy, this time over car-battery sales. *The Wall Street Journal,* p. B3. Retrieved August 12, 2003, from http://proquest.umi.com/pqdweb

California accuses Sears of bilking auto service customers. (1992, August). *National Petroleum News,* pp. 21–22. Retrieved August 12, 2003, from http://proquest.umi.com/pqdweb

Fuchsberg, G. (1994, March 7). Retailing: Sears reinstates sales incentives in some centers. *The Wall Street Journal,* p. B1. Retrieved August 12, 2003, from http://proquest.umi.com/pqdweb

Hass, N. (1993, January 19). Truths of commission. *Financial World,* pp. 28–29. Retrieved August 12, 2003, from http://proquest.umi.com/pqdweb

Patterson, G. A. (1992a, June 18). New Jersey says Sears advised excess car repairs. *The Wall Street Journal,* p. A5. Retrieved August 12, 2003, from http://proquest.umi.com/pqdweb

Patterson, G. A. (1992b, June 23). Retailing: Sears's Brennan accepts blame for auto flap. *The Wall Street Journal,* p. B1. Retrieved August 12, 2003, from http://proquest.umi.com/pqdweb

Patterson, G. A. (1992c, October 2). Sears is dealt a harsh lesson by states: Mishandling of auto-repair inquiries proves costly. *The Wall Street Journal,* p. A9. Retrieved August 12, 2003, from http://proquest.umi.com/pqdweb

Quinn, J. (1992, October). Employee motivation: Repair job, Sears Auto Centers shift to rewarding customer service. *Incentive,* pp. 40–46. Retrieved August 12, 2003, from http://proquest.umi.com/pqdweb

Williams, L. C., Jr. (2002/2003). Business ethics: An oxymoron? *Communication World, 20*(1), 26–32. Retrieved August 12, 2003, from http://proquest.umi.com/pqdweb

Yin, T. (1992, June 12). Retailing: Sears is accused of billing fraud at auto centers. *The Wall Street Journal,* p. B1. Retrieved August 12, 2003, from http://proquest.umi.com/pqdweb

CHAPTER 3

The Role of Leaders in Influencing Unethical Behavior in the Workplace

Linda Klebe Treviño

Michael E. Brown

After years of focusing on explaining and predicting positive employee attitudes (e.g., job satisfaction, employee commitment) and behaviors (e.g., employee citizenship, work performance), organizational behavior researchers have increasingly turned their attention to understanding what drives costly misconduct in organizations (Bennett & Robinson, 2000; Giacalone & Greenberg, 1997; Robinson & Bennett, 1995; Robinson & O'Leary-Kelly, 1998; Treviño, 1986; Vardi & Wiener, 1996). Although researchers have used a variety of terms to describe such employee behavior (e.g., deviance, antisocial behavior, misbehavior, counterproductive behavior, unethical behavior), all of them share a concern with counternormative behavior intended to harm the organization or its stakeholders (O'Leary-Kelly, Duffy, & Griffin, 2000).

Unethical behavior in organizations has been widely reported in the wake of many recent high-profile corporate scandals. As researchers and practitioners consider what may be driving such behavior, leaders are coming under increasing scrutiny not only because many senior executives are accused of having committed unethical acts but also because of the role that leaders at all levels are thought to play in managing the ethical (and unethical) conduct of organization members. For example, Bernie Ebbers, the former chief executive officer of WorldCom, was hailed as a great leader for growing the company into a telecommunications superpower.

Ebbers, however, was later discredited for his failure to provide moral leadership as WorldCom became engulfed in financial scandals that resulted in the largest bankruptcy in U.S. history (for more on Ebbers, see Case 3). As Turner, Barling, Epitropaki, Butcher, and Milner (2002) suggest, organizational researchers are increasingly interested in the "moral potential of leadership" (p. 304). The assumption is that a leader who exerts moral authority should be able to influence followers' ethical behavior.

Theory and research suggest that leaders should, and do, influence organizational ethics. The normative business ethics literature has focused on cases (e.g., Donaldson & Gini, 1996) or prescriptions regarding what leaders *should* do to provide ethical leadership (e.g., Ciulla, 1998; Freeman, Gilbert, & Hartman, 1988; Rost, 1995). The descriptive business ethics literature has reported that executive leaders set the ethical tone at the top of organizations (Murphy & Enderle, 1995) and shape their formal and informal ethical cultures (Treviño, 1990; Treviño & Nelson, 2004). Executive leaders have been found to play an important role in communicating ethical standards and using rewards and punishments to reinforce normatively appropriate conduct (Treviño, Hartman, & Brown, 2000). In addition, senior management's concern for ethics has been shown to influence an organization's values or compliance-oriented approach to ethics management and its integration of ethics into everyday activities such as performance appraisals (Weaver, Treviño, & Cochran, 1999a, 1999b). Leaders have also been found to influence employees' ethical conduct. For example, employees' perception that executives and supervisors sincerely care about ethics has been associated with the amount of unethical conduct observed in the organization (Treviño, Weaver, Gibson, & Toffler, 1999). However, despite this evidence suggesting that leaders "matter" when it comes to organizational ethics, the specific role of leadership in influencing unethical behavior in the workplace has yet to be fully explicated.

In this chapter, we explore theoretical reasons why leaders should play an important role in influencing followers' ethical and unethical behavior. Specifically, we look at this relationship from cognitive moral development, social learning, and social exchange perspectives. Next, we consider leadership styles and how they have been linked to ethics in the leadership literature (e.g., transformational/charismatic leadership). Next, we discuss our recent research on the development of an ethical leadership construct. We conclude with recommendations for future research.

Why Leaders Are Important: Insights From Cognitive Moral Development Theory

To understand why leaders are important for understanding ethical and unethical behavior in organizations, we first turn to moral psychology and particularly to cognitive moral development theory (Kohlberg, 1969). Kohlberg's theory, widely cited as the leading theory in the field of moral development, focuses on how individuals reason through ethical dilemmas and how they decide what is right.

Although Kohlberg studied the moral development of children and young adults, his students (e.g., Rest, 1986) and others have studied adults in work settings.

According to Kohlberg (1969), people reason at six stages that can be understood in terms of three broad levels: preconventional, conventional, and principled. Preconventional individuals (the lowest level) are concerned with avoiding punishment and a "one hand washes the other" kind of reciprocation. Principled individuals (the highest level) make decisions autonomously by looking inside themselves and are guided by principles of justice and rights. But we know from decades of research that the large majority of adults reason at the conventional level of cognitive moral development (for summaries of research on moral development, see Rest, 1986; Rest, Narvaez, Bebeau, & Thoma, 1999; for a summary of research on moral development in the professions, see Rest & Narvaez, 1994). Such conventional-level individuals look outside themselves to rules and laws and to the expectations of significant others in their environments for guidance when determining the ethically right thing to do. Because these conventional-level individuals represent the large majority of workers, immediate supervisors should be among the most important sources of moral guidance for these employees, and we can expect that they will look to leaders for cues about what behavior is appropriate and inappropriate.

It is also important to note that moral reasoning has been associated with ethical and unethical conduct in a number of studies. Individuals at the principled level of moral development are less likely to engage in negative behaviors such as cheating and stealing, whereas those at lower levels are more likely to engage in such behaviors and are more susceptible to outside influences (e.g., Greenberg, 2002; for a review, see Treviño, 1992). Although other outside influences, such as peers (Zey-Ferrell & Ferrell, 1982; Zey-Ferrell, Weaver, & Ferrell, 1979), and formal organizational systems, such as ethics codes and training programs (Greenberg, 2002; Treviño et al., 1999), affect ethical behavior, leaders should be a key source of ethical guidance due to the authority role they play. In fact, leaders' level of moral reasoning has been shown to influence the moral reasoning used by group members in their decision making (Dukerich, Nichols, Elm, & Vollrath, 1990), and leadership style has been shown to influence conformity in ethical decision-making frameworks in work groups (Schminke, Wells, Peyrefitte, & Sebora, 2002). The next step, then, is to attempt to better understand some of the theoretical processes by which leaders are likely to influence such behavior.

How Leaders Influence Employee Ethical and Unethical Behavior

We discuss several theoretical explanations for how leaders influence ethical and unethical behavior. We offer a social learning perspective to suggest that leaders influence ethical and unethical conduct through modeling processes, and we offer a social exchange perspective to suggest that subordinates are likely to reciprocate with positive behavior when they and their leaders are involved in relationships that are based on admiration and trust.

Social Learning

Social learning has been used to understand how leaders influence followers more generally. House (1977), Bass (1985), and Kouzes and Posner (1987) all have referred to role modeling as essential leader behavior. In particular, charismatic or transformational leaders (discussed in detail later) are thought to influence followers, at least in part, through modeling and identification processes (Avolio, 1999; Avolio, Bass, & Jung, 1999; Kelman, 1958).

A social learning perspective (Bandura, 1977) suggests that leaders influence their followers by way of modeling processes. Modeling is acknowledged to be one of the most powerful means for transmitting values, attitudes, and behaviors. Employees learn what to do, as well as what not to do, by observing their leaders' behavior and its consequences. Leaders are likely to be models by virtue of their assigned role, their status and success in the organization, and their power to affect the behavior and outcomes of followers.

Clearly, modeling by leaders can influence followers to be ethical or unethical. Leaders who engage in unethical behaviors create a context supporting parallel deviance (Kemper, 1966), meaning that employees observe and are likely to imitate the inappropriate conduct. If leaders are observed "cooking the books," enriching themselves at the expense of others, or lying to customers or suppliers, followers learn that such behavior is expected. If leaders are rewarded for unethical conduct, the lesson for followers becomes particularly strong. Consider some chief executive officers, such as WorldCom's Bernie Ebbers and Enron's Ken Lay, who were celebrated by financial analysts and the media as exceptional executive leaders who defied conventional wisdom as they continually surpassed Wall Street's short-term financial expectations. They were publicly hailed and financially rewarded for achieving extraordinary financial outcomes, and no one seemed to care what means they used to achieve those outcomes. We should not be surprised to find that their subordinates followed their leads and became increasingly adept at inventing new (and sometimes unethical) ways in which to contribute to these outcomes.

Employees can also learn to be ethical by observing leaders who stand up for doing what is right, especially if the leaders are successful in doing so. For example, a chief executive who communicates with employees about a decision not to invest in a highly corrupt foreign country because it would require employees to engage in inappropriate behavior such as bribery is sending an important signal about what is appropriate and expected of followers. Similarly, an executive who shuts down machinery to ensure employee or product safety makes it clear that doing the right thing is expected even if it means short-term losses.

Leaders' power to influence may be particularly effective because leaders make decisions about the rewards and punishments that are imposed on employees, and followers learn vicariously by observing what happens to others. People in organizations pay close attention to rewards and punishments (Arvey & Jones, 1985; Kanfer, 1990; Treviño, 1992), and these contribute to modeling effectiveness because they are socially salient. Modeling theory argues that consequences (rewards and punishments) facilitate learning in an anticipatory and vicarious manner. Consequences inform observers about the benefits of modeled ethical behavior as well as about the negative effects of modeled inappropriate behavior. So, not only are leaders role models themselves, but they also make others into models by rewarding appropriate conduct and disciplining inappropriate conduct (Gini, 1998; Treviño, Brown, & Hartman, 2003). This seems especially important to the management of unethical conduct. We would not want every employee to have to personally experience punishment for inappropriate conduct so as to learn that such behavior is unacceptable. By observing how other employees are rewarded and punished, many employees can learn these important lessons vicariously.

Relying on justice and social learning theories, Treviño (1992) emphasized the key social implications of punishment in organizations. Discipline sends powerful signals about the value of organizational norms and leaders' willingness to stand behind them. Employees who are trying to do the right thing expect misconduct to be punished harshly, and they are disappointed if it is not. For example, if an employee who downloads pornography to his office computer is quickly terminated, other employees will get the clear message that such behavior will not be tolerated and that rules against it are being enforced in the organization. Employees' sense of retributive justice (Hogan & Emler, 1981) will be satisfied (Treviño, 1992; Treviño & Ball, 1992), and they will be less likely to engage in such behavior themselves. However, if such behavior is allowed to continue, employees will question management's sincerity and whether the organization's rules mean what they say.

Similarly, vicarious rewards can send powerful messages supporting ethical or unethical conduct. If an employee who pulled the handle to stop a potentially dangerous machine from harming a coworker is celebrated for his or her caring, observers learn that such behavior is appropriate, expected, and appreciated in the organization. Alternatively, if that same employee is punished because stopping the machine means missing short-term production quotas, employees will learn that short-term production quotas are more important than employee safety and that they are expected to behave accordingly. Finally, if a salesperson who is known to lie to customers is made "Salesperson of the Year," given a fat bonus, and sent on a Hawaiian vacation, employees will learn that lying to customers is rewarded, making such behavior more likely. Thus, employees are susceptible to leaders' influence to engage in appropriate or inappropriate behavior by learning from the leaders' own modeling of such behavior and by learning vicariously from how other employees' behavior is rewarded and punished.

The social learning approach suggests a mostly instrumental understanding of what drives unethical behavior in organizations. It argues that because of leaders' authority role and the power to reward and punish, employees will pay attention to and mimic leaders' behavior, and they will do what is rewarded and avoid doing what is punished in the organization. The rewards and punishments need not be direct but also can be learned vicariously by observing how others in the organization are rewarded and disciplined.

Social Exchange

Instrumental exchange is not the only way in which leaders can influence followers' ethical and unethical behavior. The quality of the interpersonal treatment that employees receive from leaders is also likely to be an important factor. Typically, high-quality leader–employee relationships are characterized as social exchanges as opposed to transactional ones. According to Blau (1964), transactional exchanges are characterized by quid pro quo logic and are governed by contract so that all terms and obligations are specified in advance and are enforceable by third parties. As a result, obligations governed by transactional exchange have a contractual tone and do not depend on trust between the parties. In a transactional exchange relationship, a supervisor relies on legitimate power to influence employees through the use of rewards or punishments, and employees can be expected to perform their duties as directed but to do little more.

In contrast, social exchange relationships entail future obligations that are unspecified and are enforced by norms of reciprocity (Gouldner, 1960). Without the protection of contractually specified obligations, the perceived trustworthiness of the partners and the fairness of the exchange become important for developing and maintaining lasting relationships. With social exchange, the obligation to reciprocate is voluntary (i.e., not contractually specified), and the benefits obtained may be nonmonetary. The rewards exchanged may be spontaneous (e.g., attraction, gratitude, respect). In addition, individuals in social exchange relationships tend to identify with the other parties in the exchange relationships. Parties engage in social exchange willingly, and reputation plays an important role in ensuring that the norms of fairness governing the exchange are not violated. Although the risks of exploitation and one-sidedness are high, a social exchange relationship develops over time with increased trust (Whitener, Brodt, Korsgaard, & Werner, 1998) and can be mutually beneficial for the parties involved as well as for the larger organization in which they work. Typically, leaders engage in both social and transactional exchanges with subordinates (Bass, 1985). Studies have shown that these two dimensions are strongly correlated (Avolio, 1999), although the dimensions can lead to different outcomes.

Perceived Fairness

Perceived fairness is particularly important for the development of a social exchange relationship (Konovsky & Pugh, 1994), especially in the context of a leader–subordinate relationship (Pillai, Schriesheim, & Williams, 1999). When employees believe that they are treated fairly in a social exchange relationship (Konovsky & Pugh, 1994), they are motivated to give more of themselves—affectively, cognitively, and/or behaviorally—in support of their supervisor and the group or organization that he or she represents. Fair treatment engenders satisfaction and loyalty among employees, making it less likely they will be motivated to harm their supervisor, group, or organization.

Social exchange is closely linked to both procedural and interactional fairness (Moorman, Blakely & Niehoff, 1998; Pillai et al., 1999). Interactional fairness refers to employees' perceptions of the degree to which they are treated with respect and dignity by authority figures (Bies & Moag, 1986). Perceived interactional justice should be particularly important to the development of a social exchange relationship between supervisors and subordinates because supervisors interact with their subordinates and make decisions that affect them every day. Although immediate supervisors may have little impact on the development of organizational procedures (procedural justice), they are likely the most important influence on employees' perceptions of whether the employees are treated with dignity and respect in the organization. When leaders treat employees well, they initiate social exchange processes, creating a sense of obligation among subordinates and motivating them to reciprocate. Subordinates may reciprocate by way of organizational citizenship behaviors, particularly those aimed at their supervisor (Malatesta & Byrne, 1997; Masterson, Lewis-McClear, Goldman, & Taylor, 2000; Niehoff & Moorman, 1993; Wayne, Shore, Bommer, & Tetrick, 2002), or by refraining from behaviors aimed at harming their leader, work group, or organization.

Alternatively, perceived unfair treatment can provoke strong negative reactions from employees. Greenberg (1990) found that employees reacted to perceived unfair pay cuts and interpersonally insensitive explanations from management by stealing from the organization, just one of many studies that have linked perceived unfairness with counterproductive employee behaviors (Konovsky, 2000). In response to perceived injustice, employees may engage in interpersonal and organizationally directed retaliation, including sabotage (Ambrose, Seabright, & Schminke, 2002; Bennett & Robinson, 2000; Robinson & Bennett, 1997; Treviño & Weaver, 2001) in an attempt to rebalance the scales of justice. One might expect an employee to target the source of the injustice, but an employee will be unlikely to retaliate against a leader overtly because such retaliation will most likely lead to formal sanction or punishment. Instead, we expect that employee retaliation will be covert and broader, including behaviors such as falsifying expense reports, abusing sick time, lying to the supervisor, and misusing company time and other resources. Research has found that unfair treatment by an individual, especially by a supervisor, can result in retaliation against either the person or the organization as a whole (Ambrose et al., 2002; Rupp & Cropanzano, 2002).

Trust in Supervisor

Social exchange relationships between leaders and followers are built on trust. Trust in leaders is especially important for employees due to their weak and subordinate positions relative to their supervisors (Kramer, 1999). Furthermore, leaders influence important outcomes such as pay, promotion, and satisfying work conditions. Employees face uncertainty about these outcomes and whether their leaders will allocate them fairly (Kramer, 1996). Furthermore, employees are dependent on their supervisors as representatives of higher organizational authority. When employees trust their leaders, the employees are more willing to engage in voluntary behaviors that benefit the organization (Podsakoff, MacKenzie, Paine, & Bachrach, 2000). A recent meta-analysis found that employees' trust in their leaders was associated with many positive outcomes (Dirks & Ferrin, 2002), including citizenship behaviors (Konovsky & Pugh, 1994) such as altruism, civic virtue, conscientiousness, courtesy, and sportsmanship as well as job satisfaction and satisfaction with their leaders. We can think of citizenship behaviors (which help the work group and organization) as representing the opposite of organizationally and interpersonally harmful behaviors. Therefore, as citizenship behaviors increase, unethical behaviors should decrease. Negative outcomes should be lower if employees trust their leaders because, as argued earlier, the leaders represent the organization to direct reports. Furthermore, although trust has been found to be more strongly related to work attitudes than to job performance (Dirks & Ferrin, 2002), the relationship of trust with unethical employee behaviors is likely to be strong because, theoretically, trust is more closely related to such behaviors than to more general job performance.

Liking and Affection for Supervisor

The leader–member exchange literature has focused on the importance of high-quality relationships between employees and their leader (Dansereau, Graen, & Haga, 1975; Graen & Cashman, 1975). In this literature, high-quality relationships are frequently characterized by employee liking and admiration of their leader (Schriesheim, Castro, & Cogliser, 1999). When employees have a high-quality relationship with their manager, they have been found to be less likely to engage in retaliation (Liden, Sparrowe, & Wayne, 1997). Alternatively, when employees have a poor exchange relationship with their supervisor, negative outcomes can result (Fairhurst, 1993). Some have argued that if employees dislike or are frustrated with a supervisor, they will retaliate in surreptitious ways by harming the organization through sabotage or by being aggressive with coworkers (Fairhurst, 1993; Liden et al., 1997; Zahn & Wolf, 1981). Again, we expect that employees will be less likely to engage in overt retaliation against a supervisor who they dislike because doing so would most likely lead to formal sanction or punishment. Rather, such frustration and dislike for a supervisor is likely to lead to covert (i.e., "behind-the-back") harmful behaviors aimed at coworkers or the organization (Bennett & Robinson, 2000).

Leadership Styles and Employee Ethical/Unethical Behavior

Now that we know something about the theoretical processes that are important to leaders' influence on followers' ethical and unethical behavior, we turn to the leadership literature to see what it can tell us about this relationship.

Transformational and Charismatic Leadership

The organizational leadership literature has addressed leadership's moral dimension primarily through the transformational and charismatic leadership dimensions (Kanungo & Mendonca, 1996). In the broader leadership literature,

Burns (1978) distinguished transformational leadership from transactional approaches. He argued that transformational leaders encourage followers to embrace moral values and to act in the interest of the collective rather than self-interest. He cited Kohlberg's (1969) theory of cognitive moral development, Maslow's (1954) hierarchy of human needs, and Rokeach's (1973) theory of values to explain transformational leaders' influence. Transformational leaders are thought to raise followers' level of moral development and to focus followers' attention on higher level needs and values.

In contrast, transactional leaders rely on rewards and punishments to direct followers' behavior. Kanungo and Mendonca (1996) argued that transactional approaches are inconsistent with moral leadership because transactional approaches ignore followers' needs and aspirations and that transactional leaders focus on the status quo rather than on an inspiring vision of the future and may be motivated by their own achievement and power rather than followers' needs.

Bass (1985) translated Burns's (1978) work on transformational leadership for the organizational behavior literature and, with Avolio (Bass & Avolio, 2000), developed a multidimensional transformational leadership construct with the following dimensions: individualized consideration, intellectual stimulation, idealized influence, and inspirational motivation. The idealized influence dimension is the most clearly "moral" dimension, with its focus on setting a good example, communicating moral values, and sacrificing self-interest for the benefit of the group.

Transformational leadership has been associated with many positive outcomes such as workers' satisfaction with work and the leader, organizational commitment, citizenship behaviors, and job performance (Fuller, Patterson, Hester, & Stringer, 1996; Lowe, Kroeck, & Sivasubramaniam, 1996; Yukl, 2002). However, researchers have just begun to study the influential mechanisms that mediate between leader behavior and these outcomes. Transformational leaders, by way of the idealized influence component, are thought to influence followers to develop a collectivistic orientation rather than a selfish one, to internalize moral values transmitted by the leader, and to increase followers' self-efficacy (Shamir, House, & Arthur, 1993).

The inspirational motivation component of transformational leadership combines with idealized influence to represent the "charismatic" aspect of transformational leadership. With inspirational motivation, leaders use symbols to present an attractive and optimistic vision of the future. Conger and Kanungo (1998) proposed that charismatic leaders would influence followers by arousing their personal identification with the leaders (Pratt, 1998). The charismatic leadership literature (House, 1977) argues that charismatic leaders link the organization's mission with followers' self-concept, including a sense of moral virtue (Gecas, 1982). Similar to transformational leaders, charismatic leaders are thought to emphasize the collective and the value of being part of something larger than themselves.

Thus far, the research to document these mediating mechanisms has produced mixed results. For example, Kark, Shamir, and Chen (2003) found that transformational leadership was related to personal identification with the leader and to social identification with the work unit, although personal identification with the leader had the stronger effect. But Dvir, Eden, Avolio, and Shamir (2002) failed to support their hypothesis that transformational leaders influence followers to develop a collectivistic orientation or to internalize moral values. Similarly, Shamir, Zakay, Breinin, and Popper (1998) found a negative relationship between leader charisma and follower self-efficacy, and their research provided only weak support for the proposition that charismatic leaders influence followers by inspiring them to work for the collective interests of the group. Furthermore, although a recent study found that transformational leaders are higher in moral reasoning (Turner et al., 2002), we do not yet have evidence that transformational leaders transmit this higher moral reasoning to their followers.

Clearly, more theoretical and empirical work will be needed to fully understand the processes by which transformational and charismatic leaders influence followers and any relationship between these leadership styles and ethics-related outcomes. One problem with understanding the relationship with ethics-related outcomes may be that transformational and charismatic leadership approaches presume "charismatic" appeal and/or "transformative" processes that may or may not be necessary to influence followers' ethical conduct (Treviño et al., 2003).

Another problem concerns the potential darker manifestations of transformational and charismatic leaders. Bass (1985) acknowledged that transformational leaders can wear "white hats or black hats." In addition, others have argued that both transformational and charismatic leaders can be self-centered and manipulative in the means they use to achieve their goals (Parry & Proctor-Thomson, 2002). Bass and Steidlmeier (1999) distinguished between pseudo-transformational leaders, who are self-interested and lack moral virtue, and "authentic" transformational leaders, who are more clearly "moral" leaders.

Others have coined the term "authentic leadership" to refer to a broad leadership construct that they propose to be the "root concept underlying all positive approaches to leadership and its development" (May, Chan, Hodges, & Avolio, 2003, p. 2). May and colleagues (2003) argued that authentic leaders have the ability to judge ethical dilemmas from multiple stakeholder perspectives and see their leadership role as including ethical responsibility. In addition, authentic leaders are self-aware and transparent in their decision making as well as in their intentions to act ethically. Authentic leaders can be, but are not necessarily, charismatic and/or transformational, but they are courageous enough to act on their ethical intentions and to sustain ethical action despite countervailing pressures.

Ethical Leadership

Because we sought to establish empirical grounding for further research on an ethical dimension of leadership, we have focused our attention on the development of a construct we call "ethical leadership." We conducted interviews with 20 senior executives (mostly chief executives) and 20 ethics officers in large business organizations. We asked them to describe the characteristics and behaviors of an ethical leader with whom they had worked closely during their careers. The good news is that all of them quickly thought of someone, suggesting that ethical leadership is not a rare phenomenon in today's business organizations. Similarly, a majority of respondents to the National Business Ethics Survey agreed that their supervisors and executive leaders model ethical behavior (Joseph, 2000).

Systematic content analysis of our interview data suggested that ethical leaders are both "moral persons" and "moral managers" (Treviño et al., 2000). We think of the "moral person" as representing the "ethical" part of the term "ethical leadership," and we think of the "moral manager" as representing the "leadership" part of that term.

Ethical leaders are thought to be moral persons because they are honest and trustworthy, take good care of their people, and do the right things in both their personal and professional lives. They make decisions based on values and ethical decision rules, and they are fair and concerned about stakeholders' interests and long-term outcomes.

As moral managers, ethical leaders are clear about their expectations of followers. They are visible role models of ethical behavior, communicate with their people about their ethical and values-based expectations, and use the reward system to hold followers accountable for ethical conduct.

Ethical leaders are also socially salient in their organizations. Ethical leaders stand out from what can be described as an "ethically neutral" background in many business organizations where the intent focus on the financial bottom line can easily drown out other messages (Treviño et al., 2003).

It is important to note that the executives we interviewed rarely described ethical leaders as either transformative or visionary, terms that are consistent with the transformational and charismatic leadership literatures. In addition, ethical leaders clearly use the reward system to support ethical conduct, suggesting that ethical leadership includes a dimension more consistent with transactional leadership approaches. Thus, although overlap certainly exists between ethical leadership and the transformational and charismatic leadership constructs, some important differences remain.

Understanding ethical leadership in this way makes sense if we consider the proposed theoretical processes underlying the relationship between leadership and employee ethical conduct: social learning and social exchange. In accordance with a social learning perspective, ethical leaders are described as being visible ethical role models who stand out from an ethically neutral landscape. They behave ethically in their personal and professional lives, and they make decisions based on ethical principles and the long-term interest of multiple stakeholders. Followers are likely to personally identify with such a visible role model of ethical conduct and to pattern their own behavior after that of the leader.

In addition, ethical leaders send clear messages to organizational members about expected behavior and use the reward system to hold everyone accountable to those expectations. By clearly rewarding ethical conduct and disciplining unethical conduct, they allow for vicarious learning to take place. This aspect of ethical leadership depends on social learning and can be viewed as more transactional (than transformational) because followers behave ethically and refrain from unethical conduct largely due to the observed consequences.

However, ethical leadership is also consistent with a social exchange perspective. Ethical leaders were described as being trustworthy and as treating their people with care, concern, and fairness. As such, they are likely to create social exchange relationships with their subordinates, who can be expected to reciprocate this care and fair treatment by engaging in citizenship behaviors and by refraining from unethical conduct. In addition, using the reward system to support ethical conduct is consistent with followers' perceptions of organizational justice. By disciplining unethical conduct, the leaders are upholding organizational norms and supporting the values of those who obey the rules. Thus, ethical leaders are likely to influence their followers to engage in ethical conduct and to refrain from unethical conduct by way of multiple processes that rely on both transformational and transactional approaches to leadership. This finding is contrary to the view that transactional approaches are inconsistent with ethical leadership (Kanungo & Mendonca, 1996).

Discussion

In this chapter, we have focused on the role of leadership in influencing employees' ethical and unethical conduct. We argued that because most employees are at the conventional level of cognitive moral development, they are looking outside themselves for guidance in ethical dilemma situations. Leaders, especially first-line supervisors, should be a key source of such guidance due to their proximity to their followers and their power to influence subordinate outcomes. We then outlined a number of theoretical processes, particularly social learning and social exchange, that are proposed to underlie this relationship between leader and follower ethical outcomes. We also reviewed the leadership literature for insight into relevant leadership styles and found that although transformational/charismatic leaders are proposed to be moral leaders, the empirical evidence for their influence on ethics-related outcomes remains scanty. Finally, we reviewed our own work on an ethical leadership construct that more tightly links leadership characteristics and practices to ethics-related outcomes.

Potential Limitations on the Role of Leadership

We hope that we have convinced the reader that leadership is enormously important and deserves more attention in our attempts to understand employee ethical and unethical behavior. However, we should also put the role of leaders in a broader context and understand its potential limitations, all of which are open to empirical testing.

We expect that some employees will be less influenced by leaders than will others. For example, employees who are at the principled level of cognitive moral development are expected to behave in accordance with internally held principles of justice and rights. Therefore, their ethical conduct should be less influenced by what specific leaders do or say. If faced with "unethical" leadership, principled individuals are more likely than others to try to change the situation, blow the whistle, or leave.

Employees at the lowest levels of cognitive moral development (preconventional) should be less influenced by leaders than by reward system contingencies.

When thinking about right and wrong, preconventional individuals think mostly about obedience and punishment avoidance or instrumental exchange (i.e., a "one hand washes the other" kind of relationship). Therefore, preconventional individuals will likely pay more attention to what will happen to them if they engage in a particular behavior than they will attend to leaders' behavior or expectations. Still, to the extent that leader expectations are tied to reinforcement contingencies, preconventional individuals can be expected to do what is expected of them by leaders.

Leader and follower demographics may also be significant. We suspect that ethical leadership may be less influential in homogeneous settings where leaders and their followers share values based on age and cultural similarity. Yet with the development of an increasingly diverse workforce in the United States, ethical leadership should become even more important.

Supervisory leaders may be more or less influential depending on characteristics of their work group such as size and type of work. For example, the larger the span of control, the more difficult it may be to communicate ethical standards and to hold work group members accountable. Furthermore, if employees work in the field and not under a leader's direct supervision (e.g., sales representatives), a leader's ability to influence them may be diminished simply because the leader is less visible or salient due to less frequent communication.

Individual leaders may also be less influential to the extent that the organization has a strong ethical climate and culture that incorporates formal and informal systems to support ethical conduct (Treviño, 1990; Treviño, Butterfield, & McCabe, 1998; Victor & Cullen, 1988). For example, since the implementation of the U.S. Sentencing Guidelines in 1991 (see www.ussc.gov), the majority of large business organizations have developed formal systems such as codes of conduct, ethics and legal compliance training programs, and telephone advice and reporting lines that answer employees' questions about appropriate conduct in ambiguous situations and that allow employees to anonymously report misconduct they observe (Joseph, 2000). To the extent that these formal systems are supported by other formal organizational systems such as performance management systems and norms of daily business practice, unethical conduct should be lower (Joseph, 2000; Treviño et al., 1999). On the one hand, a strong ethical context can be thought of as providing a kind of substitute for ethical leadership; thus, individual leaders may have less influence on their direct reports in such settings. On the other hand, in a strong ethical context, leaders are expected to provide ethical guidance. So, their efforts simply become part of the larger ethical environment that supports and encourages ethical conduct.

Alternatively, some organizations have a strong culture and climate that supports unethical conduct. In such an environment, it is unclear how much a single supervisory-level leader can do to change the situation. Anecdotal evidence suggests that only a chief executive may have the power to change such an unethical culture. Take the example of Douglas Durand. Durand had worked for 20 years at Merck & Company, where he was a senior regional director in 1995. Merck had a strong ethical culture where ethics and social responsibility were taken seriously. Durand accepted a lucrative offer to become the vice president of sales at TAP

Pharmaceuticals. Once he arrived, he quickly discovered a culture where sales representatives bribed doctors, did not account appropriately for free samples, and engaged in Medicare fraud. Durand tried to change the culture first by appealing to the sales representatives' ethics and by using the reward system to reinforce ethical conduct. However, his efforts were not supported by senior management, and he began to feel increasingly marginalized. In desperation and fear that he too would be implicated in the fraud, he finally determined that he had no choice but to blow the whistle on the company and leave. After years of investigation, the company was convicted and paid a record $875 million fine, and Durand collected a large part of the fine under the federal whistle-blower statute. Even at his fairly high executive level in the organization, he was unable to change a culture that focused exclusively on the bottom line and supported unethical and illegal conduct (Treviño & Nelson, 2004).

Levels of Leadership

Another question for future research relates to levels of leadership. Much leadership research does not distinguish between the executive and supervisory levels, although such a distinction is likely to be important for leaders' influence on ethics-related outcomes. Our published qualitative research focused on characteristics of executive-level ethical leaders. We conducted follow-up interviews with M.B.A. students that focused on supervisory ethical leadership, and we found that these informants characterized supervisory ethical leaders in similar ways. But some differences do stand out. Based on our executive ethical leadership data, we inferred four types of executive leader: ethical leader (high on the moral person and moral manager dimensions), unethical leader (low on both dimensions), hypocritical leader (high on the communication of an ethics agenda but not perceived to be a strong moral person), and ethically neutral leader (low on the moral manager dimension and not clearly high or low on the moral person dimension) (Treviño et al., 2000).

Executives are perceived from a distance. As a result, ethical leadership is largely a reputational phenomenon whereby the social salience of their "ethical" leadership is particularly important (Treviño et al., 2003). Executives must work to stand out from a background filled with other messages. If they are not visible ethical role models who communicate a strong ethics and values message and hold followers accountable for ethical conduct, executives are likely to be perceived as ethically neutral. Followers simply do not know where such executives stand. However, supervisory leaders are seen quite differently. Most employees work closely with their supervisors every day and have a clearer understanding of the ethical dimension of their leadership based on direct observation and experience. As a result, supervisory ethical leaders are likely to be seen in more black-and-white terms as either ethical or unethical leaders.

It is also unclear whether executive or supervisory leadership is more important in influencing ethical and unethical conduct. We suspect that both are required, but for different complementary reasons. For example, senior executives set the tone "at the top" and create and maintain organizational culture, including an organization's ethical culture and climate (Treviño, 1990; Victor & Cullen, 1988). Through their impact on the performance management system and their support (or lack of support) for ethics-related resources, organizational members—including supervisors—receive powerful messages about the importance of ethical conduct in the organization. Supervisors translate those messages and make them real through their daily treatment of followers and by setting daily expectations. When supervisory leaders reinforce the messages from the top, the positive influence on ethical conduct should be strongest. However, if supervisors contradict these messages, followers are forced to make a difficult choice. We suspect that most followers will choose to do what is expected by their supervisors unless the ethical culture is so strong that the followers believe that reporting unethical supervisors will be supported.

Conclusion

Leaders receive much of the credit for success and also shoulder most of the blame for ethical failures in organizations. Given their visible positions of authority, responsibility for shaping formal organizational policies, ongoing interactions with employees, and control over important rewards and punishments, leaders should play an important role in influencing employees' ethical and unethical conduct. In this chapter, we have proposed that leaders influence such conduct primarily by way of social learning and social exchange processes. Through modeling, leaders influence followers by demonstrating high ethical standards in their own conduct and by using the reward system to teach employees vicariously about the outcomes of ethical and unethical behavior in the organization. Furthermore, admired leaders who are seen as trustworthy, and who treat employees fairly and considerately, will develop social exchange relationships that result in employees reciprocating in positive ways. We hope that these insights will help to guide future research.

References

Ambrose, M. L., Seabright, M. A., & Schminke, M. (2002). Sabotage in the workplace: The role of organizational justice. *Organizational Behavior and Human Decision Processes, 89,* 947–965.

Arvey, R. D., & Jones, A. P. (1985). The use of discipline in organizational settings: A framework for future research. In L. L. Cummings & B. M. Staw (Eds.), *Research in organizational behavior* (Vol. 7, pp. 367–408). Greenwich, CT: JAI.

Avolio, B. J. (1999). *Full leadership development: Building the vital forces in organizations.* Thousand Oaks, CA: Sage.

Avolio, B. J., Bass, B. M., & Jung, D. I. (1999). Re-examining the components of transformational and transactional leadership using the Multifactor Leadership Questionnaire. *Journal of Occupational and Organizational Psychology, 72,* 441–462.

Bandura, A. (1977). *Social learning theory.* Englewood Cliffs, NJ: Prentice Hall.

Bass, B. M. (1985). *Leadership and performance beyond expectations.* New York: Free Press.

Bass, B. M., & Avolio, B. J. (2000). *Multifactor Leadership Questionnaire.* (Distributed by Mind Garden, Redwood City, CA)

Bass, B. M., & Steidlmeier, P. (1999). Ethics, character, and authentic transformational leadership behavior. *Leadership Quarterly, 10,* 181–218.

Bennett, R. J., & Robinson, S. L. (2000). Development of a measure of workplace deviance. *Journal of Applied Psychology, 85,* 349–360.

Bies, R. J., & Moag, J. S. (1986). Interactional justice: Communication criteria of fairness. In R. J. Lewicki, B. H. Sheppard, & M. H. Bazerman (Eds.), *Research on negotiation in organizations* (Vol. 1, pp 43–55). Greenwich, CT: JAI.

Blau, P. M. (1964). *Exchange and power in social life.* New York: John Wiley.

Burns, J. M. (1978). *Leadership.* New York: Harper & Row.

Ciulla, J. (1998). *Ethics, the heart of leadership.* Westport, CT: Quorum Books.

Conger, J., & Kanungo, R. (1998). *Charismatic leadership in organizations.* Thousand Oaks, CA: Sage.

Dansereau, F., Graen, G., & Haga, W. J. (1975). A vertical dyad linkage approach to leadership within formal organizations: A longitudinal investigation of the role making process. *Organizational Behavior and Human Performance, 13,* 46–78.

Dirks, K. T., & Ferrin, D. L. (2002). Trust in leadership: Meta-analytic findings and implications for research and practice. *Journal of Applied Psychology, 87,* 611–628.

Donaldson, T., & Gini, A. (1996). *Case studies in business ethics.* Englewood Cliffs, NJ: Prentice Hall.

Dukerich, J. M., Nichols, M. L., Elm, D. R., & Vollrath, D. A. (1990). Moral reasoning in groups: Leaders make a difference. *Human Relations, 43,* 473–493.

Dvir, T., Eden, D., Avolio, B. J., & Shamir, B. (2002). Impact of transformational leadership on follower development and performance: A field experiment. *Academy of Management Journal, 43,* 735–744.

Fairhurst, G. T. (1993). The leader–member exchange patterns of women leaders in industry: A discourse analysis. *Communication Monographs, 60,* 321–351.

Freeman, R. E., Gilbert, D. R., & Hartman, E. (1988). Values and the foundations of strategic management. *Journal of Business Ethics, 7,* 821–835.

Fuller, J. B., Patterson, C. E., Hester, K., & Stringer, D. Y. (1996). A quantitative review of research on charismatic leadership. *Psychological Reports, 78,* 271–287.

Gecas, V. (1982). The self-concept. In R. H. Turner & J. F. Short (Eds.), *Annual review of sociology* (Vol. 8, pp. 1–33). Palo Alto, CA: Annual Reviews.

Giacalone, R. A., & Greenberg, J. (1997). *Antisocial behavior in organizations.* Thousand Oaks, CA: Sage.

Gini, A. (1998). Moral leadership and business ethics. In J. B. Ciulla (Ed.), *Ethics, the heart of leadership* (pp. 27–45). Westport, CT: Quorum Books.

Gouldner, A. W. (1960). The norm of reciprocity. *American Sociological Review, 25,* 161–178.

Graen, G., & Cashman, J. F. (1975). A role making model of leadership in formal organizations: A developmental approach. In J. G. Hunt & L. L. Larson (Eds.), *Leadership frontiers* (pp. 143–165). Kent, OH: Kent State University Press.

Greenberg, J. (1990). Employee theft as a reaction to underpayment inequity: The hidden costs of pay cuts. *Journal of Applied Psychology, 75,* 551–558.

Greenberg, J. (2002). Who stole the money and when? Individual and situational determinants of employee theft. *Organizational Behavior and Human Decision Processes, 89,* 985-1003.

Hogan, R., & Emler, N. P. (1981). Retributive justice. In M. J. Lerner & S. C. Lerner (Eds.), *The justice motive in social behavior* (pp. 125–143). New York: Plenum.

House, R. J. (1977). A 1976 theory of charismatic leadership. In J. G. Hunt & L. L. Larson (Eds.), *Leadership: The cutting edge* (pp. 189–207). Carbondale: Southern Illinois University Press.

Joseph, J. (2000). *Ethics Resource Center's National Business Ethics Survey,* Vol. 1: *How employees perceive ethics at work.* Washington, DC: Ethics Resource Center.

Kanfer, R. (1990). Motivation theory and industrial and organizational psychology. In M. D. Dunnette & L. M. Hough (Eds.), *Handbook of industrial and organizational psychology* (2nd ed., Vol. 1, pp. 75–170). Palo Alto, CA: Consulting Psychologists.

Kanungo, R. N., & Mendonca, M. (1996). *Ethical dimensions of leadership.* Thousand Oaks, CA: Sage.

Kark, R., Shamir, B., & Chen, G. (2003). The two faces of transformational leadership: Empowerment and dependency. *Journal of Applied Psychology, 88,* 246–255.

Kelman, H. C. (1958). Compliance, identification, and internalization: Three processes of attitude change. *Journal of Conflict Resolution, 2,* 51–60.

Kemper, T. D. (1966). Representative roles and the legitimization of deviance. *Social Problems, 13,* 288–298.

Kohlberg, L. (1969). State and sequence: The cognitive-development approach to socialization. In D. Goslin (Ed.), *Handbook of socialization theory and research* (pp. 347–480). Chicago: Rand McNally.

Konovsky, M. A. (2000). Understanding procedural justice and its impact on business organizations. *Journal of Management, 26,* 489–511.

Konovsky, M. A., & Pugh, S. D. (1994). Citizenship behavior and social exchange. *Academy of Management Journal, 37,* 656–669.

Kouzes, J. M., & Posner, B. Z. (1987). *The leadership challenge: How to get extraordinary things done in organizations.* San Francisco: Jossey–Bass.

Kramer, R. M. (1996). Divergent realities and convergent disappointments in the hierarchical relation: The intuitive auditor at work. In R. M. Kramer & T. R. Tyler (Eds.), *Trust in organizations* (pp. 216–246). Thousand Oaks, CA: Sage.

Kramer, R. M. (1999). Trust and distrust in organizations: Emerging perspectives, enduring questions. *Annual Review of Psychology, 50,* 569–598.

Liden, R. C., Sparrowe, R. T., & Wayne, S. J. (1997). Leader–member exchange theory: The past and potential for the future. In G. R. Ferris (Ed.), *Research in personnel and human resources management* (Vol. 15, pp. 47–119). Greenwich, CT: JAI.

Lowe, K. B., Kroeck, K. G., & Sivasubramaniam, N. (1996). Effectiveness correlates of transformational and transactional leadership: A meta-analytic review of the MLQ literature. *Leadership Quarterly, 7,* 385–425.

Malatesta, R. M., & Byrne, Z. S. (1997, April). *The impact of formal and interactional justice on organizational outcomes.* Poster session at the meeting of the Society for Industrial and Organizational Psychology, St. Louis, MO.

Maslow, A. (1954). *Motivation and personality.* New York: Harper.

Masterson, S. S., Lewis-McClear, K., Goldman, B. M., & Taylor, M. S. (2000). Integrating justice and social exchange: The differing effects of fair procedures and treatment on work relationships. *Academy of Management Journal, 43,* 738–748.

May, D. R., Chan, A. Y. L., Hodges, T. D., & Avolio, B. J. (2003). Developing the moral component of authentic leadership. *Organizational Dynamics, 32,* 247–260.

Moorman, R. H., Blakely, G. L., & Niehoff, B. P. (1998). Does perceived organizational support mediate the relationship between procedural justice and organizational citizenship behavior? *Academy of Management Journal, 41,* 351–357.

Murphy, P., & Enderle, G. (1995). Managerial ethical leadership: Examples do matter. *Business Ethics Quarterly, 5,* 97–116.

Niehoff, B. P., & Moorman, R. H. (1993). Justice as a mediator of the relationship between methods of monitoring and organizational citizenship behavior. *Academy of Management Journal, 36,* 527–556.

O'Leary-Kelly, A. M., Duffy, M. K., & Griffin, R. W. (2000). Construct confusion in the study of antisocial behavior at work. *Research in Personnel and Human Resources Management, 18,* 275–303.

Parry, K., & Proctor-Thomson, S. B. (2002). Perceived integrity of transformational leaders in organizational settings. *Journal of Business Ethics, 35,* 75–96.

Pillai, R., Schriesheim, C. A., & Williams, E. S. (1999). Fairness perceptions and trust as mediators for transformational and transactional leadership: A two-sample study. *Journal of Management, 25,* 897–933.

Podsakoff, P. M., MacKenzie, S. B., Paine, J. B., & Bachrach, D. G. (2000). Organizational citizenship behavior: A critical review of the theoretical and empirical literature and suggestions for future research. *Journal of Management, 26,* 513–563.

Pratt, M. G. (1998). To be or not to be: Central questions in organizational identification. In D. A. Whetten & P. C. Godfrey (Eds.), *Identity in organizations: Building theory through conversation* (pp. 171–207). Thousand Oaks, CA: Sage.

Rest, J. R. (1986). *Moral development: Advances in research and theory.* New York: Praeger.

Rest, J. R. & Narvaez, D. (Eds.). (1994). *Moral development in the professions.* Hillsdale, NJ: Lawrence Erlbaum.

Rest, J. R. Narvaez, D., Bebeau, M. J., & Thoma, S. J. (1999). *Postconventional moral thinking; A neo-Kohlbergian approach.* Mahwah, NJ: Lawrence Erlbaum.

Robinson, S. L., & Bennett, R. J. (1995). A typology of deviant workplace behaviors: A multidimensional scaling study. *Academy of Management Journal, 38,* 555–572.

Robinson, S. L., & Bennett, R. J. (1997). Workplace deviance: Its definition, its manifestation, and its causes. In R. J. Lewicki, R. J. Bies, & B. H. Sheppard (Eds.), *Research on negotiation in organizations* (Vol. 6, pp. 3–27). Greenwich, CT: JAI.

Robinson, S. L., & O'Leary-Kelly, A. M. (1998). Monkey see, monkey do: The influence of work groups on the antisocial behavior of employees. *Academy of Management Journal, 41,* 658–672.

Rokeach, M. (1973). *The nature of human values.* New York: Free Press.

Rost, J. C. (1995). Leadership: A discussion about ethics. *Business Ethics Quarterly, 5,* 129–136.

Rupp, D. E., & Cropanzano, R. (2002). The mediating effects of social exchange relationships in predicting workplace outcomes from multifoci organizational justice. *Organizational Behavior and Human Decision Processes, 89,* 925–946.

Schminke, M., Wells, D., Peyrefitte, J., & Sebora, T. C. (2002). Leadership and ethics in work groups. *Group & Organization Management, 27,* 272–293.

Schriesheim, C. A., Castro, S. L., & Cogliser, C. C. (1999). Leader–member exchange (LMX) research: A comprehensive review of theory, measurement, and data-analytic practices. *Leadership Quarterly, 10,* 63–113.

Shamir, B., House, R., & Arthur, M. B. (1993). The motivation effects of charismatic leadership: A self-concept based theory. *Organization Science, 4,* 1–17.

Shamir, B., Zakay, E., Breinin, E., & Popper, M. (1998). Correlates of charismatic leader behavior in military units: Subordinates' attitudes, unit characteristics, and superior's evaluation of leader's performance. *Academy of Management Journal, 43,* 387–409.

Treviño, L. K. (1986). Ethical decision making in organizations: A person–situation interactionist model. *Academy of Management Review, 11,* 601–617.

Treviño, L. K. (1990). A cultural perspective on changing and developing organizational ethics. In R. Woodman & W. Passmore (Eds.), *Research in organizational change and development* (Vol. 4, pp. 195–230). Greenwich, CT: JAI.

Treviño, L. K. (1992). The social effects of punishment in organizations: A justice perspective. *Academy of Management Review, 17,* 647–676.

Treviño, L. K., & Ball, G. A. (1992). The social implications of punishing unethical behavior: Observers' cognitive and affective reactions. *Journal of Management, 18,* 751–768.

Treviño, L. K., Brown, M., & Hartman, L. P. (2003). A qualitative investigation of perceived executive ethical leadership: Perceptions from inside and outside the executive suite. *Human Relations, 55,* 5–37.

Treviño, L. K., Butterfield, K. B., & McCabe, D. L. (1998). The ethical context in organizations: Influences on employee attitudes and behaviors. *Business Ethics Quarterly, 8,* 447–476.

Treviño, L. K., Hartman, L. P., & Brown, M. (2000). Moral person and moral manager: How executives develop a reputation for ethical leadership. *California Management Review, 42,* 128–142.

Treviño, L. K., & Nelson, K. A. (2004). *Managing business ethics: Straight talk about how to do it right* (3rd ed.). Hoboken, NJ: John Wiley.

Treviño, L. K., & Weaver, G. R. (2001). Organizational justice and ethics program follow-through: Influences on employees' harmful and helpful behavior. *Business Ethics Quarterly, 11,* 651–671.

Treviño, L. K., Weaver, G. R., Gibson, D. G., & Toffler, B. L. (1999). Managing ethics and legal compliance: What works and what hurts. *California Management Review, 41*(2), 131–151.

Turner, N., Barling, J., Epitropaki, O., Butcher, V., & Milner, C. (2002). Transformational leadership and moral reasoning. *Journal of Applied Psychology, 87,* 304–311.

Vardi, Y., & Wiener, Y. (1996). Misbehavior in organizations: A motivational framework. *Organization Science, 7,* 151–165.

Victor, B., & Cullen, J. B. (1988). The organizational bases of ethical work climates. *Administrative Science Quarterly, 33,* 101–125.

Wayne, S. J., Shore, L. M., Bommer, W. H., & Tetrick, L. E. (2002). The role of fair treatment and rewards in perceptions of organizational support and leader–member exchange. *Journal of Applied Psychology, 87,* 590–598.

Weaver, G. R., Treviño, L. K., & Cochran, P. L. (1999a). Corporate ethics programs as control systems: Managerial and institutional influences. *Academy of Management Journal, 42,* 41–57.

Weaver, G. R., Treviño, L. K., & Cochran, P. L. (1999b). Integrated and decoupled corporate social performance: Management commitments, external pressures, and corporate ethics practices. *Academy of Management Journal, 42,* 539–552.

Whitener, E. M., Brodt, S. E., Korsgaard, M. A., & Werner, J. M. (1998). Managers as initiators of trust: An exchange relationship framework for understanding managerial trustworthy behavior. *Academy of Management Review, 23,* 513–530.

Yukl, G. A. (2002). *Leadership in organizations* (5th ed.). Upper Saddle River, NJ: Prentice Hall.

Zahn, G. L., & Wolf, G. (1981). Leadership and the art of cycle maintenance: A simulation model of superior–subordinate interaction. *Organizational Behavior and Human Performance, 28,* 26–49.

Zey-Ferrell, M., & Ferrell, O. C. (1982). Role set configuration and opportunity as predictors of unethical behavior in organizations. *Human Relations, 35,* 587–604.

Zey-Ferrell, M., Weaver, K. M., & Ferrell, O. C. (1979). Predicting unethical behavior among marketing practitioners. *Human Relations, 32,* 557–569.

Bernard Ebbers: Innovative Leader or Reckless Risk Taker

I n 1998, Bernard Ebbers, then chief executive officer of WorldCom, was named one of *Network World*'s 25 most powerful people in the telecommunications industry. Through the 1990s, Ebbers's WorldCom had acquired many companies and merged with others in a quest to build a worldwide telecommunications giant from a headquarters based in Mississippi.

As Ebbers became a major player in a rapidly growing industry, he cultivated a maverick image as an industry outsider in cowboy boots leading his troops to the top of the mountain. Although he was not seen as an Internet prophet who foretold of the inevitable dominance of cyberspace, Ebbers displayed a simple charm that led key staff members to describe him as a charismatic leader who inspired extraordinary levels of personal loyalty and high employee performance.

"When he enters a room, he is like a rock star," one WorldCom employee said. "People wanted to touch him, shake his hand. He created tremendous wealth, at least on paper. People revered him."

AUTHOR'S NOTE: This case was prepared by Roland Kidwell (Niagara University) as the basis for classroom discussion. It was developed from accounts that are listed in the bibliography at the end of the case. All names of individuals and the organization are real.

Within a few years of achieving industry prominence, the WorldCom bubble burst. A man who challenged the status quo in worldwide telecommunications through more than 70 mergers and acquisitions, including a multibillion-dollar deal to take over the much larger MCI, Ebbers was unceremoniously removed by his company's board of directors in 2002. That summer, allegations of accounting fraud surfaced, WorldCom entered into what was then the largest bankruptcy in the United States, and within a few months the company name became MCI.

From Small Beginnings to Industry Powerhouse

The story of Bernie Ebbers was once described by author George Gilder as "one of the most fascinating, improbable, and inspiring in North American business." To Gilder, who examined networking and telecommunications in his 2000 book *Telecosm,* Ebbers displayed "the magic of entrepreneurial vision and temerity." Ebbers quickly moved from motel chain owner to fiberoptic network magnate, leading commentators to dub him the "Ted Turner of the Internet."

Ebbers was born in Edmonton, in western Canada, during the early 1940s. After flunking out of two other colleges, the 6-foot-4-inch Ebbers was offered a basketball scholarship at Mississippi College, where he eventually graduated with a physical education degree. At the small liberal arts school, Ebbers learned a valuable lesson from his coach: "With hard work, dedication, a commitment to principles, and a commitment to Jesus Christ, life can be worthwhile."

After graduation, Ebbers married a local woman and decided to stay in Mississippi. He got his start in business by purchasing rural motels, financing the purchases with large helpings of money borrowed from friends. In 1982, the breakup of telecommunications giant AT&T offered an important opportunity to Ebbers and his business associates. Ebbers became an original investor in LDDS, a company that purchased long-distance service wholesale from AT&T and resold it to individual customers at retail prices.

The company was not immediately successful. It lost money and racked up debt for the first 2 years. At that point, in 1985, Ebbers gained control of LDDS by using equity from his motel chain. Shortly afterward, he was named chief executive officer and began to seek new sources of capital and to cut the costs of operations. Along the way, large amounts of debt financing caused him little concern.

Murray Waldron, one of Ebbers's original partners, described him as "the most focused leader I'd ever seen."

Ebbers, who saw himself as a marketing expert, hired engineering and accounting expertise to assist in his efforts to make LDDS profitable. Part of that turnaround effort involved rapid expansion. According to Gilder, Ebbers adopted economies of scale as a means to success; Ebbers purchased or rented larger volumes of bandwidth, thereby reducing unit costs. This strategy was accomplished through rapid expansion—purchasing regional long-distance resellers and integrating them into the system. In 1989, LDDS merged with Advantage, a publicly traded company that held a small long-distance business. The newly acquired public status of LDDS allowed the company to expand by trading its stock for assets. More acquisitions followed.

Eventually, Ebbers's growth strategy led to vertical integration. In 1994, LDDS purchased its key network supplier, Wiltel, the nation's fourth-largest fiber-optic network. This purchase allowed Ebbers to obtain the name WorldCom, which was the moniker of Wiltel's European subsidiary. Wiltel was purchased for LDDS stock and paid for by cuts in operating costs that resulted from the merger.

Expansion did not end there. The new WorldCom made additional network purchases that allowed the company to start building a fiber-optic network across Europe and to boast of owning one of the largest Internet service providers in the world. In 1998, the multibillion-dollar purchase of MCI, which was three times the size of WorldCom, gave the company additional industry clout and resources.

"It's actually a very, very enjoyable exercise," Ebbers once said of his rash of acquisitions. "After you do enough of them, it kind of becomes part of your culture."

In WorldCom's heyday, Ebbers controlled "the world's most menacing business challenge to the world's telecom industry," according to Gilder's account. That industry included corporations such as AT&T, British Telecom, Sprint, GTE Communications, and the Bell regional operating companies.

WorldCom's stock surged in 1999, reaching $75 a share. After the MCI acquisition, the company, led by Ebbers, continued its efforts to create a lean and mean amalgamation, selling off two of MCI's five corporate jets, cutting expense accounts of former MCI people, and (most significantly) axing 2,000 of the company's 75,000 jobs.

As his industry status increased, Ebbers was viewed by colleagues and members of the local community in Mississippi as a responsible business leader who was willing to give back to the community. He taught Sunday school at his local Baptist church, served meals to the needy at a Jackson restaurant, and lived modestly in a prefabricated home. He invested most of his wealth in company stock.

"He is absolutely one of the most incredible human beings I have come in contact with," said Diana Day, who worked with Ebbers for nearly 20 years. "The Lord was his CEO, as (He) is all of ours."

"Bernie Ebbers is my mentor," LeRoy Walker, Jr., a businessman and community leader, once told Jesse Jackson, according to an account in *Time* magazine. Jackson had attacked Ebbers during a speech at historically black Tougaloo College, accusing him of failing to provide money for Mississippi's black students while spending billions to buy MCI. Walker, a Tougaloo board member, explained to the social activist that Ebbers had given the college more than $1 million, new information technology, and computers to be used by disadvantaged black youth in the local community.

Another View of Ebbers's Leadership

Not everyone was thrilled about Ebbers's capabilities and priorities. Although Ebbers's professed hatred of corporate bureaucracy led to significant reductions in staff as new companies were acquired, the company chief executive purchased a 164,000-acre ranch and 20,000 head of cattle in British Columbia.

As new companies were absorbed, critics argued, WorldCom did not effectively realize the savings that had been suggested as the reason why the takeovers made business sense in the first place. Acquisitions occurred so quickly that there was no time to properly integrate new companies into WorldCom. Employees at WorldCom meetings would often introduce themselves by the company where they had originally worked, for example, "Happy to meet you. I'm legacy–MCI."

While WorldCom moved to make its largest proposed acquisition of all— that of Sprint—Ebbers did not endear himself to international competitors when he attacked the European telecommunications players that he claimed were lagging behind North America: "Most of the companies in Europe would not be survivors in a transaction" between U.S. and European telecommunications companies, he said. Ebbers expressed impatience with, and disdain for, those who questioned WorldCom's direction.

Based on stories that were related to the media about Ebbers, his management philosophy focused obsessively on keeping down costs. He questioned why expensive bagels, rather than cheaper food, were served at company meetings. He replaced the coffee supplier with vending machines when he discovered that the company was spending $3 million a year on coffee. He announced that he would videotape employees' walks on an exercise track at company headquarters to document whether they were taking too many breaks. He banned color copies because he deemed them too expensive. He personally turned off lights to shave energy bills and adjusted thermostats in WorldCom's offices, putting them 2 degrees higher during the summer and 2 degrees lower during the winter.

These cost-cutting tales conflicted with Ebbers's alleged generosity in loaning money for the purchase of company stock; he provided personal loans to key senior executives for that purpose. One former senior manager told the *Financial Times* that Ebbers offered $80,000 to $300,000 loans to as many as 50 top executives. These loans were not put in writing, but it was understood that they would be repaid.

"All those guys drank Bernie's Kool-Aid," one anonymous WorldCom source said in a *Financial Times* analysis of the company. The source likened the situation to the infamous Jim Jones's religious cult mass suicide of the 1970s.

Company observers said that power became concentrated among a few people in the upper echelon, including Scott Sullivan, chief financial officer; Ron Beaumont, chief operating officer; and Diana Day, senior vice president of customer service. Other executives who joined the company through its acquisitions were shunted to the background. These "outsiders" viewed the company as lacking the professional management and operating systems that would be expected in an organization of its size. They claimed that the mammoth company ran like an entrepreneurial start-up.

Regulatory Problems, Deflated Stock, and Disgrace

Because of the use of company stock to finance most of WorldCom's continuing run of acquisitions, it was crucial for the company to keep the stock price high. Thus, company officials found it extremely important to meet Wall Street's expectations of what the company earnings should be. Ebbers and Sullivan frequently attended industry analyst conferences, where they made presentations touting the company and its rising stock price. When the stock price declined during the general telecommunications stock downturn, it was inevitable to some that the company would go bust.

"Everybody always felt like there was no room for error," a former executive told the *Financial Times*. "Once, we missed [earnings] by 1 cent, and the stock nearly [collapsed]. That was an error that lived with 'the Bern' for a long time. He went on a rampage. He would be completely nasty, condescending, and arrogant."

In 1999, WorldCom moved to take over Sprint, making a $115 billion bid to acquire the rival carrier. The bid exceeded the $80 billion proposed merger of the Exxon and Mobil oil companies. Ebbers's long-term strategy in acquiring Sprint, along with MCI in 1998, was to upgrade their Internet facilities and engage larger competitors on a worldwide basis with a streamlined Internet capability. However, in both cases, U.S. regulatory agencies stepped in, claiming that WorldCom was attempting to monopolize the industry. Regulators forced WorldCom to sell MCI's Internet facilities to Cable & Wireless of Britain and barred acquisition of the Sprint network. Some observers, including Gilder, said that the government's failure to allow WorldCom to pursue its strategy led to the company's downfall.

At the least, such regulatory actions did not aid Ebbers in turning his organization into a strong company that would be able to cope with economic fluctuations and a stock market downturn that would make additional acquisitions unfeasible. By April 2002, calls for Ebbers's dismissal increased as the company stock slid from a market value of $180 billion in 1999 to $8 billion 3 years later, and a Securities and Exchange Commission investigation into WorldCom's accounting practices began. Ebbers was also questioned about

$400 million in low-interest loans that he had secured earlier from the company's board of directors, ostensibly to buy more stock.

"With Bernie, it was live by the sword, die by the sword," said Alex Peters, manager of Franklin Global Communications Fund. "He has certainly assembled a valuable set of assets. The question is, will he be able to get a fair price for them in the end?"

When Ebbers was finally forced out by the board's outside directors, he still refused to concede that the company had significant problems. At that point, WorldCom stock was selling for approximately $2.50 a share.

Fraud, Bankruptcy, and Recriminations

Within 2 months of Ebbers's departure, allegations of financial fraud surfaced and led to the firing of Sullivan. An internal audit found that the company had fabricated profitable numbers to ensure that its stock price stayed high. In June 2002, John Sidgmore, who took over as chief executive officer for Ebbers, announced that an "irregularity" had been found in the way in which the company had been accounting for its capital expenses. An ensuing investigation by accountants for WorldCom found that $3.8 billion in operating costs had been incorrectly classified as capital expenditures over a 15-month period that began in 2001. The inaccuracy increased reported cash flow and profits, leading the company to falsely report a $1.4 billion profit in 2001 and a $130 million profit for the first 3 months of 2002.

As the investigation continued, more reporting problems were uncovered, leading the company to admit that it had overstated its earnings by more than $9 billion since 1999. Five company officials, including Sullivan, were charged with criminal fraud, but for many months investigators' efforts to link Ebbers to illegal activity were unsuccessful. Despite WorldCom's high-tech nature, Ebbers did not use e-mail and usually responded to e-mails from his staff with phone calls.

Within a month of disclosing its accounting misdeeds, WorldCom, faced with $41 billion in debt, filed for reorganization in federal bankruptcy court. The largest bankruptcy in U.S. history affected creditors, business clients, 20 million consumers, and 80,000 employees around the world. Lawsuits related to the company's downfall continue, as do investigators' attempts to implicate Ebbers in the accounting fraud.

WorldCom's board voted in September 2002 to ask the bankruptcy court to rescind Ebbers's severance agreement, which awarded him $1.5 million a year for life. Lawyers for the board argued that the agreement was void because Ebbers knew the company was insolvent at the time the agreement was reached.

In June 2003, a report prepared by an independent law firm with the aid of MCI (formerly WorldCom) board members cited tremendous pressure at WorldCom to keep revenues up so as to meet Wall Street's expectations.

Although the company was legitimately growing at 5 to 10% each quarter, one MCI board member said, that figure was boosted to 10 to 15% to meet analysts' expectations. The report asserted that only a few top executives at WorldCom directed the fraudulent accounting, but it identified Ebbers as the creator of a culture that gave birth to the fraud.

On March 2, 2004, federal authorities charged Ebbers with conspiracy, securities fraud, and filing false financial statements. Sullivan agreed to plead guilty to similar charges and to testify against Ebbers in exchange for receiving a less severe sentence. Two months later, Ebbers was accused of falsifying six regulatory filings just before WorldCom's collapse.

Discussion Questions

1. To what extent were the actions of Bernard Ebbers indicative of leadership, and to what extent did Ebbers display destructive deviant behavior? Provide examples of leadership and deviant behavior from the case.

2. How did Ebbers influence his managers and employees to engage in deviant unethical behavior? How could he have used his influence and leadership style to avoid deviant behavior among subordinates?

3. Identify some theoretical linkages between Ebbers's leadership style as practiced and the behavior that occurred within WorldCom.

4. The law firm report identified Ebbers as the source of a culture that resulted in the company's accounting fraud. How did Ebbers's leadership style contribute to the values and actions of key managers? How could key managers perform their jobs effectively and ethically in the WorldCom culture?

5. Consider the characteristics of the ethical leader described in Chapter 3. How does such a leader encourage ethical behavior among managers and employees and, at the same time, obtain successful organizational results? Could Ebbers have used these characteristics to accomplish his goals at WorldCom? Explain.

Bibliography

Another cowboy bites the dust. (2002, June 27). *Economist.com*. Retrieved August 22, 2003, from http://proquest.umi.com/pqdweb

Boyd, D. P. (2003). Chicanery in the corporate culture: WorldCom or world con? *Corporate Governance, 3*(1), 83–85. Retrieved August 22, 2003, from http://proquest.umi.com/pqdweb

Catan, T., Kirchgaessner, S., Larsen P. T., & Ratner, J. (2002, December 18). Bernie Ebbers: Before the fall. *FT.com*. Retrieved August 22, 2003, from http://proquest.umi.com/pqdweb

Edwards, B., & Speer, J. (2003, June 10). Analysis: Report on Bernie Ebbers' role in WorldCom collapse. *Morning Edition* (National Public Radio transcript). Retrieved August 22, 2003, from http://proquest.umi.com/pqdweb

Gallant, J. (1997–1998, December 29–January 5). The 25 most powerful people in networking. *Network World,* pp. 44–56. Retrieved August 22, 2003, from http://proquest.umi.com/pqdweb

Gilder, G. (2000). *Telecosm: How infinite bandwidth will revolutionize our world.* New York: Free Press.

Gilder, G. (2001, August 6). Tumbling into the Telechasm. *The Wall Street Journal,* p. A12. Retrieved August 22, 2003, from http://proquest.umi.com/pqdweb

Haddad, C., & Borrus, A. (2002, September 23). What did Bernie know? The feds are hot on Ebbers' trail, but so far he's playing it cool. *BusinessWeek,* pp. 75–76. Retrieved August 22, 2003, from http://proquest.umi.com/pqdweb

Haddad, C., Foust, D., & Rosenbush, S. (2002, July 8). WorldCom's sorry legacy: Its downfall may hurt rivals and kill telecom competition. *BusinessWeek,* pp. 38–40. Retrieved August 22, 2003, from http://proquest.umi.com/pqdweb

Ho, D. (2004, March 3). Criminal charges cap WorldCom chief's fall. *Atlanta Journal–Constitution,* p. A1. Retrieved March 16, 2004, from LexisNexis database

Kirchgaessner, S. (2003, July 18). Investigators circle Ebbers associates. *Financial Times,* p. 30. Retrieved August 22, 2003, from http://proquest.umi.com/pqdweb

Kirchgaessner, S., & Larsen, P. T. (2002, August 26). Life under watchful eye of Ebbers: An arch micromanager claims he missed a developing scandal. *Financial Times,* p. 20. Retrieved August 22, 2003, from http://proquest.umi.com/pqdweb

Kirchgaessner, S., & Waters, R. (2002, April 25). Death of bull market leaves Ebbers in the dust: Once the most feared man in the telecom industry because of his aggressive acquisition strategy, the once high-flying WorldCom chief has now been brought back down to earth with a bump. *Financial Times,* p. 28. Retrieved August 22, 2003, from http://proquest.umi.com/pqdweb

Kupfer, A. (1997, December 8). Why Bernie Ebbers wants to be the Internet's Mr. Big. *Fortune,* pp. 214–216. Retrieved August 22, 2003, from http://proquest.umi.com/pqdweb

Padgett, T. (2002, May 13). The rise and fall of Bernie Ebbers. *Time,* pp. 56–57. Retrieved August 22, 2003, from http://proquest.umi.com/pqdweb

Schwartz, N. D. (1999, February 1). How Ebbers is whipping MCI WorldCom into shape. *Fortune,* p. 152. Retrieved August 22, 2003, from http://proquest.umi.com/pqdweb

Waters, R. (1999, October 9). Mobile phone mogul: Man in the news Bernie Ebbers: The maverick former basketball coach has used his Wall Street fan club to build a global telecom group. *Financial Times,* p. 15. Retrieved August 22, 2003, from http://proquest.umi.com/pqdweb

Waters, R. (2002, May 1). Ebbers is forced out of WorldCom: Brash dealmaker falls victim to outside directors after collapse of share price. *Financial Times,* p. 1. Retrieved August 22, 2003, from http://proquest.umi.com/pqdweb

CHAPTER 4

Badmouthing the Company

Bitter Employee or Concerned Corporate Citizen?

Robert J. Bies

Thomas M. Tripp

I had to go public with this information. The company had "screwed" me and my team. They didn't care about us. The company got what it deserved.

—Manager, consumer products company

I didn't want to "leak" the information to the press, but I had no other choice. No one would listen to me, even though my complaints were supported by facts. I know my action put the company in a "bad light," but I wanted to save it from even further damage by remaining silent. This company is my family and my life.

—Manager, telecommunications company

During the past few years, many companies and government agencies have found themselves to be the targets of negative publicity brought on by employees who provided "damaging" information about the organizations to the public and the press. Prominent examples include Sherron Watkins, who raised concerns about financial practices at Enron (Witt & Behr, 2002), and Colleen Rowley, the Federal Bureau of Investigation (FBI) agent who wrote FBI Director Robert Mueller a memo detailing how the bureau ignored warnings of terrorist activities before the attacks of September 11, 2001 (Ratnesart & Weisskopf, 2002). Although the individuals making this information public viewed themselves as concerned organizational citizens, they were viewed as bitter employees by the executives leading those organizations.

As the introductory quotations suggest, people may have different motivations for bringing to public light damaging information about their organizations and their leaders. It could be a bitter employee motivated to "get even," as the first quotation suggests. Or, it could be a concerned organizational citizen trying to save the company, as the second quotation suggests. In either case, such "bad-mouthing" of the company, so to speak, should be viewed as an act of revenge (Bies & Tripp, 1996, in press); that is, it is an action intended to "right" a "wrong," regardless of the employee's motivation. The primary focus of this chapter is to understand and analyze badmouthing of the company through the lens of revenge theory and research.

A growing body of research on revenge (Bies & Tripp, 1996, 1999, in press; Bies, Tripp, & Kramer, 1997; McLean Parks, 1997; Tripp & Bies, 1997) and related topics, such as retaliation (Allred, 1999; Skarlicki & Folger, 1997), has yielded insight into this phenomenon. As with the world of practitioners, a similar split perspective on revenge has been found among scholars and researchers. Whereas many scholars conceptualize revenge as behavior that is, by definition, "deviant" in nature (Robinson & Bennett, 1995), others argue that such a conceptualization reflects an ideologically biased view of revenge, one that has truncated academic and managerial understanding and analysis of revenge (Bies & Tripp, in press). Although revenge *can* be counterproductive behavior, it can *also* be constructive and productive behavior (Bies & Tripp, 1998). Sometimes, revenge serves a purpose that is useful not only to the avengers but also to their victims, the bystanders, and even the organization itself when it corrects or stops workplace injustices that the formal system was unable or unwilling to deal with (Bies & Tripp, 1998). Indeed, when such injustices are stopped, one often witnesses improved employee morale and productivity (Tripp & Bies, 1997).

In this chapter, we examine revenge and its consequences in organizations. We begin our analysis with a review of findings from our research on revenge. In the second section, we present our stakeholder perspective on revenge (Bies & Tripp, 1998), a framework that can provide a more textured analysis of revenge, in general, and of badmouthing, in particular. In the final section, we explore the implications of our analysis for scholars and practitioners. Throughout these three sections, we apply our previous work to the context of badmouthing in organizations, using new examples from a recent study on organizational badmouthing by the first author.

Toward a Better Understanding of Badmouthing the Organization: Insights From Empirical Studies on Revenge

Bies and Tripp (in press) reviewed the growing body of research on revenge, and from that analysis five tentative conclusions emerged, each with implications for understanding badmouthing. Specifically, revenge is a provoked act, emotions are figural elements in the act of revenge, the act of revenge has a rationality and morality, the emotions of revenge are shaped by social cognitive dynamics, and the act of revenge can take many forms. We elaborate on these conclusions in the following subsections.

Revenge Is a Provoked Act

Research on revenge has produced converging findings that revenge is a provoked behavior (Allred, 1999; Bies & Tripp, 1996; Skarlicki & Folger, 1997). One source of provocation is *goal obstruction* (Buss, 1962; Neuman & Baron, 1997). The mere frustration of goal attainment in organizations can lead to acts of revenge in response (Morrill, 1992). For example, the feeling that Watkins's career mobility was being obstructed at Enron was one of the motivations behind her "going public" with the information about Enron accounting practices (Witt & Behr, 2002).

But badmouthing can also be motivated by justice concerns. For example, another source of provocation is *violation of rules, norms, and promises.* Employees are motivated to badmouth the organization when the formal rules of the organization have been violated (Bies & Tripp, 1996). Other examples of rule violation include organizational authorities changing the rules or criteria of decision making after the fact (Bies & Tripp, 1996) and a formal breach of a contract occurring between an employee and an employer (Bies & Tyler, 1993).

Breaches of social and equity norms can also provoke and motivate badmouthing. Examples of a social norm violation include bosses or coworkers making promises but then breaking them or even lying outright (Bies & Tripp, 1996) and disclosing private confidences or secrets to others inside or outside the organization (Bies, 1993). Examples of equity norm violations include bosses or coworkers shirking their job responsibilities, taking undue credit for a team's performance, and outright "stealing" ideas (Bies & Tripp, 1996).

Another source of provocation is *status and power derogation* (Bies & Tripp, in press). Several studies suggest that attempts to derogate a person's status or power can motivate revenge (Bies & Tripp, 1996). For example, bosses who are hypercritical, overdemanding, and overly harsh—even cruel—in their dealings with subordinates over time can motivate badmouthing of the bosses and their organizations

(Bies & Tripp, 1996, 1999). Other incidents that might motivate badmouthing include destructive criticism (Baron, 1988), public ridicule intended to embarrass a subordinate or coworker (Morrill, 1992), and wrongful accusation of an employee by a boss or peer (Bies & Tripp, 1996).

Emotions Are Figural Elements in the Act of Revenge

One of the consistent findings about revenge is the central role of emotions in such behavior. Most studies of revenge have focused on anger as the figural element in revenge (e.g., Allred, 1999), an emotion that is triggered by an assignment of blame for perceived harm or wrongdoing (Bies et al., 1997). Bies and Tripp (in press) identified other important facets of the emotions of revenge that are relevant to the current analysis: *a sense of violation, intensity,* and *enduring nature.*

A sense of violation is more than mere "unmet expectations." Indeed, the violation is much deeper, reflecting a violated psyche or sense of sacred self (Bies, 2001). A telecommunications company executive, in an ongoing study being conducted by the first author, articulated this feeling of violation as follows: "I believed them. I trusted them. Then, they betrayed me by giving the job to someone outside the company. I no longer believe. I no longer trust."

In many cases, Bies and Tripp (in press) found that the feelings of violation often give way to very intense, action-oriented emotions. Indeed, people talk about the intensity of the emotions they experience, often belying a strong visceral response of physiological and psychological pain. For example, the initial emotions are often described as quite hot and volatile, characterized by expressions of pain, anger, and rage, and these emotions are often at the root of badmouthing (Bies & Tripp, 1996).

Furthermore, the emotions of revenge can create a psychological and physiological stranglehold on an individual. The emotions of revenge can endure over time, sometimes for days, weeks, or even months, if not longer. Indeed, the emotions of revenge can act like a "social toxin" (Hornstein, 1996), "poisoning" the individual's professional and personal lives over time. A consumer products company executive, in an ongoing study being conducted by the first author, described the experience in these words: "The anger consumed me. It was all I could think about. I had to badmouth them. I had to get it out of my system."

The Act of Revenge Has a Rationality and Morality

Whether an action or outcome triggers the revenge motive depends on how one makes sense of, or cognitively processes, the harm or wrongdoing (Bies et al., 1997). In particular, to provide a moral basis for revenge (i.e., it is not just a harm but also an injustice or a wrongdoing), the assignment of blame is critical (Folger & Cropanzano, 2001). If an individual can place blame on some agent of the organization, that person will likely construe the action as a personal attack (Bies, 2001). Following Cahn (1949), the attack is viewed as an act of aggression that will trigger emotions that are often described vividly (e.g., furious, enraged, hate). In other words, badmouthing is viewed as a *legitimate* and *rational* act of self-defense in response to an injustice or a wrongdoing by another (Bies & Tripp, 1996).

There is also clear and consistent empirical evidence that revenge has its own moral imperative (Bies & Tripp, 1996; McLean Parks, 1997). First, in many cases, revenge is a response to a perceived injustice or wrongdoing (Skarlicki & Folger, 1997). Badmouthing often is in response to the organization's failure to correct an injustice (Bies & Tripp, 1996). Second, revenge is most often intended to restore justice. For instance, while engaging in badmouthing, people reported a strong belief that they were doing the right thing; that is, they were "doing justice" (Tripp & Bies, 1997). Third, although the act of badmouthing may serve self-interest, it often serves other interests and is usually justified in moral terms (Bies & Tripp, 1998), as it was in the case of Watkins at Enron (Witt & Behr, 2002).

The Emotions of Revenge Are Shaped by Social Cognitive Dynamics

Research on revenge has identified several cognitive processes that can bias the blame assignment process (Bies et al., 1997) and, thus, shape badmouthing behavior. First, there is the *overly personalistic attribution* (Bies & Tripp, 1996), that is, when individuals overattribute sinister and malevolent motives to others' actions (e.g., "She wasn't just being careless or even just selfish—she was mean-spirited," "She was out to get me—it wasn't just business, it was personal"). Such an attributional bias often motivates badmouthing (Bies & Tripp, in press).

A second important cognitive process contributing to individuals' perceptions that they are being intentionally harmed or singled out unfairly is the *biased punctuation of conflict* (Bies et al., 1997). Biased punctuation of conflict refers to a tendency of individuals to construe the history of conflict with others in a self-serving and provocative fashion. For example, in a tit-for-tat feud, each party perceives itself as the avenging victim and perceives its opponent as the aggressor against whom one must defend. In other words, the one who is badmouthing the organization or one of its leaders views that action as a response to a specific harm but might not remember any action on his or her own part that may have contributed to the specific harm to which he or she is responding (and vice versa on the part of the leader or organization).

Third, a cognitive process that often acts to amplify the emotions of revenge is *rumination and obsession* (Bies et al., 1997). Indeed, we find that rumination and obsession are often at the foundation of more extreme emotions that can motivate badmouthing (e.g., bitterness, hatred). Furthermore, rumination and obsession can become even more intense and enduring when they are reinforced in social gatherings where people vent their emotions (Bies & Tripp, 1996), which Morrill (1992) referred to as "bitch sessions." When badmouthing occurs in such sessions, along with the social support given by others in the sessions, it often provides greater motivation to go even more public with the badmouthing (Bies et al., 1997).

The Act of Revenge Can Take Many Forms

Badmouthing is but one of many forms of revenge (Bies & Tripp, in press) and is one that is grounded in a retributive justice motivation (Hogan & Emler, 1981), that is, to harm the perpetrator. In Bies and Tripp (1996) and Tripp and Bies (1997), we found retributive elements not only in badmouthing the organization or its leaders but also in public complaints designed to humiliate another person, public demands for apologies that are intended to embarrass the organization or its leaders, whistle-blowing, and litigation. Badmouthing, whistle-blowing, and litigation might not always be intended to harm the perpetrator. Indeed, it might be intended to stop the wrongdoing, perhaps even in the hope of reforming the organization (as with pollution or unsafe work practices) or restoring justice (Bies & Tripp, 1996).

The Consequences of Revenge: A Stakeholder View

The argument underlying the current analysis is that whether the revenge, in general, or the badmouthing, in particular, is good or bad depends on one's interests and vantage point. With such a perspective, it leads us to a "stakeholder view" of revenge (Bies & Tripp, 1998). It is this perspective that guides our analysis of badmouthing.

Building on Bies and Tripp (1998), the stakeholder framework for analyzing revenge has two dimensions. The first dimension indicates who is affected by the revenge act. Three different stakeholders may be affected: *the avenger, the perpetrator,* and *the organization.*[1] The second dimension reflects the perceived functionality of the revenge response. Responses are perceived as either *constructive*, in that a stakeholder benefits from the act of revenge, or *destructive*, in that a stakeholder suffers some harm from the act of revenge. Table 4.1 illustrates the taxonomy. A discussion of each cell follows.

Table 4.1   The Stakeholder Framework for Analyzing Revenge

	Perspective		
	Avenger	*Perpetrator*	*Organization*
Constructive			
Destructive			

Constructive for the Avenger

Getting even can help the avenger both materially and psychologically. *Material benefits* may include obtaining greater visibility for one's successes, securing critical resources, and eliminating underperforming coworkers. For example, a global defense company executive, in an ongoing study being conducted by the first author, stated, "By badmouthing other executives about their inefficiency and corruption in department operations, I got promoted—and as a bonus to the company, saved it thousands of dollars." A number of avengers reported benefiting their companies by collecting and reporting the evidence required to get underperforming coworkers fired (Tripp & Bies, 1997). By no longer depending on such unreliable coworkers, they argued, they could work more effectively and efficiently (Bies & Tripp, 1996).

Psychological benefits are those outcomes that improve an employee's emotional state. Some examples may include restored social status/identity, increased self-esteem, and released frustration (Bies & Tripp, 1999). Even when the avenger believes that badmouthing will not result in organizational change or career advancement, revenge can still provide psychological relief. For example, a manufacturing company executive, in an ongoing study being conducted by the first author, reported, "I just couldn't hold in my anger about the corrupt practices of top management, so I badmouthed the company to friends and family. It didn't change the situation, but I felt better. It released some the pressure inside of me."

Constructive for the Perpetrator

Badmouthing can, in some cases, provide the perpetrator with corrective feedback that particular behaviors or attitudes hurt others or are inappropriate (Bies & Tripp, 1996). Leaders often are unaware of the harms they commit against their employees. In other words, the leaders do not know that they have become "perpetrators." In some cases, when the information gets back to the leaders, it can motivate behavior change (Bies & Tripp, 1996).

But for such badmouthing to be constructive, a key consideration is that the information must be from "anonymous sources" or else retribution may be imminent (Bies & Tripp, 1999). For example, a manufacturing company executive, in an ongoing study being conducted by the first author, stated, "I try to be enlightened. I know people badmouth their bosses. It is human nature. So, I try to build in anonymous feedback opportunities for my people beyond that of 360-degree feedback. I want to hear the badmouthing before it escalates out of control."

Constructive for the Organization

In some cases, badmouthing can be constructive for the organization and its members. For example, badmouthing may embolden others to speak out, thereby acting as a catalyst for organizational change (Bies & Tripp, in press). Tripp and Bies (1997) found that many respondents in their study believed that acts of revenge, including badmouthing, benefited others. Some respondents claimed that in engaging in revenge, including badmouthing corporate "bullies," they "stood up" for others who could not stand up for themselves. Furthermore, badmouthing unproductive and mischievous coworkers often led to the removal of those individuals, resulting in greater efficiencies for their companies (Tripp & Bies, 1997).

Badmouthing the organization or its leaders can prove to be dangerous, however, because retaliation is often targeted at those who badmouth the organization or its leaders (Bies & Tripp, 1998). Thus, rather than public badmouthing where one's identity is known, the negative information is typically "leaked" without a trace of authorship (Bies & Tripp, 1999). For example, a global defense company executive, in an ongoing study being conducted by the first author, reported the following:

> I knew of the corruption and the lies, but it needed to go public. Nobody knew I had copies of the files, which was the key to my success. The information just "appeared" in the mailbox of the ombudsman of the company, and it led to a "housecleaning" operation at the company. The ombudsman's office got all of the credit, but that was okay with me. I still had my job, and things changed for the better here.

Destructive for the Avenger

Badmouthing can hurt the avenger both materially and psychologically. Materially, the avenger may lose desirable tasks or job assignments or even lose his or her job (Bies & Tripp, 1999). Also, visible acts of revenge, such as badmouthing, may tarnish an avenger's reputation as "professional." Indeed, respondents in the Tripp and Bies (1997) study reported that the most common negative judgment about their acts of revenge, including badmouthing, was that such behavior is "unprofessional."

Psychologically, the avenger may lose control of his or her own thoughts and emotions. Badmouthing is an emotional act that may consume the attention of the avenger. Indeed, in many cases, revenge (or the desire for revenge) is a time-consuming, obsessive process that drains the avenger emotionally (Matthews, 1988). Furthermore, if the badmouthing occurs among friends and colleagues who further reinforce one's feelings, such support may lead to more obsession and rumination, further draining one's emotional energy (Tripp & Bies, 1997).

Destructive for the Perpetrator

As the target, the perpetrator suffers the sting of the revenge act. However, sometimes the perpetrator may suffer even more as unintended consequences occur. Many avengers reported that they took too much risk in that they did not, or could not, predict all of the consequences of their actions (Tripp & Bies, 1997). For example, a consumer products company executive, in an ongoing study being conducted by the first author, recounted the following: "We had badmouthed the boss all the time to anyone and everyone who was willing to listen. All this badmouthing led to our boss having an emotional breakdown when his boss confronted him about the situation. That was not what we expected or wanted."

Destructive for the Organization

Badmouthing can trigger a series of events resulting in unintended, yet seriously damaging, consequences for the organization as well (Bies & Tripp, 1998). For example, a government executive, in an ongoing study being conducted by the first author, reported the following story:

> I had been badmouthing the agency to my friends because the agency head was playing favorites and it cost me an assignment that would have brought me great visibility and recognition. What I didn't realize, until it was too late, was that one of my friends passed along some of my comments, including names of people in the agency, to one of their friends in the press. This resulted in a newspaper story that not only cost the agency head his job, but many of us, including me, got reassigned to different departments and lesser jobs. I did not mean for this to happen, but it did. I have to live with that the rest of my life.

Understanding Those Who Badmouth the Company: Implications for Theory and Practice

In developing approaches to dealing with revenge (including badmouthing) in organizations, one must understand what motivates revenge in the first place (Bies & Tripp, in press). One approach views revenge as the behavior of an employee who is a malcontent. In the employee as *malcontent* approach, it is assumed that all acts of revenge are the product of inherently aggressive employees who are simply "bad eggs." That is, those who engage in revenge are psychologically troubled individuals imbued with aggressive traits. Thus, an organization's response is to identify and remove such employees before they can cause damage (Bies & Tripp, in press).

The other approach views revenge more as a function of injustices and managerial abuses in the workplace and, thus, is referred to as the *malpractice* approach. In the malpractice approach, the focus is more on environmental triggers of revenge such as reactions to unjust attributes of the workplace environment, including abusive bosses. From this perspective, revenge is more likely if the formal organization system fails to correct the injustices or abuses. Conversely, as Bies and Tripp (in press) argued, by focusing on eliminating those triggers, acts of revenge may be less likely. Similarly, creating a just workplace—one that promotes distributive, procedural, and interactional justice and also brings justice to those who do injustice—should also lessen the likelihood of revenge.

Obviously, both the malcontent and malpractice perspectives yield insights into the dynamics of revenge.[2] We call for a unification of these two approaches to study revenge in all of its forms as the result of both individual traits and environmental triggers. After all, not every employee responds to the same provocations in the same contexts in the same way. However, rather than getting into a classic "trait versus situation" debate over how much variance of aggressive behavior is explained by individual differences, it is better to look at the interaction between traits and situations.

Recently, scholars have begun to move in the direction that we are endorsing. For example, Fox, Spector, and Miles (2001) examined the interaction effects between job stressors (including injustices), affective traits, and counterproductive work behaviors (CWBs). They found that affective traits (trait anger and trait anxiety) weakly moderated the relationship between injustice and CWBs and that chronically angry and/or anxious victims are more likely to avenge an injustice than are calmer victims. Those are important findings because they provide compelling empirical evidence to practitioners and scholars as to how to understand and deal with revenge. More specifically, practitioners and scholars should focus on both individual traits and environmental triggers.

Fox and colleagues (2001) provided a discussion of broader practical implications of their findings, which are consistent with the perspective taken in this analysis. Specifically, they concluded,

> Still, our findings suggest that organizations may be able to reduce the levels of work behaviors that undermine their effectiveness by developing human resource policies and practices that take into consideration their possible emotional effects on employees. . . . The implications of this study suggest an alternative to the predominant "selection" solution to CWB, in which individuals with certain personality tendencies that may predict CWBs are screened out of the organization during the selection process. (p. 306)

Conclusion

We agree with our colleagues in the field that acts of badmouthing can be counterproductive and destructive. However, we are concerned that in their focusing primarily on individual traits, as well as framing and defining all acts of badmouthing as counternormative, they pay insufficient attention to environmental triggers of badmouthing or to situations where badmouthing is beneficial or even serves the common good (Bies & Tripp, in press). Indeed, we are suggesting that our colleagues (and practitioners) may be guilty of the actor–observer bias (Jones & Nisbett, 1972).

Recognizing the existence of these biases and their impact on analysis by scholars and practitioners further highlights the importance of our stakeholder perspective on revenge. This perspective necessarily broadens the focus of attention of scholars and practitioners alike. Indeed, as the stakeholder perspective demonstrates, revenge can be destructive, but it can also be constructive. It all depends on one's interests and vantage point.

Notes

1. This list of stakeholders is by no means exhaustive. For example, society at large is sometimes affected by badmouthing when, for instance, related behavioral norms are reinforced or eroded. Also, geographic or business communities often benefit from whistleblowing when a dangerous or unfair problem is eradicated.

2. The malpractice perspective has been neglected by most authors. Bies and Tripp (in press) detailed the various reasons why it has been neglected. The main reason, we argue, is that scholars also suffer from a biased punctuation of conflict; that is scholars frame the phenomena, and thus their subsequent analysis, only around the response (e.g., badmouthing) instead of including in their framework the provocation (e.g., an abusive boss).

References

Allred, K. G. (1999). Anger driven retaliation: Toward an understanding of impassioned conflict in organizations. In R. J. Bies, R. J. Lewicki, & B. H. Sheppard (Eds.), *Research on negotiations in organizations* (Vol. 7). Greenwich, CT: JAI.

Baron, R. A. (1988). Negative effects of destructive criticism: Impact on conflict, self-efficacy, and task performance. *Journal of Applied Psychology, 73,* 199–207.

Bies, R. J. (1993). Privacy and procedural justice in organizations. *Social Justice Research, 6,* 69–86.

Bies, R. J. (2001). Interactional (in)justice: The sacred and the profane. In J. Greenberg & R. Cropanzano (Eds.), *Advances in organizational behavior* (pp. 89–118). Stanford, CA: Stanford University Press.

Bies, R. J., & Tripp, T. M. (1996). Beyond distrust: "Getting even" and the need for revenge. In R. M. Kramer & T. Tyler (Eds.), *Trust in organizations* (pp. 246–260). Thousand Oaks, CA: Sage.

Bies, R. J., & Tripp, T. M. (1998). Revenge in organizations: The good, the bad, and the ugly. In R. W. Griffin, A. O'Leary-Kelly, & J. Collins (Eds.), *Dysfunctional behavior in organizations: Non-violent dysfunctional behavior* (Vol. 23, Part B, pp. 49–67). Stamford, CT: JAI.

Bies, R. J., & Tripp, T. M. (1999). Two faces of the powerless: Coping with tyranny. In R. M. Kramer & M. A. Neale (Eds.), *Power and influence in organizations* (pp. 203–220). Thousand Oaks, CA: Sage.

Bies, R. J., & Tripp, T. M. (in press). The study of revenge in the workplace: Conceptual, ideological, and empirical issues. In S. Fox & P. E. Spector (Eds.), *Counterproductive workplace behavior: Investigations of actors and targets.* Washington, DC: APA Press.

Bies, R. J., Tripp, T. M., & Kramer, R. M. (1997). At the breaking point: Cognitive and social dynamics of revenge in organizations. In R. A. Giacalone & J. Greenberg (Eds.), *Antisocial behavior in organizations* (pp. 18–36). Thousand Oaks, CA: Sage.

Bies, R. J., & Tyler, T. (1993). The "litigation mentality" in organizations: A test of alternative psychological explanations. *Organization Science, 4,* 352–366.

Buss, A. H. (1962). *The psychology of aggression.* New York: John Wiley.

Cahn, E. (1949). *The sense of injustice.* New York: New York University Press.

Folger, R., & Cropanzano, R. (2001). Fairness theory: Justice as accountability. In J. Greenberg & R. Cropanzano (Eds.), *Advances in organizational behavior* (pp. 1–55). Stanford, CA: Stanford University Press.

Fox, S., Spector, P. E., & Miles, D. (2001). Counterproductive work behavior in response to job stressors and organizational justice: Some mediator and moderator tests for autonomy and emotions. *Journal of Vocational Behavior, 59,* 291–309.

Hogan, R., & Emler, N. P. (1981). Retributive justice. In M. J. Lerner & S. C. Lerner (Eds.), *The justice motive in social behavior* (pp. 125–143). New York: Plenum.

Hornstein, H. A. (1996). *Brutal bosses and their prey.* New York: Riverhead Books.

Jones, E. E., & Nisbett, R. E. (1972). The actor and the observer: Divergent perceptions of the causes of behavior. In E. E. Jones, D. E. Kanouse, H. H. Kelley, R. E. Nisbett, S. Valins, & B. Weiner (Eds.), *Attribution: Perceiving the causes of behavior* (pp. 79–94). Morristown, NJ: General Learning Press.

Matthews, C. (1988). *Hardball: How politics is played—told by one who knows the game.* New York: Summit Books.

McLean Parks, J. M. (1997). The fourth arm of justice: The art and science of revenge. In R. J. Lewicki, R. J. Bies, & B. H. Sheppard (Eds.), *Research on negotiation in organizations* (Vol. 6, pp. 113–144). Greenwich, CT: JAI.

Morrill, C. (1992). Vengeance among executives. *Virginia Review of Sociology, 1*, 51–76.

Neuman, J. H., & Baron, R. A. (1997). Aggression in the workplace. In R. A. Giacalone & J. Greenberg (Eds.), *Antisocial behavior in organizations* (pp. 37–67). Thousand Oaks, CA: Sage.

Ratnesart, R., & Weisskopf, M. (2002, June 3). How the FBI blew the case. *Time*, pp. 24–32.

Robinson, S. L., & Bennett, R. J. (1995). A typology of deviant workplace behaviors: A multidimensional scaling study. *Academy of Management Journal, 38*, 555–572.

Skarlicki, D. P., & Folger, R. (1997). Retaliation in the workplace: The roles of distributive, procedural, and interactional justice. *Journal of Applied Psychology, 82*, 434–443.

Tripp, T. M., & Bies, R. J. (1997). What's good about revenge? The avenger's perspective. In R. J. Lewicki, R. J. Bies, & B. H. Sheppard (Eds.), *Research on negotiation in organizations* (Vol. 6, pp. 145–160). Greenwich, CT: JAI.

Witt, A., & Behr, P. (2002, July 29). Dream job turns into a nightmare: Skilling's success comes at a high price. *The Washington Post*, p. A1.

Web Revenge on HealthSouth Corporation

Richard Scrushy, HealthSouth Corporation's chief executive officer, had no idea that he and his company were under attack until he was pulled aside by analysts at a 1998 investor conference and questioned about postings on a Yahoo! discussion board.

As with thousands of other financial discussion forums in cyberspace, shareholders, potential investors, and just about anyone else could post questions and comments about a company's performance and stock price. However, the postings on the HealthSouth board had become increasingly vicious. Anonymous postings alleging poor health care practices, billing fraud, financial impropriety, and unfair treatment of employees had caught the attention of the stock analysts.

The Internet had become the perfect weapon of tech-savvy individuals, particularly ex-employees who had gripes with their former companies. For example, ex-employees of Intel constructed the website *www.faceintel.com* for alleging discriminatory practices. At *www.f—edcompany.com,* sensitive internal company memos could be posted by whistle-blowers or those who simply sought revenge. According to a posting on the Internet gripe site *www.vault.com,* the New York-based financial services firm, Morgan Stanley, operated like a "sweatshop."

Scrushy saw himself as the latest victim of this disgruntled group. "Here I am, the CEO of a multibillion-dollar company, and I'm having to answer

AUTHOR'S NOTE: This case was prepared by Christopher L. Martin (Centenary College of Louisiana) as the basis for classroom discussion. It was developed from accounts listed in the bibliography at the end of the case. All names of individuals and the organization are real.

about what some weirdo has said on a message board," he told the *Wall Street Journal*.

Perhaps Scrushy was an easy target. HealthSouth had become the nation's largest chain of rehabilitation hospitals and clinics, and Scrushy was the highest paid executive in the health care industry. He was an aggressive, self-made millionaire who started the company in 1984 with three friends and $55,000. However, a *New York Times* interview with current and former associates of Scrushy described him as "a megalomaniac . . . who ruled by top-down fear, threatened critics with reprisals, and paid his loyal subordinates well." He owned four homes, a 92-foot yacht, and three dozen cars, including two Rolls-Royces and a Lamborghini.

As HealthSouth stock reached its high of $31 in April 1998, Scrushy bragged that his firm had once again beat the quarter's earnings estimate. However, in September of that year, after he and other key HealthSouth executives had sold millions of dollars worth of their stock, the company announced it would miss the estimates for 1998 and 1999 due to Medicare changes. The stock lost more than half its value, and the electronic bulletin boards lit up.

Scrushy was outraged by the anonymous postings and sought to identify and sue the attackers. HealthSouth subpoenaed *Yahoo!* records on each of the board's more than 300 anonymous posters. *Yahoo!* turned over only 20 records, arguing that the request was overly broad. Among the bulletin board posters who were unmasked were two former HealthSouth employees, Peter Krum and Kimberly Landry.

Krum, who had been a food service manager at HealthSouth's Nittany Valley rehabilitation hospital in Pennsylvania, began bashing his former employer by suggesting that its managers lacked ethics and that the "house of cards" was about to collapse. Then, in subsequent postings, the attacks got personal. He accused Scrushy of bilking Medicare. Furthermore, Krum spoke of wife swapping and of having sex with Scrushy's wife, writing that "soon Dick's wife will dump him and be able to give me her full attention."

HealthSouth brought suit, charging that Krum tried to "undermine public faith in a company and blacken reputations [and] had libeled the company, its chairman, and his wife." Krum was also criminally charged by the state of Pennsylvania with "harassment by communication."

Because Krum had posted his anti-HealthSouth message from a university computer during work hours, he lost his job as a food and beverage manager at Pennsylvania State University. As part of a settlement, the criminal harassment charges were dropped. However, he was asked to sign an affidavit stating that his claims were "thoughtless lies" told as a result of "my childish desire to be recognized as important by other posters on the bulletin board." Furthermore, he wrote a letter of apology to Scrushy and donated both $50 per week and 3 hours of community service to a charity of HealthSouth's choice for a 2-year period.

The lesson to be learned, according to Scrushy and his legal team, was that the Internet is not a safe haven for people taking potshots at HealthSouth.

Landry was next on the list. In 1998, Landry was a marketing executive with HealthSouth in Baton Rouge, Louisiana. She believed that Scrushy and other executives had been laughing at shareholders after the 1998 drop in the stock. She became aware of this because she was having an affair with one of the executives at the time.

In its defamation suit against Landry, HealthSouth cited postings in which she called Scrushy a "bozo" and a "crook." "Screwshe [sic] and his Cronies get off on power and position instead of having sex." She predicted that company stock would decline because too much money had been paid for its new surgery centers, and she accused HealthSouth of inappropriate Medicare admissions.

However, Landry was not as easily quieted as Krum. She demanded access to corporate and personal financial records to prove that her postings were correct. In April 2003, HealthSouth moved to drop its defamation lawsuit. As reported in the *New York Times,* the company made the decision not because of the merits of the case but because it believed that pursuing the lawsuit was not an appropriate use of its resources. Landry's lawyer said that she planned to sue HealthSouth for malicious prosecution.

Five months later, on November 4, 2003, Assistant Attorney General Christopher A. Wray of the Criminal Division of the U.S. Department of Justice announced that Scrushy had been charged in an 85-count indictment stemming from a wide-ranging scheme to defraud investors about HealthSouth's financial condition. The indictment alleged that Scrushy "personally participated in the preparation of financial statements and other financial documents" that made the company appear to be more successful than it actually was.

Between 1996 and 2003, internal reports from HealthSouth's corporate accounting staff revealed that the company routinely failed to "make the numbers" and produce income to meet Wall Street's expectations.

According to the indictment, Scrushy and other HealthSouth executives devised a plan to inflate earnings through false and fraudulent statements in the company's income statements and balance sheet accounts. Allegedly, $2.7 billion in fictitious earnings was added during this time frame.

The Department of Justice further noted that Scrushy received $7.5 million in base salary, $53 million in bonuses, and stock options valued at $206 million, all directly or indirectly tied to the company's financial performance during this period.

As Landry once observed, Scrushy may have gone to such lengths to shut down cyber critics such as her because he feared that any investigation would reveal that the charges contained some truth. As Landry's attorney asserted to the *Wall Street Journal* in 1999, "The truth is an absolute defense, and the truth will come out."

Today, Scrushy has turned to the very medium that may have contributed to the collapse of his empire. He has taken his side of the story to the Internet. The site, *www.richardmscrushy.com,* proclaims his innocence in the HealthSouth scandal and promises to reveal the truth. In an interview with the *Birmingham News,* Scrushy's attorney, Thomas Sjoblom, said that the website was launched to "level the playing field. . . . People have been asking us what our side of the story is, and people have been wondering when there's misinformation out there, why it hasn't been corrected. We need to straighten out the record."

Discussion Questions

1. Were the actions of Peter Krum and Kimberly Landry in making Web attacks on HealthSouth morally justified? Why or why not?

2. Use the Bies and Tripp revenge framework in Chapter 4 to analyze the constructive and/or destructive actions taken by Krum and Landry against HealthSouth, employing different stakeholder perspectives.

3. Was the decision by HealthSouth to pursue legal action against Krum and Landry the most appropriate means of dealing with the problem of badmouthing by way of the Web? Explain.

4. Some companies attempt to combat electronic badmouthing of their organizations by allowing anonymous employee posts on the companies' intranets. Integrating information from Chapter 4 into your answer, evaluate the pros and cons of this strategy as a means of dealing with poor employee morale.

Bibliography

Abelson, R., & Freudenheim, M. (2003, April 20). The Scrushy mix: Strict and so lenient. *The New York Times,* sec. 3, p. 1.

Ackman, D. (2003, March 3). For years, HealthSouth could do no wrong. *Forbes.com.* Retrieved December 15, 2003, from www.forbes.com/2003/03/31/cx_da_0331 topnews.html

Gibbs, T. (1998, November 8). Internet attacks bring man charges, suit, suspension. *Pittsburgh Post Gazette,* p. 1.

Gibbs, T. (1999, April 29). State College man pays large penalty for Internet attack on company. *Post-Gazette.com.* Retrieved December 15, 2003, from www.post-gazette.com/regionstate/19990429net7.asp

Goodman, S. (2003, October 30). Scrushy takes PR campaign to the web. *Birmingham News,* p. A1.

Leonard, B. (1999, November). Cyberventing. *HR Magazine,* pp. 34–39.

Moss, M. (1999, July 17). Online: CEO exposes, sues anonymous online critics. *The Wall Street Journal,* p. B1.

Taubs, S. (2003, November 5). Scrushy indicted on 85 counts. *CFO.com.* Retrieved December 15, 2003, from www.cfo.com/article.cfm/3010823?f=related.

CHAPTER 5

Withholding Effort at Work

Understanding and Preventing Shirking, Job Neglect, Social Loafing, and Free Riding

Nathan Bennett

Stefanie E. Naumann

Throughout modern times, business cycles have contributed to organizational conditions with well-understood implications for the employee–employer relationship. During "boom" periods, qualified employees are scarce and expensive. During these periods, employers express concern about maintaining competitive pay and benefits practices, protecting their "investment" in human resources, creating and maintaining an attractive work environment, and minimizing turnover. During "bust" periods, qualified labor becomes much more easily found, and employers focus on minimizing the cost of human resource "overhead," downsizing, maximizing operational efficiency, and optimizing the performance of remaining employees. Although macroeconomic conditions are arguably the key driver of these approaches, similar patterns of employment practices can also be attributed to the competitive position, life cycle stage, and/or traditions of a focal organization (Ferris, Hochwarter, Buckley, Harrell-Cook, & Frink, 1999).

In both the best and worst of times, content and configuration of employment practices play an important role in determining the nature of the "psychological contract" between employees and employers. In some instances, the conditions that are created allow employees to conclude that it is at least rational—and perhaps even reasonable—to provide less than their full effort. Withholding of effort at work, in its various forms, has been labeled "production deviance" (Robinson & Bennett, 1995). The purpose of this chapter is to introduce the reader to the various forms that this withholding of effort takes, to discuss its implications for organizations, and to highlight management's role in its prevention. Certainly, managing employee performance is a central aspect of managerial work. Managers are rightly concerned that subordinates provide fair effort. When effort is withheld, individual and organizational performance may be reduced. In addition, coworkers who observe an individual withholding effort without facing adverse consequences will quickly determine that they are being treated inequitably. Among the predictable reactions to such a conclusion are additional reductions in effort, morale problems, and perhaps departures from the organization.

A growing body of organizational behavior research has been conducted to identify the factors that cause employees to withhold effort (Albanese & Van Fleet, 1985; Karau & Williams, 1993, 1997; Kidwell & Bennett, 1993, 2001; Kidwell & Robie, 2003; Miles & Klein, 2002). Several forms of withholding effort on the job have been identified. These forms differ in regard to either (a) the performance context in which the withholding of effort occurs (e.g., an employee working alone or in a work group) or (b) the employee motivation behind the withholding of effort. All end in the same place, that is, with employees withholding effort that their supervisor expects for proper fulfillment of their work responsibilities. At the same time, the unique contextual and motivational components of each form provide cues about the steps that managers might properly view as remedies. For that reason, we begin with a brief description of each form of withholding effort.

Withholding Effort

Shirking

The first two forms of withholding effort, shirking and job neglect, focus on a performance context where an individual employee is working alone. *Shirking* is a term whose development can be traced to the economics literature and has been defined as an increase in the tendency to supply less effort in the presence of some incentive to do so (Jones, 1984; Leibowitz & Tollison, 1980). Essentially, shirking occurs when an employee determines that he or she can create more "leisure time" and will face no negative consequence for doing so. The assumption underlying the shirking literature is that employees will shirk when employers are not monitoring them. Employees are thought to reduce their work effort because their interests do not necessarily match those of the organization (Judge & Chandler, 1996). In fact, it has been suggested that employees prefer larger amounts of on-the-job free time for a given wage and will shirk when the utility gained from shirking exceeds that gained from working. Accordingly, managerial policies that limit the incentive to shirk have been designed to enhance either the cost of shirking or the value of working.

Much of the shirking research in the economics field has focused on the use of various compensation policies to decrease shirking: (a) paying above-market wages to elevate the cost of job loss and to deter shirking in contexts where it is hard for managers to directly monitor employees (e.g., Cappelli & Chauvin, 1991; Krueger, 1991) and (b) tournaments where employees compete for desirable top-paying assignments (Lazear & Rosen, 1981). In the organizational behavior field, expectancy theory (Vroom, 1964) and equity theory (Lawler, 1968) have been used to justify the use of compensation policies to decrease shirking. According to expectancy theory, employees will work harder if they perceive that hard work will be rewarded. For that reason, various compensation policies make explicit to employees that their efforts will not go unnoticed. Equity theory suggests that employees who believe that they are overrewarded in comparison with their coworkers may increase work effort to establish equity. On the other hand, those employees who believe that they are underrewarded may react through shirking. Consequently, employee perceptions as to the "fairness" of reward systems are expected to play a role in employee decisions to withhold effort.

The empirical research on shirking has found that the compensation policies suggested by the economics and organizational behavior literatures do, in fact, have an impact on shirking. Whereas the bulk of this shirking research has focused on organizational-level determinants of shirking, little research has examined why employees in the same organization or work group would shirk. The exception to this is a study that focused on individual-level determinants of shirking (Judge & Chandler, 1996). Interestingly, this study did not find a link between how closely supervisors monitored employees' behavior and employees' level of shirking. Instead, the study found that job satisfaction and general life satisfaction negatively affected shirking. Employees who are unhappy with their jobs, or with their lives in general, are more likely to withdraw from their jobs through shirking. Thus, paying attention to the factors associated with subordinates' job dissatisfaction is another way in which to deter employee shirking. Although the managerial implications for job satisfaction are clear, the finding about general life satisfaction indicates that shirking is not wholly determined by organizational practices. In sum, carefully designed compensation policies and attention to subordinates' job satisfaction can be effective deterrents of employee shirking, yet other factors not under the organization's direct control (e.g., general life satisfaction) may also contribute to an employee's level of shirking.

Job Neglect

The second form of withholding effort that occurs in an individual performance context is *job neglect*, that is, a tendency for employees to passively allow conditions at work to deteriorate through a focus on nonwork interests. Job neglect involves the withholding of effort in favor of a focus on other interests.

Someone who spends work time managing a personal portfolio of auctions on eBay, for example, is guilty of job neglect. This form of job neglect has recently been labeled "cyberloafing" (Lim, 2002). Apparently, such job neglect is prevalent. A recent study reported that 30% to 40% of employees' work time is spent using the Internet for non-work-related purposes (Verton, 2000).

Understood in this way, job neglect is easily conceptualized as a particular form of shirking behavior. It may manifest itself through decreased effort, increased absenteeism or lateness, or decreased speed of work. Job neglect has been measured by asking employees the degree to which they avoid work by speaking with coworkers, offering less effort than they know they can, intentionally steering clear of their supervisors, taking more frequent and longer breaks than is allowed, making deliberate mistakes, and arriving at work late (Leck & Saunders, 1992; Rusbult, Farrell, Rogers, & Mainous, 1988).

Organizational commitment and satisfaction with work, supervision, pay, promotion, and coworkers are among the attitudes expected to be negatively related to job neglect. Research has suggested that those who withhold effort from their jobs passively through job neglect believe that the options of selecting more active responses to being unhappy with their work environment (e.g., leaving the organization, complaining to a supervisor) are either too risky or of no use (Withey & Cooper, 1989). Specifically, employees who believe that it would be difficult to transfer their skills to another job would have high exit costs and, thus, would be more likely to neglect their jobs than to leave. Similarly, employees who think that voicing their job dissatisfaction (e.g., through complaining to a supervisor) would result in penalties are expected to instead respond through job neglect. In addition, employees with an external locus of control do not believe that they have control over the decisions in their lives (i.e., a more active response would be useless) and, thus, would also respond to job dissatisfaction passively through job neglect.

Whereas most job neglect research has focused on both extrinsic motivators (e.g., pay) and intrinsic motivators (e.g., satisfaction resulting from high achievement levels), some recent studies have found that elements of an employee's job context (e.g., the employee's relationship with the boss, characteristics of the employee's work group) also affect job neglect. Kidwell and Bennett (2001) found that employees were less likely to neglect their jobs if they perceived that their bosses exhibited expertise and consideration. Research on leader–member exchange (e.g., Sparrowe & Liden, 1997) has suggested that employees have expectations about what their supervisors should do in exchange for their job effort. Employees with supervisors who do not provide what is expected (e.g., expertise, consideration) are likely to exhibit greater levels of job neglect.

A related component of an employee–employer relationship that can affect job neglect concerns equity perceptions. Lim (2002) suggested that employees surf the Internet during work hours as a form of retribution against the organization (i.e., to correct what they view as injustice). This justification, referred to as neutralization, implies that when employees think that their managers have not recognized their contributions (e.g., working extra hours to complete an assignment), they will retaliate by spending work time on nonwork interests (Lim, 2002). Using the Internet for personal purposes during work hours is often thought of as a simple way in which to get back at the organization because it is convenient and somewhat easy to hide.

In addition to the employee–employer relationship, another job context area associated with job neglect involves characteristics of an employee's work group. The Kidwell and Bennett (2001) study found that employees were less likely to neglect their jobs if they perceived that their work groups exhibited altruistic behaviors. Examples of altruistic behaviors include helping coworkers with heavy workloads and helping newcomers to "learn the ropes." When employees perceive that their work groups are altruistic, they do not want to endanger the spirit of solidarity and emotional bonding within their groups by neglecting their jobs. Similarly, the study found that employees working in cohesive groups were less likely to neglect their jobs (Kidwell & Bennett, 2001). Members of cohesive work groups identify strongly with one another and are committed to their tasks. A strong group norm of cohesiveness is likely to prevent employees from defying their groups and neglecting their jobs.

Taken as a whole, the findings of the Kidwell and Bennett (2001) and Lim (2002) studies highlight the importance of *noneconomic* motivations in influencing job neglect. Variables such as consideration, altruism, cohesiveness, and equity are noneconomic motivators, which involve helping others or preserving relationships with others, as opposed to economic motivators, which are based on things such as a rational cost–benefit analysis of monetary reward or punishment.

Shirking and job neglect can occur in virtually any context. The next two forms of withholding effort, however, are unique to work groups. The common feature of these two forms of withholding effort is a group performance context structured in such a way that there is great difficulty in identifying individual contributions.

Social Loafing

Social loafing occurs in a group context and can be defined as a tendency to reduce effort because the nature of the focal task makes it impossible for others to determine individual contribution (Kerr & Bruun, 1983). In a meta-analytic review of social loafing research, Karau and Williams (1993) noted that the phenomenon has been observed on cognitive (e.g., brainstorming), physical (e.g., rope pulling, shouting), evaluative (e.g., ratings of performance), and perceptual (e.g., computer simulations) tasks.

That same body of research has generated six somewhat interrelated explanations for the presence of social loafing. Social impact theory (Latané, 1981) proposed that social loafing occurs when a request for effort is made of multiple "targets" rather than of a single target. This is similar to the predictions of Jackson and Williams (1985), whose arousal reduction explanation posits that the presence of others is "drive reducing"; that is, the fact that other employees are involved reduces the pressure on a single employee to perform. A third explanation involves whether or not individuals can "hide in the crowd" as opposed to having their contributions easily identified (e.g., Davis, 1969; Williams, Harkins, & Latané, 1981). Fourth, the dispensability of effort view (Kerr & Bruun, 1983) suggests that individuals will loaf when they conclude that their own effort is not essential to the production of the group's work. Fifth, the matching of effort view (cf. Jackson & Harkins, 1985) posits that individuals "match" their efforts to those they expect from coworkers so as to avoid being played for "suckers" (cf. Schnake, 1991). Finally, the self-attention perspective (Mullen, 1983) suggests that individuals pay less attention to their work effort due to an increased self-awareness caused by the group performance context.

Karau and Williams (1993) identified a number of factors that increase the likelihood that social loafing will occur. In summary, their results indicate that social loafing is more likely when (a) individual output cannot be evaluated (see also Gagne & Zuckerman, 1999; George, 1992), (b) the tasks involved are viewed as unimportant, (c) a group performance comparison is not available, (d) individuals are working with strangers on a group task, (e) individuals have reason to suspect their fellow group members will perform well without their personal contribution, and/or (f) individuals see their potential contributions as redundant with those offered by other group members. Subsequent research has also identified the lack of incentives (George, 1995), lack of individual evaluations (Karau & Williams, 1993), low group cohesiveness (Duffy & Shaw, 2000; Karau & Hart, 1998), and low-quality leader–member relations (Murphy, Wayne, Liden, & Erdogan, 2003) to be associated with higher levels of social loafing. In a recent multilevel study of 23 work groups in two organizations, increases in social loafing were related to larger group size and decreased group cohesiveness, whereas at the individual level of analysis, increased task interdependence and decreases in distributive justice and task visibility were linked to greater degrees of social loafing (Liden, Wayne, Jaworski, & Bennett, 2004).

Free Riding

Free riding refers to social loafing that occurs when an individual is able to obtain some benefit from the group without contributing a fair share of the costs associated with the production of that benefit (Albanese & Van Fleet, 1985; Olson, 1965). Students will recognize this phenomenon as one that often plagues group class projects. When all group members receive the same grade from the evaluation of a group project regardless of individual contributions, the situation is ripe for free riders (Brooks & Ammons, 2003). In organizations, circumstances where group members are recognized or rewarded *as a group* are likely to produce free riding as well. Because the individual still participates in whatever "reward" the group earns, the free rider enjoys that benefit without bearing a fair share of the costs required to obtain it (e.g., Albanese & Van Fleet, 1985). In fact, when the reward is indivisible and can be obtained through others' work, the decision to withhold effort is economically rational.

In the near term, free riding might not result in lower group performance. After all, the free rider is counting on his or her share of the group reward and has chosen to withhold effort only because he or she can do so at no cost. Over time, however, coworkers of free riders have been found to be less committed to group goals, have lower levels of individual performance, set lower goals for their own achievement, and constitute groups whose performance suffers (Miles & Klein, 2002). Miles and Klein (2002) suggested that free riding, if left unchecked, creates a "spiral of negative consequences" for organizations.

Challenges for Managers

The process through which these forms of production deviance develop is clear. First, individuals determine, for varied reasons, that withholding of effort is a viable personal performance strategy. Next, they withhold effort (a) to restore their sense of being treated equitably, (b) to make available time to pursue other interests, (c) because there is no "cost" in terms of either a sanction or a reduced reward, and/or (d) simply because they can. Then, to the extent that withholding of effort is noticeable to coworkers, a negative impact on the coworkers' attitudes and behaviors is expected to develop over time. If this situation is left unchecked, negative consequences with regard to production norms may be felt. In addition to reduced productivity, one would expect an increase in turnover and other withdrawal behaviors as well as lower morale. In the aggregate, the potential cost of production deviance for an organization may be substantial.

Before turning attention to the remedies that managers should consider in addressing withholding of effort, it is important to note that diagnosing it is not always an easy task. It is precisely this difficulty of diagnosis that creates the opportunity for employees to withhold effort in the first place. Although there are performance contexts in which withholding of effort is more easily seen (e.g., a situation where performance measures are assessed objectively and where accepted productivity norms exist), many employees perform tasks that do not lend themselves to such clear observation. A second challenge is that managers may conclude that employees' performance is unacceptable but might not immediately know the best explanation why. Although effort may be the best explanation, there are other explanations for low performance that are unrelated to effort. Before designing a course of action, managers need to accurately diagnose the underlying cause for the performance decrement.

Fundamentally, there are four explanations for low performance: (a) lack of appropriate effort, (b) lack of ability, (c) task difficulty, and (d) chance. Our focus in this chapter is on lack of effort. Suggestions for managers to deal with our topic of interest are discussed in what follows. In contrast to the recommendations for an effort explanation of a performance decrement, lack of ability issues are best addressed by training or reassigning employees, whereas task difficulty issues are best addressed by breaking a task into less difficult components or by providing additional resources. Poor performance explained by bad luck (e.g., an unforeseeable change in market conditions, a personal crisis) might not be particularly manageable, and because the constellation of forces that led to the bad luck is unlikely to reappear in a recognizable manner, the situation might not require managerial intervention.

In comparing the managerial remedies for various sources of a performance decrement, it becomes clear that misunderstanding the underlying cause will likely lead to the selection of an inappropriate remedy. Clearly, efforts to correct a performance decrement that is truly due to lack of effort using an inappropriate remedy, such as breaking the task into less difficult increments or providing more training, are not likely to work. Similarly, trying to "fix" a withholding effort problem when an employee's performance problems are caused by other factors is also unlikely to produce the desired results.

That said, the review of the literature earlier indicated that there are many reasons why individuals choose to withhold effort on the job. Clearly, work context plays the key role in that it provides cues to employees that withholding of effort is tolerated, rational and to be expected, and/or undetectable. Furthermore, the conclusion that withholding effort generally has negative consequences for both the organization and the perpetrator's coworkers is easily understood. In sum, when employee withholding of effort is left unchecked, there are certainly deleterious impacts on productivity and morale. Fortunately, this is one form of workplace deviance that managers generally have some ability to address. For example, by paying close attention to the way in which work groups are constructed, jobs are designed, and rewards are distributed, managers can minimize the incentives for the withholding of effort and thereby redress its negative consequences for organizational effectiveness and employee morale. In the paragraphs that follow, we discuss suggestions for managers concerned with reducing the likelihood of employee withholding of effort on the job. Our approaches fall into four categories: style of supervision, job design, incentive systems, and employee selection.

Style of Supervision

One conclusion that might be reached from our discussion of withholding effort is that the answer is to simply supervise employees more closely. If employees sense that managers will quickly detect reduced effort, and if managers deliver negative consequences for that reduction of effort, employees should be deterred from reducing their effort. During the past 20 years, organizations have experimented with various technologies to monitor employee performance as a way of deterring employees from withholding effort on the job (Chalykoff & Kochan, 1989). For example, organizations have installed software to count keystrokes per minute among data entry employees and have installed cameras in break areas, restrooms, and employee dressing areas. However, monitoring has not been the panacea that some predicted it might be (e.g., Judge & Chandler, 1996), and many employees view such measures as an invasion of their privacy.

The business press has recently devoted attention to employees' responses to monitoring through creating ways in which to appear to be working hard when one actually is not (Spencer, 2003). For instance, remote control technology allows employees to open documents on their office computer screens while they are away from their offices. Timer features in software allow e-mails to be sent during the middle of the night while employees sleep. So, just as technology has afforded organizations the opportunity to monitor employee performance more closely, it has also enhanced the ability of employees to disguise their withholding of effort.

Methods to increase direct supervision through more traditional methods have also proven to be difficult. Simply put, direct supervision is expensive. It requires that managers have a narrower span of control, effectively increasing the need for greater numbers of more expensive employees. Certainly, large numbers of employees work in positions that are inherently difficult to monitor (e.g., outside sales and service). Thus, given the problems associated with direct supervision as a means of deterring withholding of effort, more fruitful methods include attention to job design, reward systems, and employee selection. These alternatives are discussed in the following subsections.

Job Design

With regard to job design, the key contributor to withholding of effort is an inability to identify individual contribution to the performance of a task. Naturally, then, one recommendation for those seeking to curtail the withholding of effort is to pay careful attention to the way in which work is allocated across jobs. To the extent that individuals can be held accountable for the performance of a discrete piece of work, the opportunities to withhold effort are mitigated. Employees experiencing role ambiguity are not likely to understand how their personal activities at work relate to their tasks, goals, and procedures for performing well. Thus, employees might not exert full effort until they understand exactly how to perform their tasks. Group size and performance norms might affect the degree to which employees understand their roles (Kidwell & Bennett, 2001).

Another job design issue related to withholding effort is goal setting. As noted previously, one explanation for why individuals expend less effort on group tasks involves matching their performance to that of other group members. When group members believe that others will exert low effort, social matching may drive them to decrease their own effort. Consequently, the total group performance would likely be low. In this case, group members' attempts to achieve equity in effort lead to withholding of effort. One study offered preliminary evidence that setting goals can reduce the likelihood of social matching and, thus, of withholding effort. In a laboratory study, Leeuwen and Knippenberg (2002) found that a specific group goal acted as an alternative standard for determining a group member's performance. When a group goal was present, the majority of the participants' perceptions of a fair contribution seemed to be determined by the goal instead of by their expectations of other group members' performance. Thus, the presence of a specific standard may shape group members' perceptions about what performance level is viewed as equitable and, as a result, may reduce the likelihood of withholding effort.

A related job design issue regarding withholding effort concerns task interdependence. Task interdependence is the extent to which group members rely on each other to conduct their jobs (Kiggundu, 1981). Interdependence varies across groups, increasing as workflow goes from pooled (i.e., the work from each individual is added to that done by others for a group total), to sequential (i.e., each employee is one step in a multistep production process similar to an assembly line), to reciprocal (i.e., the group's work product is the result of a number of multiparty interactions) interdependence (Thompson, 1967). As task interdependence increases, it becomes more difficult to detect withholding of effort. Thus, those interested in preventing employees from withholding effort should consider the level of task interdependence surrounding the job in question.

Incentive Systems

Another suggestion for managers concerned about reducing the likelihood of employee withholding of effort on the job involves incentive systems. Managers should strengthen the linkage between exerting effort and performing a job well. Expectancy theory (Vroom, 1964) suggests that establishing a connection between effort and performance is critical to understanding whether employees will be motivated to exert effort. If a worker perceives no link between exerting effort and performing a job well, it follows that the worker would not be motivated to exert effort or might exert less effort.

Managers can strengthen the effort–performance linkage in a number of ways, including (a) provision of clear instructions at the outset of the task; (b) timely, accurate, and constructive performance feedback during and after the task; and (c) provision of sufficient resources for task completion. Expectancy theory also suggests that employees will be less likely to withhold effort if they think that their effort will be rewarded. It is important to keep in mind that although the financial reward itself is important, employee perceptions of the equity of performance–reward linkages are equally critical. Recall that equity theory suggests that employees who believe that they are overrewarded in comparison with their coworkers may boost their work effort to achieve equity. Conversely, those employees who think that they are underrewarded may react by withholding effort. Thus, managers should use an incentive system that (a) establishes a clear link between effort and performance and (b) rewards high effort in ways that are perceived as equitable.

In addition, managers should not focus only on financial rewards in deterring job neglect and shirking. Research points to the role of employees' expectations of their supervisors in influencing withholding of effort. Employees with supervisors who take steps to provide what is expected (e.g., expertise, consideration) are more likely to reciprocate through lower levels of withholding effort.

Employee Selection

With regard to employee selection, managers should select work group members with high perceptions of altruism and cohesiveness. Recall that research has found that employees perceiving a high level of altruism and cohesiveness in a group are less likely to withhold effort (Kidwell & Bennett, 2001). Perceptions of group cohesiveness and altruism are important factors that affect employees' decisions to exert full effort or withhold it because group members who help one another and are committed to the group's work tend to bond together emotionally. Such employees are thought to have a desire to support the group's sense of camaraderie and do not want to endanger it by neglecting their jobs. Thus, managers should not view financial rewards as the sole contributor to how much effort is exerted and should also consider the role that work group characteristics play in shaping employees' decisions about how much effort to exert in their jobs.

Once managers have selected employees who are not likely to withhold effort, they should expose these employees to a high-performance culture during the socialization process (Schein, 1984). In so doing, managers may promote the value that the organization places on high performance and may teach employees the appropriate ways in which to avoid and manage withholding effort problems. In a high-performance culture, managers attract and retain employees who not only have the skills required to do their jobs but also are so energized by the organization's core values that they "give 110%" (Rosenthal & Masarech, 2003). This culture serves to attract those who fit in with it and serves to deter those who believe that they do not fit in with such a culture; thus, withholding of effort may be prevented.

Ethical Issues in the Withholding of Effort

One theme explored in this book is the consideration of ethical issues in the management of deviant behavior at work. In that regard, the withholding of effort presents an interesting case. There are two major sets of ethical questions that merit consideration.

First, is an employee who provides less than full effort in return for his or her wages behaving unethically? In other words, is it enough to meet minimum performance expectations—to "hit the numbers"—and not to make a complete effort for a higher level of performance? Said differently, is it fair for an employer to expect an employee's best effort, or should that employer be content with satisfactory effort?

Second, our discussion has implied that the work expected by the employer is itself of an appropriate nature. Recently, however, we have seen many examples of employers requesting that employees perform tasks that the larger community views as inappropriate (e.g., Bing, 2002; Thomas, 2002). In such cases, does withholding of effort become a form of disobedience that would be applauded outside the walls of these firms? If so, does this require that we be careful about creating a workplace where the structures to prevent the withholding of effort are so strong as to distort employee perceptions of ethical corporate behavior?

Conclusions

Our review has shown that there are numerous and varied reasons why employees might conclude that it is rational to withhold effort on the job. Whether withholding of effort occurs (a) to compensate for a sense of inequitable treatment, (b) to create "free time" for undertaking activities of a more personal interest, or (c) "just because it can," withholding of effort creates two basic problems for organizations. First, the focal employees are not providing the organization with what it expects. Second, if left unchecked, the withholding of effort may create the negative performance spiral among coworkers predicted by Miles and Klein (2002).

In total, the costs of withholding effort may be substantial (e.g., decreased productivity, morale problems, turnover). To help managers deter employee withholding of effort, a number of suggestions were offered. First, because managers are not always able to directly observe employees withholding effort, managers need to carefully diagnose any performance decrement to properly assess its root cause. An incorrect diagnosis will lead to an ineffective remedy. Then, in those instances where managers determine that withholding of effort is the cause of the performance decrement, a number of potential actions involving job design, reward systems, and employee selection may be useful. Through careful consideration of the cues contained in the work context, managers can reduce the incidence of employee withholding of effort and its potentially damaging effects.

References

Albanese, R., & Van Fleet, D. D. (1985). Rational behavior in groups: The free-riding tendency. *Academy of Management Review, 10,* 244–255.

Bing, S. (2002, February 18). Lessons from the abyss. *Fortune,* pp. 49–50.

Brooks, C. M., & Ammons, J. L. (2003). Free riding in group projects and the effects of timing, frequency, and specificity of criteria in peer assessments. *Journal of Education for Business, 78,* 268–273.

Cappelli, P., & Chauvin, K. (1991). An interplant test of the efficiency wage hypothesis. *Quarterly Journal of Economics, 106,* 769–787.

Chalykoff, J., & Kochan, T. A. (1989). Computer-aided monitoring: Its influence on employee satisfaction and turnover. *Personnel Psychology, 42,* 807–834.

Davis, J. H. (1969). *Group performance.* Reading, MA: Addison–Wesley.

Duffy, M. K., & Shaw, J. D. (2000). The Salieri syndrome: Consequences of envy in small groups. *Small Group Research, 31,* 3–23.

Ferris, G. R., Hochwarter, W. A., Buckley, M. R., Harrell-Cook, G., & Frink, D. D. (1999). Human resource management: Some new directions. *Journal of Management, 25,* 385–415.

Gagne, M., & Zuckerman, M. (1999). Performance and learning goal orientations as moderators of social loafing and social facilitation. *Small Group Research, 30,* 524–541.

George, J. M. (1992). Extrinsic and intrinsic origins of perceived social loafing in organizations. *Academy of Management Journal, 35,* 191–202.

George, J. M. (1995). Asymmetrical effects of rewards and punishments: The case of social loafing. *Journal of Occupational and Organizational Psychology, 68,* 327–338.

Jackson, J. M., & Harkins, S. G. (1985). Equity in effort: An explanation of the social loafing effect. *Journal of Personality and Social Psychology, 49,* 1199–1206.

Jackson, J. M., & Williams, K. D. (1985). Social loafing on difficult tasks: Working collectively can improve performance. *Journal of Personality and Social Psychology, 49,* 937–942.

Jones, G. R. (1984). Task visibility, free riding, and shirking: Explaining the effect of structure and technology on employee behavior. *Academy of Management Review, 9,* 684–695.

Judge, T., & Chandler, T. D. (1996). Individual-level determinants of employee shirking. *Industrial Relations, 51,* 468–486.

Karau, S. J., & Hart, J. W. (1998). Group cohesiveness and social loafing: Effects of a social interaction manipulation on individual motivation within groups. *Group Dynamics: Theory, Research, and Practice, 2,* 185–191.

Karau, S. J., & Williams, K. D. (1993). Social loafing: A meta-analytic review and theoretical integration. *Journal of Personality and Social Psychology, 65,* 681–706.

Karau, S. J., & Williams, K. D. (1997). The effects of group cohesiveness on social loafing and social compensation. *Group Dynamics: Theory, Research, and Practice, 1,* 156–168.

Kerr, N. L., & Bruun, S. (1983). The dispensability of member effort and group motivation losses: Free rider effects. *Journal of Personality and Social Psychology, 44,* 78–94.

Kidwell, R. E., Jr., & Bennett, N. (1993). Employee propensity to withhold effort: A conceptual model to intersect three avenues of research. *Academy of Management Review, 18,* 429–456.

Kidwell, R. E., Jr., & Bennett, N. (2001). Perceived work context and employee job neglect. *American Business Review, 19*(2), 64–74.

Kidwell, R. E., Jr., & Robie, C. (2003). Withholding effort in organizations: Toward development and validation of a measure. *Journal of Business and Psychology, 17,* 537–561.

Kiggundu, M. N. (1981). Task interdependence and the theory of job design. *Academy of Management Review, 6,* 499–508.

Krueger, A. B. (1991). Ownership, agency, and wages: An examination of franchising in the fast food industry. *Quarterly Journal of Economics, 106,* 75–101.

Latané, B. (1981). The psychology of social impact. *American Psychologist, 36,* 343–356.

Lawler, E. E., III. (1968). *Motivation in work organizations.* Pacific Grove, CA: Brooks/Cole.

Lazear, E. P., & Rosen, S. (1981). Rank-order tournaments as optimum labor contracts. *Journal of Political Economy, 89,* 841–864.

Leck, J. D., & Saunders, D. M. (1992). Hirschman's loyalty: Attitude or behavior? *Employee Responsibilities and Rights Journal, 5,* 219–230.

Leeuwen, E. V., & Knippenberg, D. V. (2002). How a group goal may reduce social matching in group performance: Shifts in standards for determining a fair contribution of effort. *Journal of Social Psychology, 142,* 73–86.

Leibowitz, A., & Tollison, R. (1980). Free riding, shirking, and team production in legal partnerships. *Economic Inquiry, 18,* 380–394.

Liden, R. C., Wayne, S. J., Jaworski, R. A., & Bennett, N. (2004). Social loafing: A field investigation. *Journal of Management, 30,* 285–304.

Lim, V. K. G. (2002). The IT way of loafing on the job: Cyberloafing, neutralizing, and organizational justice. *Journal of Organizational Behavior, 23,* 675–694.

Miles, J. A., & Klein, H. J. (2002). Perception in consequences of free riding. *Psychological Reports, 90,* 215–225.

Mullen, B. (1983). Operationalizing the effect of the group on the individual: A self-attention perspective. *Journal of Experimental Social Psychology, 19,* 295–322.

Murphy, S. M., Wayne, S. J., Liden, R. C., & Erdogan, B. (2003). Understanding social loafing: The role of justice perceptions and exchange relationships. *Human Relations, 56,* 61–84.

Olson, M. (1965). *The logic of collective action: Public goods and the theory of groups.* Cambridge, MA: Harvard University Press.

Robinson, S. L., & Bennett, R. J. (1995). A typology of deviant workplace behaviors: A multidimensional scaling study. *Academy of Management Journal, 38,* 555–572.

Rosenthal, J., & Masarech, M. A. (2003). High performance cultures: How values can drive business results. *Journal of Organizational Excellence, 22*(2), 3–18.

Rusbult, C. E., Farrell, D., Rogers, G., & Mainous, A. G. (1988). Impact of exchange variables on exit, voice, loyalty, and neglect. *Academy of Management Journal, 31,* 599–627.

Schein, E. H. (1984). Coming to a new awareness of organizational culture. *Sloan Management Review, 25*(2), 3–16.

Schnake, M. E. (1991). Equity in effort: The "sucker effect" in co-acting groups. *Journal of Management, 17,* 41–55.

Sparrowe, R. T., & Liden, R. C. (1997). Process and structure in leader–member exchange. *Academy of Management Review, 22,* 522–552.

Spencer, J. (2003, May 15). Shirk ethic: How to fake a hard day at the office—White-collar slackers get help from new gadgets; the faux 4 a.m. e-mail. *The Wall Street Journal,* p. D1.

Thomas, C. W. (2002). The rise and fall of Enron. *Journal of Accountancy, 193*(4), 41–47.

Thompson J. D. (1967). *Organizations in action.* New York: McGraw–Hill.

Verton, D. (2000, December 18). Employers OK with e-surfing. *ComputerWorld,* p. 16.

Vroom, V. H. (1964). *Work and motivation.* New York: John Wiley.

Williams, K., Harkins, S., & Latané, B. (1981). Identifiability as a deterrent to social loafing: Two cheering experiments. *Journal of Personality and Social Psychology, 40,* 303–311.

Withey, M. J., & Cooper, W. H. (1989). Predicting exit, voice, loyalty, and neglect. *Administrative Science Quarterly, 34,* 521–539.

The Low-Quality Loafers

J ust a few weeks after his appointment as unit manager at Talaveras Industries, Bowman Vance was informed by the plant superintendent that his section and its employees had been selected for a continuous quality improvement (CQI) program.

CQI was a new approach at Talaveras, and if Vance was successful at implementing the program within 1 year, the unit would gain quality certification, an important external recognition of product quality and work process improvement. In addition, if the program worked, it would be extended to the rest of the 300-employee company.

There were 25 employees in Vance's unit. Of these, 20 were union members and the others were assistant managers and clerical staff members. Consultants who were experts in statistical process control, self-directed teams, and other elements of the quality program were brought in to discuss these issues with the union employees and build momentum for the change to a quality process improvement program.

The union workers were skeptical of the program at first, but thanks to the enthusiasm of Vance, the two union stewards, and other key employees, the program implementation began and was quite well received during the first 6 weeks. Of the 20 union employees, most attended and participated in team-building activities, learned about building quality into the process, came to regular meetings, and generally understood and accepted the need for change and the principles behind it relatively quickly.

A trio of older workers did not. Lucas Bradford, 58 years of age, had worked at Talaveras for 25 years. He was content to do the minimum amount

AUTHOR'S NOTE: This case was prepared by Roland Kidwell (Niagara University) as the basis for classroom discussion. It is based on an actual organization investigated by the author. The names of all characters and the organization are fictitious, as are some details, to protect the identities of the individuals and the organization involved.

of work and instead focused on his off-hour activities. He came to work on time, put in minimal effort, would not go out of his way to try anything new, and was the first one out the door to get to his boat at the lake during the summer months or to get out into the woods during hunting season. He regularly failed to show up for meetings regarding the quality effort. When the stewards asked him about this, Bradford said he would try to attend in the future, but he did not make an appearance. Otherwise, his work was a bit below average.

Marv Goldberg, 55 years of age and a 30-year Talaveras employee, actively opposed the quality effort. He came to the regular meetings and talked about the lack of need for change, how this was being forced on the union employees, and how it was unfair of the company to ask employees who were doing their jobs to make changes. "We put in the effort to make a quality product; we don't need to change the way we do things to satisfy a bunch of outside consultants and gurus," he said at one meeting. The other employees generally shrugged off his comments and paid little attention. Goldberg had few friends at the company and was generally isolated from the other employees. His job performance was significantly below average.

Joe Machiano, 60 years of age and a 35-year Talaveras employee, had a small crafts business that he operated at night and during weekends. He sold wood carvings during his off hours. When he should have been at the meetings, he was in the break room carving figurines for his part-time business. When he was invited to the meetings or otherwise to participate in the quality effort, he said that he was going to retire soon and that the changes were not going to play a role in his future, so he found them a waste of time. His job performance was generally below average.

Three months into the program, morale among other employees started to dip. There was grumbling about the three employees who were not attending the meetings. The message that the three men were sending to management was, "We've been here for years. This is not what we signed up for when we came here. This is not fair."

Other union employees who had been with the company just as long as Bradford, Goldberg, and Machiano participated fully in the continuous improvement effort and wondered whether the three laggards were hurting the overall productivity of the unit. Vance, his assistants, and the union representatives realized that more employees needed to be hired to pick up the slack, but the plant superintendent had given strong signals that new hiring was not going to happen anytime soon.

After months of subtle encouragement from Vance and his assistants, Vance spoke to the three men individually. Each worker said that he did not see the need for accepting the program and would not change his behavior, complaining that it wasn't fair because they were not being paid anything extra to become involved in the program. Although the answers were similar, Vance was convinced that the three men were not engaging in a concerted organized effort.

Vance again went to the management and asked that he be supported in an effort to discipline or fire the three employees. The plant superintendent said that it would be too expensive to fight the union on this and that so long as the men were doing the minimum, they could not be seriously punished. The superintendent also said that Vance could not add staff members, at least until the next budget year. Although the union stewards were openly supportive of Vance and the quality effort, they privately told him that they would have to defend the employees if any disciplinary action took place.

A week later, James Omatao, a young employee, confronted Vance in his office. "This loafing is not fair to the rest of us who are working our butts off to make this quality thing happen," Omatao told the unit manager. "We're getting tired of having to pick up the work and cover for the mistakes of these slackers. What are you going to do about it, Mr. Vance?"

Discussion Questions

1. Is this a case of deviant behavior in the workplace? Explain.

2. Using Chapter 5 as your guide, explain whether withholding effort is occurring in this case. If so, which type?

3. Is it fair for the company to expect that the three longtime employees will change their behavior to meet the quality effort? Why or why not?

4. Evaluate the behavior of the three longtime employees in terms of ethics and fairness. Evaluate the behavior of Bowman Vance in terms of ethics and fairness.

5. Based on information included in Chapter 5 and other sources available to you, what might Vance do about this situation that would be both effective and ethical?

CHAPTER 6

Managing Noncompliance in the Workplace

Danielle E. Warren

R ecent scandals in business shed light on the importance of employee noncompliance to organizational success and failure. Large corporations have suffered unimaginable losses and fines, and have faced bankruptcy, due to the actions of noncompliant employees. During the mid-1990s, a young trader, Nick Leeson, worked for the Singapore office of a large British financial institution, Barings Bank. Through a series of bad investments, he found himself in a situation with extreme losses that he chose to hide in a phony client account, an action that violated organizational, as well as legal, rules. The size of his losses grew with time, and his actions eventually forced Barings Bank, one of the United Kingdom's oldest financial institutions, into bankruptcy.

On the other hand, noncompliant actions can also save organizations if the behavior involves alerting upper management to impending dangers or refusing to proceed in a process that will lead to harm. Unfortunately, upper management often does not properly discern differences in types of noncompliance such that the warnings or actions of the noncompliant employees may be dismissed and the employees may be labeled "troublemakers." In the B. F. Goodrich case involving the development of aircraft brakes for the U.S. government, engineer objections regarding brake failure and design flaws fell on deaf ears. The engineers associated with the project refused to sign the final qualification report describing the safety tests for the brakes because they believed that the statistics contained in the report

AUTHOR'S NOTE: This research was funded by the Prudential Business Ethics Center.

were falsified and that the brakes would fail and the failure could be deadly. The brakes were delivered to the customers and failed in initial tests by the government (Vandivier, 1996).

How are the acts of noncompliance at Barings Bank and B. F. Goodrich similar? How are they different? Both cases describe situations where employees ignored organizational directives and, in so doing, exhibited noncompliant behavior. Should management respond to all noncompliant behavior in the same manner? Most would argue the Barings Bank trader should not be treated in the same way as the engineers at B. F. Goodrich. Clearly, the noncompliant behavior differed in important and significant ways; therefore, the respective management responses should vary accordingly.

Although the examples of Barings Bank and B. F. Goodrich were related to serious outcomes for the organizations involved, not all noncompliance involves extreme consequences. However, it is difficult to know whether a particular act of noncompliance will lead to a larger, more dangerous outcome for an organization. Thus, managers are best off being aware of noncompliance, the ways in which it occurs in organizations, and strategies for managing such behavior. This chapter includes an in-depth discussion of four types of noncompliance: ignorance about rules, ignorance about rule application, opportunistic noncompliance, and principled noncompliance.

The first form of noncompliance, *ignorance about rules,* involves employees who accidentally break organizational rules or procedures because they do not know that the rules exist. These employees do not know the rules; therefore, they do not intentionally violate them. This form of noncompliance is similar to the second form in that it also involves a lack of intention. In the second instance, referred to as *ignorance about rule application,* employees know the rules but do not know whether the rules apply to them. The third form of noncompliance differs markedly from the first two forms in that employees understand that they are breaking the rules but do so for opportunistic reasons. This third form of noncompliance is referred to as *opportunistic noncompliance.* The fourth form of noncompliance is conceptually close to opportunistic noncompliance in that it involves intentional behavior, but the motivation is substantially different. In this situation, employees exhibit noncompliance but are motivated by ethical principles or moral beliefs. Employees believe that the organizational rules are unfair or morally wrong; therefore, they exhibit noncompliance as a form of protest. This form of noncompliance is referred to as *principled noncompliance.*

Behavior that falls into any of these four categories of noncompliance can pose a serious threat to an organization. None of these categories precludes behavior with potentially disastrous consequences. Thus, it is important to understand strategies for managing each type of noncompliance.

Each form of noncompliance must be managed in a way that addresses the unique issues associated with the behavior. As indicated in the previous descriptions, not all forms of noncompliance involve the same motivations. The first step in managing noncompliance is to understand what causes each type of noncompliance. Therefore, a discussion of noncompliance antecedents is provided.

To facilitate the comparison of types of noncompliance, the same examples are presented in each section to highlight the differences among the four categories.

Ignorance About Rules

Examples

In Example 1 (travel agencies), an employee who works for a manufacturing firm needs to plan a managerial tour of the international factories. The employee calls a friend at a local travel agency to assist in the travel arrangements. However, the employee does not realize that the company has a strict policy regarding travel agencies. Employees are required to use only agencies that appear on the "approved" list of agencies.

In Example 2 (confidential information), an employee works on new product development at a large telecommunications firm. The employee is excited about the new product and the work involved. At a family celebration, the employee shares information regarding a work assignment with friends and family members, not realizing that the firm has a detailed policy protecting confidential information.

Of the four types of noncompliance, the least amount of research exists on this type of noncompliance. The most relevant research exists on the mistakes in organizations (Vaughn, 1999). Some employee mistakes, such as ignorance about rules, involve unintentional deviance from organizational rules or directives. Most studies of employee mistakes, however, focus on individuals who know the organizational rules but break them accidentally (Vaughn, 1999).

Strategy for Managing

Education

In many instances, employees are never exposed or introduced to the full set of organizational rules. Some organizational rules or norms are tacit; that is, they reside in the minds of the organizations' leaders but do not appear in written form. This creates difficulties for newcomers who need to learn these rules over time. For instance, during the investigation of a scandal involving hospital waiting lists in the United Kingdom, it was found that "the deputy chief executive Liz Parker was new to her responsibilities and was unaware of the rules about waiting lists" (BBC News, 2003). Ideally, employees would be exposed to all applicable rules on entering an organization, but in many organizations, this task is too difficult, too overwhelming, or too time-consuming.

Instead, many employers give new employees a set of organizational rules, such as a code of conduct, and ask them to sign a document indicating that they agree to abide by the rules (Conference Board Report 986, 1996; De George, 1995;

Paine, 1996; Weaver, Treviño, & Cochran, 1999). Many organizations provide employees with binders that contain the organizational rules, but these may fall short in that rules may be updated and so the binders need to be kept current. Furthermore, employees may find the binders to be daunting and difficult to navigate when ethical dilemmas arise. Even if employees read the documentation thoroughly, they are bound to forget much of what they read unless the information is particularly relevant to their positions in the organizations.

Firms differ in their approaches to teaching the rules (Conference Board Report 986, 1996; Paine, 1996; Weaver et al., 1999). Some resort to classes. In some cases, an organization will require new hires to pass a test on the organizational rules so as to ensure that every employee has read and retained information regarding the rules. Yet even tests do not guarantee that employees will always know the rules given that employees may forget the rules or the rules may change between the time at which employees enter the organization and the time at which they break organizational rules.

In response, organizations have taken steps to better organize their rules and policies in ways that are more accessible to their employees. One approach involves computer software and online databases that allow employees to search on subjects or topics pertaining to their specific dilemmas. The databases may include country laws as well as organizational rules. The U.S. Office of Government Ethics (2003a) and the U.S. Department of Defense (2003) offer Web-based interactive ethics training on a variety of subjects, including gift giving between government employees, receiving gifts from outside sources, and misusing positions.

A video containing a variety of situations may exhibit the expectations of a firm better than written words. Videos are particularly useful for communicating organizational expectations when the rules are vague or difficult to apply (Business for Social Responsibility, 2003). Individuals have a natural inclination to learn behavior by watching the behavior of peers. Videos take advantage of this inclination by allowing employees to learn vicariously through the stories displayed in the videos. Hackman (1992) explained, "One of the most powerful ways for a group to help its members learn skills and role behaviors is by providing for them models of appropriate behavior" (p. 226).

Just as employees often learn by watching other employees, videos displaying role-playing are a useful means of educating employees on situation-specific rule applications. A video containing a variety of situations often will exhibit the expectations of a firm better than written words. Thus, the video provides a work context for the abstract rules. For instance, the U.S. Office of Government Ethics uses training videos to provide employees with guidance when judging appropriate behavior in the workplace. One video, titled *The Battle for Avery Mann*, traces the ethical dilemmas encountered by a typical government worker while conducting his work (U.S. Office of Government Ethics, 2003b). In addition to videos, some firms rely on board games to aid in the learning of organizational rules, whereas others use role-playing exercises (Business for Social Responsibility, 2003; Conference Board Report 986, 1996).

Sanctions

Just as ignorance of the law is not an acceptable excuse in the judicial system, ignorance of organizational rules might not fully excuse an employee's behavior. The reason behind holding employees accountable for knowing the rules is important not only for the focal employee but also for the employees who work in the same environment. Employees often learn by watching peers. Treviño (1992) explained, "The observation of a punishment event leads to the formation of punishment expectancies by the observer and, consequently, to inhibition of the punished behavior" (p. 647). A system that allows ignorance as an excuse provides no incentive for employees to learn and abide by the rules. Under such a system, any employee who broke an organizational rule could claim ignorance and be excused.

Deterrence theory suggests that employees decide whether or not to break the rules by weighing the benefits of breaking the rules against the likelihood of getting caught and the severity of the sanctions (Piliavin, Thornton, Gartner, & Matsueda, 1986). In this particular instance of noncompliance, sanctions might not matter because the employees are not consciously considering the decision of whether or not to break the rules. The threat of severe sanctions, however, may provide an incentive for learning the rules. Arguably, if the sanctions are severe, employees may learn the rules merely out of fear. In addition to sanction severity, employees must believe that the sanctions are likely to be applied if they exhibit noncompliance. If employees believe that management is unlikely to detect noncompliant behavior, the threat of severe sanctions will not deter noncompliance because the assignment of sanctions is unlikely.

Regardless of whether or not employees knew the rules or the sanctions were certain or severe enough, firms may still choose to assign sanctions, assess fines, or dismiss the employees. The decision depends on whether or not the employees *should* have known the rules.

A sanction system alone, however, is not an effective tool for managing employee noncompliance in the long run (Paine, 1996; Treviño, Weaver, Gibson, & Toffler, 1999). Research suggests that sanctions encourage employees to find loopholes in the rules (Treviño et al., 1999). Tenbrunsel and Messick (1999) suggested that organizational initiatives that emphasize sanctions and monitoring enact a "business" decision frame rather than an "ethics" decision frame, causing individuals to approach dilemmas as calculated business decisions rather than as decisions involving ethical or moral concerns.

Furthermore, employees may resent sanctions if the employees are not involved in the punishment system or if the desired behavior is unattainable. Paine (1996) explained, "An overemphasis on potential sanctions can be superfluous and even counterproductive. Employees may rebel against programs that stress penalties, particularly if they are designed and imposed without employee involvement or if the standards are vague or unrealistic" (p. 499). This is one reason why Becton Dickinson included international employees when they developed and introduced global organizational rules (Paine, 1998).

Managers, however, should be sensitive to the intentions of employees. An employee who accidentally breaks the rules should not be treated in the same way as an employee who intentionally breaks the rules. Managers need to take into account that employees in these situations did not doubt the importance of the rules; they just did not know that the rules existed. In law, individuals who do wrong intentionally are held more accountable than are those who do so unintentionally. This philosophy should extend to managerial assignment of blame and the punishment of employees (Strudler & Warren, 2001).

From a practical standpoint, management needs to consider the suitability of the sanctions because if employees believe that a sanction or punishment does not fit the wrongdoing (e.g., harsh punishment for an unintentional infraction), the focal employee, as well as those who know of the event, will respond negatively (Treviño, 1992). If a manager unfairly or harshly punishes employees, the employees may choose to withhold effort at work, distrust management, or even leave the organization. Thus, the organization may lose high-quality employees due to management's response to noncompliance.

Ignorance About Rule Application

Examples

In Example 1 (travel agencies), an employee who works for a manufacturing firm needs to plan a managerial tour of the international factories. The employee calls a friend at a local travel agency to assist in the travel arrangements. The employee knows that the company has a strict policy regarding travel agencies but does not realize that the policy applies to international travel.

In Example 2 (confidential information), an employee works on new product development at a large telecommunications firm. The employee is excited about the new product and the work involved. At a family celebration, the employee shares information regarding a work assignment with friends and family members, not realizing what attributes of the new product are considered to be confidential.

In many instances of noncompliance, individuals know the rules of the organization but do not fully understand how the rules apply to their specific jobs or responsibilities. Either they believe that the rules do not apply to them due to their specific roles, or the language of the rules makes it difficult to apply the rules to everyday business situations.

Some managers assume that organizational rules do not apply to them due to the nature of their work. For instance, information technology managers are accustomed to managing sensitive or private information of the employees in their corporations. They may have access to employee e-mail accounts, passwords, and computer files. They might not realize that rules regarding privacy apply to them because they normally manage information with restricted access. Likewise, human resources managers who typically access the personnel files of employees might not realize that certain personal information is restricted even for them.

Other managers, due to their status or positions in their organizations, may believe that the rules do not apply to them. For instance, a salesperson might not believe that rules regarding meal allowances apply to employees who entertain clients. Hackman (1992) explained, "Occupants of some roles have far more behavioral latitude than do others" (p. 242). Such latitude may lead employees to believe that certain rules do not apply to them.

Strategy for Managing

In these situations, the employees know the rules; they just do not realize that the rules apply to them. Managers should focus on teaching employees how the rules apply to their work. For instance, corporate codes of conduct often mention the Foreign Corrupt Practices Act, but few employees know the laws or how to apply them to their work. Paine (1998) described a scenario at Becton Dickinson where "a physician considering BD's [Becton Dickinson] diagnostic equipment for his hospital laboratory would like to go for instrument training in California and afterwards to visit Disneyland with his family" (p. 1). Whereas the Foreign Corrupt Practices Act describes clear distinctions between facilitating payments and taking bribes, the application of the law to this particular situation may be less clear for an employee. Donaldson (1996) explained, "The pronouncement that bribery is unacceptable is useless unless accompanied by guidelines for gift giving, payments to get goods through customs, and 'requests' from intermediaries who are hired to ask for bribes" (p. 55). Thus, the rules often are difficult to apply to specific work situations.

Education

Unlike the previous form of noncompliance (ignorance about the rules), employees who exhibit this type of noncompliance know the rules but are unsure about how to apply them to their work. Thus, education would focus specifically on the application of rules. For instance, manufacturing employees should provide training on the application of rules in their work environment and the ethical dilemmas that employees face on the factory floor. Similarly, information technology employees should receive training that is useful to their work. White and Lam (2000) suggested surveying employees about job-specific ethical dilemmas and then using the dilemmas to create educational simulations whereby the organizations communicate how employees should respond to such scenarios. Videos and role-playing tailored to the work environment would be particularly effective. Other firms encourage employees to learn the rules by having them teach the rules to others in their organizations (Business for Social Responsibility, 2003).

Those who work in international locations are particularly vulnerable to noncompliance because they may be working in settings where the local environments promote cultural practices that clash with their organizations' rules. In some cases, the local cultural practices also conflict with the local laws, and employees who follow local customs might break not only U.S. laws but also local laws (Donaldson & Dunfee, 1999). These employees should receive training that reflects the difficulties that they may face when complying with organizational rules while respecting local culture and country laws. One approach involves using respected local country managers to train employees in the local language. These managers understand the local culture, so they are better able to communicate the organization's directives, and these managers' reputations lend legitimacy to the messages contained in the organization's training (Business for Social Responsibility, 2003).

Sanctions

Much like the previous form of noncompliance, sanctions may be ineffective because employees are not consciously considering the decision of whether or not to break the rules. The threat of severe sanctions, however, may provide employees with an incentive to learn the rule application. The firm may still choose to assess fines or dismiss these employees. It depends on whether or not the employees should have known that the rules applied to them.

Similar to the employees who fall into the "ignorance about rules" category, the employees who fall into the "ignorance about rule application" category do not doubt the importance of the rules; they just did not know that the rules applied to them or their work. The next two forms of noncompliance differ from the previous two in that they involve intentional rule breaking and require more complex responses from management.

Opportunistic Noncompliance

Examples

In Example 1 (travel agencies), an employee who works for a manufacturing firm needs to plan a managerial tour of the international factories. The employee calls a friend at a local travel agency to assist in the travel arrangements. The employee knows that the company has a strict policy regarding travel agencies and that employees are required to use only agencies that appear on the "approved" list, but the employee wants to give business to the friend's travel agency because the friend will provide a kickback for placing the order.

In Example 2 (confidential information), an employee works on new product development at a large telecommunications firm. The employee is excited about a new product and the work involved. At a family celebration, the employee shares information with a competitor despite a strong company policy regarding confidential information. The employee hopes to be hired away by the competing firm.

As these examples illustrate, employee noncompliance sometimes occurs because employees intentionally break rules for personal gain or opportunism. This type of noncompliance is the most threatening to the organization because the employee's rule behavior is motivated by destructive or negative intentions. Examples of this include not only minor rule infractions, such as tardiness and dress code violations, but also criminal behaviors, such as theft and fraud (Greenberg, 1990, 1997; Robinson & Bennett, 1995; Warren, 2003).

Strategy for Managing

Opportunistically noncompliant employees know the organizational rules but choose to disregard them. They do so to benefit themselves, their organizations, or a combination of both. For example, at Salomon Brothers, the noncompliant actions of one trader caused a series of events that were devastating for the firm. Paul Mozer placed a bid in the U.S. Treasury Securities Auction that extended beyond the allowable amount per firm. He lied to the Treasury and claimed that the extra portion was for one of Salomon's clients. Mozer's actions, coupled with management's reactions, precipitated more than $290 million in fines for Salomon (Crane & Williams, 1992; Thornton, 2002). If Mozer's behavior had gone undetected, both he and the firm would have financially benefited from bidding beyond the limit imposed by the Treasury.

If employees are noncompliant for personal gains (e.g., stealing company property), this is the most threatening form of noncompliance to the organization because the employees' interests are completely misaligned with those of the organization. Vardi and Wiener (1996) discussed this distinction in their research on misbehavior where they addressed the importance of employee intentions. They theorized that the antecedents to misbehavior intended to benefit employees themselves differ greatly from those to misbehavior intended to benefit the organization. The main distinction in antecedents lies in the employees' identification and commitment to the organization. Vardi and Wiener suggested that misbehaviors exhibited with the intention of benefiting the organization "are anchored in ideology and values and are carried out by individuals who strongly identify with their organization, its mission, and its leadership and who often are willing to sacrifice self-interests for such causes" (p. 158).

An example of opportunistic noncompliance focused on organizational gain is demonstrated in the Royal Caribbean case. Employees at Royal Caribbean wanted to avoid the expense associated with properly disposing of waste aboard their ships, so they devised a secret bypass pipe for illegally discarding waste (Rosenzweig, 1999; U.S. Department of Justice, 1998). These actions violated organizational procedures as well as environmental laws. The employees' behavior was eventually discovered, and the company incurred an $18 million fine for environmental crimes. In this case, the employee actions apparently were for the firm's benefit because it is not clear how the employees personally benefited from the illegal dumping of waste.

To better understand the factors leading to unethical decisions at work, social psychologists conduct controlled experiments. Many argue that unethical decision making is caused by a combination of situational factors in the workplace and individual differences of the employees (Hegarty & Sims, 1978, 1979; Treviño & Youngblood, 1990). Hegarty and Sims (1978) found that rewards for unethical behavior and increased competition, as well as certain personality variables such as locus of control, had a negative effect on ethical decision making. In another laboratory study, Hegarty and Sims (1979) found that the presence of certain organizational factors, such as a letter from the chief executive officer supporting ethics and an organizational ethics policy, reduced the levels of unethical decision making displayed by study participants. Thus, laboratory studies may help to pinpoint the factors that lead employees to exhibit opportunistic noncompliance.

If the noncompliance is widespread, the organization may want to examine the work environment. Organizational objectives might be unrealistic and difficult to reach without breaking the rules. Thus, employee noncompliance may be the result of unattainable organizational objectives. Does the current incentive structure compete with the rules of the organization? When mechanics at Sears Automotive were accused of inappropriately conducting repairs on customer vehicles, an investigation revealed that an organizational quota system played an important role in encouraging the mechanics' behavior. The mechanics needed to meet a certain quota of repairs to qualify for compensation. The mechanics found it difficult to meet these quotas by conducting their work legitimately, so they recommended unnecessary repairs, fabricated repairs, and did not properly complete the repairs (Paine, 1996; Paine & Santoro, 1993; see also Case 2).

Although an employee may exhibit noncompliance for the sake of the organization, there is still a significant difference between opportunistic noncompliance for the organization and principled noncompliance. Those who opportunistically break the rules, either for the organization's gain or for their own gain, are not concerned with the morality of the organizational rules. A principled noncompliant employee objects to the rules and, possibly, the inequities that result from their application. An opportunistic noncompliant employee is not morally objecting to the rule or questioning its fairness; the employee is just trying to find a shortcut for organizational or personal gain. Thus, although the engineers at Royal Caribbean may have bypassed organizational standards in a way that temporarily benefited the organization, their motives were not morally motivated. They did not adapt the plumbing because they questioned the morality of the organizational standards; rather, they did so to find an easier way in which to dispose of waste.

Education

As with the other forms of noncompliance, management should consider education as a means of preventing future noncompliance. Unlike employees who exhibit noncompliance due to a lack of knowledge about rules and their application, employees who exhibit opportunistic noncompliance know the rules but choose to break them, so the educational focus should be somewhat different. Education for opportunistic noncompliance should center on the purpose of rules, with particular attention paid to the seriousness of rule violations. As with the other forms of noncompliance, management may use classes, tests, videos, and/or simulations to educate employees.

Sanctions

In this particular instance, sanctions are applicable because the employee is knowingly breaking the rules for opportunistic reasons. Sanctions may include fines, suspension, or dismissal. Just as management needs to be careful not to harshly punish the employee who unintentionally breaks the rules, the employee who exhibits opportunistic noncompliance should be punished accordingly. The suitability of the punishment is important for the fair treatment not only of the focal employee but also of the coworkers who witness the event. Researchers have found that employees expect punishments to fit infractions and that if employees believe that management's sanctions lack severity, they will react negatively and possibly intervene to further punish a noncompliant employee (Treviño, 1992).

Principled Noncompliance

Examples

In Example 1 (travel agencies), an employee who works for a manufacturing firm needs to plan a managerial tour of the international factories. The employee calls a friend at a local travel agency to assist in the travel arrangements. The employee knows that the company has a strict policy regarding travel agencies and that employees are required to use only agencies that appear on the "approved" list. However, the employee does not use one of the approved agencies due to their inadequate service and unreliable scheduling. The employee is concerned that the travelers will be stranded without proper transportation and lodging at international locations.

In Example 2 (confidential information), an employee works on new product development at a large telecommunications firm. The employee is concerned about the failure of the product in safety tests and is concerned that the information has not been communicated to upper management. The employee shares confidential information regarding product attributes with senior management despite restrictions on sharing confidential product information with employees outside the project.

In both examples, the employees are concerned with quality and are attempting to change their workplaces to encourage higher standards and improve business. The employees' behavior may cause their firms to change their rules on travel agencies and confidentiality policies. These individuals may provide important information about inadequate or outdated rules. Becker (1963) referred to individuals as "moral entrepreneurs" because they are a source of new rules. Or, they may expose situations where the rules do not provide adequate guidance. Most important, in these instances, employees are engaging in their environment and trying to change it in ways that they consider to be appropriate or morally correct. If managers harness this type of energy properly, they may tap a powerful human resource.

Principled noncompliance aligns with other constructs in the management literature, such as organizational citizenship behavior (Van Dyne, Graham, &

Dienesch, 1994), taking charge behavior (Morrison & Phelps, 1999), and extra-role behavior (Van Dyne & LePine, 1998), in that the employee voluntarily and intentionally attempts to improve the organization. Principled noncompliance differs from these constructs, however, because it involves deviance from the organization's directives. Those who exhibit organizational citizenship, taking charge behavior, and extra-role behavior are acting in ways that deviate in the sense that they surpass managerial expectations but still correspond with organizational directives. These kinds of behavior would generate praise and attract positive attention, whereas principled noncompliance may generate concern and negative attention.

Management constructs that are conceptually closer to principled noncompliance include constructive deviance (Warren, 2003), functional disobedience (Brief, Buttram, & Dukerich, 2001), tempered radicalism (Meyerson & Scully, 1995), counter-role behavior (Staw & Boettger, 1990), positive deviance (Spreitzer & Sonenshein, 2003), and principled organizational dissent (Graham, 1986). These constructs, along with principled noncompliance, may focus on an employee who resists the current organizational system with the intent of improving the organization or aligning the organization's system with what the employee feels is morally correct. This motivation is thoroughly explored and analyzed in the whistle-blowing literature.

Whistle-blowing involves an employee's objection to organizational practices or directives and may be based on principle or opportunism, depending on the motivation of the whistle-blower. Whistle-blowing based on false claims is a form of revenge or sabotage and is more closely aligned with opportunistic noncompliance, whereas whistle-blowing rooted in moral objection aligns with principled noncompliance (Miceli & Near, 1997; Near & Miceli, 1995).

This objection may be internal (i.e., within the organization) or external (i.e., outside the organization). Employees who blow the whistle externally may dramatically affect the future of the company and, in some cases, the future of the industry. This effect is demonstrated by the noncompliance of Jeffrey Wigand, a scientist who had worked as an executive for the Brown & Williamson tobacco firm. Wigand broke a confidentiality agreement with his former employer when he disclosed information on the harmfulness of tobacco during a broadcast of the television program *60 Minutes* and, at a later point, during a legal deposition (Enrich, 2001; Miller, 1995). Wigand was the highest ranking employee to blow the whistle on the tobacco industry, and his actions are viewed as an impetus to a wave of litigation against the tobacco industry. As one news story reported, "Wigand's damning court testimony helped pave the way for a 1998 'master settlement' in which the industry agreed to pay $206 billion to 46 states for smoking related medical expenses" (Enrich, 2001, p. 70). Wigand's actions were helpful to society but harmful to the organization.

Meyerson and Scully (1995) introduced a construct, tempered radicalism, which is another form of principled noncompliance yet differs from external whistle-blowing in that it involves employee commitment to the organization and an attempt to change the organization from within. Meyerson and Scully explained that tempered radicals are "individuals who identify with and are committed to their organizations and are also committed to a cause, community, or ideology that is fundamentally different from, and possibly at odds with, the dominant culture of their organization" (p. 586). These authors' assumption is that employees will remain loyal to the organization, a situation that is more desirable than the employees sharing negative organizational information with individuals outside the organization. However, Meyerson and Scully did not address the ways in which employees may attempt to change the organization and whether or not the changes are desirable. This is an important aspect of managing principled noncompliance and is discussed in the next section.

Strategy for Managing

Managers certainly do not want to treat an employee who exhibits principled noncompliance in the same way as they treat an employee who exhibits opportunistic noncompliance. If the employee's concerns are valid, the organization can respond and rectify the situation. If the employee's concerns are the result of misinformation or lack of knowledge regarding a complex situation within the organization, employee education may be a good approach to managing the situation. For instance, an employee might believe that a company product is unsafe, but the employee might not realize that safety is actually tested and certified at a later point in the production process.

Education

If the employee is misguided in his or her understanding of the rules or the values supporting the rules, education is a good strategy for managing the situation. The education should focus on the purpose of rules and the seriousness of rule violations. As with the other forms of noncompliant behavior, management should consider reeducating the employee using courses, videos, role-playing, and/or online training. Unlike ignorance about rules or ignorance about rule application, this type of noncompliance involves an intentional opposition to the rules themselves. Assuming that the employee fully understands the organizational rules and how the organization expects them to be applied to the employee's work context, the education should focus on learning the purpose or meaning behind the rules rather than on learning the rules or rule application. In other words, the employee who exhibits principled noncompliance needs to understand the organizational values and principles supporting the organizational rules.

Consulting With Upper Management

In this situation, upper management might want to be involved in the adjustment of rules or in the creation of new ones. If an employee is blowing the whistle internally, management needs to be careful not to dismiss the employee's behavior because the next step might be external whistle-blowing. In most situations, the organization is better off managing an internal whistle-blower than an external whistle-blower because if the employee blows the whistle externally, the organization will lose control over the situation and face a restricted set of options for responding to the whistle-blower. External whistle-blowing places the organization in a defensive position where it needs to respond to the media, federal agencies, and investors. In addition to needing to manage the publicity and scrutiny associated with an organizational scandal, the organization might be more blameworthy and might suffer larger punishments for wrongdoing if the employee had tried to exercise voice by internally blowing the whistle but received no support from management. Thus, the organization has more flexibility in responding to a crisis if the whistle-blowing occurs internally.

Many organizations understand the benefits of keeping whistle-blowing incidents internal and thus create programs and work environments that foster employee comfort in sharing dissenting views within the organization. For instance, Martin Marietta uses an extensive ethics program that encourages employee voice. Paine (1996) explained, "By providing an alternative channel for raising such concerns, Martin Marietta is able to take corrective action more quickly and with a lot less pain. In many cases, potentially embarrassing problems have been identified and dealt with before becoming a management crisis, a lawsuit, or a criminal investigation" (p. 501).

There are circumstances where an employee is opposed to an organizational directive for moral reasons and displays principled noncompliance, but the moral reasoning of the employee is objectionable to the organization. For instance, an employee might be passionately dedicated to restricting the gender or race of an organization and, therefore, hires only candidates of a particular gender or race. Thus, the employee exhibits principled noncompliance by breaking organizational rules regarding equal opportunity employment. Although the employee's noncompliance may rest on personal moral principles, the organization should not attempt to adjust organizational rules to embrace the employee's beliefs. The organization should educate the employee on the organization's values and how they relate to the rules. If the employee refuses to comply with the organizational rules, the employee probably does not belong in the organization. Not only does this employee violate the organizational rules, but the employee's behavior also violates the values of the larger society and puts the organization at legal risk. Although this behavior is still considered to be principled noncompliance because the employee is acting on moral beliefs, management needs to be able to differentiate principled noncompliance that will improve the organization from principled noncompliance that will result in dysfunctional consequences for the organization.

Sanctions

Management should consider the reasons for rule violations and decide whether or not the rules are outdated or inappropriate. If management wants to keep the rules in place, sanctions should be considered as a means of deterrence.

Summary

One employee objects to delivering a faulty product to a consumer, whereas another employee embezzles money. What do these employees have in common? They both exhibit behavior that deviates from organizational directives, and both may be considered troublemakers from the organization's perspective. On further consideration, management may realize how the objection to delivering the faulty product can help the organization in the long run.

Table 6.1 summarizes the four types of noncompliance that have been discussed in this chapter. All forms of noncompliance involve situations where employees did not follow an organization's rules, and at first glance, all infractions may look similar. As suggested in the chapter, a closer examination of employee intentions reveals very different situations requiring specific managerial responses. It is also important to understand when employees are trying to improve the organization and when they are behaving opportunistically. As discussed in the chapter, principled noncompliance is often dismissed or not properly considered. The introductory example of the B. F. Goodrich brake scandal illustrates how employee warnings are not always heeded even though the messages are valuable to the future of the organization. Although all forms of noncompliance may result in difficulties for the

Table 6.1 Types of Noncompliance

Type of Noncompliance	Description	Intentional?	Strategy for Managing
Ignorance about rules	Employee does not know the rules	No	Educate employee on the rules and how they apply to the employee's work environment
Ignorance about rule application	Employee does not understand when rules apply	No	Educate the employee on the application of rules to the employee's specific work environment
Opportunistic noncompliance	Employee intentionally breaks rules for personal or organizational benefit	Yes	Examine situational and individual factors affecting noncompliance; depending on cause and severity of noncompliance, assign sanctions, suspend, or dismiss
Principled noncompliance	Employee intentionally breaks rules based on moral principles	Yes	Reexamine rules for flaws; if rules are appropriate, educate employee on the rules' purpose and how the rules reflect the organization's values

organization, principled noncompliance is a unique situation where the employee is taking an active role in changing the organization—generally for the better. Thus, this type of behavior should be embraced by the organization.

A number of exceptions apply to the guidance on managing noncompliance described in this chapter and illustrated in Table 6.1. Managerial responses to certain forms of noncompliance, such as violence, require more than education even if the employee did not realize that there was a specific organizational rule against it. Employee violence entails a specific set of antecedents that require careful consideration and specific managerial responsiveness (Neuman & Baron, 1997; O'Leary-Kelly, Griffin, & Glew, 1996; see also Martinko, Douglas, Harvey, & Joseph, this volume).

Other exceptions may include situations where the employee works in an area that requires high safety and has zero tolerance for mistakes (e.g., nuclear power plant, flight control deck). Although the employee might not intentionally break organizational rules, the organization may still choose to dismiss the employee due to the extreme risk associated with employee mistakes.

Managers who want to create systems that guard against all four types of non-compliance should consider strong education systems that not only emphasize the rules and how they apply to employees' specific work contexts but also stress the purpose of the rules and how they correspond to the organization's values. As a means to deterrence, employees should fully understand the sanctions associated with rule infractions as well as the monitoring systems for tracking infractions. Thus, the education should contain a mixed focus with both values and compliance orientations (Paine, 1996; Treviño et al., 1999). Treviño and colleagues (1999) reported that this is the most commonly used approach taken by organizations. Proponents of this approach suggest that employees will be less likely to focus on loopholes around the rules if they focus on organizational values such as integrity (Paine, 1996).

The first two categories, ignorance about rules and ignorance about rule application, are easier to rectify because employees are not intentionally challenging the current rule system. The final two categories, opportunistic noncompliance and principled noncompliance, involve intentional noncompliance that raises serious questions about employees' motives and the organization's response. Ultimately, managers need to be cautious when responding to acts of noncompliance because the response could mean the difference between saving the organization and ruining it.

References

BBC News. (2003, July 4). Waiting lists "fiddled" for years. Retrieved November 20, 2003, from http://news.bbc.co.uk/2/hi/uk_news/england/north_yorkshire/3043810.stm

Becker, H. S. (1963). *Outsiders: Studies in the sociology of deviance.* New York: Free Press.

Brief, A. P., Buttram, R. T., & Dukerich, J. M. (2001). Collective corruption in the corporate world: Toward a process model. In M. E. Turner (Ed.), *Groups at work: Theory and research* (pp. 471–499). Mahwah, NJ: Lawrence Erlbaum.

Business for Social Responsibility. (2003). *Ethics training.* Retrieved December 12, 2003, from www.bsr.org/bsrresources/whitepaperdetail.cfm?documentid=437

Conference Board Report 986. (1996). Corporate ethics practices: An international survey of ethics codes and programs. In T. Donaldson & P. H. Werhane (Eds.), *Ethical issues in business: A philosophical approach* (pp. 507–509). Upper Saddle River, NJ: Prentice Hall.

Crane, D. B., & Williams, M. W. (1992). *Salomon and the Treasury Securities Auction.* Boston: Harvard Business School Press.

De George, R. T. (1995). *Business ethics.* Englewood Cliffs, NJ: Prentice Hall.

Donaldson, T. (1996). Values in tension: Ethics away from home. *Harvard Business Review, 74,* 48–62.

Donaldson, T., & Dunfee, T. W. (1999). *Ties that bind: A social contracts approach to business ethics.* Boston: Harvard Business School Press.

Enrich, D. (2001, August 20). Jeffrey Wigand: The insider who blew smoke at Big Tobacco. *U.S. News & World Report,* p. 70.

Graham, J. (1986). Principled organizational dissent: A theoretical essay. In B. M. Staw & L. L. Cummings (Eds.), *Research in organizational behavior* (Vol. 8, pp. 1–51). Greenwich, CT: JAI.

Greenberg, J. (1990). Employee theft as a reaction to underpayment inequity: The hidden cost of pay cuts. *Journal of Applied Psychology, 75,* 561–568.

Greenberg, J. (1997). The STEAL motive: Managing the social determinants of employee theft. In R. A. Giacalone & J. Greenberg (Eds.), *Antisocial behavior in organizations* (pp. 85–108). Thousands Oaks, CA: Sage.

Hackman, J. R. (1992). Group influences on individuals in organizations. In M. D. Dunnette & L. M. Hough (Eds.), *Handbook of industrial and organizational psychology* (pp. 199–268). Palo Alto, CA: Consulting Psychologists Press.

Hegarty, W. H., & Sims, H. P. (1978). Some determinants of unethical decision behavior: An experiment. *Journal of Applied Psychology, 63,* 451–457.

Hegarty, W. H. & Sims, H. P. (1979). Organizational philosophy, policies, and objectives related to unethical decision behavior: A laboratory experiment. *Journal of Applied Psychology, 64,* 331–338.

Martinko, M. J., Douglas, S. C., Harvey, P., & Joseph, C. (2005). Managing organizational aggression. In R. E. Kidwell, Jr., & C. L. Martin (Eds.), *Managing organizational deviance* (pp. 237–259). Thousand Oaks, CA: Sage.

Meyerson, D., & Scully, M. (1995). Tempered radicalism and the politics of ambivalence and change. *Organization Science, 6,* 585–600.

Miceli, M., & Near, J. (1997). Whistle-blowing as antisocial behavior. In R. A. Giacalone & J. Greenberg (Eds.), *Antisocial behavior in organizations* (pp. 37–67). Thousands Oaks, CA: Sage.

Miller, M. (1995, March 2). The Barings debacle. *Los Angeles Times,* p. A12.

Morrison, E. W., & Phelps, C. C. (1999). Taking charge at work: Extrarole efforts to initiate workplace change. *Academy of Management Journal, 42,* 403–419.

Near, J. P., & Miceli, M. P. (1995). Effective whistle-blowing. *Academy of Management Review, 20,* 679–708.

Neuman, J. H., & Baron, R. A. (1997). Aggression in the workplace. In R. A. Giacalone & J. Greenberg (Eds.), *Antisocial behavior in organizations* (pp. 37–67). Thousands Oaks, CA: Sage.

O'Leary-Kelly, A. M., Griffin, R. W., & Glew, D. J. (1996). Organization-motivated aggression: A research framework. *Academy of Management Review, 21,* 225–253.

Paine, L. S. (1996). Managing for organizational integrity. In T. Donaldson & P. H. Werhane (Eds.), *Ethical issues in business: A philosophical approach* (pp. 494–507). Upper Saddle River, NJ: Prentice Hall.

Paine, L. S. (1998). *Becton Dickinson: Ethics and business practices (A)*. Boston: Harvard Business School Press.

Paine, L. S., & Santoro, M. (1993). *Sears Auto Centers (A)*. Boston: Harvard Business School Press.

Piliavin, I., Thornton, C., Gartner, R., & Matsueda, R. L. (1986). Crime, deterrence, and rational choice. *American Sociological Review, 51,* 101–119.

Robinson, S., & Bennett, R. (1995). A typology of deviant workplace behaviors: A multidimensional study. *Academy of Management Journal, 38,* 555–572.

Rosenzweig, D. (1999, July 22). Cruise line fined $18 million for dumping waste at sea. *Los Angeles Times,* p. A6.

Spreitzer, G., & Sonenshein, S. (2003). Becoming extraordinary: Empowering people for positive deviance. In K. Cameron, J. Dutton, & R. Quinn (Eds.), *Positive organizational scholarship* (pp. 207–224). San Francisco: Berrett–Koehler.

Staw, B. M., & Boettger, R. (1990). Task revision: A neglected form of work performance. *Academy of Management Journal, 33,* 534–559.

Strudler, A., & Warren, D. E. (2001). Authority, heuristics, and the structure of excuses. In J. M. Darley, D. M. Messick, & T. Tyler (Eds.), *Social influence and ethics* (pp. 155–173). Mahwah, NJ: Lawrence Erlbaum.

Tenbrunsel, A. E., & Messick, D. M. (1999). Sanctioning systems, decision frames, and cooperation. *Administrative Science Quarterly, 44,* 684–707.

Thornton, E. (2002, December 16). Wall Street's fine mess. *BusinessWeek Online.* Retrieved January 8, 2004, from www.businessweek.com/bwdaily/dnflash/dec2002/nf20021216_5177.htm

Treviño, L. K. (1992). The social effects of punishment in organizations: A justice perspective. *Academy of Management Review, 17,* 647–676.

Treviño, L. K., Weaver, G. R., Gibson, D. G., & Toffler, B. L. (1999). Managing ethics and legal compliance: What works and what hurts. *California Management Review, 41,* 131–151.

Treviño, L. K., & Youngblood, S. A. (1990). Bad apples in bad barrels: A causal analysis of ethical decision making behavior. *Journal of Applied Psychology, 75,* 378–385.

U.S. Department of Defense. (2003). *2003 annual online ethics training.* Retrieved December 20, 2003, from www.defenselink.mil/dodgc/defense_ethics/2003ethics_training

U.S. Department of Justice. (1998). Cruise line sentenced for fleet-wide conspiracy of dumping oil and lying to the Coast Guard. Retrieved December 1, 2003, from www.usdoj.gov/opa/pr/1998/October/478_enr.htm

U.S. Office of Government Ethics. (2003a). *Computer and Web-based ethics training.* Retrieved December 26, 2003, from www.usoge.gov/pages/comp_web_trng/comp_web_trng.html

U.S. Office of Government Ethics. (2003b). *Ordering information for OGE publications, videos, and software.* Retrieved December 26, 2003, from www.usoge.gov/pages/misc_files/orderinfo.html#anchor-

Van Dyne, L., Graham, J. W., & Dienesch, R. M. (1994). Organizational citizenship behavior: Construct redefinition, measurement, and validation. *Academy of Management Journal, 37,* 765–802.

Van Dyne, L., & LePine, J. A. (1998). Helping and voice extra-role behaviors: Evidence of construct and predictive validity. *Academy of Management Journal, 41,* 108–119.

Vandivier, K. (1996). The aircraft brake scandal. In T. Donaldson & P. H. Werhane (Eds.), *Ethical issues in business: A philosophical approach* (pp. 345–356). Upper Saddle River, NJ: Prentice Hall.

Vardi, Y., & Wiener, Y. (1996). Misbehavior in organizations: A motivational framework. *Organization Science, 7,* 151–165.

Vaughn, D. (1999). The dark side of organizations: Mistake, misconduct, and disaster. *Annual Review of Sociology, 25,* 271–305.

Warren, D. E. (2003). Constructive and destructive deviance in organizations. *Academy of Management Review, 28,* 622–632.

Weaver, G. R., Treviño, L. K., & Cochran, P. L. (1999). Corporate ethics practices in the mid-1990's: An empirical study of the Fortune 1000. *Journal of Business Ethics, 18,* 283–292.

White, L. P., & Lam, L. W. (2000). A proposed infrastructural model of the establishment of organizational ethical systems. *Journal of Business Ethics, 28,* 35–42.

Noncompliance at Dow Chemical

During the summer of 2000, Dow Chemical fired dozens of its employees and reprimanded hundreds of others in Michigan and Texas for failing to obey the company's harassment policy. Following employee complaints about sexually explicit and otherwise offensive e-mail, Dow management reviewed thousands of company employee e-mail accounts and disciplined workers who violated the policy. The terminated employees had sent or forwarded offensive e-mail.

According to accounts of an incident published in the *Los Angeles Times,* Dow dismissed John, a 25-year company veteran, for sending illicit e-mails, including one that contained a picture of a nude man and a female dwarf.

Another longtime employee, Tom, received his termination after sending an e-mail that showed a woman and a horse engaged in a sex act.

A third employee, Angie, was dismissed after she sent an e-mail that showed a man cutting his finger off with a paint scraper.

All three of these former Dow employees did not comply with what seemed to be clear company policy. Two months before the investigation into e-mail abuse began at its Michigan plant, Dow had mailed to employees a 30-page booklet that outlined the company's harassment policies. Page 5 of the booklet listed behavior that the company would not tolerate, including using e-mail "to view or pass along inappropriate material (particularly relative to race, ethnicity, gender, disability, religion, or of a sexual nature)."

AUTHOR'S NOTE: This case was prepared by Roland Kidwell (Niagara University) as the basis for classroom discussion. It was developed from accounts listed in the bibliography at the end of the case. All names of individuals and the organization are real.

In what one Dow human resources manager confidentially described to the writer of this case as the "worst experience of my career," Dow fired at least 70 employees and reprimanded hundreds more at facilities in Texas and Michigan because the workers sent e-mail considered sexually explicit or violent through the company's computer system.

After an internal investigation and consultation with ethics specialists led to the large dose of terminations and disciplinary actions, many of the fired employees complained that they had not followed the policy because they had not seen the booklet or had tossed it out without reading it.

Other employees did not understand why the company was making such a fuss. They viewed forwarding "humorous" e-mail in the same vein as posting risqué pictures in the locker room, telling off-color jokes at the water cooler, and engaging in other forms of what they believed to be harmless banter. In a long-standing tradition of passing around photos and copying lewd cartoons on company machines, the employees believed that their behavior was acceptable so long as these items were not forced on others unwillingly. They saw it as typical of what goes on in a factory with a predominantly male workforce.

In the past, most organizations had not permitted conduct such as passing around pictures of nude women and telling sexually distasteful jokes and stories, but they had not explicitly taken action against such behavior. As sexual harassment laws and court rulings have evolved, however, passive acceptance by organizations is no longer the norm. To defend themselves against potential charges of sexual harassment, organizational managers have decided that they should be proactive in halting situations that may be considered potentially abusive.

E-mail jokes, photos, and cartoons leave a permanent record, just as recorded employee phone calls, computer keystrokes, and video surveillance cameras provide a log of employee activity to company supervisors focused on improving productivity and efficiency. In addition, organizations are now connected to an electronic global community where all kinds of dubious material can be transmitted into and from an organization's e-mail system. To managers investigating complaints, the beneficial element of e-mail is the permanent record that apparently makes clear that the employee was not complying with the policy. Managers apparently do not need to take evidence from a complainant, a suspect, and witnesses and then decide whose story to believe.

During recent years, hundreds of workers in similar circumstances have lost jobs at organizations such as Xerox, the New York Times, and Merck after company officials—fearful that e-mail abuse may lead to sexual harassment charges by other employees—inspected the electronic trail. One protest from an employee can lead to the investigation of thousands of e-mail accounts.

Following an employee's complaint about seeing something offensive on the company e-mail system, Dow conducted extensive electronic surveillance and disciplined the employees after reviewing thousands of computer records that documented violations of the policy. At first, officials from the unions that represented many of the workers could watch as company employees checked the e-mail system, but when the investigation expanded, they were no longer allowed to be in the room, according to the union officials. Kent Holsing, a union vice president, observed the checks for a day. He told the *Los Angeles Times* that something must have happened later that day. "The next morning I got there, and they said, 'This just got bigger.' We were no longer allowed to participate."

At Dow's facility in Freeport, Texas, Charlie Singletary, business manager for the International Union of Operating Engineers Local 564, said the company had gone on a witch hunt regarding the e-mail. Singletary said that many of the firings could have been avoided if the company had done a better job of training its employees on what was considered to be improper and prohibited by company policy. The operating engineers union had 1,000 or so members at the Freeport plant.

In Michigan, the Dow investigation quickly became so large that company officials decided to take a record of the company's computer network for the date the employee complaint was received. Instead of looking at individual e-mail accounts and following up on e-mail from those accounts, the network snapshot looked at all 7,500 employees in the Midland plant, that is, at anyone who had a company e-mail account. Employees who heard about the probe tried to delete files and clean out improper e-mail from their accounts, but the snapshot made those actions too late.

The company focused on roughly 600 workers whose accounts contained what Dow considered to be inappropriate e-mail. The next step for the company was determining how to punish the workers who were not compliant with company policy. The punishment focused largely on two factors: the content of the material and what the employees had done with it. The most serious type of material was that depicting "overt sexual acts or deviant behavior." Employees who had e-mailed the most egregious material to others or had brought it into the plant in the first place were terminated.

Union officials and others who examined Dow's actions suggested that the company should have issued a warning about noncompliance with company policy before terminating workers. Some of these critics viewed the firings as unfair because they resulted from a "first offense" and because they occurred soon after the new company policy was distributed to employees who had not been disciplined previously for this type of behavior, which had once been considered a normal part of the culture. Providing warnings before termination would have led to the elimination of inappropriate e-mail, according to these observers. Dow officials said that they believed the warnings were adequate and that the policy would not be taken seriously if employee noncompliance was permitted.

Several of the affected employees claimed that they had not sent e-mail in violation of the policy. At least one claimed that he had not broken the rules because he did not know how to send e-mail. The employee, Brian, said that another worker had seen him open an obscene e-mail and that the other employee had forwarded it to others. But the company found the e-mail in Brian's "sent" folder and assumed that he was responsible. Brian was offered a last chance at reinstatement if he admitted guilt, accepted a year's probation, and promised to comply with the policy in the future. Claiming he did no wrong, Brian refused to admit guilt, declined the company offer, and was fired.

The firings shocked the workers, who had been expecting less severe punishment—at best a warning, at worst a suspension. After all, racy pictures and sexist jokes had always been a big part of life at the factory, although they had not been sent by e-mail.

Ken Lumbert, a longtime Dow employee, showed a *Los Angeles Times* reporter thousands of pages of such material that he had collected in binders over the years. "This is what goes on in a factory," Lumbert said. "You can't mold this into a sweet little office complex."

Three of the fired employees made similar statements to the reporter. "It's a human nature thing," Angie said. "We're not perverts. We're all pretty normal."

Tom believed that the punishment did not fit the crime. "It was like a life sentence for a first-time offense," he said.

John said that he would have had no problem complying with company policy if he had known the consequences. "If you want to believe I'm a pornography person or whatever, go ahead," he said. "But my morals have always been good. And I would never have even looked at e-mail if I thought it would have meant my job."

Discussion Questions

1. Using Table 6.1, how would you categorize the type of noncompliance that occurred in this case? From management's perspective? From the workers' perspective?

2. What factors were involved in the employees' failure to comply with the company's harassment policy?

3. In light of the information provided in Chapter 6, discuss the behavior of the employees at Dow and the company's disciplinary action.
   a. Was the employees' behavior deviant and negative? Did it have any constructive functional elements?
   b. Does the punishment the employees received fit their level of noncompliance to policy? Was the punishment fair and equitable? Why or why not?

4. How could the Dow harassment policy have been implemented and enforced more effectively, that is, to ensure increased compliance among the workforce, to reduce sexual harassment, and to reach higher levels of perceived fairness?

Bibliography

Carrns, A. (2000, February 4). Prying times: Those bawdy e-mails were good for a laugh—until the ax fell; The close-knit staff shared jokes but didn't realize the bosses were watching—A special funnies folder. *The Wall Street Journal,* pp. 1, 8. Retrieved December 11, 2003, from http://proquest.umi.com/pqdweb

Dow Chemical to fire workers for violating its policy on e-mail. (2000, August 23). *The Wall Street Journal,* p. B4. Retrieved May 3, 2001, from http://proquest. umi.com/ pqdweb

Miller, G. (2001, January 28). Fired by Big Brother: Fearing sexual harassment lawsuits, Dow Chemical Co. in Michigan fired workers who forwarded lewd e-mail—Could your company do the same? *Los Angeles Times Magazine.* Retrieved December 11, 2003, from www.latimes.com

Olafson, S. (2000, September 14). Dow fires 24 for e-mail abuse, 235 reprimanded at Freeport facility. *Houston Chronicle,* p. A31. Retrieved May 3, 2001, from http://proquest.umi.com/pqdweb

Richards, D. (2000, August 28). Dow disciplines employees for violating e-mail policy. *Chemical Market Reporter,* pp. 7, 41. Retrieved December 11, 2003, from http:// proquest.umi.com/pqdweb

Swanson, S. (2001, August 20). Beware: Employee monitoring is on the rise— Employee privacy gives way to business needs for electronic surveillance. *Information Week,* pp. 57–58.

CHAPTER 7

The Difficulties of Telling the Truth at Work

Steven L. Grover

People lie. We know that they lie because we catch them. After all, if a lie is never caught, how can we know it occurred? People lie for a variety of reasons, and the results vary in their magnitude, ranging from the little white lies that lubricate social discourse to the lies that result in major corporate financial catastrophes.

This chapter explores the landscape populated by liars and, in so doing, pokes into the woods of other unethical behaviors and questions the very existence of a "normal" ethical business life. To help the reader to understand lying, the chapter looks at the psychological literature on how people interact as well as how they express themselves nonverbally. It also examines the specific organizational behavior and business ethics literatures, which together are the landmarks along the honesty and dishonesty parade.

Some of the questions that this chapter seeks to illuminate are as follows:

1. Why do people lie?

2. Do some people lie more than others?

3. How can we tell whether people are lying?

4. What, if anything, can organizations do about lying, either proactively or retroactively?

What Is Meant by "Lying"?

The first step toward understanding truth telling and lying is to define the conceptual domain. One definition of lying is "to speak untruthfully with intent to mislead or deceive" (HarperCollins, 2001), a conceptualization that requires one to *state* the fact and know that it is incorrect so as to qualify as a lie. Following this strict definition of lying disqualifies reports of misinformation, such as gossip, that one believes to be true. Experts on lying, such as Bok (1978) and Ekman (1985), often distinguish between concealment and deception. *Deception* refers to outright lying along the lines of the formal definition just presented. The car salesman who says that a car was driven by an old lady on Sundays, when in fact he bought the car from a teenager, is telling an outright lie and is deceiving. However, the car salesman is engaging in *concealment* when he says, "I'm not sure who exactly drove the car, but it doesn't look like it has had much use. Maybe it has mostly been driven by an old lady."

The distinction might not be that important because concealment and deception are likely to have similar causes, yet some—such as philosopher Immanuel Kant—might argue that concealment is not wrong. What becomes important in this chapter is that the way in which people react to concealment is different from how they react to deception, whether they are the perpetrator or the recipient of the message. This section has given a behavioral definition of lying, yet the term is pejorative and has negative ethical connotations. Therefore, the next section considers some of the moral underpinnings of honesty and dishonesty.

The Morality of Lying

Not all lies are immoral. Some lies, in fact, might be told to help a person or an institution (Bok, 1978). Nurses lie to help patients (Grover, 1993b) by telling them that they are not as sick as they really are. Sometimes lying is the more positive moral choice because the lie might improve the human condition, whereas telling the truth might harm it.

The intent of lies constitutes a moral component (Jones, 1991). Lies meant to harm or take advantage of another person are in a different class from social white lies or lies meant to help someone. Sometimes people do not want others to get certain information in business. Sometimes people do not really need another opinion, so it might be better if that opinion were obfuscated. For example, if a person is making an important sales pitch and asks a colleague immediately beforehand whether he or she thinks their chances are good, it would do no good to give an honest opinion of "No, we don't have a chance." Therefore, it is an important point that not all lies are bad.

On the other hand, we depend on honesty in business transactions, and there are pragmatic consequences to incorrect information. The very essence of an organization is information flowing among people, making the quality and veracity of the information critical (Galbraith, 1973). From an information point of view, if the production manager tells the sales manager that "2,000 pairs of shoes can be delivered by Friday," all kinds of decisions may hinge on that information, making its veracity critical. The sales manager will then make promises to clients, and a financial manager may make projections based on the information. If the information were a lie (e.g., if the production facility had too few workers or too little leather), a pyramid of decisions built on that information would collapse. On a day-to-day basis, then, clear informational honesty and accuracy can be quite important to organizations.

Trust is another reason why truthfulness is important in organizations. Interactions in business rely on trust, and dishonesty hinders trust. In the shoe example just cited, the production manager has a relationship with the sales manager based on some level of trust. If the production manager has a history of being honest and accurate, the sales manager will trust that person and trust the information presented by that person. On the contrary, if the production manager has a history of providing flawed information, the person receiving that information is unlikely to risk putting himself or herself out on a limb as a result of the information. In this example, the reason for the inaccuracy of information is not so critically essential to trust in the information. Whether the misinformation derives from the production manager simply making a lot of mistakes or from being overly optimistic or pessimistic with ambiguous data does not really matter because the result of reduced trust in the information will be the same, illustrating the importance of honesty in organizations.

Why Do People Lie?

One of the primary questions surrounding deception has to do with the motivation to lie. From an armchair philosopher's point of view, any kind of lying is strange behavior because lying is viewed as morally wrong and people find out about lies. Lying presumably affects liars' moral reputations negatively. Hence, maintaining a positive self-image should eschew lying, but people do lie anyway. The reader can probably identify personal experiences with lies, for example, being told something and later finding it not to be true.

Situational Factors

During the 1920s, Hartshorne and May (1928) conducted a series of studies purporting to explore the dishonest personality. Their aim was to identify the type of people who were more prone to lying, cheating, and stealing. The aim of the study perhaps fit along with a mentality at the time that there were "good people" and "undesirables." In a series of studies with adults and children, the researchers hypothesized that people who went to church had solid moral character and would be less likely to engage in the unethical behaviors that were presented to them.

Contrary to their expectations, Hartshorne and May (1928) found that moral behavior was strongly influenced by the situations that people faced. For example, children who were placed in a room with tasty cookies were more likely to steal and eat that food when there was no adult around to catch them in the act. The researchers found individual differences and finally concluded that the situation influenced honesty. Likewise, contemporary studies of lying behavior in organizations have found situational determinants of ethical behavior. People who are placed in certain situations are more likely to lie than are people who are not placed in those situations.

One situational theory of honesty uses role conflict to explain lying (Grover, 1993a). Role theory, sometimes called a dramaturgical approach, explains people's lives as acting out a set of roles (Goffman, 1956). In an organization, for example, the same person might play the role of manager, father, friend, and husband on the same day, and each of these roles has certain expectations attached to it. For example, the role of manager has a fiduciary responsibility attached to it, along with the responsibility to make the hard decisions and perhaps to provide for some forward movement of one's part of the organization.

People have an amazing ability to respond to the demands of a role. Although there may be an imposter syndrome when people begin a new professional role, most people adopt the role's characteristics. For example, a professor, on the first day of teaching, may have some sense of shock when standing in front of the classroom or lecture hall with the expectation that he or she is knowledgeable. However, class begins when the person playing the leading role says class begins, and students—who are also playing roles—respond to the direction set by the teacher. To illustrate the point, in a classroom or lecture hall of hundreds of students, if the person in front says that he or she wants the class to split up with the women sitting on one side and the men sitting on the other, the students are likely to do so with only a little grumbling.

People play multiple roles simultaneously, producing conflicts among the various role expectations. There are a number of different types of role conflict (Grover, 1993a; Rizzo, House, & Lirtzman, 1970). Professional role conflict is the conflict between what the job or the manager on a job expects and what the profession expects people to do. In the practice of medicine, there are prescribed techniques for dealing with certain disease symptoms, but there are conflicting constraints of cost, time, and staffing placed on the institution that translate into demands made on the medical professional. For example, the ideal treatment for someone who has become hypothermic is to flush the person with a warmed intravenous solution. The cost of the machine to provide that warm intravenous solution is quite high, however, and the hospital might want to limit its use, creating a bit of a conflict between providing the patient with ideal treatment and meeting institutional financial obligations.

One way in which people resolve role conflicts is through lying. For example, if you are torn between two lovers, you can tell the truth to one lover and lie to the other. Perhaps you could say "I'm really in love with you" and dash off with one lover while telling the other lover that you have a "mysterious illness and will be leaving the country for treatment." This resolves a conflict. It does not remove the conflict, and it does not address the conflicting situation. However, it does reduce the internal distress that most people experience when they are being torn or drawn in different directions.

One study of professional nurses found that nurses lied as a way of resolving conflict (Grover, 1993b). Nurses lied in their charting when they were asked by physicians or the hospital to do things that went against good nursing practice. They seemed likely to behave according to a well-known nursing standard, ignoring the demands placed on them by the hospital, but then when they reported their behavior in the charts, they forced the charts to correspond with the demands. For example, in that study, nurses fed hungry neonates more baby formula than was prescribed because the babies were hungry, but then the nurses reported that they had fed the babies the prescribed amount in the charts.

People face various types of conflict in their working lives. Sometimes a conflict is as simple as that between being a student and being a part-time employee. Students in one study identified with this conflict and reported that they would lie about their required class attendance if they were expected to be at work at the same time (Grover & Hui, 1994). The role conflict explanation of honesty seems to be quite robust in explaining lying under a variety of circumstances (Grover, 1993a).

Self-interest is another explanation for lying and unethical behavior. Self-interest is central to a host of social science theories; for example, behaviorism and most of neoclassical economics premise themselves on the assumption that humans do things that are favorable to themselves. People repeatedly eat food that tastes good to them and may make decisions of all sorts, including moral ones, that favor themselves. People behave in their own self-interest, and their views of the world are influenced by that self-interest. An egocentric bias creates perceptions of fairness and unfairness to the extent that it benefits the individual self (Greenberg, 1981). For instance, people prefer a tax cut that benefits them and tend to perceive that type of tax cut as more fair than one that does not benefit them. Therefore, people's ethical judgments may be clouded when individuals are directly involved with the action or the result of an ethical action.

The fact that people's ethics are influenced by their self-interest poses difficulties for organizations. For example, many firms use goal setting to manage employee performance, creating situations in which it benefits an employee to accomplish his or her goals. Schweitzer, Ordonez, and Douma (2004) demonstrated that one of the nonperformance effects of setting goals was dishonesty. People lied more about performance when goals were set for them, and this was particularly true for people who fell just short of their goals.

Role conflict and self-interest, moreover, may be viewed as competing theories of why people lie. Grover and Hui (1994) conducted a study in which the two theories were compared to assess the question of whether self-interest or role conflict predicted lying behavior. It is intriguing that the study found support for both theories. Students lied when there was a conflict leading them to lie, as one would expect in support of role conflict theory. Students also lied when there was a benefit from doing so in the form of course credit, as one would expect in support of self-interest theory. Because the two things—role conflict and reward—were manipulated separately, one could compare their individual and combined influences. Of course, the two factors added together, so that people lied the most when there was role conflict and a benefit or reward for lying. However, they also combined as a multiplicative interaction, meaning that the existence of reward and role conflict together helps the two to potentiate each other beyond the level one would expect from simply adding the two effects.

The practical implication of the finding is support for the notion that people do not lie every time it benefits them to do so. There must first be some *opportunity,* which probably means a situation in which one is not likely to be caught lying. Second, there should be some benefit to lying. Perhaps it is only in fiction that people make up fanciful tales for absolutely no ends or purposes. Third, there is probably some impetus found in the situation, such as role conflict, that pushes a person to tell a lie. Situations present people with difficulties that appear to have no obvious alternative resolutions.

Individual Differences

Opportunity, benefit, and conflict are characteristics of situations that engender lying. However, not everyone lies when he or she has the opportunity, something to gain, or a difficult dilemma. Individual difference factors relate to lying propensity.

Moral maturity is an individual difference that might account for why some people lie and others do not. One of the dominant ways in which to assess moral development is based on Kohlberg's (1969) theory of cognitive moral development. In contrast to other theories of emotional or spiritual moral development, Kohlberg's theory is based on models of cognitive development, tracing changes in the ways in which people think as they mature. Kohlberg's theory identifies three sequential levels of moral development: preconventional, conventional, and principled. Most adults operate at the conventional or principled level. Moral development theory does not provide behavioral prediction; rather, it predicts the cognitive basis for decisions. Conventional-level moral thinkers, who compose the bulk of the workforce, are strongly influenced and guided by the dictates of situations in which they find themselves. In contrast, principled-level moral thinkers evaluate situations, the reasons for rules, and how and why those rules were developed before making moral decisions and taking actions. For example, people who work on loading docks that have informal cultures encouraging theft evaluate the reasons for the antitheft rules, determine who theft harms, and then decide whether to support or violate the rules. At the very highest level, principled people adopt a self-chosen set of universal ethical principles.

A couple of studies of workplace lying have investigated the interaction between situation and moral development. Grover (1993b) found that nurses at the principled level were less influenced by the role conflict situation than were nurses at the conventional level. That study did not find a main effect for moral development; that is, people did not lie any more or any less as a function of their moral development scores. Rather, conventional-level nurses were much more influenced by the role conflict situation, whereas the existence of a role conflict made no difference to principled nurses. This result was conceivably due to principled nurses' greater ability to cope with moral ambiguity. Principled nurses may take a principled position on their nursing care drawing on a universal set of, in this case, nursing principles. Pragmatically, there are many different ways in which to resolve role conflict, and lying is just one of them. More principled nurses could change the situation and follow their professional obligation by confronting the boss or physician issuing the order to get that order changed in the patient's interest.

Principled people often may be less influenced by situations in their lying behavior. Most people find themselves at the conventional level of moral development, follow the established procedures or rules, and are comfortable with the status quo. Although people may lie to benefit themselves, they most likely follow the patterns of others before them. Sometimes it is easier for people to lie their way out of sticky situations. The problem, of course, is that lies can take on lives of their own. A person who lies must continually create stories that fit the lie until he or she finally gets caught, gives up, or lets the storyline die.

Another individual difference that affects lying behavior is Machiavellianism. This personality characteristic, or (more appropriately) individual difference, is loosely based on Machiavelli's Renaissance prescriptions to the prince on how to lead (Christie & Geis, 1970). Those instructions advocated being a kindly despot but being despotic nonetheless. The personality measure that borrows the name from Machiavelli takes the flavor of a focus on the end result as opposed to the means to that end. In terms of lying research, people who are highly Machiavellian are more likely to lie to accomplish some goal. In a study of sales representatives, more Machiavellian sales representatives were more likely to lie concerning an internal company rule than were their less Machiavellian counterparts (Grover & Enz, 2004). Although highly Machiavellian people lied more in general and across conditions, people who were lower in this trait were influenced by whether there was a formal rule against the particular lie.

Does Everyone Lie?

So far, this chapter has noted how situations such as role conflict influence lying and that some people react more strongly to these situations than do other people. However, there are situations in which nearly everyone lies. It might be useful to consider these situations. People may lie immediately and without thinking when they are caught doing something they should not be doing, even if the infraction is quite minor. For example, imagine that a coworker sees you reading something that is off-limits to you but that is not particularly secret. You react in a guilty manner and make up an excuse that you were looking for some document on the coworker's desk when in fact you had simply been distracted by the color of the report that you are not supposed to be reading. There are probably a host of situations that would lead a majority of people toward dishonesty. The remainder of this section focuses on negotiation situations.

Negotiations are rife with deceit. The distributive negotiation, or one over the distribution of money or other resources, seems to conjure a competitive schema. In some cultures, the other party is commonly characterized and labeled as the opponent or enemy. Moreover, a competitive spirit underscores the social exchange process of negotiation. Empirical studies have represented this competitive and potentially dishonest orientation of the negotiation, finding that the competitive versus cooperative spirit surrounding the negotiation has an impact on honesty. The negotiation arena has received substantial research attention, and part of that research touches on issues of honesty. The general findings that are described in what follows are that people will lie freely in the competitive situation—and even more so when they are confronted directly—but will lie much less when they trust the other party and have an extended relationship.

In a series of studies, Aquino and colleagues (Aquino, 1998; Aquino & Becker, 2002; Grover & Aquino, 1999) documented that people will deceive in a distributive negotiation, finding that approximately 70% of M.B.A. students lied during a negotiation exercise. In those studies, participants were explicitly asked about "the length of the contract," and the liars misrepresented the contract duration as something exceeding 3 years when in fact they knew it to be just 3 years. Participants said that the price offered depended on the payoff period. The strength of demands created by the negotiation situation is amazing given that, in classroom and laboratory situations, people lied with very little personal benefit. The only tangible benefit to lying was the possibility of getting a small cash incentive for arriving at the best price, but this incentive was paid only to one member of the class or to a large experiment group on a random basis. It seems startling that people would risk suffering the potential loss of reputation and esteem for nearly no tangible gain. Therefore, one conclusion is that the negotiation situation in the United States brings on a competitive spirit that is strong and leads to dishonesty.

Although it might seem as though a person should be able to gain honesty by confronting people directly, the results of empirical studies indicate that this does not seem to be the case. People lie to an even greater extent when they are asked direct questions. In the negotiation studies just discussed, people lied when they were asked directly about the length of the contract. Another study found that asking people questions curtailed lies of omission but actually increased lies of commission (Schweitzer & Croson, 1999). The apparent reason for this finding is that lies of omission are passive and can be quietly "swept under the table"; people can pretend to have agreement on a certain set of facts that have not been completely spelled out and can be quite happy with one another. When a person starts to spell out those facts completely, however, the person is faced with having to tell a complete lie. By that point, the person might have escalated his or her own commitment to "winning" the negotiation and, therefore, committing to the lie. Part of these negotiation studies is their "one-off" or single interaction nature in which people demonstrate little commitment to a long-term relationship. People are more interested in honesty when a long-term relationship is expected, perhaps because they can be hurt by their own lies in the future.

Boles, Croson, and Murnighan (2000) found that in repeated interaction bargaining, deception bred ill will even to a degree beyond economic benefit. When people had been lied to during an earlier round, they subsequently gave the liars a worse deal, even if doing so meant not achieving an agreement. The authors explained this psychological and emotional outcome as a certain irrationality that pervades the emotional business of negotiating. However, people were much more honest when they believed that there would be repeated rounds of the experiment. The practical application to real-life situations is clear: In repeated interactions, people tend to treat each other with trust and honesty. Moreover, doing business with the same party repeatedly over time breeds trust (Mayer, Davis, & Schoorman, 1995). Because the other party has performed well and done what it said it would do, the same performance is expected in the future. People are less likely to deceive a trusted party because doing so would harm the relationship at a greater cost than in one-off interactions.

Consequences of Lying

Given that lying is commonplace in the negotiation situation, it seems reasonable to consider the consequences of having lied for the liar. Because lying is generally socially unacceptable and violates trust, people need to find means of justifying their actions. Cognitive dissonance helps to interpret this with the notion that people have difficulty in holding conflicting thoughts at the same time; therefore, liars need to provide some kind of neutralization or justification for their lies to neutralize the effects of the lies on their self-concepts. Aquino and Becker (2002) found that people who had lied in the purchasing agent negotiation study altered their perceptions of the other party; that is, liars in the negotiation rated the abilities of their opponents consistently lower than did people who had not lied.

It is largely speculative to go beyond the claim that people will neutralize their behavior by rationalizing the behavior as positive. It also seems reasonable that people will try to cover up their lies. Lies lead to more lies because people have a need to appear to be consistent. Within a company, lies are likely to escalate. If people are not honest with one another, and the lies lead to more lies, one would expect the general level of dishonesty in the company to escalate as well. Clearly, an organization with an extremely high level of dishonesty might have difficulty in functioning. The information flowing around the organization is flawed; therefore, the very organization, which could be conceptualized as nothing more than sets of information (Galbraith, 1973), may cease to exist.

Trust and mistrust flow from honesty and dishonesty. Trust is defined as making oneself vulnerable to another person or party (Rousseau, Sitkin, Burt, & Camerer, 1998). Any relationship between people can be described in terms of the level of trust between the individuals. Trust is extremely important in many of life's circumstances that require one person to make himself or herself vulnerable to another (Mayer et al., 1995). For instance, undergoing dental surgery requires the patient to have a certain level of trust in the surgeon because the patient must open his or her mouth and remain still for the procedure to begin. If the patient has no base level of trust in the surgeon—or, even worse, mistrusts the surgeon—the procedure is unlikely to occur because most people are unlikely to go to a dentist who they do not trust.

Trust results from a relationship built over time and repeated interactions. Relationships that have a long history of successful and honest interactions hold a higher level of trust. For example, when you engage a contractor to do a job for you, and then the contractor performs the activity according to the contract for the agreed-on price, you are likely to trust that contractor and continue the relationship. In repeated interactions, this trust would grow until it is somehow betrayed. Intentional deception is a way of betraying trust.

We learn from the negotiation context that lying betrays trust, and we know from other literature that trust is very difficult to rebuild once an intentional betrayal has occurred (Bottom, Gibson, Daniels, & Murnighan, 2002). People generally avoid relationships in which trust has been violated, and they tread very carefully when they must continue to interact with mistrusted people. In the organizational context, continuous relationships are quite important. If organizations are merely sets of relationships (some formal and some informal), honesty in the organization will influence the strength of at least some of those relationships and lying will deteriorate these bonds. So, it seems obvious in reality that honesty is important to successful organizational functioning.

What Can Organizations Do About Honesty?

This leads to the question of what companies should or can do about honesty. If we assume that honesty should be encouraged for the good of the organization or its very existence, what can be done to create honesty? One of the first knee-jerk reactions should be to encourage honesty. Intuitively, it seems that organizational culture should affect honesty. However, the empirical studies do not seem to capture this effect. In a laboratory study of sales agents, culture was manipulated so that a person worked in either an honest culture or a dishonest culture. In addition, the existence of formal rules pertaining to the issue over which one might lie was manipulated (Grover & Enz, 2004). In that study, personality proved to be a better predictor of lying behavior than did culture, with the highly Machiavellian individuals being more likely to lie across conditions. There was also a personality-by-situation interaction in which people with a low tolerance for ambiguity looked toward the formal rules to guide their behavior when the culture told them to behave honestly.

Developing a so-called honest culture might do nothing more than drive lying beneath the surface of the organization. Manipulating culture in a negotiation study found that in the honest culture condition, people lied about lying (Grover & Aquino, 1999). The culture had no effect on the occurrence of lying about the price or length of a contract in the negotiation; instead, it affected how people reported to the experimenter at the end of the study. After the negotiation, when participants completed a postexperiment questionnaire, liars in the honest culture condition lied about having lied significantly more often than did liars in the neutral culture condition. Presumably, those people felt some sort of guilt that they needed to assuage in the honest climate by presenting themselves as honest folks, possibly a neutralization strategy.

Impression Management

A large and growing literature employing the term "impression management" uses the metaphor to suggest that actors in organizations actively and usefully manage, or create, images of themselves. This literature identifies a number of behaviors intended to affect how others perceive a person without really affecting how the person does his or her job. These behaviors include self-promotion and ingratiating oneself to the boss and others.

Various kinds of self-promotion, such as talking about oneself and one's accomplishments (Kacmar, Carlson, & Bratton, 2004), might seem a bit unseemly to the naive observer. However, reputation in most complex occupations is difficult to assess based on actual performance or ability; therefore, people rely on these impressions. People who do a job well or just satisfactorily are difficult to differentiate from people who are excellent at the job. Impression management generally works to bolster one's reputation and advancement in the company. A host of research suggests that people have more positive attitudes toward people who use impression management techniques (Harrell-Cook, Ferris, & Dulebohn, 1999; Turnley & Bolino, 2001).

When does impression management cross a boundary and become deceptive? We see and hear about this happening in the news. There are numerous examples of people in the public domain who have attempted to enhance their reputations with embellished credentials. Ronald Zarrrella, chief executive officer of Bausch & Lomb, claimed a nonexistent M.B.A. on his résumé (Wayne, 2002), and Lena Guerrero resigned from the Texas Railroad Commission when her faked educational credentials were discovered ("Texas Official Resigns," 1992; see also Cases 7.1 and 7.2).

In most cases, however, the distinction is not so clear. One woman who had just started her first sales job lasted only 2 weeks because she believed that she had to lie to the customers. She commented to the author, "The salespeople who were most successful made outright lies on a frequent basis and then were successful and earned the highest commission incentives." On the other hand, a marketing department employee recently referred to similar behavior as "knowing your customer and presenting information salient to that customer." When people play the politics of an organization, when they jockey for position, and when they use information to their advantage, it might not always be totally "honest."

Most political players recognize that there are various shades of honesty in their normal behavior. For example, they may fail to give one person information, they may portray another situation as positive when in fact it is not so, and they generally present information strategically so as to make themselves look good (Judge & Bretz, 1994; Kacmar et al., 2004). People usually are not aware of the truthfulness of these behaviors unless they step back and observe themselves from a distance. In the heat of daily organizational life, people do not abstractly think, "Oh, is this a totally honest way of presenting this information to this particular group of people?" People continuously balance the different roles and responsibilities they encounter on a daily basis. One person's lying might be another person's impression management.

Is Lying Natural?

Some level of dishonesty is perhaps endemic to organizational life and not particularly to contemporary organizational life. Charles Dickens's 19th-century business characters, for example, were not depicted as upstanding pillars of the community. Lying could be conceptualized as a consequence of success in organizational life. Put differently, the construction of a contemporary organization might engender dishonesty.

Organizations are inherently political (Pfeffer, 1992). Difficult decisions need to be made using ambiguous information at best. Choosing people to do jobs, moreover, is fraught with ambiguity, and the candidates who present themselves in the most positive light to the decision makers are likely to be successful. Perhaps that presentation of self is political, perhaps it is impression management, or perhaps it is lying (or perhaps only in the worst cases it is lying). But whatever one calls it, success in organizations is *partly* due to the manner in which people present themselves, engendering the potential for dishonesty and success to work together, meshing like a cog and chain. The system then becomes self-perpetuating in that the people who have risen to powerful positions will be making decisions with ambiguous information and might value the same behaviors that worked for them.

Whereas this portrayal of organizational life might seem cynical, it is important to consider how the organization works as a system to encourage or discourage honesty. It is too easy for pundits to claim that they want honesty in organizations when the entire system may perpetuate and inadvertently reward some level of dishonesty dressed up as impression management.

People of a certain type get hired and promoted, and individuals will, in a self-interested fashion, make themselves appear to be hirable or promotable; in other words, they will manage their impressions. All people do it when they write their résumés. People place on their résumés things that make them look good. If sales at the store they managed increased 20% in 1 year, they write that down on their résumés. It makes them look like performers. In American culture, this positive self-presentation is highly accepted. Americans expect people to speak for themselves and to demonstrate their accomplishments.

Cultures vary widely on this dimension. In more collectivistic cultures, for example, standing out might not be seen as a good thing and being part of a group might be seen as a positive. New Zealand has a culture in which the so-called "tall poppies" get mowed down; not only is presenting oneself as superior not encouraged, it is faced with a vindictive wrath. In yet another subculture, the native New Zealand Maori culture holds a dim view of speaking for oneself. It is seen as very bad form to speak highly or positively about oneself. It is believed that if a person has positive characteristics, other people who know the person well will speak of those qualities on his or her behalf.

So, how does impression management relate to lying? In the example, a store manager noted that the store's sales increased 20%. Maybe that was due to increased traffic based on the four new stores that opened nearby, or maybe it was paired with a 5% drop in profit from discounting. A person might not mention these things on a résumé, and this is a concealment type of dishonesty.

How Much Honesty Do We Want?

Now, there is a dilemma. It seems that the obvious answer is that we want a lot of honesty all the time. However, we know from a couple of studies that creating honest environments or cultures actually drives dishonesty beneath the surface (e.g., Grover & Aquino, 1999). Moreover, one way of being dishonest is for an employee to lie to a customer and then tell coworkers how and why he or she did it. It is quite another matter for an employee to work in the total honest culture situation and lie to a customer for the exact same reasons and then be held to a standard so strong that the employee cannot reveal that he or she has engaged in this perhaps harmless and justifiable lie. One can imagine that it is potentially psychologically harmful to the individual to have these indiscretions bottled up inside with no outlet to express them.

Internal harm aside, the question for managers is how much they really want honesty. Honesty/Dishonesty is a multilayered phenomenon with few easy answers. Most people and organizations benefit from understanding that there are reasons for lies. We can understand why people might lie and can help them to cope with those lies. It also allows managers to remove the barriers to honesty and the precursors to lying. We can attempt to create situations in which people do not feel torn apart by diverging allegiances.

For example, one should be able to behave in a professional manner without violating the rules, norms, or expectations of the company. Managers and leaders will benefit from aligning their expectations so that they get honest answers and reports from the people with whom they interact. Moreover, managers need to model that same honesty, which is called leader integrity. Whereas leader integrity appears in the literature over and over, it still has received insufficient attention. It is clear that people expect their leaders to behave honestly and ethically (Kouzes & Posner, 2002) and that transformational leader behaviors are associated with a sense of integrity (Parry & Proctor-Thomas, 2002). Further research is needed to discern the elements of honesty that affect leadership perceptions and effectiveness. However, at this point, we can say with some certainty that people will at least be perceived as better leaders if they promote the perception that they are honest.

Asking people to be honest leaders, however, might be a bit overly simplistic. Leaders need to conceal things under certain circumstances. They cannot be perfectly honest all of the time, making this a multilayered issue. At the core of leadership integrity might lie the ethical sensibility with which people behave. The intentions of leaders or of other people in the organization may be as important as their actual behavior. If one focuses on lying, the actual lie is seen as a really bad thing only in virtue ethics and Kantian ethics. Most philosophers recognize that there are times when lying is the best thing to do (Bok, 1978) or when the leader had no choice other than to lie. The intent of the leader in these cases, however, is extremely important. Did the leader intentionally lie to staff members so as to deceive and take advantage of them, or did the leader lie to staff members so as to resolve some other situation? The area of leader integrity is open to future research, but at this point it seems reasonable to say that people want their leaders to be honest and consistent, even though this might not always be possible.

Detecting Lies

One of the interesting paradoxes concerning lying is how and when people can tell that others are lying to them. Some nonverbal cues are clearly linked to lying, but they are not the cues that most people would associate with lies. Most people believe that certain symbols, such as swaying from side to side, having shifty eyes, and stammering, indicate that people are lying. However, these cues are more clearly associated with anxiety, creating a false correlation with lying. Many people are clearly nervous when they are telling lies, especially when they are lying to an authority source such as a judge or a police officer.

Nonverbal behavior researchers have identified other cues associated with lying. Pupil constriction is one of the most profound and consistent nonverbal cues associated with lying. Pupil control is an autonomic response, with a person's pupils dilating in the dark and on attraction to another person. When people are exposed to identical photographs that contain different-sized pupils, the photographs with the larger pupils are consistently rated as more attractive. Likewise, when viewing photographs rated as attractive, raters' own pupils dilate. In contrast, pupils consistently constrict when people are lying (DePaulo, Stone, & Lassiter, 1985).

The fact that people's pupils consistently constrict when they lie is not entirely useful. Even armed with this knowledge, it is difficult to see a person's pupils. One must be physically very close to the person to see the pupils, and even then, one must focus on the pupils, and this is not what most people focus on while engaged in conversations. Even trained interrogators and police officers, who believe that they can tell when someone is lying, cannot consistently separate liars from truth tellers. In one study, interrogators identified liars at no better than a chance level (Vrij, 1993). The message for managers and students of organizations, then, is that people will lie, but we can have little confidence in our ability to tell when they are lying to us. Therefore, the reasons why people lie and the more macroorganizational issues that influence honesty become important as the tools available to promote honesty.

Conclusion

Lying is the status quo, and we should reasonably expect that it will remain so. As students and participants of organizations, we are better off attempting to understand dishonesty than attempting to eradicate it. Understanding dishonesty should provide the realization that other people succumb to the temptations caused by conflicting expectations and benefits or rewards. Closer examination of dishonesty demonstrates that it violates trust and leads to even more dishonesty. Understanding the antecedents and consequences of lying, moreover, should allow the reader to influence situations so as to reduce lying and its impact.

References

Aquino, K. (1998). The effects of ethical climate and the availability of alternatives on the use of deception during negotiation. *International Journal of Conflict Management, 9,* 195–217.

Aquino, K., & Becker, T. E. (2002, August). *How individual and situational factors influence the use of neutralization strategies in the aftermath of lying.* Paper presented at the meeting of the Academy of Management, Denver, CO.

Bok, S. (1978). *Lying: Moral choice in public and private life.* New York: Random House.

Boles, T. L., Croson, R. T. A., & Murnighan, J. K. (2000). Deception and retribution in repeated ultimatum bargaining. *Organizational Behavior and Human Decision Processes, 83,* 235–259.

Bottom, W. P., Gibson, K., Daniels, S. E., & Murnighan, J. K. (2002). When talk is not cheap: Substantive penance and expressions of intent in rebuilding cooperation. *Organization Science, 13,* 497–513.

Christie, R., & Geis, F. L. (1970). *Studies in Machiavellianism.* New York: Academic Press.

DePaulo, B. M., Stone, J. I., & Lassiter, G. D. (1985). Deceiving and detecting deceit. In B. R. Schlenker (Ed.), *The self and social life* (pp. 323–370). New York: McGraw–Hill.

Ekman, P. (1985). *Telling lies: Clues to deceit in the marketplace, politics, and marriage.* New York: Norton.

Galbraith, J. R. (1973). *Designing complex organizations.* Reading, MA: Addison–Wesley.

Goffman, E. (1956). *The presentation of self in everyday life.* Edinburgh, UK: University of Edinburgh.

Greenberg, J. (1981). The justice of distributing scarce and abundant resources. In M. J. Lerner & L. L. Lerner (Eds.), *The justice motive in social behavior* (pp. 289–316). New York: Plenum.

Grover, S. L. (1993a). Lying, deceit, and subterfuge: A model of dishonesty in the workplace. *Organization Science, 4,* 478–495.

Grover, S. L. (1993b). Why professionals lie: The impact of professional role conflict on reporting accuracy. *Organizational Behavior and Human Decision Processes, 55,* 251–272.

Grover, S. L., & Aquino, K. (1999, June). *When people lie in organizations: The psychological and behavior consequences of lying in dyadic negotiations.* Paper presented at the meeting of the International Association of Conflict Management, San Sebastián-Donostia, Spain.

Grover, S. L., & Enz, C. A. (2004). *How do the rules of the company, the company's culture, and individual personal characteristics influence how much people lie or tell the truth?* Unpublished manuscript, University of Otago, Dunedin, New Zealand.

Grover, S. L., & Hui, C. (1994). The influence of role conflict and self-interest on lying in organizations. *Journal of Business Ethics, 13,* 295–303.

HarperCollins. (2001). *Collins' concise dictionary.* New York: Author.

Harrell-Cook, G., Ferris, G. R., & Dulebohn, J. H. (1999). Political behaviors as moderators of the perceptions of organizational politics–work outcomes relationships. *Journal of Organizational Behavior, 20,* 1093–1105.

Hartshorne, H., & May, M. A. (1928). *Studies in the nature of character.* New York: Macmillan.

Jones, T. M. (1991). Ethical decision making by individuals in organizations: An issue-contingent model. *Academy of Management Review, 16,* 366–395.

Judge, T. A., & Bretz, R. D., Jr. (1994). Political influence behavior and career success. *Journal of Management, 20*(1), 43–66.

Kacmar, K. M., Carlson, D. S., & Bratton, V. K. (2004). Situational and dispositional factors as antecedents of ingratiatory behaviors in organizational settings. *Journal of Vocational Behavior, 65,* 309–331.

Kohlberg, L. (1969). Stage and sequence: The cognitive–developmental approach to socialization. In D. A. Goslin (Ed.), *Handbook of socialization research* (pp. 347–480). Chicago: Rand McNally.

Kouzes, J. M., & Posner, B. Z. (2002). *The leadership challenge* (3rd ed.). San Francisco: Jossey–Bass.

Mayer, R. C., Davis, J. H., & Schoorman, F. D. (1995). An integrative model of organizational trust. *Academy of Management Review, 20,* 709–734.

Parry, K. W., & Proctor-Thomas, S. B. (2002). Perceived integrity of transformational leaders in organizational settings. *Journal of Business Ethics, 35*(2), 75–96.

Pfeffer, J. (1992). *Managing with power.* Boston: Harvard Business School Press.

Rizzo, J. R., House, R. J., & Lirtzman, S. I. (1970). Role conflict and ambiguity in complex organizations. *Administrative Science Quarterly, 15,* 150–163.

Rousseau, D., Sitkin, S. B., Burt, R. S., & Camerer, C. (1998). Not so different after all: A cross-discipline view of trust. *Academy of Management Review, 23,* 393–404.

Schweitzer, M. E., & Croson, R. T. A. (1999). Curtailing deception: The impact of direct questions on lies and omissions. *International Journal of Conflict Management, 10,* 225–248.

Schweitzer, M., Ordonez, L., & Douma, B. (2004). Goal setting as a motivator of unethical behavior. *Academy of Management Journal, 47,* 422–432.

Texas official resigns over falsified résumé. (1992, September 26). *The New York Times,* p. A5.

Turnley, W. H., & Bolino, M. C. (2001). Achieving desired images while avoiding undesired images: Exploring the role of self-monitoring in impression management. *Journal of Applied Psychology, 86,* 351–360.

Vrij, A. (1993). Credibility judgments of detectives: The impact of nonverbal behavior, social skills, and physical characteristics on impression formation. *Journal of Social Psychology, 133,* 601–610.

Wayne, L. (2002, October 19). Bausch & Lomb executive admits to falsified résumé. *The New York Times,* p. C2.

George O'Leary's Résumé

T he University of Notre Dame's winning football tradition dates back to Coach Knute Rockne and the renowned "Four Horsemen" during the first part of the 20th century. Notre Dame's sports website touts the school's football success, which includes eight National Collegiate Athletic Association (NCAA) football championships since the Associated Press established the award in 1936. Legendary coaches Frank Leahy, Ara Parseghian, Dan Devine, and Lou Holtz guided Notre Dame to NCAA national championships. The job of Notre Dame head coach, although filled with pressure to produce winning teams every year, is one of the most coveted positions in any sport.

"I believe there are two great coaching jobs in all of sports, one being the manager of the New York Yankees and the other being the head football coach of Notre Dame," George O'Leary told a cheering campus crowd after being named coach on December 9, 2001. Before picking O'Leary to return Notre Dame to its championship tradition, the school's athletic director, Kevin White, and his associates interviewed 50 people who were sure that O'Leary's honesty, character, and ability were excellent.

Born on August 17, 1946, O'Leary, the grandson of Irish immigrants, began putting together his coaching résumé 22 years later at his high school alma mater in Central Islip, New York. From 1968 to 1974, he was an assistant at Central Islip, becoming head coach in 1975. He moved on to head coach at

AUTHOR'S NOTE: This case was prepared by Roland Kidwell (Niagara University) as the basis for classroom discussion. It was developed from accounts listed in the bibliography at the end of the case. All names of individuals and organizations are real. A version of this case is included in Kidwell, R. E., Jr. (2004). "Small" lies, big trouble: The unfortunate consequences of résumé padding, from Janet Cooke to George O'Leary. *Journal of Business Ethics, 51,* 175–184.

another New York high school, Liverpool, where his teams posted a 37-8-1 record in five seasons. "Your dedication, ethics, and loyalty are recognized by everyone," the high school's executive principal, David Kidd, wrote in a letter to O'Leary.

After his success at Liverpool, O'Leary jumped to the college ranks at Syracuse University. At Syracuse, the résumé problems that eventually would cost him his dream job began. On a personal information form, in attempting to emulate achievements of fellow assistants, he falsely identified himself as a 3-year letter winner in football at the University of New Hampshire, where he had graduated in 1968. On a personal data sheet, he added 17 graduate credits to the 31 he had already obtained.

O'Leary's coaching stint at Syracuse was a major success, and he eventually became assistant head coach. From there, O'Leary was hired as defensive coordinator at another university, Georgia Tech. He went on to coach defense for the San Diego Chargers in the National Football League (NFL) and was named head coach of Georgia Tech in 1994. None of the schools or individuals who hired him after his Syracuse job asked to see his résumé. However, when Georgia Tech's sports information department interviewed O'Leary in 1987, he added a master's degree from New York University to his list of accomplishments. The false master's degree showed up in both the Georgia Tech media guide and, eventually, in the Notre Dame press release announcing his appointment as head coach.

O'Leary's teams continued to accomplish on the field. As an assistant at Georgia Tech, O'Leary coached the Yellow Jackets to a share of the NCAA championship. When he was an NFL assistant in San Diego, the Chargers went to a Super Bowl. After he returned to Atlanta as Georgia Tech's head coach, his teams went to several bowl games and he was named conference coach of the year twice and national coach of the year once. Even after these successes, he made no effort to correct the false information about his college letters and his master's degree from the school's publicity material.

"Ah, the guys in the sports information department at Syracuse told me to make it look good," he reportedly told his wife, who had noticed the inaccurate information about his college playing career. "I don't know how it got in there. I gotta get it out," he said to his parents, according to a *Sports Illustrated* account. The dubious biographical form seemed to conflict with O'Leary's reputation as a religious man, a Roman Catholic of such modesty that he kept his coaching awards hidden from view until his secretary at Georgia Tech displayed them.

As the 2001 season came to an end, Notre Dame fired its previous coach, who had failed to bring the team to contention for a national title. Within days, the athletic director called O'Leary with a job offer. Notre Dame wanted him to be the school's new head coach. It was a dream come true for O'Leary.

Notre Dame fans celebrated O'Leary's arrival on the South Bend, Indiana, campus by wearing "By George, It's O'Leary" T-shirts. In a public welcoming ceremony at the school arena, the university president called O'Leary a man of integrity. White, the athletic director, described his choice for the job as a winner who could restore the program to national championship caliber.

The résumé problems quickly surfaced when a sports reporter for a New Hampshire newspaper began working on a story about how a former New Hampshire football player had made good by attaining the head coaching position at Notre Dame. Unfortunately, when the reporter interviewed several former New Hampshire players, he found that they could not remember O'Leary, whose name did not even appear in old football game programs.

After only 2 days on the job, O'Leary faced questions about his past that had been directed toward Notre Dame officials by the media. They asked why O'Leary's biographical information stated that he had three football letters from New Hampshire when it was revealed in a newspaper article that he had never played there. They asked why a newspaper reporter had a document—the personal information form from Syracuse—indicating that O'Leary himself had provided the inaccurate information. They asked whether there were any other falsities among his stated achievements.

O'Leary almost immediately offered to resign as his résumé embellishments and related questions continued to surface. After first refusing to accept his resignation, Notre Dame officials subsequently agreed. A school that is as concerned about its academic reputation as it is about its football success could not have a head coach who was associated with any academic fraud. O'Leary and the university he loved parted company, and he made a statement of regret only 5 days after the public celebration had welcomed him to the campus.

In a resignation statement reprinted on the *South Bend Tribune* website, O'Leary said,

> Many years ago, as a young married father, I sought to pursue my dream as a football coach. In seeking employment, I prepared a résumé that contained inaccuracies regarding my completion of course work for a master's degree and also my level of participation in football at my alma mater. These misstatements were never stricken from my résumé or biographical sketch in later years. . . . I regret that I did not call these facts to the attention of the university during their search. It now seems, therefore, that in keeping with my philosophy of personal accountability for these errors, I resign my position and deeply apologize for any disappointment I have caused the university, my family, and many friends.

Within days, White took full responsibility for dropping the ball in O'Leary's hiring. "It has been the most challenging, difficult time [not in] my professional career, but in my life," he said on his radio show. "I feel very responsible for not making this thing work better, and that's all on me."

Before hiring O'Leary, Notre Dame had agreed to pay $1.5 million to buy out his contract at Georgia Tech. After the coach resigned, this agreement became void, leaving O'Leary to negotiate the buyout clause with his old school. Although Notre Dame did not have to buy out the expensive contract, the school suffered adverse publicity across the nation due to the O'Leary fiasco. Within a few weeks, however, Notre Dame hired Stanford University's Tyrone Willingham as its head football coach. Willingham became the first black head football coach in the history of Notre Dame, and his teams' successes in subsequent seasons led the faithful to quickly forget what might have been.

When O'Leary was named to the Notre Dame post, nine Georgia Tech assistants were left uncertain about their futures in coaching. Several of them had planned to follow O'Leary to Notre Dame, but that bubble burst with O'Leary's resignation. However, within 6 months, all nine assistants had found jobs, some of them in better positions than they had at Georgia Tech.

O'Leary also did not stay unemployed for long. He was hired within a few weeks as defensive line coach and assistant head coach of the NFL's Minnesota Vikings. His biography on the Vikings website did not mention college football letters, a master's degree, or his 5 days as Notre Dame head coach. The introduction read,

> George O'Leary comes to the Minnesota Vikings after a very successful tenure as the head coach at Georgia Tech. O'Leary will coach the defensive line and also is the assistant head coach. A native of Central Islip, N.Y., he was Vikings' head coach Mike Tice's high school football coach at Central Islip High.

In December 2003, O'Leary returned to the college ranks when he was hired as the head football coach at Central Florida University.

Discussion Questions

1. Based on the information included in this case and in Chapter 7, did George O'Leary lie or were his actions an example of impression management? Explain your answer.

2. Evaluate the reasons for O'Leary's actions regarding the false information that appeared on his résumé. Were his actions based on self-interest or role conflict? Explain.

3. Should O'Leary have resigned his head coaching position at Notre Dame? Was this too harsh a price for him to pay for his actions? Why or why not?

4. Discuss the ethical behavior of O'Leary. If he had corrected the mistakes in his biography while he was head coach at Georgia Tech, would such actions have made him more ethical? Why or why not?

5. Are the colleges and universities where O'Leary worked at least partially responsible for what happened to him? Explain your answer.

Bibliography

Haugh, D. (2001, December 15). O'Leary resigns: "Breach of trust," "puff piece" unearths bio inaccuracies. *www.southbendtribune.com.* Retrieved May 15, 2002, from http://proquest.umi.com/pqdweb

Hollis, J. (2002, July 21). All O'Leary's ex-assistants in good jobs. *Atlanta Journal–Constitution,* p. D9. Retrieved July 30, 2002, from http://proquest.umi.com/pqdweb

Moran, M. (2001, December 17). Irish AD feels "very responsible" in O'Leary case. *USA Today,* p. C4. Retrieved May 15, 2002, from http://proquest.umi.com/pqdweb

O'Leary's resignation statement. (2001, December 15). *www.southbendtribune.com.* Retrieved May 15, 2002, from http://proquest.umi.com/pqdweb

Smith, G. (2002, April 8). Lying in wait. *Sports Illustrated,* pp. 70–87.

Wong, E. (2001, December 10). O'Leary accepts task of reviving Notre Dame. *The New York Times,* p. 8. Retrieved May 15, 2002, from http://proquest.umi.com/pqdweb

Wong, E. (2002, January 1). Notre Dame names Willingham. *The New York Times,* p. D1. Retrieved May 15, 2002, from http://proquest.umi.com/pqdweb

Janet Cooke and the *Washington Post*

T he *Washington Post* was founded in 1877, but its reputation as an outstanding newspaper with significant editorial and political power in the U.S. capital and the world was solidified nearly 100 years later. During the early 1970s, the *Post*'s Watergate scandal stories, which many credit for precipitating the resignation of President Richard Nixon, earned it a reputation as a journalistic watchdog of the national government. Robert Woodward and Carl Bernstein, the reporters who broke the Watergate stories, and the newspaper's editor, Ben Bradlee, became international celebrities due to their work. The *Post* was awarded journalism's highest honor, a Pulitzer Prize, for its Watergate stories, 1 of 18 Pulitzers won by the newspaper or its staff members while Bradlee served as editor.

During Bradlee's editorship, "creative tension" came into being at the *Post*. "It pitted reporter against reporter, editor against editor, in a daily contest in which the prize was space on the front page. . . . Those who found the pace overwhelming were made to feel unwelcome," wrote Tom Kelly, author of a book about the newspaper. The *Post* publisher's biographer said that Bradlee set a tone that promoted the "holy s—" story, so named because readers could be expected to utter those words when seeing such a story in print. The pressure to produce resulted in outstanding journalism—and sometimes fiction—appearing in the *Post*'s pages.

AUTHOR'S NOTE: This case was prepared by Roland Kidwell (Niagara University) as the basis for classroom discussion. It was developed from accounts listed in the bibliography at the end of the case. All names of individuals and organizations are real. A version of this case is included in Kidwell, R. E., Jr. (2004). "Small" lies, big trouble: The unfortunate consequences of résumé padding, from Janet Cooke to George O'Leary. *Journal of Business Ethics, 51,* 175–184.

"Janet Cooke is a beautiful black woman with dramatic flair and vitality, and an extraordinary talent for writing," Bradlee wrote in his 1995 autobiography. Several years earlier, in 1979, Bradlee had been in his office reading unsolicited applications for reporting positions when he came across Cooke's—age 25 years, Phi Beta Kappa from Vassar College, master's in literature, fluency in French and Italian, a writing award for work at the *Toledo Blade,* member of the National Association of Black Journalists. Unknown to Bradlee, only some of it was true.

Bradlee sent the letter and résumé along to Woodward, who was now the newspaper's Metro editor, suggesting that Cooke be hired before the *New York Times* or another top newspaper could snap her up. "Female Phi Beta Kappa graduates of Seven Sisters colleges who can write the King's English with style don't grow on trees, white or black, and we were a decade into our commitment to increase the number and quality of minorities and women on the staff," Bradlee later wrote. In her interviews at the *Post,* Cooke impressed several of the editors who spoke with her, but one said that she was a little "too Vassar" for his tastes. However, before hiring Cooke, *Post* officials did not contact Vassar to confirm that she was a graduate.

Cooke, raised as a member of an upper middle-class family in Toledo, Ohio, started in the Metro Weekly section in January 1980. The Weekly was the bottom rung of the *Post,* a kind of proving ground for new reporters. New arrivals found the pressure to produce, and Cooke wrote 52 byline articles during her first 8 months. A few months after she began working at the Weekly, Cooke started looking into a story about a new kind of heroin that was circulating on the streets of Washington, D.C. She then informed an editor that she had heard about an 8-year-old heroin addict and was encouraged to get an interview and write a story about him. One of the editors told her that this was the kind of story that would be on the front page of the newspaper. She spent several months trying to find the boy, believing that publication of the story would be her chance to win a promotion at the newspaper, possibly to the full-fledged Metro staff.

After weeks of unsuccessfully searching for the young addict, "it dawned on me that I could simply make it all up. I just sat down and wrote it," Cooke told writer Mike Sager several years later. The eventual story about the addict "Jimmy," his mother, and her live-in boyfriend Ron, who allegedly injected Jimmy with heroin while the reporter watched, was published in September 1980.

The story began, "Jimmy is 8 years old and a third-generation heroin addict, a precocious little boy with sandy hair, velvety brown eyes, and needle marks freckling the baby-smooth skin of his thin brown arms." Once the story was published, the public's reaction was immediate outrage and concern.

The D.C. police launched a search for Jimmy but were unsuccessful in locating him. They later declared that the boy did not exist, and the same suspicions resided among some members of the *Post* newsroom. Those suspicions did not deter the *Post* leadership from nominating the story for a Pulitzer Prize at the end of the year.

The story won the Pulitzer Prize in April 1981, and then the story quickly began to unravel. The *Toledo Blade* and the Associated Press (AP) began preparing biographical information about Cooke after the announcement of the prize. The *Blade*'s biography and the AP story were radically different because the former was based on its own personnel records about Cooke and the latter was based on information that Cooke had supplied on her Pulitzer application, which had exaggerated her credentials beyond her original résumé submitted to the *Post*.

The *Blade* story reported that Cooke spent a year at Vassar and graduated from the University of Toledo, whereas the AP story listed her as a magna cum laude Vassar graduate. The AP story reported that Cooke attended the Sorbonne in Paris, whereas the *Blade* story did not mention this. Cooke's original résumé listed fluency in two languages, whereas her Pulitzer application added Spanish and Portuguese. Cooke added six more writing awards to the biography she submitted to the Pulitzer board.

The falsification of Cooke's résumé and Pulitzer biography raised suspicions about the truth of the Jimmy story. Cooke was confronted by several editors, and she admitted falsifying her credentials but initially maintained that her story about Jimmy was true. She later explained that her father's strictness in her upbringing and in his total control of her family members' lives had created an atmosphere that often led to lying and deceit.

"The conclusion I've come to is that lying, from a very early age, was the best survival mechanism available," she told Sager 15 years later. "And I became very good at it. It was like, do you unleash the wrath of Dad's temper, or do you tell something that is not exactly true and be done with it?" She used this "talent" and moral perspective to prepare her résumé for the *Post*. She said her goal was to portray herself as a super black woman.

Cooke continued to maintain the truth of the Jimmy story. Accompanied by another reporter, she attempted to find the house where the boy and his mother lived. An inquisition of Cooke by several *Post* editors continued into the evening and the next morning. Finally, she was left alone with David Maraniss, one of the *Post* editors. "There is no Jimmy and no family. It was a fabrication. I want to give the prize back," she admitted to Maraniss. She quickly submitted a resignation letter to the *Washington Post*. Bradlee later wrote, "I can't explain now why I let her resign rather than fire her on the spot for the grossest negligence."

"It's the editor's fault," recalled Eugene Patterson, a Pulitzer board member who voted against awarding a prize to the story. "It didn't smell right, and that's why I wondered why somebody at the *Post* didn't sniff it."

After her resignation, Cooke dropped out of public sight and did not discuss her story with reporters for nearly 15 years. She married a lawyer, moved to Paris with him, eventually divorced, and returned to the United States. In 1996, she was employed for $6 an hour at a boutique in a Michigan mall. A $1.5 million motion picture deal based on her life story resulted from her *GQ* interview with Sager. The deal has yet to result in a movie about Cooke appearing at local theaters, but she is guaranteed a share of the proceeds if the film is ever made.

Despite the possibility of her story being immortalized in film, Cooke is regarded as a symbol of the worst in American journalism just as, according to Bradlee, the term "Watergate" symbolizes the best that journalism has to offer.

Discussion Questions

1. Identify the deviant behaviors that occurred in this case and who committed them. Explain your answer.
2. Discuss ethical lapses committed by Janet Cooke and by the editors of the *Washington Post.*
3. What systems could the newspaper have put in place to ensure that Cooke could not fabricate the Jimmy story? What role did the organization's ethical value system play in the failure of the editors and managers to take those actions?
4. What role did moral development play in Cooke's dishonest behavior?
5. Can Cooke's behavior in this case be morally justified? Explain.

Bibliography

Bradlee, B. (1995). *A good life: Newspapering and other adventures.* New York: Simon & Schuster.

Dutka, E. (1996, May 28). Janet Cooke's life: The picture-perfect tale: The saga of the Pulitzer Prize hoaxer proves to be a big lure to Hollywood—and the ex-reporter resurfaces to tell her story. *Los Angeles Times,* p. A1. Retrieved May 16, 2002, from http://proquest.umi.com/pqdweb

Elvin, J. (2000, April 24). Whatever happened to . . . *Insight on the News,* p. 34. Retrieved May 16, 2002, from http://proquest.umi.com/pqdweb

Felsenthal, C. (1993). *Power, privilege, and the* Post: *The Katherine Graham story.* New York: Putnam.

Kelly, T. (1983). *The imperial* Post: *The Meyers, the Grahams, and the paper that rules Washington.* New York: William Morrow.

Perlstein, R. (2001). The big lie. *Columbia Journalism Review, 40*(4), 91. Retrieved May 16, 2002, from http://proquest.umi.com/pqdweb

Sager, M. (1996, June). Janet's world. *GQ,* pp. 200–211.

CHAPTER 8

Bullying and Harassment in the Workplace

Gina Vega

Debra R. Comer

Bullying has always been part of the human condition. History is rife with references to abuse of power and unnecessary or excessive force. The classic bully story is of Joseph and his brothers, a tale of envy and hostility. Joseph, his father's favorite, was thrown into a pit and left alone by his older brothers. When they returned repentant to retrieve him later, he was gone and presumed dead. In fact, he had been "rescued" by Egyptian slavers.

This crude display was refined over the centuries. However, the refinement of bullying to include various forms of legally defined social harassment is a relatively recent phenomenon, dating back to the U.S. Civil Rights Act of 1964. Bullying is not illegal in the United States, whereas it is illegal in many other countries.

Bullying is not benign teasing, nor does it include the off-color jokes, racial slurs, or unwelcome advances that are the hallmarks of legally defined harassment. Workplace bullying is a pattern of destructive and deliberate demeaning of coworkers or subordinates that reminds one of the activities of the "schoolyard bully." Unlike the schoolyard bully, however, the workplace bully is an adult who is usually aware of the impact of his or her behavior on others. Bullying in the

AUTHORS' NOTE: Parts of this chapter are based on Vega. G., & Comer, D. R. (2003, October). *Sticks and stones may break your bones, but words can break your spirit: Bullying in the workplace.* Paper presented at the 10th Annual Vincentian Conference Promoting Business Ethics, New York.

workplace, often tacitly accepted by the organization's leadership, can create an environment of psychological threat that diminishes corporate productivity and inhibits individual and group commitment.

Bullying Versus Harassment

It is important to differentiate between bullying and harassment, both of which are forms of personal abuse. The two examples that follow help to clarify the difference between harassment and bullying on an interpersonal level.

Anita Hill and Harassment

The following is taken from the testimony of Anita Hill, a University of Oklahoma law professor, at the U.S. Senate hearings on the nomination of Clarence Thomas to the Supreme Court on October 11, 1991:

In 1981, I was introduced to now Judge [Clarence] Thomas by a mutual friend. Judge Thomas told me that he was anticipating a political appointment and asked if I would be interested in working with him. He was, in fact, appointed as Assistant Secretary of Education for Civil Rights. After he had taken that post, he asked if I would become his assistant, and I accepted that position. . . .

After approximately 3 months of working there, he asked me to go out socially with him. What happened next and telling the world about it are the two most difficult things, experiences of my life. It is only after a great deal of agonizing consideration and a number of sleepless nights that I am able to talk of these unpleasant matters to anyone but my close friends.

I declined the invitation to go out socially with him and explained to him that I thought it would jeopardize what at the time I considered to be a very good working relationship. I had a normal social life with other men outside of the office. I believed then, as now, that having a social relationship with a person who was supervising my work would be ill advised. I was very uncomfortable with the idea and told him so.

I thought that by saying "no" and explaining my reasons, my employer would abandon his social suggestions. However, to my regret, in the following few weeks he continued to ask me out on several occasions. He pressed me to justify my reasons for saying "no" to him. These incidents took place in his office or mine. They were in the form of private conversations which would not have been overheard by anyone else.

My working relationship became even more strained when Judge Thomas began to use work situations to discuss sex. On these occasions, he would call me into his office for reports on education issues and projects, or he might suggest that because of the time pressures of his schedule, we go to lunch to a government cafeteria. After a brief discussion of work, he would turn the conversation to a discussion of sexual matters. His conversations were very vivid. . . .

On several occasions, [Judge] Thomas told me graphically of his own sexual prowess. Because I was extremely uncomfortable talking about sex with him at all, and particularly in such a graphic way, I told him that I did not want to talk about these subjects. I would also try to change the subject to education matters or to nonsexual personal matters, such as his background or his beliefs. My efforts to change the subject were rarely successful. . . .

For my first months at the [Equal Employment Opportunity Commission], where I continued to be an assistant to Judge Thomas, there were no sexual overtures. However, during the fall and winter of 1982, these began again. The comments were random and ranged from pressing me about why I didn't go out with him to remarks about my personal appearance. I remember him saying that some day I would have to tell him the real reason that I wouldn't go out with him.

He began to show displeasure in his tone and voice and [in] his demeanor in his continued pressure for an explanation. He commented on what I was wearing in terms of whether it made me more or less sexually attractive. The incidents occurred in his inner office at the EEOC. (Hill, 1991)

Celia Zimmerman and Bullying

The following account is excerpted from an article in *Massachusetts Lawyers Weekly* (Pfaffenbach, 2000):

The plaintiff, Celia G. Zimmerman, filed a complaint at MCAD [Massachusetts Commission Against Discrimination] against the defendants, Direct Federal Credit Union and its president and CEO [chief executive officer], David Breslin.

Shortly after delivering her complaint to Breslin, the plaintiff alleged that her situation at the credit union deteriorated.

For example, although the plaintiff, as a member of management, had regularly attended annual meetings, she was not asked to attend the annual meeting in March 1997.

When the plaintiff was called upon to attend meetings, she testified that her attempts to participate in the meetings were ignored by Breslin.

After the plaintiff gave notice of her intention to pursue her discrimination claim in court, a company meeting was called in which Breslin spoke about "integrity" and commented that he would have expected some employees would have already left the employ of the credit union.

The plaintiff and some fellow employees testified that they believed these comments were directed specifically at her.

In November 1997, the plaintiff was asked to give a presentation at a board meeting. Breslin updated the members of the board on the status of the plaintiff's lawsuit immediately before she made her presentation.

After this incident, the plaintiff never attended another board meeting.

In early 1998, the plaintiff was assigned the goal of improving the compliance function at the credit union.

To complete this task, she attended a compliance training course aimed at all areas of compliance issues, including year 2000 compliance.

However, when the credit union formed a team to deal with year 2000 issues, the plaintiff was assigned the task of doing spreadsheets.

In early December 1996, the plaintiff began keeping a journal. In 1997, she learned that she would have to produce the diary to the defendants during the discovery phase of litigation.

The diary contained passages describing conversations the plaintiff had with her co-workers in which they expressed sympathy for her situation.

After the diary was produced, the plaintiff testified that she witnessed senior managers and other people who were mentioned in the diary being called into the defendant's office and leaving "visibly shaken."

After these events, the plaintiff alleged that she began to feel overwhelmed and unable to concentrate.

Harassment Versus Bullying: Specificity Makes the Difference

The main difference between harassment and bullying on an interpersonal level lies in specificity (Pryor & Fitzgerald, 2003). In fact, Einarsen (1999) referred to bullying as "generic harassment." Title VII protects specific classes of workers from specific types of aggression. Under the law, Anita Hill should have been protected from sexual pursuit by her employer. Workers are protected from persecution or discrimination based on religion, race, ethnicity, sexual orientation, age, and Vietnam veteran status, any of which may result in actionable events.

However, the same worker who is tormented, along with other nonprotected workers, in a generally demeaning or insulting pattern is not protected by the law in the United States. If an individual registers a complaint about this type of behavior, he or she is likely to be branded as hypersensitive, a troublemaker, or unable to take a joke. The case of *Celia Zimmerman v. Direct Federal Credit Union* is unusual because it validates the legitimacy of protection from workplace bullying practices in the United States. Under most circumstances, the target of the workplace bully receives neither protection from the bully nor recognition of the legitimacy of the target's complaint.

Bullying that results from hyperattentiveness to performance statistics, overt or covert threats to security, abuse or misapplication of personnel policies, and/or forced choices in assignments is also common behavior in many organizations. This type of bullying can be referred to as organizational bullying or institutional bullying (Liefooghe & Davey, 2001). Little has been written directly about organizational bullying; instead, most research has focused on the individual interactions between bully and victim. However, it is prudent to be aware of the potential within an organization for an individual to use power inappropriately and to create, through the rigid application of rules and protocols, an environment that supports and sustains bullying on both organizational and individual levels. This is discussed later in the chapter.

There are many definitions of workplace bullying. The one used here is

unwanted, offensive, humiliating, undermining behavior towards an individual or groups of employees. Such persistently malicious attacks on personal or professional performance are typically unpredictable, irrational, and often unfair. This abuse of power or position can cause such chronic stress and anxiety that people gradually lose belief in themselves, suffering physical ill health and mental distress as a result. (Rayner, Hoel, & Cooper, 2002, p. xi)

This definition comports well with similar definitions internationally (Bernardi, 2001; Costigan, 1998; Einarsen, Hoel, Zapf, & Cooper, 2003; Glendinning, 2001; Namie, 1999; Pemberton, 2000; Zapf, 1999).

Sexual Harassment and Title VII

Title VII of the Civil Rights Act made it illegal to base employment decisions (e.g., hiring, promotion, dismissal) on employees' race, color, religion, sex, or national origin. Later legislation similarly protected older people (Age Discrimination in Employment Act of 1967), pregnant women (Pregnancy Discrimination Act of 1978), and people with disabilities (Americans with Disabilities Act of 1990). Title VII does not specifically mention sexual harassment, but the courts have ruled that sexual harassment is a form of discrimination and, thus, is illegal. Indeed, two kinds of sexual harassment violate Title VII, according to guidelines issued in 1980 by the Equal Employment Opportunity Commission (EEOC). In *quid pro quo* harassment, a subordinate's job benefits and security are made contingent on the subordinate's compliance with his or her superior's sexual demands. The second form, hostile work environment harassment, may be more difficult to establish. As Justice O'Connor ruled in *Harris v. Forklift Systems* (1993),

Whether an environment is "hostile" or "abusive" can be determined only by looking at all the circumstances. These may include the frequencies of the discriminatory conduct; its severity; whether it is physically threatening or humiliating or a mere offensive utterance; and whether it unreasonably interferes with an employee's work performance.

The Supreme Court decided in the *Harris* case that it is not necessary to experience psychological harm to find that there is a hostile environment. Instead, a plaintiff's attorney must demonstrate only that a reasonable person assuming the plaintiff's perspective would deem the behavior sufficiently offensive. In two 1998 cases, *Burlington Industries v. Ellerth* and *Faragher v. City of Boca Raton,* the Supreme Court ruled that employers are responsible for taking preventive action against and remedying sexual harassment. In contrast to the clear legal protections against sexual harassment, most Americans enjoy no such safeguards against bullying in their workplaces. Indeed, researchers and legislators in the United States lag markedly behind their European counterparts in their awareness of bullying at work.

The Increased Interest in Workplace Bullying

Ironically, it was an American who first reported on workplace bullying. Brodsky's (1976) work was overlooked for years. Nonetheless, as Keashly and Jagatic (2003) observed, Americans have amassed an extensive literature on various forms of hostile and offensive workplace behaviors that can inform the understanding of bullying at work. Their research includes a disturbing list of bullying behaviors distributed through verbal and physical categories.

The physical categories make only limited mention of personal physical threat ("physically assaulted"); instead, they focus on being "glared at; . . . theft or destruction of property; deliberately assigned work overload; deliberately consuming resources needed by target; expected to work with unreasonable deadlines, lack of resources; causing others to delay action in matters of importance to target" (Keashly & Jagatic, 2003, p. 137). The verbal abuse includes

> name calling, use of derogatory terms; subject to insulting jokes; belittled intellectually, talked down to; criticized harshly, attacked verbally in private or public; put down in front of others; sworn at; lied to, deceived; yelled at, shouted at; interrupted when speaking, working; pressured to change personal life, beliefs, opinions; flaunting status; treated unfairly; subject to false accusations; rumours; attempts made to turn others against the target; you or your contributions ignored; silent treatment; had memos, phone calls ignored; been given little or no feedback, guidance; deliberately excluded; failing to pass on information needed by the target. (pp. 136–137)

This extensive collection of behaviors composes the aggressive pattern that our working definition presents.

In 1986, Leymann, a family therapist whose experiences with family conflicts aroused his interest in workplace conflict, used the term "mobbing" to describe bullying in the workplace (Leymann, 1986). The radio documentaries and book of Andrea Adams, a journalist, introduced the concept of workplace bullying to the United Kingdom (Adams, 1992). Leymann's (1986) term (borrowed from the English "mob" to describe aggressive group behavior) "was later adopted in the German-speaking countries and The Netherlands as well as in some Mediterranean countries, whilst 'bullying' became the preferred term in English-speaking countries" (Einarsen et al., 2003, p. 5). Adams's broadcasts (in which listeners and callers shared their personal circumstances as victims of bullies), coupled with subsequent newspaper articles, legitimized bullying as a type of unfair workplace discrimination in the United Kingdom (Lee, 2000).

Meanwhile, interest in the topic spread to other European countries. According to Leighton (2001), "The natural assumption in Britain and in other parts of the

[European Union] is that bullying is a workplace problem. Bullying is seen to be detrimental to an individual employee, and this should prompt a legal remedy for that individual" (p. 97). The Dignity at Work Bill of 1999 was created to protect U.K. employees from bullying.

Nonetheless, Yamada (2003) asserted, "Australia, the U.K., and the U.S. have not enacted legal protections specifically in response to workplace bullying. Rather, efforts to obtain legal relief must be based primarily on a patchwork of statutory and common law measures governing discrimination, personal injury, wrongful discharge, and workplace safety" (p. 400). Yamada commended Sweden's Victimization at Work Ordinance of 1993 as an appropriate legal response to workplace bullying. This ordinance contains language to prevent workplace bullying, protect employees who try to address bullying, compensate targets/victims, and penalize bullies as well as the employers that permit their transgressions.

Targets, Perpetrators, and Effects of Workplace Bullying

Bullying can take many forms. In its most destructive incarnation, its spirit-crushing techniques can deform targets' self-images and their ability to conduct business normally (Crawford, 1999; Namie, 1999). As tolerance for bullying expands within an individual as a result of continued exposure, a cycle of demoralization begins. The victim might feel incompetent to combat or even confront the bully. As the victim becomes less and less confident, the bully pushes more and harder. This cycle often continues until the victim gives up and resigns. According to one study, three of four victims and witnesses to bullying simply quit or are driven out of the organization (Namie, 1999).

The face-to-face bullying behaviors described previously, along with the more subtle electronic bullying that may confront victims at their desktops through hostile or misleading e-mails, can be directed toward individuals on the basis of gender, race, religion, or age. It has been suggested that victims of bullying usually are unassertive, are conflict avoidant, and make little effort to be "part of the group." Some research suggests that such bullying behaviors tend to be directed most often toward the more vulnerable individuals in these categories (Coyne, Seigne, & Randall, 2000; Zapf, 1999). One study concluded that, based on characteristics that map on the "Big Five" personality traits (extraversion, emotional stability, agreeableness, conscientiousness, and culture), victims of bullying tend to be submissive, shy, neurotic, and literal-minded (Coyne et al., 2000). If that is accurate, we might be tempted to blame the victim rather than the bully for disagreeable behavior. However, given the prevalence of the phenomenon and the reports of nonvictims having witnessed bullying, as well as the conclusions of that study being disputed by other, equally reputable researchers (Leymann, 1996), this seems unlikely. Besides, as Hoel, Rayner, and Cooper (1999) discussed, victims' responses to personality assessment instruments may, in part, reflect their traumatic experiences at the hands of bullies.

In addition, bullying appears to be an equal opportunity activity, both as bully and as target. In a survey conducted by the Workplace Bullying & Trauma Institute (Namie, 1999), bullies were women (46%) nearly as often as they were men (54%). Other studies show similar results. The largest such study, conducted in 2000 by the University of Manchester Institute of Science and Technology (UMIST), showed that men and women were bullied at nearly the same rate, although women tended to report bullying more readily (see also Einarsen & Skogstad, 1996; Hoel & Cooper, 2000; Leymann, 1996; Rayner, 1997; Vartia & Hyyti, 2002). Zapf, Einarsen, Hoel, and Vartia (2003) concluded that women do not seem to be at greater risk for being victimized due to gender role socialization. They asserted, however, that women's risk of being bullied may be higher because they are more likely to hold subordinate status and to be perceived as unwanted intruders in male workplaces. Based on the ages of the victims, bullying also tended to extend over longer periods of time with increasing ages of the targets (Rayner et al., 2002).

Furthermore, position within the company or rank within the work group can provide a rationale for the badgering that is often the calling card of the bully (Fuller, 2003). The UMIST study showed that 75% of bullying is done by managers, whereas other studies indicated that at least 50% of bullying was done by managers (Rayner et al., 2002) and as much as 89% of bullying was done by individuals whose ranks in their organizations were higher than those of the victims (Namie, 1999).

The UMIST study showed that bullying by colleagues is a prevalent activity. In higher education, women were bullied as often by colleagues as by managers, and 40.8% of all women in the study (approximately 2,500 total) identified colleagues as the bullies (Rayner et al., 2002). Whereas Scandinavian studies reported that bullying by colleagues occurs about as often as does bullying by superiors, British researchers found that bullying is done predominantly by superiors (Zapf et al., 2003). Moreover, in a sample of Finnish prison officers, women were bullied more often by their coworkers than were men (Vartia & Hyyti, 2002).

When colleagues bully, their actions are often directed to individuals who do not "fit in" or who violate the group norms: "A person may . . . be singled out and bullied due to the fact that he or she belongs to a certain outsider group" (Einarsen et al., 2003, p. 18). This includes workers who work more (or less) diligently than the others and those who adhere more (or less) closely to the organizational rules. It also includes people who are generally disliked due to some personal characteristic such as unattractiveness, irritating personal habits, or simply wearing the wrong clothes (Rayner et al., 2002). The method of bullying focuses primarily on exclusion and social isolation. These are effective means of eliminating the uncomfortable presence of the target. This bullying by colleagues may be the result of competition among coworkers for advancement and promotion, or it may simply be attributed to human pack mentality, the basis for which is survival, ambition, and fear.

Power, Organizational Structure, and Bullying

Whether a matter of individual behavior or institutional carelessness, bullying is closely tied to power and organizational structure. In organizations where bullying is endemic, a hierarchical structure that reinforces power differences, along with acceptance of indoctrination and initiation rites as closely tied to the socialization process for new members, may exist (Archer, 1999). Archer's (1999) research indicates that such behavior is learned, if not sponsored, by the organization and that targets accept it as a prerequisite to acceptance. In other words, the bullying is tradition. Organizations that foster and perpetuate workplace bullying exhibit certain specific characteristics. They tend to use top-down management styles, create a separation between superiors and subordinates, reward effectiveness with promotion regardless of leadership ability, encourage internal competition, and establish a culture of fear (Glendinning, 2001).

Organizations that have rigid hierarchies and top-down management structures depend on obedience to rules, loyalty to the company, and dependence on supervisors, managers, and leaders to direct the action (Liefooghe & Davey, 2001). Placing the power for change and direction solely in the upper levels of the hierarchy lends itself to the abusive use of such power. In addition, it supports highly controlling behavior on the part of the organizational leaders such that the needs, feelings, emotions, and affective preferences of subordinates may be overlooked or blatantly disregarded in the interest of efficiency. The focus on control, in turn, creates a culture that accepts bullying relationships (Rayner et al., 2002). According to Liefooghe and Davey (2001), the arbitrariness of the implacable quantitative measurement of output can render managers blind to the human needs of workers and preferences of customers as they focus on the numbers rather than on the implications of those numbers. Workers may be treated so impersonally that a kind of "covert bullying" can result (Liefooghe & Davey, 2001).

Corporate culture, or the ways in which things are done in an organization, can be explained through an examination of the often-repeated stories, myths, rituals, and protocols that organizational members exhibit. This is often referred to as corporate anthropology and is a method that many consultants use to gain an understanding of organizational structure and operations. Some companies have developed a reputation for hard bargaining, aggressive marketing practices, task-based leadership, and highly competitive business practices. Some renowned "tough" bosses have the additional reputation for bullying practices to promote hard work and commitment.

According to *Fortune* magazine's list of America's toughest bosses (Dumaine, 1993), the seven toughest American chief executive officers (Steven Jobs of Apple Computer, Linda Wachner of Warnaco, T. J. Rodgers of Cypress Semiconductor, Herbert Haft of Dart Group, Jack Connors of Hill Holiday, and Bob and Harvey Weinstein of Miramax) used tactics such as intimidation, micromanagement, humiliation, violence, threats, aggression, shouting, overcontrol, and general meanness to terrorize employees into compliance and hard work. With evidence of numerous acquisitions of other companies and, for the most part, healthy ratios, the companies that these chief executives led have shown considerable financial success despite (or possibly due to) their reportedly tyrannical management styles. The relationship between organizational bullying and corporate performance may serve as one explanation for the persistence of the former, especially in a global marketplace with tough competition. That is, organizational bullying happens because it apparently works.

Why Submit to Bullying?

For some people, the importance of working for a successful company may outweigh the importance of maintaining their own self-respect. When confronted by aggressive and demeaning behavior, their sense of loyalty and desire for acceptance not only may keep them from complaining but also may convince them that "paying one's dues" is the cost of personal success. In the 1995 film *Swimming with Sharks,* the long-suffering personal assistant to a Hollywood studio executive can finally take no more abuse. Spent from paying his dues, he retaliates against his quintessential bully of a boss in a series of violent and threatening acts. In a self-perpetuating cycle, former victims make sure that others pay their dues as well. Their loyalty to the organization, spurred as it is by self-interest, reinforces the acceptability of poor management behavior as a cost of doing business.

Even managers who are innocent of any desire to bully their subordinates may fall prey to the temptation when hierarchical organizations equate obedience with loyalty (Crawford, 1999). In fact, the normalizing or institutionalization of bullying behavior can be the result of an undue emphasis on doing things "the company way" so as to both maintain tradition and socialize group members. In such environments, the human resources department, which normally would be the first line of defense against bad management, tends to be useless to protect employees from the abuse. The bully may be senior to the personnel in human resources, or human resources may be indifferent to the problem because it must deal with more urgent issues (Glendinning, 2001). The ability of the human resources department to investigate complaints of bullying may also be severely limited by frequent requests from victims to protect their confidentiality.

If an organization prefers not to protect its employees from such bullying, or if the bullying originates in the highest echelons, the organization ordinarily ignores the behavior completely by failing to establish a confidential means of complaint, a formal protocol that protects the complainant from hostile response or retaliation, or an accurate record-keeping control system (Rayner et al., 2002). For employees who are reluctant to fight the system, the organization then becomes complicit in the abuse.

Group Bullies

Some widely accepted work structures, such as self-managed work teams, lend themselves to bullying behavior by the group rather than by a manager. When rewards are given for team achievement rather than for individual achievement, the reward itself is based on the efforts of the weakest link. The worker who is less energetic, who has family or other external responsibilities, or who is simply unwilling to work as hard as the rest of the group will be a drag on group success and may find himself or herself badgered, pressured, and bullied by the rest of the team to meet or surpass organizational goals. Thus, these so-called free riders may be encouraged to participate to a greater extent in the work of the team, but they are just as likely to withdraw even further when confronted with aggressive responses from team members. This process of self-discipline works well for the managers but less well for the workers, all of whom are being manipulated.

The Impact of Bullying and Harassment

Impact on the Organization

The negative impacts of bullying and harassment on the organization and the individual are impressive. Organizational costs due to bullying have included the resignation of valuable personnel, reduced productivity, and a loss of creativity and innovation. Efficiency is likely to decline as extra sick days are taken. These costs tend to have a domino effect, creating additional organizational impact. Other workers (nontargets) may be drawn into the fray and suffer personal stress that has a negative impact on their productivity as well. This domino effect has been documented in British studies. In one such study conducted in 1997, the researchers found that 70% of witnesses to bullying felt stressed and 22% of witnesses left their jobs altogether (Rayner et al., 2002).

Legal countermeasures by employees can deflect organizational operational funds to legal defense funds, and potential unemployment insurance and workers' compensation claims can lead to adverse consequences for the financial bottom line (Glendinning, 2001). The greatest organizational cost is the loss of qualified personnel (Rayner et al., 2002), requiring an extensive hiring and training process for new workers. That cost has been estimated at U.S. $30,000 to $100,000 for each individual subjected to bullying (Sheehan & Barker, 1999). Considering that 75% of targets of bullying in the United States have claimed that the only way in which to stop the bullying was to leave the organization (Namie & Namie, 2000), the total financial impact on the organization can be staggering.

Impact on the Individual

The impacts of bullying on the individual are frightening. Bullying affects people's health and well-being to an alarming extent. Studies in Norway, Sweden, Finland, the United Kingdom, and the United States clearly point to the relationship between bullying and depression, anxiety, aggression, insomnia, psychosomatic effects, stress, and general physical and mental ill health (Coyne et al., 2000; Glendinning, 2001; Namie, 1999; Rayner et al., 2002; Zapf, 1999).

The linking of bullying with posttraumatic stress disorder (PTSD) and/or prolonged duress stress disorder (PDSD) by Einarsen and Matthiesen (1999) and Leymann (1996) further solemnifies the negative effects of bullying. These two conditions arise as an aftereffect of stressful experiences and can have symptoms that include reliving the stressful event or flashbacks of the event when the victim is under stress for any reason. PTSD can be particularly debilitating for an individual who must continue working in the stressful environment or in proximity to the bully who targeted him or her. Personality and character can be distorted as a result of such continued exposure, and personality changes can occur (Rayner et al., 2002).

According to the Einarsen and Mathiessen (1999) study, more than three quarters of victims of severe bullying qualify for a diagnosis of PTSD. These victims experience the breakdown of the assumptions that support our normal view of the world, as described by Janoff-Bulman (1992). The three fundamental assumptions that we hold are as follows:

1. The world is benevolent.

2. The world is meaningful.

3. The self is worthy.

The combination of these component beliefs provides people with a sense of security that begins during childhood and continues throughout their lives. However, when repeated activities challenge and destroy people's assumptions, their view of the world may shift. A sense of benevolence may be replaced by a sense of paranoia, the meaningfulness of existence may come into question, and people's perception of their own worthiness may be challenged. When collegial support is not forthcoming, people feel further abandoned and begin to wonder whether they "deserve" the treatment they have gotten from bullies. The long-term effects of being victimized can create in targets a need to protect their self-images by working harder and longer and by strengthening their self-respect through any means available to them. In worst-case scenarios, bullying has been linked to suicide in studies in the United Kingdom and Norway (Rayner et al., 2002).

Global Implications

Workplace bullying has received considerably more attention in other countries than in the United States. In the United Kingdom, the Andrea Adams Trust was established in 1997 as the world's first nonpolitical, non-profit-making charity that deals solely with the issue of workplace bullying. This organization is widely supported and has served as the model for similar organizations in other countries, promoting understanding about bullying, providing resources for victims/targets of bullying behavior, and performing research about the phenomenon and how to address it.

A 1999 study of 1,100 National Health Service workers reported that 38% of the study participants had experienced bullying within the previous year (Coyne et al., 2000), and union studies have indicated that 66% of workers had either experienced bullying or witnessed it during the preceding 6 months (Namie & Namie, 2000). In the United Kingdom, the unions have played a significant role in publicizing the problem and in seeking solutions. The Manufacturing, Science, and Finance (MSF) Union was instrumental, through its Campaign Against Bullying at Work (launched in 1994), in creating interest in changing U.K. law. In

1997, the Dignity at Work Bill was first introduced to the House of Lords, where it failed (Sheehan & Barker, 1999). The bill was then reintroduced, in 2001, with greater success.

Workplace bullying has been so pervasive in Australia that a government task force was commissioned to study the trend. Its 2002 *Report of the Queensland Government Workplace Bullying Taskforce* indicated that incidents of bullying have been widespread in the country. Data in this study were collected qualitatively and identified the following "common" behaviors:

> rude, foul, and abusive language; repeatedly threatening dismissal; constant criticism; assigning meaningless tasks; humiliating and demanding conduct in front of other workers; ridicule; taunts; confusing and contradictory instructions or constantly changing instructions; undermining work performance; isolating and excluding persons from various work activities; leaving offensive messages on e-mail; blocking an employee's promotion; overloading of work; unexplained rages; unjustified criticism; withholding of information; hiding documents or equipment; setting impossible deadlines; excluding workers on a regular pattern; threatening action that could result in loss. (Workplace Health and Safety, 2002, p. 11)

This laundry list of abuses described the harassment behavior experienced by targets in Australia in more general terms than were presented earlier. However, neither the impact nor the implications of the behavior on targets is diminished by the more general terms. The report concluded with a set of 19 recommendations to stem the workplace bullying behaviors, including reminders about the existence of several laws protecting workers from abuse.

Scandinavian studies indicate that between 8.6% (Norway) and 10.1% (Finland) of workers experience bullying (Coyne et al., 2000). In Sweden, concerns were so great as to pass an ordinance in 1997 as part of the Swedish Work Environment Act to prohibit bullying or mobbing (Sheehan & Barker, 1999). Although these numbers might appear small in comparison with others, the reader should be aware that workplace mobbing was first studied in Sweden during the 1970s by Leymann, and he began publishing on the topic during the 1980s. Two decades later, workplace bullying is still a problem that has required legislation in Sweden (enacted in 1994) and in Norway (through its Work Environment Act). In the United States, various studies have reported that between 38% and 90% of the workforce has experienced bullying at some point in their work lives (Glendinning, 2001). However, no legislation has been enacted to protect workers from bullying.

National Cultural Tendencies

What is the basis for these disparate responses to bullying across different societies? An answer could lie within national cultural tendencies and whether workplace bullying is committed by supervisors or peers. The cultural dimension of power distance, identified in cross-cultural research of 50 countries and three general regions by Hofstede (1997), is particularly relevant to this discussion (see also Thorne & Jones, this volume).

Power distance describes the way in which people with varying degrees of power relate to one another, that is, the relationship between people with unequal status. The power distance index (PDI) was developed through answers to three key questions pertaining to the frequency of employees' being afraid to express disagreement with management, subordinates' perception of their boss's actual decision-making process, and subordinates' preference for their boss's style (Hofstede, 1997). When reverse-ranked by PDI (with lower scores indicating higher acceptance of unequal distributions of power), Norway and Sweden tied at 47/48, followed by Finland at 46, Great Britain at 44, Australia at 41, and the United States at only 38. The higher the power distance (and the lower the PDI ranking), the more likely it is that hierarchy is accepted, subordinates expect to be told what to do, privileges for managers are the norm, inequalities are expected and tolerated, and values are authoritarian. In addition, larger power distance signals an acceptance of the philosophy of "might makes right" and that power is based on the ability to use force, autocracy is the managerial model, and the importance of the role of the manager is paramount (Hofstede, 1997).

The preceding rankings suggest that U.S. workers are marginally more comfortable with autocratic bosses than are workers in the other listed countries and, possibly, are more willing to accept their fiats, which might include bullying. When coupled with data from Scandinavia showing that more mobbing is done by peers and data from the United States showing that more bullying is done by managers, it is perhaps understandable that workers do not join together to insist that management respect workplace dignity. Even so, this may be surprising given the traditional emphasis in America, as well as in some Western European countries, on blurring the lines of status in organizations.

Keeping Bullying Under Control

The cost of bullying to society, as well as to individuals and organizations, can be significant. Alienation, unemployability, disaffection, and court involvement have broad economic and social implications. It is in everyone's best interest to keep the impact of bullying under control. Although legal protections from workplace bullying are important (Yamada, 2003), the role of the organization in deterring (vs. condoning) bullying cannot be overstated (Vartia, Korppoo, Fallenius, & Mattila, 2003):

> The response to workplace bullying is an organizational issue, and the conditions in which individuals are able to bully is [sic] also an organizational responsibility. The organization may encourage, through its work practices and structure, the base behaviors of men and women to surface. (Crawford, 2001, p. 23)

Any organization that truly wishes to discourage bullying needs a policy explicitly stating that bullying will not be tolerated:

A policy makes a clear statement about what an organization thinks, its relationship with staff, and how it expects people to work within its culture. It also makes clear what is considered acceptable behavior and what will not be tolerated. . . . Without a policy which legitimizes complaint[s] about bullying, it is difficult for staff to raise issues about their bullying manager or colleague. (Richard & Daley, 2003, p. 247)

Hubert (2003) likewise views an antibullying policy as a necessary condition for resolving complaints. Without such a policy, he explains, it is not possible to intervene on behalf of bullied targets. Beyond a policy statement, Hubert argued, an organization should have a code of conduct that provides concrete examples of desirable and forbidden behaviors. The very process of developing the code of conduct helps to raise awareness of inappropriate interactions.

Of course, written documents are effective only insofar as employees know about them and believe that upper management stands behind them: "Having a policy is a huge step forward, but concern about bullying needs to be lodged in people's minds, not in the written word" (Crawford, 2001, pp. 24–25). Glendinning (2001), highlighting the role of internal human resources professionals in promoting a bully-free workplace, recommended apprising job applicants that civility and respect are key, carefully checking the references of prospective hires and emphasizing that treating coworkers with dignity is fundamental. Once individuals have joined an organization, they can benefit from training sessions that explain the company's antibullying policy, tell them how and where to report bullying incidents, and clarify where to find support for themselves or other targets (Richard & Daley, 2003). Indeed, employees need to know where to turn if they are the targets of bullying as well as what consequences they will face if they bully others.

Rains (2001) described the "peer listening scheme" developed by the Royal Mail (Britain's post office) in response to bullying. Peer listeners were painstakingly recruited, selected, and trained to serve as informal "compassionate experts" who advise their coworkers on bullying and harassment policies and procedures in their workplace. The implementation of this program signaled to employees that top management was committed to eradicating bullying. Even in organizations that have not instituted such an extensive network of peer listeners, a "contact officer" or "confidential counselor" may be available. This contact person listens empathically to a target's situation, recommends appropriate medical and/or psychological help for the target, and helps the target to consider and decide among possible ways in which to proceed in accordance with company antibullying policy (Hubert, 2003; Richard & Daley, 2003). Employees might find it easier to speak to a contact person than to approach a manager or union official.

Hubert (2003) recommended that, in response to a bullying situation, the target should try an informal intervention, proceeding to a more formal one only later if needed. In certain cases, a "bully" truly might have no inkling that his or her behavior is offensive to a target. In instances involving such a "bully in a china shop," an explanation and perhaps some minimal coaching might suffice to provide enlightenment and modify behavior.

If the victim is not confident enough to approach the bully, an impartial mediator may deliver the message. However, mediation is not without its problems: "If the victim 'wins,' the offender may have feelings of rancor as well as wishes for revenge" (Hubert, 2003, p. 309). In fact, when an informal strategy is ineffective at resolving, or not viable to resolve, a bullying situation, the target may make a formal complaint. The complaint is then considered by a grievance committee, which weighs the information provided by the victim, the accused, and any witnesses to determine the merits of the complaint (Hubert, 2003). When these more formal interventions are used, more substantial training and rehabilitation are typically required to alter inveterate patterns of inappropriate behavior.

Glendinning (2001) asserted that if bullying continues, the bully should be transferred to a position that provides less opportunity to bully (e.g., a nonsupervisory capacity) or even terminated. As Hubert (2003) noted, however, when the bully is valuable to the organization, antibullying protocol may fall by the wayside as the target becomes a scapegoat: "The offender remains in the organization, [and] the victim leaves, sometimes due to illness, sometimes through dismissal" (p. 310). Moreover, other organizational members may conclude that bullying is rewarded.

Tehrani (2003) pointed out another, often overlooked difficulty in resolving claims of bullying: Although in some cases there is a "clear bully/victim relationship" (p. 280), who is bullying whom is often not immediately obvious. An employee who exhibits negativistic passive aggressive behaviors and adopts a victimized point of view may bully others indirectly. Indeed, McIlduff and Coughlan (2000) and Unterberg (2003) identified the problematic impacts of the negativistic personality type on workplace behavior. When the target of this type of bully strikes back, the bully may portray himself or herself as a wronged victim. It may be that the strikingly high rates of reported bullying are inflated because individuals who perceive and label themselves as wronged victims of bullies are, in fact, the real perpetrators. An organizations needs to determine if a "victim" is actually the root of the problems that he or she portrays.

When Bullying Is a Good Thing

All this being said, there are occasions when the activities described as "bullying" are appropriate management and/or collegial behavior. A careful look at organizational norms can bring to light circumstances that compel the behavior we have identified as bullying. Norms are the ordinary behaviors in organizations that allow people to function without many surprises during daily operations. Departures from these norms are considered to be "deviant behavior," and practitioners of such deviance are often shunned or marginalized. It is important to note that deviance in some circumstances can be considered normal behavior in others.

For most of this chapter, we have made the assumption that bullying behavior is negative, deviant, and unacceptable. Being mocked, berated in public, sworn at, and treated unfairly, as well as having one's work denigrated, all are unpleasant and, some would say, uncivilized acts. Yet some organizations routinely depend on these as training methods, geared both to desensitizing individuals to criticism and to creating in recipients an automatic response to the orders or commands of supervisors. Particularly in dangerous situations where lives may be at risk, such as those faced by the military and by paramilitary groups such as firefighters, archetypical bullying behavior is the lifesaving norm. In such organizational cultures, there is no more powerful motivator than avoiding exclusion from the group (Archer, 1999). The reason for this is the importance of teamwork in the success of the mission. Only rarely do military or paramilitary organizations permit individual action; the team model is both stronger and safer when conducting dangerous activities.

However, for such a model to work, it is necessary that team members set aside their personal preferences and strive to act as one unit. Guerillas and suicide bombers aside, a paramilitary worker without a unit is useless. One way in which to discourage independent, and thus dangerous, action is to make very clear the undesirability of acting alone. Although public humiliation may be counterintuitive, it is accepted as a valuable learning tool by managers and recruits alike. In a process that is reminiscent of fraternity hazing, recruits are subjected to extremes of behavior along with their physical challenges. Those who fail (known in other circles as "targets" or "victims") are deemed as weak links and are unable to find working partners or teams that will accept them. This protects the rest of the team from erratic responses that may lead to physical threat.

Positive bullying is not limited to environments where workers are in personal danger. Other hierarchical structures also support, if not actively encourage, bullying by those in charge. Hospital emergency rooms and operating theaters, staffed by doctors, nurses, and medical technicians, often function in this way. The overarching goal in medical environments is to protect the lives of the patients. All other concerns melt away in the face of this mission. In the process, those in charge (normally physicians) waste no time on the amenities of human interaction. Physicians are trained to be in charge, to take charge, and to take responsibility for human lives. Speed and immediate response to medical orders take precedence over other priorities, and it is expected that those who report to physicians are aware of this and can deal with it. Task leader style rather than relationship leader style is common in medical environments; consequently, few victims make formal complaints. Dangerous overwork of interns and residents has been reported in the press, but there are few complaints about general bullying abuse that occurs as a matter of course. When bullying is accepted as "normal," people dare not complain.

The Ethics of Bullying

Bullying can be good business in certain circumstances, as just identified, but even in those circumstances questions arise as to its ethical acceptability. A full discussion of the ethical implications of bullying is beyond the scope of this chapter. However, we can consider several normative ethical frameworks, such as utilitarianism, deontology, the ethics of care, and virtue ethics, as well as the way in which bullying might be addressed by these frameworks.

According to utilitarian theories, a behavior is considered ethical when it results in more benefits than drawbacks. These theories are commonly used in business to justify certain actions, such as layoffs and reorganizations, that might be deemed unacceptable to certain groups of people due to the secondary impacts of such actions. Anyone who has been unfortunate enough to be on the receiving end of a corporate downsizing recognizes that whatever is done to sustain organizational life can have a concomitant negative effect on an individual's capacity to survive. The protection of the many requires, in this instance, the sacrifice of the few. Is this sacrificial approach to worker rights transferable to the arena of bullying and harassment? The answer is complex. If we accept the economic theory of utility (i.e., the value that can be placed on an object or action), we must accept that bullying can serve an organizational purpose. The sustainability of a business is the prime responsibility of its managers, and if bullying behavior can result in more economic success than would be possible otherwise, bullying can be part of the managerial repertoire.

If we reject the concept of utility in favor of a deontological approach, the sacrifice of an individual's dignity or employment is out of the question. Deontological theories suggest universal values—what is good for one is good for all, and what is required of one is required of all. Deontologists would remind us that people are to be respected under all circumstances and that their human dignity demands considerate treatment. If bullying were acceptable under some conditions, it would have to be acceptable under all conditions. Universal bullying would create a system of anarchy and, thus, would violate deontological principles. It is critically important that those in hierarchical relationships respect the autonomy of those lower in the hierarchy to avoid using them as pawns, or as means, to an organizational end.

The rationality inherent in these two major normative theories ignores the psychological foundations of a third important approach, that of the ethics of care. The ethics of care derives from feminist ethics or ethics based on the connection between moral agents and society. This form of ethics suggests that people cannot be considered in the abstract as fungible but rather must be respected as individuals. This leads to a focus on relationships rather than on the rights and duties of utilitarianism and deontology, and it considers all parties to the relationships as personal equals rather than as contractual associates. The result is a response to the needs and welfare of all members of society, suggesting that bullying is beyond the pale as it elevates one party to the detriment of another party.

The virtues inherent to the ethics of care originate from the classical philosophy of Aristotle, which focuses on the development of character as a mark of the moral person. What would virtue ethics suggest about bullying and what it says about character? The development of strong moral character is an intentional act; virtues are not innate or genetic inheritances. One way in which to obtain virtues is to practice them by living a virtuous life. This is not as tautological as it may appear. Because we know that a virtuous life demands prudence, justice, courage, and self-restraint, practicing those virtues can instill them into people's character. Once these virtues are instilled, individuals will be able to act like "good" people. Good people make good decisions and virtuous decisions. These virtuous decisions exclude the exploitation of others as a form of injustice. Hence, bullying is not permissible.

Although it is appealing to view these frameworks and their approaches in matrix form, the mutual exclusivity of their foundations does not permit this. What we can do instead is to bear in mind the primary goal. If the goal is organizational survival, we may naturally lean toward a utilitarian perspective. But if the goal is human survival, we must engage one of the other perspectives. If jobs are integral to human survival, bullying can be *valid* but it cannot be considered acceptable.

One more ethical consideration demands our attention. As we have seen, some organizations support bullying, whereas others only condone it. Which position is more dangerous to morale? Which position is more threatening to employees? We would argue that there is no difference between supporting and condoning bullying behaviors in the workplace. Both result in the same feelings of victimization and helplessness, and of frustration and fear, regardless of formal or emergent organizational policies. There are some conditions whose existence alone permeates an entity; they cannot be quantified or validated. Like digital transmission, they are either "on" or "off." Among these are pregnancy, job termination, conviction of a crime, and personal redemption. There is no such thing as accepting a "little bit" of bullying.

References

Adams, A. (1992). *Bullying at work: How to confront and overcome it.* London: Virago Press.

Archer, D. (1999). Exploring "bullying" culture in the para-military organisation. *International Journal of Manpower, 20*(1/2), 94–106.

Bernardi, L. M. (2001, Fall). Management by bullying: The legal consequences. *Canadian Manager,* pp. 13–16.

Brodsky, C. M. (1976). *The harassed worker.* Lexington, MA: D. C. Heath.

Costigan, L. (1998). *Bullying and harassment in the workplace: A guide for employees, managers, and employers.* Dublin, Ireland: Columbia Press.

Coyne, I., Seigne, E., & Randall, P. (2000). Predicting workplace victim status from personality. *European Journal of Work and Organizational Psychology, 9,* 335–349.

Crawford, N. (1999). Conundrums and confusion in organizations: The etymology of the word "bully." *International Journal of Manpower, 20*(1/2), 86–94.

Crawford, N. (2001). Organizational responses to bullying. In N. Tehrani (Ed.), *Building a culture of respect: Managing bullying at work* (pp. 21–31). London: Taylor & Francis.

Dumaine, B. (1993, October 18). America's toughest bosses. *Fortune,* p. 38.

Einarsen, S. (1999). The nature and causes of bullying at work. *International Journal of Manpower, 20*(1/2), 16–27.

Einarsen, S., Hoel, H., Zapf, D., & Cooper, C. L. (2003). The concept of bullying at work: The European tradition. In S. Einarsen, H. Hoel, D. Zapf, & C. L. Cooper (Eds.), *Bullying and emotional abuse in the workplace: International perspectives in research and practice* (pp. 3–30). London: Taylor & Francis.

Einarsen, S. E., & Matthiesen, S. B. (1999). Symptoms of post-traumatic stress among victims of bullying at work. In *Abstracts for the Ninth European Congress on Work and Organizational Psychology* (p. 178). Helsinki: Finnish Institute of Occupational Health.

Einarsen, S., & Skogstad, A. (1996). Prevalence and risk groups of bullying and harassment at work. *European Journal of Work and Organizational Psychology, 5,* 185–202.

Fuller, R. W. (2003). *Somebodies and nobodies: Overcoming the abuse of rank.* Gabriola Island, British Columbia: New Society.

Glendinning, P. M. (2001). Workplace bullying: Curing the cancer of the American workplace. *Public Personnel Management, 30,* 269–286.

Hill, A. (1991, October 11). Testimony at U.S. Senate hearings on the nomination of Clarence Thomas to the Supreme Court. Washington, DC: Government Printing Office.

Hoel, H., & Cooper, C. L. (2000). *Destructive conflict and bullying at work.* Manchester, UK: Manchester School of Management.

Hoel, H., Rayner, C., & Cooper, C. L. (1999). Workplace bullying. In C. L. Cooper & I. T. Robertson (Eds.), *International review of organizational psychology* (Vol. 14, pp. 195–230). New York: John Wiley.

Hofstede, G. (1997). *Cultures and organizations: Software of the mind.* New York: McGraw–Hill.

Hubert, A. B. (2003). To prevent and overcome undesirable interaction: A systematic approach model. In S. Einarsen, H. Hoel, D. Zapf, & C. L. Cooper (Eds.), *Bullying and emotional abuse in the workplace: International perspectives in research and practice* (pp. 299–311). London: Taylor & Francis.

Janoff-Bulman, R. (1992). *Shattered assumptions: Towards a new psychology of trauma.* New York: Free Press.

Keashly, L., & Jagatic, K. (2003). By any other name: American perspectives on workplace bullying. In S. Einarsen, H. Hoel, D. Zapf, & C. L. Cooper (Eds.), *Bullying and emotional abuse in the workplace: International perspectives in research and practice* (pp. 131–161). London: Taylor & Francis.

Lee, D. (2000). An analysis of workplace bullying in the UK. *Personnel Review, 29,* 593–612.

Leighton, P. (2001). Dignity at work: The legal framework. In N. Tehrani (Ed.), *Building a culture of respect: Managing bullying at work* (pp. 97–114). London: Taylor & Francis.

Leymann, H. (1986). *Bullying: Psychological violence in working life.* Lund, Sweden: Student Literature.

Leymann, H. (1996). The content and development of mobbing at work. *European Journal of Work and Organizational Psychology, 5,* 165–184.

Liefooghe, A. P. D., & Davey, K. M. (2001). Accounts of workplace bullying: The role of the organization. *European Journal of Work and Organizational Psychology, 10,* 375–392.

McIlduff, E., & Coughlan, D. (2000). Understanding and contending with passive aggressive behavior in teams and organizations. *Journal of Managerial Psychology, 15,* 716–736.

Namie, G. (1999, March). *The Workplace Bullying & Trauma Institute survey results.* Paper presented at the Fourth Interdisciplinary Conference on Occupational Health and Safety, Baltimore, MD.

Namie, G., & Namie, R. (2000). *The bully at work.* Naperville, IL: Sourcebooks.

Pemberton, P. S. (2000, February 21). Bullies at work: It's nasty business that only boosts the sale of Tums. *San Diego Union Tribune,* p. D1.

Pfaffenbach, W. L. (2000, November 27). Verdict for workplace bullying is upheld: Bias claim fails, but plaintiff gets $730K. *Massachusetts Lawyers Weekly,* p. 731.

Pryor, J. B., & Fitzgerald, L. F. (2003). Sexual harassment research in the United States. In S. Einarsen, H. Hoel, D. Zapf, & C. L. Cooper (Eds.), *Bullying and emotional abuse in the workplace: International perspectives in research and practice* (pp. 79–100). London: Taylor & Francis.

Rains, S. (2001). Don't suffer in silence: Building an effective response to bullying at work. In N. Tehrani (Ed.), *Building a culture of respect: Managing bullying at work* (pp. 155–163). London: Taylor & Francis.

Rayner, C. (1997). The incidence of workplace bullying. *Journal of Community and Applied Social Psychology, 7,* 199–208.

Rayner, C., Hoel, H., & Cooper, C. L. (2002). *Workplace bullying: What we know, who is to blame, and what can we do?* London: Taylor & Francis.

Richard, J., & Daley, H. (2003). Bullying policy. In S. Einarsen, H. Hoel, D. Zapf, & C. L. Cooper (Eds.), *Bullying and emotional abuse in the workplace: International perspectives in research and practice* (pp. 247–258). London: Taylor & Francis.

Sheehan, M., & Barker, M. (1999). Applying strategies for dealing with workplace bullying. *International Journal of Manpower, 20*(1/2), 50–57.

Tehrani, N. (2003). Counselling and rehabilitating employees involved in bullying. In S. Einarsen, H. Hoel, D. Zapf, & C. L. Cooper (Eds.), *Bullying and emotional abuse in the workplace: International perspectives in research and practice* (pp. 270–284). London: Taylor & Francis.

Thorne, L., & Jones, J. (2005). Organizational deviance and culture: Oversights and intentions. In R. E. Kidwell, Jr., & C. L. Martin (Eds.), *Managing organizational deviance* (pp. 309–327). Thousand Oaks, CA: Sage.

Unterberg, M. A. (2003). Personality: Personalities, personal style, and trouble getting along. In J. P. Kahn & A. M. Langlieb (Eds.), *Mental health and productivity in the workplace: A handbook for organizations and clinicians* (pp. 458–480). San Francisco: Jossey–Bass.

Vartia, M., & Hyyti, J. (2002). Gender differences in workplace bullying among prison officers. *European Journal of Work and Organizational Psychology, 11*, 113–126.

Vartia, M., Korppoo, L., Fallenius, S., & Mattila, M-L. (2003). Workplace bullying: The role of occupational health services. In S. Einarsen, H. Hoel, D. Zapf, & C. L. Cooper (Eds.), *Bullying and emotional abuse in the workplace: International perspectives in research and practice* (pp. 285–298). London: Taylor & Francis.

Workplace Health and Safety. (2002). *Report of the Queensland Government Workplace Bullying Taskforce.* Queensland, Australia: Department of Industrial Relations.

Yamada, D. (2003). Workplace bullying and the law: Towards a transnational consensus? In S. Einarsen, H. Hoel, D. Zapf, & C. L. Cooper (Eds.), *Bullying and emotional abuse in the workplace: International perspectives in research and practice* (pp. 399–411). London: Taylor & Francis.

Zapf, D. (1999). Organisational, work group related, and personal causes of mobbing/ bullying at work. *International Journal of Manpower, 20*(1/2), 70–86.

Zapf, D., Einarsen, S., Hoel, H., & Vartia, M. (2003). Empirical findings on bullying in the workplace. In S. Einarsen, H. Hoel, D. Zapf, & C. L. Cooper (Eds.), *Bullying and emotional abuse in the workplace: International perspectives in research and practice* (pp. 103–126). London: Taylor & Francis.

Nurse Cassidy's Dilemma

Julie Ann Cogin

K ellie Cassidy loved being a nurse. She had studied for 4 years to complete her bachelor of nursing science degree at Sydney University in Australia. During her training years, she had particularly enjoyed the practical placements in several hospitals where she experienced "hands-on" patient care. During her final practical placement from the university, she was sent to Wanula District Hospital in central New South Wales. She was disappointed with this choice because she assumed that it was a small, old, and archaic hospital that presented little challenge.

As soon as Cassidy arrived at Wanula District Hospital, her disappointment changed to excitement. The hospital was well equipped, and the staff members were friendly and supportive. She was overwhelmed by the hospitality of the locals and the sense of community spirit shared by everyone she met. By the end of her 3-month rotation, she had fallen in love with the area and a local farmer, John. She hoped to secure a nursing position at Wanula after graduation from the university.

Cassidy's excellent academic record and outstanding performance appraisal during her placement ensured that she would be offered a position at Wanula District Hospital when she graduated 6 months later. She and John

---

AUTHOR'S NOTE: This case is based on an actual incident investigated by the author. The names of all characters and the hospital are fictitious, as are some details, to protect the identities of the individuals and the hospital involved.

married, and she was warmly welcomed back to the district by her hospital colleagues and the local community.

After a few years of working in a variety of specialty areas within the hospital, Cassidy obtained a supervisory position. Her effective people skills ensured that she would quickly gain the respect of her direct reports, peers, physicians, and patients alike. Her career, however, was temporarily interrupted when she took 12 months' maternity leave for the birth of her first child.

After only 6 months of leave, severe drought throughout the region meant that Cassidy had to return to work earlier than expected. The entire farming community was suffering, and income from the couple's farm was far below expectations. Although she had enjoyed being at home with her child, she was excited about the prospect of returning to nursing in a supervisory role. The newly created position entailed managing a number of student and registered nurses in addition to facilitating ongoing education sessions for nursing staff members. The hospital and her colleagues were extremely pleased to have Cassidy back.

During the first week following maternity leave, Cassidy was conducting assessments of patients with a physician, Jake Jacobson. During this time, she became very distressed and uncomfortable with Jacobson's lewd sexual innuendoes and the way in which he continually managed to brush against her. Initially, she ignored it or laughed it off, but on reflection later, it angered and annoyed her.

Cassidy resolved to find out more about Jacobson and whether this kind of incident had been reported previously. What she found out was that his medical credibility was beyond reproach and that his groundbreaking research into cancer treatment was recognized internationally. His fund-raising success had enabled the hospital to purchase much-needed medical equipment, including a linear accelerator to treat cancer patients in a new radiotherapy ward. Sophisticated technology such as this in a small rural hospital was considered to be extremely unusual. The hospital administration attributed the purchase of the linear accelerator to Jacobson's and his wife's dedication to raising funds for patient care. In their honor, the ward was named the "Jacobson Wing."

Many large city hospitals had been trying to lure Jacobson away from Wanula District Hospital over the years without success. He refused to leave due to his sense of commitment to the local farming community and strong family ties in the area (his children all attended local schools and were competitive members of several sports teams). Jacobson feared that a move to a large hospital would limit his ability to directly help individual patients and, more likely, would increase his administrative and management responsibilities (which he detested). His position at Wanula allowed him to continue with cancer research, practice innovative procedures, and set his own schedule. He enjoyed coaching one of his sons' sports teams and watching his other children compete in their matches.

Jacobson was loved and well respected by his patients; however, most staff members, especially the nurses, found him to be arrogant, aggressive, and very patronizing. As a result, he intimidated most of the staff members under his authority. While performing routine medical procedures, he regularly screamed and yelled at nurses in front of patients and their families. Jacobson justified his actions to patients by implying that the nursing staff members were incompetent.

Although Jacobson rarely left them alone to do their jobs without some interference, nurses at Wanula District Hospital were praised by other physicians for their excellence and professionalism. When inducting medical students, Jacobson instructed his recruits to stop talking to particular staff members. It was made clear that not complying with these directions would result in a poor student appraisal and an unpopular medical placement. Despite such behavior, the Wanula staff members all acknowledged the benefits to the hospital and community of Jacobson's tenure.

With this knowledge, Cassidy was very apprehensive about taking any action against Jacobson's continued sexual comments and lingering touches. She quickly discovered, however, that he had a reputation for such behavior, particularly among the nursing staff members. In fact, Cassidy had heard that a previous sexual harassment complaint made by a radiographer had resulted in that person leaving the hospital without a reference and no reprimand being given to Jacobson.

The following week, Jacobson's actions and lewd comments escalated to several remarks being directed at Cassidy's breast size and fondling of her buttocks in a joking manner. Because Cassidy did not respond to these actions, Jacobson anticipated a positive response when he suggested that Cassidy and he begin an affair. She exploded at this suggestion and told him to stop harassing and embarrassing her. Jacobson was surprised with her response and told her to "lighten up." After this exchange, Cassidy was relieved when his behavior improved for a week, but it started up again shortly thereafter.

Cassidy felt as though she could not approach anyone about her problem. She questioned how she may have contributed to the situation. Was she too familiar with Jacobson in the first instance? Did she lead him on? She considered making a report against him but quickly realized that she would rather leave a hospital than make a sexual harassment complaint against a doctor, especially one so well regarded by the medical administration and community. Cassidy was also well aware of the hierarchical structure within hospitals and the authority given to physicians.

Resignation was not an option. The value of Cassidy's and her husband's farm had dropped considerably due to the drought, and unfortunately, there were no other hospitals (or jobs) in the area to guarantee an income for the family. During the ensuing weeks, Cassidy began to feel detached from her family, friends, and colleagues due to her ever-increasing level of discomfort at work. She was frequently absent from her job, especially on the days she was scheduled to work with Jacobson. She began to make simple errors and avoid patients under Jacobson's care. In a situation where she would normally page a doctor due to a patient's deteriorating condition, she would avoid alerting Jacobson until her shift was about to end or it was absolutely necessary to summon him immediately. As a result, patient care suffered.

One day, Cassidy was unable to avoid Jacobson. Following hospital guidelines, she was required to be present during a gynecological exam that he was conducting. She became clearly disturbed when he remarked, "I'll do the next [vaginal] exam on you." Cassidy could not believe that Jacobson was puzzled when she verbally reacted following this statement. He appeared to have no idea of the impact of the remark, let alone the ramifications of such a comment.

Cassidy finally decided to speak to the area nursing manager. She detailed the continual barrage of unprofessional behavior from Jacobson on physical, mental, and emotional levels. She was distraught when the area manager implied that she had gotten herself into this situation and that Jacobson would never do anything like Cassidy had suggested. The area manager also told Cassidy that she had depleted all of her sick leave and that perhaps she should reevaluate her nursing career and her position at Wanula District Hospital.

Cassidy left the office feeling dejected and guilty that perhaps she had encouraged Jacobson's actions. As she walked past the human resources department, she happened to glance up and see a notice about sexual harassment that encouraged staff members to speak with an equal employment officer (EEO) without fear of reprisal. Cassidy found this to be ironic and believed that the hospital had no intention of following through with any complaints or implementing any EEO policies.

Things got progressively worse. Cassidy believed that Jacobson had found out about her discussion with the area nursing manager. His mannerisms now became insulting as well as offensive in front of patients. Jacobson did not allow Cassidy to perform the most basic and routine of procedures on his patients, even overtly preferring the services and care of a student nurse. Medical students under Jacobson's influence began to ostracize Cassidy. Her job hours were altered so that she was regularly scheduled for the worst shifts. In addition, her supervisory role in the hospital was being reevaluated due to cost constraints, and this would mean a lower salary. When Cassidy questioned the hospital administration about these issues, there always appeared to be valid explanations for these changes. She could prove nothing.

Discussion Questions

1. List acts of bullying and harassment that occurred in this case study. Based on the discussion of bullying and harassment in Chapter 8, explain why you categorized certain behaviors as bullying and other behaviors as harassment.

2. Discuss the actual and potential effects of harassing or bullying behavior on the people and organizations involved in this case. What actions should the hospital take against Dr. Jake Jacobson?

3. Imagine that when Jacobson was confronted about his bullying of Kellie Cassidy and other nurses, he responded, "I was merely attempting to desensitize these nurses to criticism and ensure that they would respond automatically to my orders in high-pressure situations, which are quite common at the hospital." Based on the chapter's discussion of bullying as a good thing and the facts in this case, evaluate the validity of Jacobson's response.

4. What should the hospital do to prevent situations such as this from occurring in the future? Evaluate the actions, or lack thereof, of the area nursing manager in terms of ethical behavior.

5. What should Cassidy do?

CHAPTER 9

Discouraging Employee Theft by Managing Social Norms and Promoting Organizational Justice

Edward C. Tomlinson

Jerald Greenberg

P revalent in occurrence and costly in impact, the theft of company property by employees is a serious problem for organizations, and curtailing it has been a daunting challenge for managers. Employee theft has been defined as the unauthorized appropriation of company property for personal use (Greenberg, 1995). It has been estimated that approximately three quarters of all employees have stolen from their employers on at least one occasion (McGurn, 1988) and that many do so routinely (Delaney, 1993; London House and Food Marketing Institute, 1993; Sandberg, 2003). This behavior exacts a heavy toll on corporate bottom lines. In 2001 alone, for example, employee theft cost retailers more than $15 billion (Hollinger & Davis, 2002). So insidious are the effects of employee theft that it has been estimated to account for more than 30% of business failures (Bullard & Resnick, 1983; Snyder & Blair, 1989). Importantly, repeated instances of petty theft by employees cumulatively inflict greater losses than do major, albeit more isolated, incidents of grand larceny that capture news headlines (Emshwiller, 1993; Lipman & McGraw, 1988).

Given the scope and magnitude of employee theft, it is not surprising that scholars and practitioners across many disciplines have paid widespread attention to this phenomenon. This chapter describes several primarily nonsocial causes of employee theft that have been identified along with techniques for curtailing it derived from this literature. Toward this end, the chapter begins by describing these traditional approaches to employee theft. It then contrasts these approaches with more recently developed, interpersonally oriented conceptualizations of employee theft—ones that highlight informal social processes and perceptions of fairness as underlying causal determinants. Finally, the chapter concludes by drawing on this interpersonal orientation as the basis for recommending practical strategies for managing these social and perceptual processes in a manner that discourages employees from stealing.

Traditional Nonsocial Approaches to Employee Theft

Traditionally, three major approaches to employee theft have been taken, and a different professional group has embraced each approach. These approaches are the security orientation adopted by criminologists (e.g., Bintliff, 1994; Purpura, 1998), the individual differences orientation used by industrial–organizational psychologists (e.g., Gruys & Sackett, 2003; Hackstain, Farrell, & Tweed, 2002), and the psychopathology orientation favored by clinical psychologists (e.g., Black & Larson, 2000; Wolman, 1999). Greenberg (1997a) referred to these as nonsocial approaches to employee theft because they largely ignore the interpersonal determinants of employee theft. Each orientation, along with its associated approach to deterring employee theft, is considered in turn in the following subsections.

The Security Orientation

The security orientation, which represents the perspective of many loss prevention experts (e.g., Case, 2000; Jaspan, 1974), focuses on the context in which theft occurs. This perspective posits that employee theft is largely opportunistic in nature; that is, individuals steal simply because they can (Sandberg, 2003). Accordingly, the solution lies in reducing or removing such opportunities by way of accountability, monitoring, and surveillance mechanisms (Bintliff, 1994; Purpura, 1998). For example, many companies have responded by installing security cameras, designating restricted access areas, using internal accounting control systems, and conducting regular loss prevention audits and investigations (Sennewald, 1996). These interventions strive to deter theft from occurring and/or to apprehend the culprits if and when those deterrents fail.

The security perspective embraces the assertion that the moral fabric of our society is deteriorating. Individuals, when left to their own devices, cannot be trusted to behave honorably in the absence of law enforcement mechanisms (Jones & Gautschi, 1988). However, the assumption that all individuals will steal when they have the chance to do so has a clear limitation in that many people choose not to steal even when the opportunity presents itself, whereas others steal even when security deterrents are present (Greenberg, 1997a, 1997b; Murphy, 1993).

The Individual Differences Orientation

The individual differences orientation, sometimes referred to as the "bad apples" approach, is favored by criminologists (e.g., Robin, 1969) and industrial psychologists (e.g., Ones, Viswevaran, & Schmidt, 1993) and explicitly accounts for personal determinants that are ignored by the security orientation. Specifically, this approach contends that only individuals with certain personality or demographic characteristics are inclined to engage in theft behaviors (Ash, 1991), for example, individuals who are young, facing economic pressures, and/or emotionally unstable (Hollinger & Clark, 1983). In this perspective, the solution lies in selection procedures that carefully "weed out" potentially problematic employees before they are hired (Murphy, 1993; Sackett, 1994). The individual differences orientation explains the prevalent use of honesty or integrity testing among many organizations (Miner & Capps, 1996). In this manner, human resources specialists hope to curtail or eliminate employee theft by hiring employees who are least inclined to steal.

Despite some successes (for a review, see Ones et al., 1993), this approach is far from an ideal solution to curtailing employee theft. There are several key shortcomings. For example, paper-and-pencil honesty tests have only limited ability to predict employee theft (Dalton, Metzger, & Wimbush, 1994). Moreover, heavy reliance on these tests may be misguided insofar as psychometric limitations preclude reliable and valid measures of the variables of interest (Ones et al., 1993) and may generate unacceptably high numbers of false positives (Dalton & Metzger, 1993).

A particularly serious limitation of this approach is that evidence of a relationship between some individual difference variables and employee theft does not pinpoint the exact cause of the behavior (Murphy, 1993). This, in turn, makes it difficult to identify potentially effective deterrent strategies. Consider, for example, the finding that part-time workers are more prone to theft than are full-time workers (Hollinger & Clark, 1983). This could be explained in the following ways:

- Because part-time workers generally are paid less than are their full-time counterparts, they may feel underpaid, leading them to steal in an effort to recover valuable resources that they believe they have coming to them (Greenberg, 1990).
- To the extent that part-time workers are more likely to be marginal members of society, they are more likely to associate with "bad company," leading them to steal due to their exposure to negative role models (Hollinger & Clark, 1983).
- Insofar as part-time workers are inclined to be less fully committed to their organizations than are their full-time counterparts, they may be less reluctant to steal from their organizations when given the motive and opportunity to do so (Greenberg & Scott, 1996).

In other words, some predictor variables may serve as proxies for other variables that are, in actuality, responsible for theft behavior. This underscores the inherent limitation of the individual differences orientation. Knowledge of differential predictors of employee theft does not necessarily suggest unambiguous deterrent actions.

Psychopathology Orientation

The third traditional approach is the psychopathological orientation. Derived from clinical psychologists, this approach conceives of employee theft as a manifestation of severe personality disorders (Black & Larson, 2000; Hare, 1965; Wolman, 1999). In other words, employee-thieves are psychopaths who "are prone to criminal activity because they have developed abnormal, antisocial personalities that lead them to rationalize as appropriate a broader range of activities than the nonpsychopath" (Greenberg, 1997a, p. 33). According to this approach, controlling employee theft requires careful diagnosis and treatment from mental health professionals (Lykken, 1995).

The psychopathology orientation is limited in its potential to help managers either understand or control the problem of employee theft. Most notably, it does not account for theft acts perpetrated by individuals who have not been diagnosed with any clinical disorder. In addition, insofar as the diagnostic instruments used to identify individuals with psychopathic personality disorders have not been established as valid for use in personnel selection contexts, their immediate use by human resources managers not only is legally indefensible (Gutman, 2000) but also is considered to be an unwarranted invasion of employee privacy (Decker, 1994).

Limitations of the Traditional
Nonsocial Approach to Employee Theft

Although each of the traditional approaches to employee theft—the security orientation, the individual differences orientation, and the psychopathology orientation—offers a unique insight, the three approaches share the common underlying assumption that employee theft reflects some kind of intrapersonal limitation, be it moral deviance, personality flaws, or mental illness (Mitchell, Daniels, Hopper, George-Falvy, & Ferris, 1996). The implications are that theft can be managed by carefully selecting prospective members of the workforce and/or removing opportunities for theft. However, the limited effectiveness of these approaches suggests that something more may be involved.

Further scrutiny suggests that an exclusive focus on either situational or personal variables is inadequate (cf. Treviño & Youngblood, 1990). By attributing employee theft to various internal limitations of employees, it is too easy to overlook the important social dynamics that contribute to the problem (Altheide, Adler, Adler, & Altheide, 1978; Greenberg & Scott, 1996). Moreover, managers can ignore how their own interactions with employees actually may encourage theft behavior (for an illustration, see Case 9). As a consequence, managers may fail to capture vital diagnostic information that comes with incidents of employee theft, thereby denying them the opportunity to address the true source of the problem and unwittingly allowing this behavior to continue—or, given its ostensibly tacit approval, to escalate (Lewicki, Poland, Minton, & Sheppard, 1997). Following the lead of others (e.g., Greenberg & Scott, 1996; Murphy, 1993), we believe that broader insight may be gleaned from viewing employee theft as a behavior that stems from a variety of social motives emanating from interactions with managers and colleagues. We review this approach in the following section.

Amid the widespread attention paid to nonsocial determinants of employee theft, several social scientists have called attention to the social dynamics underlying theft behavior (Cressey, 1953; Gouldner, 1954; von Hentig, 1948). During recent years, these beacons of insight have merged into a floodlight of recognition. Elsewhere (Greenberg & Tomlinson, 2004), we have identified two recurring themes in this literature: (a) informal social processes and (b) theft as a response to injustice. We review these next.

Employee Theft as a Result of Informal Social Processes

The notion that employee theft may be motivated by certain patterns of informal social influence within the workplace stands in contrast to traditional orientations regarding theft as the result of an inherent flaw in some aspect of workers themselves. The social influence approach (Greenberg, 1997a) suggests that employee theft is the inevitable result of certain normally occurring conditions. In this connection, two specific informal social processes have been identified: (a) employee theft as a reaction to the behavior of managers and (b) employee theft as a response to work group norms.

The Influence of Managers

It may come as a surprise to many managers that theft among their employees is often a result of the managers' own influence. Even as top executives struggle to contend with the scourge of employee theft, the traditional ideology predisposes them to externalize this behavior, putting it on the shoulders of workers themselves (Mitchell et al., 1996). In so doing, managers are inclined to ignore the possibility that they themselves may be at least partially to blame—and conveniently so.

Although this bias is readily understandable in view of its benefits as a defense mechanism, managers sometimes do more than tacitly permit such behavior to occur. In some cases, they proactively condone or encourage theft despite their duty to safeguard organizational assets. This was reported by Gouldner (1954) in his classic interview study of gypsum factory workers. Specifically, Gouldner found an "indulgency pattern," whereby supervisors openly permitted employees to take home tools and other items for their personal use. A similar phenomenon was noted in Ditton's (1977a) ethnographic study of British bakery workers. The theft of bread by employees was so prevalent that managers intentionally raised production levels to avoid shortages. And although managers were aware that bakery delivery drivers frequently shorted customer orders so as to supplement their wages, the managers did nothing to stop this form of theft. Similarly, interviews of garment workers revealed that supervisors regularly turned a blind eye toward their taking small items and scrap materials for personal use (Sieh, 1987).

Aside from such passive forms of supervisory influence that allow employees to steal from their organizations, some managers go a step further by actively aiding and abetting employee theft. For example, Dalton (1959) discovered that senior officials at one manufacturing plant had items specially produced for employees to take without purchasing. Several studies noted that department store managers intentionally inflicted cosmetic damage to packages so that they could justify selling the merchandise to staff members at drastically reduced prices (Altheide et al., 1978; Dalton, 1959).

Importantly, managerial support for employee theft is not without certain restrictions. Whereas the garment workers in Sieh's (1987) study were allowed to take scrap items of negligible value, there were clear prohibitions against more serious types of theft such as using company resources to produce garments to be sold privately. Similarly, although the bakery employees in Ditton's (1977a) study were tacitly permitted to pilfer loaves of bread, they were strictly prohibited from taking cash.

It is instructive to note that such managers often permit and/or promote employee theft as an informal supplement to subordinates' wages. This allows for an "invisible wage structure" (Ditton, 1977b) that provides extra compensation for low-paid jobs (Mars, 1973) and/or unsavory jobs (Altheide et al., 1978). In the vernacular, managers consider this type of appropriation as "fiddling," a legitimate form of payment that is not regarded as theft at all (Dalton, 1959). In this manner, allowing some form of employee theft is employed as a motivational tool for managers, one that is more flexible and efficient than officially sanctioned compensation systems (Altheide et al., 1978; Greenberg & Scott, 1996; Zeitlin, 1971).

In addition, managers may send the tacit signal that they condone theft behavior when they engage in theft themselves (Kemper, 1966). Because they are a central source of information regarding employees' role expectations (Wimbush, 1999), managers are salient role models who strongly influence the behavior of their subordinates (Dineen, Lewicki, & Tomlinson, 2003; Treviño & Brown, this volume). Accordingly, it is vital for managers to be vigilant of their behavior and how it may affect a climate of dishonesty (Cherrington & Cherrington, 1985).

The Influence of Group Norms

Beyond managerial influence, employee theft also is shaped strongly by the norms that are collectively established by coworkers (Horning, 1970), and research indicates that informal social norms exert a more powerful influence on employee theft than do formal organizational sanctions (Hollinger & Clark, 1982). In this connection, studies have shown that strict group norms govern the specific types and amounts of theft considered to be acceptable among groups such as electronics assembly workers (Horning, 1970), garment workers (Sieh, 1987), restaurant waiters (Hawkins, 1984), and dockworkers (Mars, 1974). Theft activities are regulated carefully so as not to exceed normatively established parameters of quantity and quality (Sieh, 1987). To maintain this practice, individuals who defy these group norms (e.g., by taking prohibited items, by exceeding acceptable amounts of permitted items) are openly criticized (Horning, 1970) or severely punished by the group, sometimes to the point of being driven to resign (Mars, 1974).

Over time, norms develop within work groups that specify the different roles played by members of work groups involved in theft (Hollinger & Clark, 1982; Mars, 1982). In this manner, work groups are particularly potent in promoting, developing, and perpetuating elaborate schemes of theft. Mars's (1974) study of British dockworkers provides an illustration. Among these workers, theft became normalized, with precise and coordinated systems developed to make it possible to steal in a methodical fashion. Receivers falsified paperwork, forklift operators stacked crates to obstruct the view of managers, and lookouts were posted to signal any imminent threat to their illicit enterprise.

The influence of these carefully regulated group norms is manifested in several ways. Indeed, although many acts of theft are committed in groups, many also are conducted as solitary activities of which other work group members may be aware (Hawkins, 1984; Horning, 1970; Robin, 1969). As a result, norms of toleration enjoin peer reporting of this behavior and motivate passive compliance. So, even when an employee does not personally desire to engage in theft behavior, he or she will be reluctant to report coworkers engaged in theft (Tatham, 1974) so as to avoid provoking the group's wrath.

However, group norms also induce the active participation of all work group members. For example, Mars (1982) found that employee theft was a regular aspect of working life and a common supplement to one's income. In fact, it was so "woven into the fabric of people's lives" (p. 17) that it was considered abnormal *not* to steal. Altheide and colleagues (1978) observed that employees would even hold informal conferences in which they shared tips on how to steal. Reciprocation sometimes also involved assisting a fellow employee in theft, with the expectation that doing so would obligate that person to reciprocate in the future.

Moreover, not only is theft so firmly embedded that it becomes considered normal, but it also is used as a way of cultivating status and approval from peers and fostering identification with the work group (Altheide et al., 1978). Because conformity to valued group norms demonstrates commitment to group standards, it legitimizes both the thief and the act of theft. Under the umbrella of a social standard, theft becomes viewed as an acceptable behavior that is dissociated from one's personal identity, making it possible to shed culpability for seemingly inappropriate behavior. Because this activity is governed by social norms, those individuals who have committed this behavior can readily maintain their self-images as honest individuals who have not done anything wrong (Greenberg, 1998; Payne, 1989). Moreover, by participating in such acts, workers stand to benefit by elevating their stature within their work groups. So strong is the social force that it also works in the opposite manner, leading to the rejection and social ostracism of those who decline to participate (Mars, 1974). This is in keeping with the general tendency for members of work groups to reinforce self-regulatory behavior (Terry & Hogg, 1999).

To promote this process, work groups actively engage in the socialization of their members to accommodate employee theft. New employees are carefully indoctrinated in theft techniques as part of their informal training with coworkers (Mars, 1974). Hollinger (1989) and Dabney (1995) found that justifications for theft are used to socialize new employees so that they have such justifications readily available *before* they ever commit a deviant act. According to Hollinger (1989), "Justifications for theft are passed from the experienced employees to the newly hired. When substantial numbers of the work force have a reservoir of easily invoked excuses for their dishonesty, we can see how theft can quickly become widespread in an organization" (p. 26).

Such collective justifications serve to neutralize or absolve any guilt stemming from employees' actions, allowing the employees to consider themselves as honest people who are not doing anything wrong (Payne, 1989). In fact, although these employees are likely to acknowledge that they did in fact take company property, they are unlikely to label their behavior as "stealing" (Greenberg, 1998). Feelings of guilt can be neutralized as employees engage in psychological rationalizations that portray theft as benign and legitimate (Sykes & Matza, 1957). For example, they may draw the following conclusions:

- They should not be considered culpable for theft of property left out in the open without proper safeguards (i.e., denial of responsibility).
- The amounts taken are so small that they will not be missed (i.e., denial of injury).
- The company is so wealthy that it makes their individual act of taking company property seem insignificant and innocuous (i.e., denial of victim).

In keeping with this, several studies have found that many employee-thieves do not regard their actions as theft and, as a result, do not experience any guilt associated with their actions (Dabney, 1995; Dalton, 1959; Ditton, 1977a; Horning, 1970; Tatham, 1974).

Finally, work groups sometimes even perpetuate their theft activities as a form of recreation. Indeed, stealing is often a source of fun, providing the thrill of "beating the system," which may enhance satisfaction with otherwise tedious and boring jobs (Latham, 2001; Mars, 1982). With this in mind, one author (Zeitlin, 1971) went so far as to encourage employee theft as a means of promoting job satisfaction.

To summarize, evidence suggests that employees steal as a reaction to various informal social processes. Specifically, employees steal from their employers because managers sometimes either turn a blind eye to such behavior, or in some instances, even promote it as a method of unsanctioned compensation. Likewise, employees steal as a means of demonstrating their conformity to group norms supporting such behavior.

Employee Theft as a Response to Injustice

A second theme that has emerged as a social determinant of employee theft is the notion that theft occurs as a result of efforts to restore justice stemming from some form of provocation. This is suggested by research indicating a correlation between self-reported employee theft and job dissatisfaction (Hollinger & Clark, 1983; Mangione & Quinn, 1975). Again, this notion is at odds with traditional ideology labeling those employees who steal as immoral thieves. Rather, employees who believe they are treated unfairly at work are likely to be angry and frustrated, and these feelings will be exacerbated if there is no viable or legitimate outlet for such emotions. When more constructive responses are unavailable or impractical, theft offers a covert way in which to respond to unfair treatment. For example, consider the admission by a convicted felon interviewed by Cressey (1953): "I had this fancy grievance against the company, and the owner was not straightening it out fast enough. . . . You might say it [my theft] was in the spirit of retaliation" (p. 59).

This kind of reaction is in keeping with a broader literature suggesting that people are inclined to model the deviance of authority figures with their own deviant behavior (Kemper, 1966). We see this, for example, in a range of deviant reactions to unjust treatment, including vandalism (DeMore, Fisher, & Baron, 1988) and hostile behavior toward others (Greenberg & Alge, 1998).

In this manner, the occurrence of employee theft also may present a signal for organizational officials to become aware of abusive managers or arbitrary and capricious policies that motivate this behavior (Lewicki et al., 1997). Managers who externalize by simplistically assuming that stealing is only a result of inadequate security measures or of workers who are morally or psychologically deficient stand to misread this signal, denying themselves the opportunity to correct it. In fact, managers' aggressively acting on these traditional assumptions may be perceived by employees as additional evidence of injustice and may incite even more deviant behavior in a dangerously escalating cycle (Bennett & Robinson, 2003; Vardi & Weitz, 2004). Thus, it is vital for managers to be alert to the effects of injustice within their organization so that they can address the root of the problem. Specifically, it is instructive to consider three specific types of fairness perceptions: (a) distributive justice, (b) interactional justice, and (c) procedural justice. The following subsections cover each of these categories with respect to relevant findings from employee theft research.

Distributive Justice Effects

Viewed as a social exchange relationship, employees develop expectations that their rewards should be proportional to the labor they contribute to their employer (Homans, 1961). This notion of distributive justice focuses on the *outcomes* allocated to employees on the basis of what they deserve. When outcomes are not distributed fairly, employees become upset and enact a course of action to change or restore balance (or equity) between their inputs to the organization and the outcomes they receive (Adams, 1965).

The work on social dynamics described earlier suggested that employees may view theft as a legitimate way in which to supplement their wages. This implies that workers believe that their official compensation is insufficient, leading them to even the score by taking more as a means of unilaterally raising their own outcomes (Greenberg, 1990, 1997b). In one study, an employee in a clothing store stated, "I feel I deserved to get something additional for my work since I was not getting paid enough" (Zeitlin, 1971, p. 26). In another study, a copper mine worker admitted to taking a wrench but justified this action as a self-rewarded compensating wage differential for hazardous working conditions (Altheide et al., 1978). Analoui and Kakabadse (1991) interviewed a female bartender whose managers had her work so late that she could not catch a bus home and then proceeded to deny her request for cab fare (a benefit commonly provided to late shift workers in such establishments). Although the woman refrained from stealing otherwise, on this occasion she pocketed a customer's payment for a drink, claiming, "I'll get a taxi and he'll pay for it" (p. 52).

These anecdotal reports are bolstered by a quasi-experiment that also demonstrated the effects of distributive injustice on employee theft. Greenberg (1990) examined employee theft in three manufacturing plants operated by the same company. Because of financial exigencies within the company, management decided to impose a 10-week 15% pay cut among employees at two of the plants. The third plant served as the control group, where demographically similar employees performed identical work but did not experience a pay reduction. This allowed a comparison of theft rates (measured by the company's internal accounting for asset shrinkage) before, during, and after the pay cut as a function of underpayment inequity.

As shown in Figure 9.1, the results showed that during the pay cut, theft rates were significantly higher in the plants experiencing the pay cut than in the control group plant. This is especially striking insofar as theft rates were consistently low among *all three* plants before and after the pay cut. This supports the argument that employees steal to raise their outcomes in response to underpayment inequity (a distributive injustice).

Interactional Justice Effects

In addition to basing their assessments of fairness on the quantity of outcomes received, employees are sensitive to the quality of interpersonal treatment they receive from their managers, referred to as interactional justice (Bies & Moag, 1986). Illustrating the potency of social treatment, Altheide and colleagues (1978) reported comments by a woman who worked at two record stores. At one store, where she believed she was mistreated by the manager, she proclaimed, "I stole there all the time. Towards the end, I did just because I didn't like him [the manager] at all" (p. 105). However, the woman's reactions were quite different in the other store, where she did not believe she was mistreated. "Working for them," she said, "you just didn't want to steal," adding, "There was no reason to. . . . You liked to work there" (pp. 105–106).

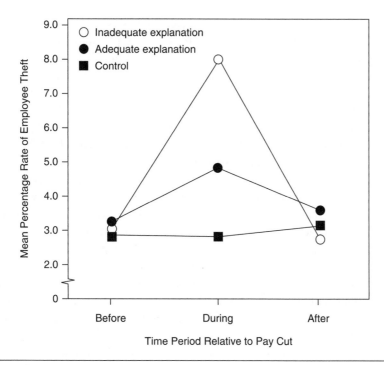

Figure 9.1   Theft Rates as a Function of Conditions in the Field Experiment by
Greenberg (1990)

SOURCE: Greenberg, J. (1990). Employee theft as a reaction to underpayment inequity: The
hidden cost of pay cuts. *Journal of Applied Psychology, 75,* 561–568. © 1990 by the American
Psychological Association. Reprinted with permission.

Greenberg's (1990) quasi-experimental study, described previously, also
established the effect of interpersonal treatment on employee theft. Specifically,
Greenberg explained that the type of explanation offered by managers ameliorated
the adverse effects of distributive injustice. These explanations were created in a
manner that varied with respect to the adequacy of the explanation given. In one
of the plants whose workers received a pay cut, constituting the adequate explanation condition, workers were provided with an elaborate explanation that justified
the decision and presented it in a manner that showed considerable social sensitivity. Specifically, the president of the company made a personal visit to announce the
decision and brought extensive supporting materials to document the rationale
for the pay cut. He also presented this information by repeatedly expressing his
remorse (e.g., "Will it hurt? Of course! But it will hurt us all alike. . . . It really hurts
me to do this, and the decision didn't come easily"). By contrast, workers who
received a pay cut in the other plant, constituting the inadequate explanation condition, received very limited information and only the most superficial expressions
of remorse. In this case, a more junior executive spoke at a brief and hastily conducted meeting, announcing the decision without describing the basis on which it
was made and doing so in a manner that was far less apologetic in tone.

During the 10-week pay cut period, the rate of theft was more than twice as high in the plant whose employees received the inadequate explanation than in the plant whose employees received an adequate explanation (Figure 9.1). A questionnaire confirmed that employees in the inadequate explanation condition felt more unfairly treated than did those in the adequate explanation condition. This evidence supports the argument that the type of interpersonal treatment that employees receive affects their willingness to steal in response to underpayment. Apparently, adding the insult of an inadequate explanation encouraged theft at levels exceeding that stimulated by the injury of underpayment (Greenberg & Alge, 1998).

Despite the compelling nature of these findings, the explanation manipulation in these studies confounded the quality of information and the sensitivity in which it was presented, rendering it impossible to tease apart their independent effects. Accordingly, Greenberg (1993) conducted a laboratory study that disentangled these elements, manipulating them independently. Participants in this study were students who were motivated to steal (because they were paid less than the promised amount for a clerical task they had been recruited to perform) and who had the opportunity to do so (because they were asked to pay themselves from an ostensibly unknown sum of money). When the participants learned that they were being underpaid for the task they had just completed, they were given explanations that were either extremely thorough and based on verifiable facts (high valid information) or extremely incomplete and based on questionable facts (low valid information). These explanations also varied in social sensitivity. In the high social sensitivity condition, the experimenter conveyed extensive remorse and concern for participants' welfare. In the low social sensitivity condition, the message conveyed by the experimenter was lacking in this respect.

Because in actuality the exact amount of money was known by the experimenter, he was able to determine the precise amount of money taken. Amounts in excess of the announced (underpaid) amount were interpreted as theft. Greenberg (1993) found that the amount of theft was affected independently by both information quality and social sensitivity. Participants stole less money when they received an explanation that contained high valid information (as opposed to low valid information) and when they received an explanation that was high in social sensitivity (as opposed to low in social sensitivity). These variables also combined in an additive fashion such that high levels of both were associated with the lowest theft, whereas participants receiving the lowest levels of both stole the most money.

Procedural Justice Effects

Procedural justice refers to people's perceptions of the fairness of the procedures used to allocate outcomes. Among the key determinants are the degree to which people are given input (or voice) in allocation decisions (Thibaut & Walker, 1975) and the extent to which decisions are made in a manner that uses accurate information applied in a consistent and unbiased fashion (Leventhal, 1976, 1980). These considerations are especially important whenever people receive undesirable outcomes (Brockner & Wiesenfeld, 1996; Colquitt & Greenberg, 2003).

To test the relationship between employee theft and procedural justice perceptions, Shapiro, Treviño, and Victor (1995) conducted a field study of employees in 18 fast-food restaurants. The management of these restaurants introduced several theft reduction interventions designed to enhance procedural justice. These included giving employees a voice in defining theft and drafting a code of ethics that prohibited it as well as tracking missing food in an accurate and publicly observable manner. Reflecting the practical value of procedural justice as a theft deterrent, the researchers found that the more employees perceived these procedures to be fair, the less food the employees subsequently stole from the restaurant (based on reports of theft by peers).

To summarize, evidence suggests that employees steal as a reaction to various sources of injustice. Specifically, employees steal from their employers to the extent that they believe that they have failed to receive levels of reward commensurate with their work contributions (i.e., distributive injustice), that they have been treated in a manner that denies them the dignity and respect they deserve (i.e., interactional injustice), and that the organizational policies used have denied them due process (i.e., procedural injustice).

Social-Based Strategies for Managing Employee Theft

To this point, we have considered the limitations of the traditional nonsocial approaches to deterring employee theft and have supplemented these orientations by explaining how two key social determinants, informal social processes and reactions to injustice, expand our understanding of the underlying causes of this behavior. Drawing on this work, we now turn to considering specific ways in ways in which these social factors can be managed in a manner that discourages employees from stealing. Although these recommendations by themselves might not deter employee theft completely, in combination they may "chip away" at it, adding incrementally to the effectiveness of more traditional approaches. As such, we present these recommendations not as substitutes for, but rather as supplements to, these already popular, albeit not totally effective, approaches. Our discussion is organized around five specific managerial recommendations.

Create Awareness of Employee Theft as a Serious Problem

Our first recommendation is that managers should set the tone for behavioral expectations by announcing the costs of stealing. The rationale underlying this recommendation is straightforward. Powerful norms established by supervisors and work groups lead employees to steal, and these are enabled by rationalizations that view some forms of theft as legitimate supplements to wages or as a benign and fully justified activity—what has been called the "invisible wage system"

(Ditton, 1977b). Accordingly, it follows that managers may be able to counter the influence of these norms by demonstrating to employees that their theft behavior is, in fact, damaging to the company, ultimately threatening their continued employment. Hollinger (1989) advocated this as follows: "The social prevention of employee theft involves convincing employees that stealing from the company is against their own best interests. . . . Employees must be helped to recognize the personal benefits derived by protecting the property and assets of their employers" (p. 40).

Research findings by Carter, Holström, Simpanen, and Melin (1988) support this advice. These investigators studied rates of employee theft in a Swedish grocery store where graphs tracking weekly rates of theft were posted in a conspicuous location. They found that the number of missing items decreased significantly following this intervention and that it remained below the preintervention baseline level throughout the study period.

These findings may be explained in three ways following from the current analyses. First, the findings are consistent with the possibility that feedback promoted employees' awareness of the costliness of the theft, thereby challenging the belief that employees were committing "a victimless crime" (or, for that matter, any "crime" at all), potentially weakening group pressures to steal. Second, the effectiveness of this intervention also may be explained in terms of the signals it sends about management's explicit condemnation of theft behavior, thereby precluding any possibility about its tacit approval. Third, to the extent that the posting procedure may have advanced perceptions of procedural justice, as indicated by Shapiro and colleagues (1995), the reduction in theft resulting from this intervention also may be explained. Although it is difficult to determine which of these mechanisms, individually or jointly, ultimately is responsible for reducing employee theft, the clear efficacy of the practice of communicating the cost of employee theft underscores its value as a deterrent technique.

Institute Codes of Ethical Conduct

In addition to creating awareness of the malignant effects of employee theft, we advocate that companies formalize codes of ethical conduct that explicitly distinguish between acceptable and unacceptable forms of behavior in the workplace (Farrell, Cobbin, & Farrell, 2002). To the extent that such codes reduce ambiguity regarding what constitutes theft, particularly with respect to items of uncertain ownership (e.g., the scrap materials reported as pilfered in studies by Horning, 1970, and Sieh, 1987), they promise to challenge the development and acceptance of informal norms promoting theft by institutionalizing desired standards of behavior (Adams, 1981). Not surprisingly, codes of ethical conduct have been found to be invaluable in creating and maintaining cultures of honesty (Niehoff & Paul, 2000), particularly when accompanied by a formal program of ethics training and an ethics office that further oversees and promotes ethical standards (Ethics Resource Center, 1994; Treviño & Nelson, 2004).

In this connection, Greenberg (2002) recently conducted an experiment among customer service representatives working in one of two branch offices in different parts of the United States. At the time of the study, one of these offices had in place an ethics program that provided employees with at least 10 hours of training in ethical principles, how those principles were expected to be applied in their jobs, practice sessions in responding to ethical issues at work, and procedures to follow when seeking additional guidance on ethical matters. The other office had no such program in effect and, thus, served as a natural control group.

After employees in both groups were underpaid for completing a survey, they were asked to pay themselves the stated amount from a bowl of coins whose exact total value was believed to be unknown by the survey administrator (following the paradigm used by Greenberg, 1993, described earlier). Extending earlier findings showing that workers are prone to steal when they believe they are underpaid, Greenberg (2002) found that this effect was attenuated when an ethics program was in place—particularly among individuals who had attained a level of cognitive moral development that enabled them to benefit from the training (Treviño & Weaver, 2003; Wells & Schminke, 2001).

It is important to note that codes of ethical conduct are most effective in reducing deviant behavior when they incorporate certain features. Specifically, in keeping with the notion that theft may be promoted by managerial support, ethical codes discourage such behavior to the extent that they operationalize management's disdain for it (Gross-Schaefer, Trigilio, Negus, & Ro, 2000). Furthermore, to the extent that employees are involved in the creation of codes of ethical conduct, they are likely to accept them as fair and adhere to them (Shapiro et al., 1995).

Use Corporate Hotlines

To further erode social norms that stand to condone and support employee theft, we also recommend that companies provide confidential hotlines that employees can call to report incidents of stealing and other forms of dishonest behavior. Growing numbers of companies have been following this practice during recent years and have found it to be a cost-effective means of curtailing theft (Addis, 1992). Hotlines allow employees to remain anonymous and avoid the social ostracism from colleagues likely to result from openly defying theft norms. In effect, hotlines provide employees with an "escape route" (Greenberg, 1997a, 1997b) through which they can subvert the effects of group-induced pressure to steal. Although hotlines might not completely eradicate theft, they are likely to weaken the stronghold of social norms that embrace it.

Hotlines also can be a useful mechanism for challenging employees' perceptions of unfairness at work. For example, to the extent that concerns about perceived unfair pay may be addressed in information provided by way of hotlines, companies enjoy opportunities to alleviate concerns about unfair treatment that threaten to result in theft. Depending on the nature and tone of the information imparted, this potentially is the case with respect to the distributive, interactional, and procedural forms of justice. For example, it is not unusual for hotlines to be used as a mechanism for enlightening employees about the procedures used to determine their pay (Folger & Greenberg, 1985). Indeed, corporate hotlines can be instrumental in assuaging perceptions of unfair pay, thereby mitigating the threat of employee theft (Shapiro et al., 1995). Moreover, the mere practice of having hotlines itself can be effective in promoting perceptions of procedural fairness that may discourage employees from stealing (Taft, 1985).

Rotate Group Membership

To the extent that social norms may encourage employee theft, it follows that practices that weaken group norms may discourage employee theft. In particular, norms may be weakened by unstable membership, in part because new group members may challenge ostensibly inappropriate standards until they are appropriately socialized (Feldman, 1984). Thus, the practice of rotating work group membership may mitigate social pressures to steal. Accordingly, we advocate this practice as a means of deterring employee theft. The underlying rationale is that rotating work group members will inhibit the development of informal group norms, including those supporting employee theft, making it difficult to indoctrinate new employees in this illicit behavior.

This same rationale has been applied to airline cockpit crews (Ginnett, 1993) to combat norms of sloppy communication that may compromise the safety and integrity of flight operations (Kanki & Palmer, 1993). In this manner, group rotation serves to maintain a high degree of vigilance and clarity. As Greenberg (1997a) described, "Just as norms permitting suboptimal communications are unlikely to develop in cockpits whose occupants frequently change, norms promoting theft are unlikely to develop in work groups whose membership is unstable" (p. 45).

Managers should be cautioned that this practice might not always be practical. This would be the case, for example, in situations where members must have a high degree of familiarity with one another so that they can coordinate their efforts (e.g., work teams). In such cases, rotating group membership threatens to weaken effectiveness in this regard. As such, this recommendation probably should be reserved for situations in which group norms are so extremely counterproductive that the benefits of promoting unstable groups readily offsets the costs of maintaining them. Clearly, this recommendation should be reserved for extreme situations.

Train Managers in Ways of Promoting Organizational Justice

Our final recommendation is that companies provide supervisors with special training in principles of organizational justice and practices that effectively promote perceptions of fairness. In view of research showing that employees steal from their companies in response to perceptions of injustice (Greenberg, 1990, 1993), it follows that promoting organizational justice may be an effective means of eliminating a key motive behind employee theft. With this in mind, we advocate the practice of training employees in practices that encourage their subordinates to perceive them as being fair (Skarlicki & Latham, in press).

To test this idea more directly, Greenberg (1999) conducted an intervention study among three discount stores in the same chain. These stores were experiencing an unusually high rate of asset shrinkage from areas accessible only to employees (e.g., stockrooms). A preexperimental survey indicated that employees believed that they were underpaid and treated in a disrespectful and insensitive manner by their managers. The survey also revealed that managers typically made no effort to explain to employees the rationales behind various decisions affecting the employees. In short, the survey suggested that workers experienced high levels of distributive, interactional, and procedural injustice and that these perceptions may have motivated the alarming degree of theft observed.

Of the three stores, one was selected at random to be administered a program of interpersonal justice training (IJT). This consisted of training managers in techniques of delegation, information sharing, respectful communication, and other fairness-related topics. This training took approximately 2 hours per week over an 8-week period and used various exercises and case studies to meet the course objectives. Importantly, no mention was ever made regarding the goal of reducing employee theft. After training, the rate of theft occurring in this experimental store was compared with the rates of theft occurring in two other stores constituting the control conditions. Managers at a second store, selected at random, received training in areas completely unrelated to organizational justice or employee theft. In addition, managers at a third store, also constituting a control group, received no training whatsoever.

It was found that IJT was instrumental in improving employees' attitudes after the training in comparison with those before the training and also in comparison with those in the other two groups. More important, the theft rate dropped from approximately 8% to 4% in the IJT group and remained at this level for 6 months after the study was completed. However, there was no change in either of the two control groups. It is remarkable that this reduction in theft did *not* occur due to typical forms of training in loss prevention methods (Tilley, Dafoe, & Putsey, 1999); rather, it occurred due to training managers in how to treat employees fairly. Training in interpersonal justice is relatively new, as are the benefits of training managers in ways of promoting justice manifested with respect to other desirable forms of behavior such as organizational citizenship behavior (Skarlicki & Latham, 1996, 1997). Still, there is good reason to promote this practice (for a review, see Skarlicki & Latham, in press).

Conclusion

In view of the severity and prevalence of employee theft, we are not surprised that practitioners have proposed a wide variety of recommendations for curtailing it. The vast majority of these, however, are grounded in traditional orientations that ignore the social motives underlying theft behavior (e.g., Tilley et al., 1999; Weiner, 1998). As a result, most managers are inclined to approach employee theft as a problem to be addressed by others, for example, specialists in fields such as criminology, security and loss prevention, and mental health. Conveniently, this frees them from having to assume any personal responsibility for the problem. However, insofar as the traditional approaches to employee theft have not totally eradicated the problem, the door remains open to consider other approaches.

The approach we have advanced here is more interpersonal in orientation and places managers squarely in a position to do something about the problem. Although this responsibility can be burdensome, we believe that the effort to follow our recommendations will be worthwhile. Moreover, we hope that by explaining the solid social scientific bases underlying our recommendations, managers will accept the possibility that they may be contributing to the very problem of employee theft that they hope to eradicate and ultimately will rise to the challenge of attacking this problem.

References

Adams, J. S. (1965). Inequity in social exchange. In L. Berkowitz (Ed.), *Advances in experimental social psychology* (Vol. 2, pp. 267–279). New York: Academic Press.

Adams, V. (1981, November). How to keep 'em honest: Honesty as an organizational policy can help prevent employee theft. *Psychology Today*, pp. 50–53.

Addis, K. K. (1992, July). Company crooks on the line. *Security Management*, pp. 36–38, 40–42.

Altheide, D. L., Adler, P. A., Adler, P., & Altheide, D. A. (1978). The social meanings of employee theft. In J. M. Johnson & J. D. Douglas (Eds.), *Crime at the top* (pp. 90–124). Philadelphia: J. B. Lippincott.

Analoui, F., & Kakabadse, A. (1991). *Sabotage*. London: Mercury.

Ash, P. (1991). *The construct of employee theft proneness*. Park Ridge, IL: SRA/London House.

Bennett, R. J., & Robinson, S. L. (2003). The past, present, and future of workplace deviance research. In J. Greenberg (Ed.), *Organizational behavior: The state of the science* (pp. 247–281). Mahwah, NJ: Lawrence Erlbaum.

Bies, R. J., & Moag, J. S. (1986). Interactional justice: Communication criteria of fairness. In R. J. Lewicki, B. H. Sheppard, & M. H. Bazerman (Eds.), *Research on negotiation in organizations* (Vol. 1, pp. 43–55). Greenwich, CT: JAI.

Bintliff, R. L. (1994). *Crime-proofing your business*. New York: McGraw–Hill.

Black, D. W., & Larson, C. L. (2000). *Bad boys, bad men: Confronting antisocial personality disorder*. New York: Oxford University Press.

Brockner, J., & Wiesenfeld, B. M. (1996). An integrative framework for explaining reactions to decisions: The interactive effects of outcomes and procedures. *Psychological Bulletin, 120*, 189–208.

Bullard, P. D., & Resnick, A. J. (1983). SMR forum: Too many hands in the corporate cookie jar. *Sloan Management Review, 24*(3), 51–56.

Carter, N., Holström, A., Simpanen, M., & Melin, K. (1988). Theft reduction in a grocery store through product identification and graphing of losses for employees. *Journal of Applied Behavior Analysis, 21*, 385–389.

Case, J. (2000). *Employee theft: The profit killer*. Del Mar, CA: John Case & Associates.

Cherrington, D. J., & Cherrington, J. O. (1985). The climate of honesty in retail stores. In W. Terris (Ed.), *Employee theft: Research, theory, and applications* (pp. 27–39). Park Ridge, IL: London House.

Colquitt, J. A., & Greenberg, J. (2003). Organizational justice: A fair assessment of the state of the literature. In J. Greenberg (Ed.), *Organizational behavior: The state of the science* (2nd ed., pp. 165–210). Mahwah, NJ: Lawrence Erlbaum.

Cressey, D. (1953). *Other people's money: A study in the social psychology of embezzlement.* Belmont, CA: Wadsworth.

Dabney, D. (1995). Neutralization and deviance in the workplace: Theft of supplies and medicines by hospital nurses. *Deviant Behavior, 16,* 313–331.

Dalton, D. R., & Metzger, M. B. (1993). "Integrity testing" for personnel selection: An unsparing perspective. *Journal of Business Ethics, 12,* 147–156.

Dalton, D. R., Metzger, M. B., & Wimbush, J. C. (1994). Integrity testing for personnel selection: A review and research agenda. In G. R. Ferris (Ed.), *Research in personnel and human resources management* (Vol. 12, pp. 125–160). Greenwich, CT: JAI.

Dalton, M. (1959). *Men who manage.* New York: John Wiley.

Decker, K. H. (1994). *Privacy in the workplace: Rights, procedures, and policies.* Palm Beach Gardens, FL: LRP Publications.

Delaney, J. (1993). Handcuffing employee theft. *Small Business Report, 18*(7), 29–38.

DeMore, S. W., Fisher, J. D., & Baron, R. M. (1988). The equity–control model as a predictor of vandalism among college students. *Journal of Applied Psychology, 18,* 80–91.

Dineen, B. R., Lewicki, R. J., & Tomlinson, E. C. (2003). *Walking the talk: A field study examining the relationship between supervisory coaching and modeling behaviors and employee discretionary behavior.* Unpublished manuscript, Ohio State University.

Ditton, J. (1977a). *Part-time crime: An ethnography of fiddling and pilferage.* London: Macmillan.

Ditton, J. (1977b). Perks, pilferage, and the fiddle: The historical structure of invisible wages. *Theory and Society, 4,* 39–71.

Emshwiller, J. R. (1993, December 3). Corruption in the bankruptcy system injures firms in need. *The Wall Street Journal,* p. B1.

Ethics Resource Center. (1994). *Ethics in American business: Policies, programs, and perceptions.* Washington, DC: Author.

Farrell, B. J., Cobbin, D. M., & Farrell, H. M. (2002). Codes of ethics: Their evolution, development, and other controversies. *Journal of Management Development, 21,* 152–163.

Feldman, D. C. (1984). The development and enforcement of group norms. *Academy of Management Review, 9,* 47–53.

Folger, R., & Greenberg, J. (1985). Procedural justice: An interpretive analysis of personnel systems. In K. Rowland & G. Ferris (Eds.), *Research in personnel and human resources management* (Vol. 3, pp. 141–183). Greenwich, CT: JAI.

Ginnett, R. C. (1993). Crews as groups: Their formation and their leadership. In E. L. Weiner, B. G. Kanki, & R. L. Helmreick (Eds.), *Cockpit resource management* (pp. 71–98). San Diego: Academic Press.

Gouldner, A. W. (1954). *Wildcat strike: A study in worker–management relationships.* New York: Harper & Row.

Greenberg, J. (1990). Employee theft as a reaction to underpayment inequity: The hidden cost of pay cuts. *Journal of Applied Psychology, 75,* 561–568.

Greenberg, J. (1993). Stealing in the name of justice: Informational and interpersonal moderators of theft reactions to underpayment inequity. *Organizational Behavior and Human Decision Processes, 54,* 81–103.

Greenberg, J. (1995). Employee theft. In N. Nicholson (Ed.), *The Blackwell encyclopedic dictionary of organizational behavior.* Oxford, UK: Blackwell.

Greenberg, J. (1997a). A social influence model of employee theft: Beyond the fraud triangle. In R. J. Lewicki, B. H. Sheppard, & R. J. Bies (Eds.), *Research on negotiation in organizations* (Vol. 5, pp. 22–49). Greenwich, CT: JAI.

Greenberg, J. (1997b). The STEAL motive: Managing the social determinants of employee theft. In R. Giacalone & J. Greenberg (Eds.), *Antisocial behavior in organizations* (pp. 85–108). Thousand Oaks, CA: Sage.

Greenberg, J. (1998). The cognitive geometry of employee theft: Negotiating "the line" between taking and theft. In R. W. Griffin, A. O'Leary-Kelly, & J. Collins (Eds.), *Dysfunctional behavior in organizations: Non-violent dysfunctional behavior* (Vol. 23, Part B, pp. 147–193). Stamford, CT: JAI.

Greenberg, J. (1999). *Interpersonal justice training (IJT) for reducing employee theft: Some preliminary results.* Unpublished data, Ohio State University.

Greenberg, J. (2002). Who stole the money, and when? Individual and situational determinants of employee theft. *Organizational Behavior and Human Decision Processes, 89,* 985–1003.

Greenberg, J., & Alge, B. (1998). Aggressive reactions to workplace injustice. In R. W. Griffin, A. O'Leary-Kelly, & J. Collins (Eds.), *Dysfunctional behavior in organizations: Violent and deviant behavior* (Vol. 23, Part A, pp. 83–117). Stamford, CT: JAI.

Greenberg, J., & Scott, K. S. (1996). Why do workers bite the hands that feed them? Employee theft as a social exchange process. In B. M. Staw & L. L. Cummings (Eds.), *Research in organizational behavior* (Vol. 18, pp. 111–155). Greenwich, CT: JAI.

Greenberg, J., & Tomlinson, E. C. (2004). The methodological evolution of employee theft research: The DATA cycle. In R. W Griffin & A. O'Leary-Kelly (Eds.), *The dark side of organizational behavior* (pp. 426–461). San Francisco: Pfeiffer.

Gross-Schaefer, A., Trigilio, J., Negus, J., & Ro, C. (2000). Ethics education in the workplace: An effective tool to combat employee theft. *Journal of Business Ethics, 26,* 89–100.

Gruys, M. J., & Sackett, P. R. (2003). Investigating the dimensionality of counterproductive work behavior. *International Journal of Selection and Assessment, 11,* 30–42.

Gutman, A. (2000). *EEO law and personnel practices.* Thousand Oaks, CA: Sage.

Hackstain, A. R., Farrell, S., & Tweed, R. G. (2002). The assessment of counterproductive tendencies by means of the California Psychological Inventory. *International Journal of Selection and Assessment, 10,* 58–86.

Hare, R. D. (1965). A conflict and learning theory analysis of psychopathic behavior. *Journal of Research in Crime and Delinquency, 18,* 12–19.

Hawkins, R. (1984). Employee theft in the restaurant trade: Forms of ripping off by waiters at work. *Deviant Behavior, 5,* 47–69.

Hollinger, R. C. (1989). *Dishonesty in the workplace: A manager's guide to preventing employee theft.* Park Ridge, IL: London House.

Hollinger, R. C., & Clark, J. P. (1982). Formal and informal social controls of employee deviance. *Sociological Quarterly, 23,* 333–343.

Hollinger, R. C., & Clark, J. P. (1983). *Theft by employees.* Lexington, MA: Lexington Books.

Hollinger, R. C., & Davis, J. L. (2002). *2001 National Retail Security Survey: Final report.* Gainesville, FL: Center for Studies in Criminology and Law.

Homans, G. C. (1961). *Social behavior: Its elementary forms.* New York: Harcourt, Brace, and World.

Horning, D. N. M. (1970). Blue-collar theft: Conceptions of property, attitudes toward pilfering, and work group norms in a modern industrial plant. In E. O. Smigel & H. L. Ross (Eds.), *Crimes against bureaucracy* (pp. 46–64). New York: Van Nostrand Reinhold.

Jaspan, N. (1974). *Mind your own business.* Englewood Cliffs, NJ: Prentice Hall.

Jones, T. M., & Gautschi, F. H., III. (1988). Will the ethics of business change? A survey of future executives. *Journal of Business Ethics, 7,* 231–248.

Kanki, B. G., & Palmer, M. T. (1993). Communication and crew resource management. In E. L. Weiner, B. G. Kanki, & R. L. Helmreich (Eds.), *Cockpit resource management* (pp. 99–136). San Diego: Academic Press.

Kemper, T. D. (1966). Representative roles and the legitimation of deviance. *Social Problems, 13,* 288–298.

Latham, G. P. (2001). The importance of understanding and changing employee outcome expectancies for gaining commitment to an organizational goal. *Personnel Psychology, 54,* 707–716.

Leventhal, G. (1976). The distribution of rewards and resources in groups and organizations. In L. Berkowitz & E. Walster (Eds.), *Advances in experimental social psychology* (Vol. 9, pp. 91–131). New York: Academic Press.

Leventhal, G. (1980). What should be done with equity theory? In K. J. Gergen, M. S. Greenberg, & R. H. Willis (Eds.), *Social exchange: Advances in theory and research* (pp. 27–55). New York: Plenum.

Lewicki, R. J., Poland, T., Minton, J. W., & Sheppard, B. H. (1997). Dishonesty as deviance: A typology of workplace dishonesty and contributing factors. In R. J. Lewicki, R. J. Bies, & B. H. Sheppard (Eds.), *Research on negotiation in organizations* (Vol. 6, pp. 53–86). Greenwich, CT: JAI.

Lipman, M., & McGraw, W. R. (1988). Employee theft: A $40 billion industry. *Annals of the American Academy of Political and Social Science, 498,* 51–59.

London House and Food Marketing Institute. (1993). *Fourth annual report on employee theft in the supermarket industry.* Rosemont, IL: London House.

Lykken, D. T. (1995). *The antisocial personalities.* Hillsdale, NJ: Lawrence Erlbaum.

Mangione, T. W., & Quinn, R. P. (1975). Job satisfaction, counterproductive behavior, and drug use at work. *Journal of Applied Psychology, 60,* 114–116.

Mars, G. (1973). Hotel pilferage: A case study in occupational theft. In M. Warner (Ed.), *The sociology of the workplace* (pp. 200–210). New York: Halsted.

Mars, G. (1974). Dock pilferage: A case study in occupational theft. In P. Rock & M. McIntosh (Eds.), *Deviance and social control* (pp. 209–228). London: Tavistock.

Mars, G. (1982). *Cheats at work: An anthropology of workplace crime.* Boston: Allen and Unwin.

McGurn, S. (1988, March 7). Spotting the thieves who work among us. *The Wall Street Journal,* p. A16.

Miner, J. B., & Capps, M. H. (1996). *How honesty testing works.* Westport, CT: Quorum.

Mitchell, T. R., Daniels, D., Hopper, H., George-Falvy, J., & Ferris, G. R. (1996). Perceived correlates of illegal behavior in organizations. *Journal of Business Ethics, 15,* 439–455.

Murphy, K. R. (1993). *Honesty in the workplace.* Pacific Grove, CA: Brooks/Cole.

Niehoff, B. P., & Paul, R. J. (2000). Causes of employee theft and strategies that HR managers can use for prevention. *Human Resource Management, 39,* 51–64.

Ones, D. S., Viswevaran, C., & Schmidt, F. L. (1993). Comprehensive meta-analysis of integrity test validities: Findings and implications for personnel selection and theories of job performance. *Journal of Applied Psychology, 78,* 679–703.

Payne, S. L. (1989). Self-presentational tactics and employee theft. In R. A. Giacalone & P. Rosenfeld (Eds.), *Impression management in the organization* (pp. 397–410). Hillsdale, NJ: Lawrence Erlbaum.

Purpura, P. P. (1998). *Security and loss prevention* (3rd ed.). Boston: Butterworth–Heinemann.

Robin, G. D. (1969). Employees as offenders. *Journal of Research in Crime and Delinquency, 6,* 17–33.

Sackett, P. R. (1994). Integrity testing for personnel selection. *Current Directions in Psychological Science, 3,* 73–76.

Sandberg, J. (2003, November 19). Office sticky fingers can turn the rest of us into Joe Fridays. *The Wall Street Journal,* p. B1.

Sennewald, C. (1996). *Security consulting* (2nd ed.). Boston: Butterworth–Heinemann.

Shapiro, D. L., Treviño, L. K., & Victor, B. (1995). Correlates of employee theft: A multi-dimensional justice perspective. *International Journal of Conflict Management, 6,* 404–414.

Sieh, E. W. (1987). Garment workers: Perceptions of inequity and employee theft. *British Journal of Criminology, 27,* 174–190.

Skarlicki, D. P., & Latham, G. P. (1996). Increasing citizenship behavior within a labor union: A test of organizational justice theory. *Journal of Applied Psychology, 81,* 161–169.

Skarlicki, D. P., & Latham, G. P. (1997). Leadership training in organizational justice to increase citizenship behavior within a labor union: A replication. *Personnel Psychology, 50,* 617–633.

Skarlicki, D. P., & Latham, G. P. (in press). Can leaders be trained to be fair? In J. Greenberg & J. A. Colquitt (Eds.), *Handbook of organizational justice.* Mahwah, NJ: Lawrence Erlbaum.

Snyder, N. H., & Blair, K. E. (1989, May–June). Dealing with employee theft. *Business Horizons,* pp. 27–34.

Sykes, G. M., & Matza, D. (1957). Techniques of neutralization: A theory of delinquency. *American Journal of Sociology, 22,* 664–670.

Taft, W. F. (1985). Bulletin boards, exhibits, hotlines. In C. Reuss & D. Silvis (Eds.), *Inside organizational communication* (2nd ed., pp. 183–189). New York: Longman.

Tatham, R. L. (1974). Employee views on theft in retailing. *Journal of Retailing, 50*(3), 49–55.

Terry, D. J., & Hogg, M. A. (1999). *Attitudes, behavior, and social context: The role of norms and group membership.* Mahwah, NJ: Lawrence Erlbaum.

Thibaut, J., & Walker, L. (1975). *Procedural justice: A psychological analysis.* Hillsdale, NJ: Lawrence Erlbaum.

Tilley, B., Dafoe, R., & Putsey, L. (1999). *Positive loss prevention.* Uxbridge, Ontario: Bob Tilley.

Treviño, L. K., & Brown, M. E. (2005). The role of leaders in influencing unethical behavior in the workplace. In R. E. Kidwell, Jr. & C. L. Martin (Eds.), *Managing organizational deviance* (pp. 69–87). Thousand Oaks, CA: Sage.

Treviño, L. K., & Nelson, K. A. (2004). *Managing business ethics: Straight talk about how to do it right* (3rd ed.). New York: John Wiley.

Treviño, L. K., & Weaver, G. R. (2003). *Managing ethics in business organizations: Social scientific perspectives.* Stanford, CA: Stanford University Press.

Treviño, L. K., & Youngblood, S. (1990). Bad apples in bad barrels: A causal analysis of ethical decision-making behavior. *Journal of Applied Psychology, 75,* 378–385.

Vardi, Y., & Weitz, E. (2004). *Misbehavior in organizations: Theory, research, and management.* Mahwah, NJ: Lawrence Erlbaum.

von Hentig, H. (1948). *The criminal and his victim.* New Haven, CT: Yale University Press.

Weiner, A. N. (1998). *How to reduce business losses from employee theft and customer fraud.* Vestal, NY: Almar Press.

Wells, D., & Schminke, M. (2001). Ethical development and human resources training: An integrative framework. *Human Resource Management Review, 11,* 135–158.

Wimbush, J. C. (1999). The effect of cognitive moral development and supervisory influence on subordinates' ethical behavior. *Journal of Business Ethics, 18,* 383–395.

Wolman, B. B. (1999). *Antisocial behavior: Personality disorders from hostility to homicide.* New York: Prometheus.

Zeitlin, L. R. (1971, June). A little larceny can do a lot for employee morale. *Psychology Today,* pp. 22–24, 26–64.

The Purloined Passwords

Ashley Tauro started work at Cranberry Investments International as a secretary just after graduating from high school in Yonkers, New York. While attending a local college, Ashley continued to work part-time, and then full-time, for the family-owned financial services firm, which manages mutual funds and performs accounting functions for companies in the United States and two other countries.

After 6 years with the company in a variety of positions, Ashley was promoted to human resources director and special projects coordinator for the firm. Cranberry Investments, owned by brothers Marshall and Lincoln Cranberry, manages more than $6 billion for more than 60 clients. When Ashley started at Cranberry, she was 1 of 10 employees. When she was promoted to human resources director, the rapidly growing company employed 40 people and had branched out to include an information technology (IT) unit that did software consulting for some of the firm's clients.

Ashley worked in the company headquarters office in New York City with approximately 30 other employees, including Paul Starnes, a member of the IT division. Because the office was small and the hours were long, Ashley and Paul found themselves working late into the evening on many occasions over a period of a few months and eventually became close friends.

Several times while working after hours, usually with no one else in the office, Ashley saw Paul do dubious things with the computer equipment,

AUTHOR'S NOTE: This case was prepared by Roland Kidwell (Niagara University) as the basis for classroom discussion. It concerns an actual organization investigated by the author. The names of all characters and the organization are fictitious, as are some details, to protect the identities of the individuals and the organization involved. A version of this case is included in Kidwell, R. E., Jr., & Kochanowski, S. M. (in press). The morality of employee theft: Teaching about ethics and deviant behavior in the workplace. *Journal of Management Education.*

including downloading software illegally, cracking into different sites, and performing other computer hack work. She learned that others at the company engaged in similar practices and that the owners did nothing to discourage the behavior because it did not harm the business and even benefited it in some cases, including the ability to use software that the company did not purchase.

The managing director of the IT division, Donald Brandeis, knew about all of this and did not appear to care, although he had not been satisfied with Paul's overall job performance. Ashley believed that both Cranberry brothers (Marshall, the president, and Lincoln, the vice president of marketing) were aware of Paul's activities and did not pay much attention to them. At one point, Ashley even overheard a couple of senior company officials laughing about Paul's ability to provide the company with free software.

One night when Ashley was working late, Paul called her over to show her something interesting about the Cranberry Investments computer system. Ashley recalled,

> I think that he wanted to impress me by showing me that he could hack into the system and obtain everybody's passwords. I didn't really want to know, but he did it anyway. And I saw a bunch of passwords. Obviously, neither of us had any bad intentions in knowing these passwords. And in fact, it was pretty much forgotten about. I don't think it was his intention to do anything with them, I think it was more that he wanted to see if he could crack them, not to get them for himself.

One password that Ashley did notice was that of a marketing manager named Rick DiPasquale, a fellow employee she had been dating during recent weeks. His password was easy for her to remember: AshleyT.

Roughly 3 weeks after this incident, Paul's relationship with his boss, Donald, had deteriorated beyond salvation. Donald believed that Paul was not meeting expectations in his job, whereas Paul believed that Donald was not clearly communicating his expectations. Donald believed that Paul did too many things without permission, whereas Paul believed that he was just taking initiative. As a result of the dispute, Paul was let go from Cranberry Investments.

A week later, Ashley was again working late and needed some information to help an offshore client in an emergency. She found that she had been provided with incorrect data and knew the place in the company computer where she could get the correct information—Rick's e-mail account. Because of their relationship outside of work, Ashley knew that Rick would not be concerned if she accessed his e-mail to get the information necessary to help a customer. As she was doing so, Donald, who was also in the office late, happened to walk by and found her in Rick's e-mail account trying to retrieve what she needed for the client.

"When the IT director asked how I was able to get into [Rick's] e-mail, I admitted that I had the password," Ashley recalled. "And when he asked how I had obtained it, I was honest about it." Although Ashley did not think that

Rick would mind her going into his e-mail due to their personal relationship, she said that no one in the office knew they were dating and so it appeared "much worse than it was."

The next day, Marshall Cranberry was informed of the breach of security, and Ashley realized that she was in big trouble. She recalled,

> I was questioned repeatedly. I had to re-hash the entire ordeal, and then they had to decide what to do with me. I was not fired. . ., but they stripped me of my management title. . . . They also informed me that because I didn't tell them I knew what Paul had done, I had compromised the security of the company and I was not going to get my bonus for the year.

The loss of the management title meant a demotion and a lower salary. The loss of the bonus was particularly upsetting because the incident happened about a month before the bonuses were to be awarded, and Ashley was in line to receive a bonus of several thousand dollars. She said,

> I ended up deciding to leave my job because I couldn't deal with having let everybody down. So, out of respect for my bosses, Marshall and his brother Lincoln, whom I had known and worked for [for] 7 years, I informed them of my plans. They didn't take too kindly to my letting them know that I was not going to accept their plans for me in the company [as a marketing support person]. So basically, I ended up getting forced out.

Before Ashley left Cranberry Investments, the company rehired Paul in the IT division. They simply could not replace all of his previous business and IT knowledge. Ashley said, "So, after reprimanding me on compromising the security of the company by not informing them what I'd witnessed Paul do, I got in trouble for using what I'd seen to get into Rick's e-mail to help a client. But I was just trying to do my job."

Discussion Questions

1. What should Ashley Tauro have done when Paul Starnes showed her the computer passwords?

2. What actions, if any, should the company have taken against Ashley? Against Paul?

3. Evaluate the actions, or lack thereof, of Ashley, Paul, Donald Brandeis, and Marshall Cranberry in terms of deviant behavior. Evaluate their actions, or lack thereof, in terms of ethical behavior.

4. How did the informal social processes that are reviewed in Chapter 9 influence the behavior of Ashley and other employees at Cranberry Investments?

5. Discuss Chapter 9's social-based strategies for combating employee theft. Identify and explain those that are relevant to this case.

CHAPTER 10

Managing Organizational Aggression

Mark J. Martinko

Scott C. Douglas

Paul Harvey

Charles Joseph

On December 30, 1999, the Radisson Hotel in Tampa, Florida, was filled with guests. Many were college football fans in town for the "Outback Bowl," whereas others had arrived early to celebrate the coming of the new millennium. All plans were abruptly put on hold at 3:10 pm, however, when a hotel employee named Silvio Izquierdo-Leyva drew a gun and began firing on coworkers. In the end, four of his fellow employees were killed and three others were seriously wounded. A fifth person was also killed by the employee moments later in a failed carjacking attempt. A stunned coworker said, "We had no [problems] with him. . . . He just snapped" ("Hotel Worker Kills Five," 1999).

Almost exactly a year later, on the day after Christmas, a man named Michael McDermott shot and killed seven coworkers at an Internet consulting company near Boston, Massachusetts. Soon after his arrest, McDermott was found to have three guns with him, including a semiautomatic rifle. Police also found the makings of a bomb in his apartment. The shootings took place several days after company officials had offered to help mediate a tax dispute between McDermott and the Internal Revenue Service ("Shooting Suspect Pleads Not Guilty," 2000).

More recently, a disgruntled ex-employee named Salvador Tapia returned to his former place of work in Chicago on August 27, 2003—6 months after he had been terminated from the firm—and fatally shot six employees of the Windy City Core Supply warehouse. Three separate gun battles with police followed before Tapia was himself shot in the back and killed. The toll almost certainly would have been higher if the gunman had not given one former coworker the option of being tied up as opposed to being killed. That man escaped and alerted the police, and the man later reported that Tapia claimed he would not hurt him because "you haven't done anything to me." As for the others, Tapia was quoted as saying, "I am going to kill them all. I want to kill everybody" ("Seven Die in Chicago Warehouse Shooting," 2003).

These stories are a small sample of the many incidents of organizational aggression that have occurred during recent years. By one count, at least 154 people have been killed in 23 workplace shootings since 1986 ("A Record of Workplace Shootings," 2003), and it is likely that the actual number is even higher. In each case, a current or former employee entered a place of business and took the lives of coworkers, often subsequently taking his or her own life. Sometimes a motive was made clear, whereas other times it was a mystery. Taken together, these facts indicate that the topic of worker safety clearly extends beyond the realm of slips, falls, and other workplace hazards.

The reader is probably familiar with common workplace slogans such as "Safety is everyone's job" and "Make safety your first priority." In cases of aggression such as those described earlier, however, the average employee is often powerless. How can a hotel maid or a warehouse worker be expected to determine whether a seemingly normal coworker is on the brink of committing murder?

In truth, most managers are probably not trained to make such determinations, and those who are trained are probably not trained well. This is at least partly due to a lack of a comprehensive theory of workplace aggression that is based on empirical research and solid principles of human behavior rather than armchair theories based on unreliable anecdotal evidence. Although these theories, commonly espoused by the news media and popular press, often sound logical on the surface, they generally gloss over the complex interactions between individual and situational factors that underlie such shocking acts of aggression. Those theories that are more scientific in nature are more rigorous but are often limited in scope and inconsistent with one another (Douglas & Martinko, 2001).

Despite these issues, it is the moral and legal responsibility of all organizations and their managers to provide employees with safe working environments. This includes protection against all forms of workplace aggression. To assist current and future managers with this task, this chapter aims to bring together recent theoretical and empirical research and findings to summarize what is known about workplace aggression. Based on this research, the chapter explains how various warning signs of impending danger can be detected to help prevent future tragedies similar to those described earlier.

Defining Organizational Aggression

There is no single agreed-on definition of organizational aggression in use among those who study this phenomenon. Some researchers use the term to refer to any behaviors that are intended to hurt coworkers or the employing organization (Neuman & Baron, 1997). Others define it as a form of deviance from the norms of an organization that puts the safety of fellow employees in jeopardy (Robinson & Bennett, 1997).

Still other definitions result from different ideas as to exactly what behaviors fall under the umbrella of organizational aggression. In the past, some authors focused on violent actions caused by factors under the organization's control (e.g., Folger & Skarlicki, 1998; O'Leary-Kelly, Griffin, & Glew, 1996), for example, retaliatory actions in response to a mean or overly demanding supervisor. More recent research, however, has also stressed the role of factors beyond the organization's control. These factors, which are discussed in detail later in the chapter, include gender, impulsivity, attribution style, and other factors unique to each individual employee. It may be argued that such factors are insignificant because an employer cannot change them, but as we argue later in the chapter, they can be used as red flags to help managers assess which employees might pose a risk for workplace aggression (Douglas & Martinko, 2001). Thus, we recognize that given certain situations at work, some people are more likely to react aggressively than are others. Our definition of organizational aggression, therefore, considers both organizational- and individual-level factors.

Based on the preceding discussion, the term *organizational aggression* is used here to refer to violent behaviors that are carried out with the intention of causing harm. These behaviors can take either physical or verbal forms and, therefore, can have either physical or psychological effects. They can be aimed at individuals (e.g., shooting people) or property (e.g., blowing up a building) with human casualties as a side effect (Martinko & Zellars, 1998).

We can also distinguish between two forms of organizational aggression: instrumental and hostile. The difference lies in the underlying motivation of the perpetrator. The first form, instrumental, describes aggression that is intended to help achieve a goal such as the attainment of money or power. An example of this type of aggression is armed robbery, a situation where violence is used or threatened to gain possession of some desired object. The other form, hostile, refers to aggression that is acted out with the sole, or primary, goal of hurting people or destroying objects (Feshbach, 1964; Martinko & Zellars, 1998). The focus of this chapter is on the hostile form of organizational aggression because this is often the form shown by disgruntled employees (Martinko & Zellars, 1998).

Theories of Organizational Aggression

Numerous theories have been developed to explain organizational aggression. Martinko, Gundlach, and Douglas (2002) provided a comprehensive summary of these theories. As their article indicates, many of the earlier theories focused on organizational factors associated with aggression.

Included among the theories are Folger and Skarlicki's (1998) popcorn model, which uses the metaphor of people as kernels of corn that are ready to "pop" given the right circumstances. Folger and Skarlicki asserted that certain circumstances, such as unfavorable organizational cultures, policies, practices, and rules as well as unfair, incompetent, or abusive leadership, precipitate incidents of aggression. A similar situational perspective was advanced by O'Leary-Kelly and colleagues (1996), who also emphasized organizational factors, such as overcrowding and controlling policies, that are predicted to drive employees to organizational aggression. A final example of situationally based perspectives is that of Baron and Neuman (1996; see also Neuman & Baron, 1997, 1998), which emphasizes that certain working conditions, such as high temperatures and workforce diversity, can increase the probability of aggression in organizations. Thus, this group of models focuses on sociological factors that organizations may control to reduce the frequency of aggressive actions.

A second group of theories emphasizes the role of individual differences as a major cause of aggressive counterproductive behaviors. Examples of the types of individual differences suggested by this approach include integrity (Ones, Viswesvaran, & Schmidt, 1993; Ones & Viswesvaran, 1998); locus of control and self-efficacy (Bennett, 1998); trait anger, anxiety, and emotion (Fox & Spector, 1999); negative affectivity and attribution style (Martinko & Zellars, 1998); and impulsivity, Machiavellianism, and self-control (Collins & Griffin, 1998). Despite their emphasis on individual differences, these perspectives also recognize that certain organizational factors, such as type of supervision and organizational policies, also play a role in precipitating aggression.

Recently, Martinko and Zellars (1998), Martinko and colleagues (2002), and Martinko (2002) proposed models that integrate these different perspectives into a comprehensive theory that explains aggressive behaviors in organizations. In particular, Martinko (2002) and Douglas and Martinko (2001) demonstrated that although many of these models of organizational aggression emphasize individual differences or situational factors, individuals' attributions regarding the causes of organizational events play an important role in determining their emotions and behaviors. Specifically, individuals who attribute their negative outcomes to external and stable causes, such as punitive managers, are much more likely to become aggressive than are individuals who attribute the same outcomes to their own internal and stable attributes, such as lack of ability.

These models contend that although individual differences may predispose individuals to aggression, individuals' interpretations (i.e., attributions) regarding the causes of organizational outcomes are the critical variables in predicting who will become aggressive. In addition, Martinko and colleagues (2002) also suggested and demonstrated that a paradigm is emerging in that nearly all of the models have the same basic components: organizational factors, individual difference factors, and some type of cognitive processing (i.e., attributions) by the aggressors. A synthesis of the models proposed by Martinko and colleagues is provided in Figure 10.1. In the next section, we provide a brief overview of the model, discuss the various components of the model, and describe how the relations depicted by the model can be managed.

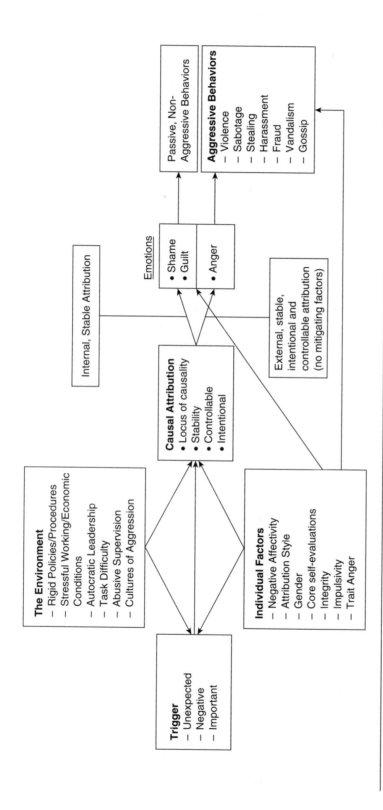

Figure 10.1 A Model of Organizational Aggression

SOURCE: Adapted from Martinko (2002), Martinko and Zellars (1998), and Martinko et al. (2002).

A Model of Organizational Aggression

Overview

The model displayed in Figure 10.1 is based on the attribution process and the elements of the various organizational aggression theories discussed previously. As indicated in the model, aggressive behavior is triggered by some negative outcome, which is followed by a causal search—the attribution process. Depending on the nature of the triggering event, as well as on the context of the situation and numerous individual factors, various attributions are made for the cause of the outcome. If an internal and stable attribution is made, such as to lack of ability, a nonaggressive emotional response, such as shame or guilt, is likely to occur. Alternatively, if the negative outcome is attributed to external factors that are considered to be stable, intentional, and controllable with no mitigating circumstances to justify them, the individual will be likely to feel anger and may retaliate with aggressive behavior.

It is important to note that this model considers both individual and organizational factors. Managers can use information on both types of variables to help ensure employee safety. As is discussed in more detail later, organizational factors can be changed to reduce the number of aggression triggers and the likelihood of external, stable, controllable, and intentional attributions made for the causes of those triggers. On the other hand, although managers cannot change individual factors, they can be made aware of those that predispose people to aggression in certain situations. In combination, this knowledge can be used to prevent tragedies from occurring.

Fleshing Out the Model

In this section we discuss the major characteristics of the model presented in Figure 10.1 to help clarify the complex interactions between people and organizations that may lead to organizational aggression. We begin with the trigger that initiates the process and then proceed to discuss the various factors that influence the process at each successive stage.

Triggers

As mentioned previously, the attribution process for aggression usually begins with a negative outcome that is unexpected and important to the perceiver. Being laid off is an example of such a trigger. Losing one's means of support is a negative outcome and is usually a matter of great importance to the person who suddenly finds himself or herself unemployed with bills to pay. People rarely plan on being fired, so this trigger also meets the criteria of being unexpected. In such a situation, the person will probably become upset and try to identify why this has happened to him or her (i.e., make attributions) and decide what he or she should do about it. Thus, the process depicted in Figure 10.1 has begun.

In addition to having one's employment terminated, numerous other triggers can occur in the workplace that are unexpected, negative, and/or important. Poor performance appraisals, for instance, may have a negative effect on employees. Disciplinary hearings and/or multiple reprimands for poor performance on the job may have similar effects. All of these examples represent outcomes that most rational people wish to avoid. Thus, their occurrence activates the process shown in Figure 10.1 in an attempt to determine the source of the outcome and to avoid it in the future.

The Environment

The environment is a source of trigger events as well as the context within which the individual contextualizes trigger events. Therefore, the environment influences both the frequency and intensity of trigger events and also provides information that the individual uses to make attributions about the causes of trigger events. Because there are countless aspects of the environment that may affect the processes leading to aggression, it is impossible to consider them all simultaneously. Instead, we have selected a list of variables that appear to be especially important, and we discuss each variable in turn.

Rigid Policies and Procedures. Rigidity is commonly cited as a factor in the now infamous U.S. Postal Service shootings that occurred during the 1990s. One example of the rigid policies is when an employee of 16 years was denied permission to leave his post to go home after learning that his house was on fire (Bensimon, 1994). It is not difficult to imagine how such a policy could lead to external and stable attributions for negative outcomes that would, in turn, lead to anger and aggressive behavior.

Stressful Working and Economic Conditions. In general, people seek to avoid psychological discomfort. One particularly prominent form of such discomfort is stress, which can result from the job itself or from factors outside the job such as the economy. To eliminate feelings of stress, it is first necessary to identify the source. Thus, the attribution process is triggered to develop a belief as to the best course of behavioral action to remedy the stress. Importantly, if the cause of stress is believed to be stable and controllable, individuals may become angry and aggressive.

Autocratic Leadership Styles. Autocratic leaders—those who give strict orders and do not accept feedback or other input from subordinates—are thought to affect perceptions of control. Bennett (1998) predicted that this form of leadership causes workers to feel as though they have no control over their success or failure on the job. The result is a tendency toward external attributions for failures.

Task Difficulty. The difficulty of a task, or at least the perceived difficulty, is thought to have a fairly direct impact on attributions (Martinko & Zellars, 1998). In the case of failing to perform a task properly, an employee performing a difficult task is likely to blame the inherent difficulty of the work regardless of the actual cause. When coworkers also believe that a task is difficult, the tendency to make external attributions for negative outcomes becomes even stronger because the attribution is supported by outside opinions.

Abusive Supervision. Abusive supervision is defined as "the extent to which supervisors engage in the sustained display of hostile verbal and nonverbal behaviors" (Tepper, 2000, p. 178). It has been shown to lead to a number of unfavorable reactions by subordinates, including psychological distress (Tepper, 2000). In the model we propose, abusive supervision acts as a trigger because it can have a direct effect on levels of psychological distress.

Cultures of Aggression. Social learning theory predicts that the culture in which a person lives or works can reinforce the use of aggressive behaviors by rewarding him or her (Bandura, 1978). People who observe others succeeding in using aggressive behaviors, either at work or outside of work, to achieve their goals will have incentive to do the same. Thus, although a culture of aggression might not affect the attributions a person makes, it may increase the likelihood of violence in response to an external, stable, and intentional attribution for a negative outcome.

Individual Differences

The goal of this subsection is to examine the individual differences that predispose individuals to be sensitive to triggers to aggression, influence people's attributional processes, and are related to emotions and aggressive tendencies. Because of space limitations and the large number of individual differences that can be included in this category, we have selected only the most salient differences and their effects for discussion.

Negative Affectivity. Research indicates that people with high levels of negative affectivity tend to focus on the negative aspects of their lives. They might perceive as negative outcomes that others might find to be only mildly negative, if at all negative (Martinko et al., 2002; Shavit & Shouval, 1977). Because of the tendency of individuals with high negative affect to harbor a negative outlook, such individuals are probably more likely to perceive negative events (i.e., triggers) and to make counterproductive attributions for negative outcomes that may lead to negative affect and aggressive behavior (Martinko et al., 2002).

Attribution Styles. Different people commonly make divergent attributions for the same outcomes. For example, consider a situation where three equally qualified people are laid off from the same jobs at the same company. The first person might believe that he was terminated because he was not as skillful and productive as he needed to be. This is an internal and stable attribution that may or may not be controllable. The second person might believe that she was a good employee but that economic reasons gave the company no choice but to let her go. This is an external, unstable, and uncontrollable attribution that implies intentionality on the part of the company but takes the mitigating factor of the economy into account. Finally, the third person might also believe that he was a good employee but that his supervisor disliked him and fired him as a result. This is an external, stable, controllable, and intentional attribution with no mitigating factors.

Why might three similar people make such different attributions? One explanation is that they have different attribution styles or tendencies to make certain types of attributions across many different situations. The first employee has what is called a pessimistic attribution style, that is, the tendency to make internal and stable attributions for failures. He blames himself whenever negative outcomes occur. Such people are more likely to feel shame or guilt than to feel angry toward others.

The second employee demonstrates the opposite trait, known as an optimistic attribution style. This is the tendency to make unstable attributions for failures. Although these attributions may also be external, uncontrollable, and unintentional (or intentional with mitigating factors, as in the example of the second employee), instability is the key dimension of the optimistic attribution style when considering negative outcomes. This is because any cause that is temporary—be it internal or external, controllable or uncontrollable, intentional or unintentional—will not hinder future attempts at success once it is gone. In this example, the employee likely believes that she will get her job back (or will get another job) when the economy recovers.

The attribution style of the third employee is of far more concern when predicting instances of aggressive behavior. Known as a hostile attribution style, it is the tendency to make external, stable, controllable, and intentional attributions with no perceived mitigating factors for negative outcomes. People with hostile attribution styles are prone to blame others for all of their failures and to become angry due to their belief that these others are intentionally orchestrating negative outcomes and will continue to do so.

Gender. Numerous studies have shown that males are more prone toward aggressive behaviors than are females (Martinko & Zellars, 1998). Although a thorough discussion about the various theories of why this is the case is beyond the scope of this chapter, it is important to know that males are generally more likely to make hostile attributions and respond aggressively to negative outcomes than are females.

Core Self-Evaluations. Core self-evaluations refer to fundamental subconscious conclusions that individuals reach about themselves, other people, and the world (Judge, Erez, & Bono, 1998; Judge, Locke, Durham, & Kluger, 1998). They consist of four major components: locus of control, self-efficacy, self-esteem, and non-neuroticism. They are believed to be closely related to the attribution process (Martinko et al., 2002) and, therefore, can be expected to influence it.

Those with an internal locus of control tend to take responsibility for their own fate and are likely to be biased toward internal attribution styles; thus, in the case of negative outcomes, hostile attributions (which require external attributions) are unlikely. On the other hand, individuals with high self-esteem or self-efficacy (i.e., faith in one's abilities) can logically be expected to have optimistic attribution styles, taking credit for success and blaming external causes for failure. As Martinko (2002) noted, although slight optimistic biases are probably healthy and motivational because they discourage depression, pronounced optimistic biases can be a problem and can lead to hostile attributions because they result in blaming failure on external sources. Thus, individuals who are extremely high on self-efficacy and self-esteem, and who have pronounced optimistic attributional biases, may be more prone to aggression than are others.

Integrity. Integrity is thought to consist of four components: emotional stability, conscientiousness, agreeableness, and reliability (Ones et al., 1993; Ones & Viswesvaran, 1998). Each of these four can logically be related to the elements of core self-evaluations just described. Emotional stability is very similar to the concept of nonneuroticism, whereas conscientiousness is related to agreeableness, self-esteem, and self-efficacy (Martinko et al., 2002). Therefore, the same relationships between conscientiousness and nonneuroticism and attributions should be expected to apply to the components of integrity. That is, both should be related to optimistic attribution styles and to both the benefits and liabilities of these styles.

Impulsivity. Impulsivity is predicted to cause certain people to be more prone to turning hostile attributions into actual aggressive behavior. This concept refers to an individual's capacity to control his or her impulses in response to negative outcomes. People who are high on impulsivity are often viewed as "hotheads" and tend to respond physically to adverse situations where most people would remain calm (Martinko & Zellars, 1998). Impulsive individuals can also be expected to make hostile attributions.

Trait Anger. Although anger is commonly thought of simply as a negative emotion, two different categories of anger exist: state anger and trait anger (Speilberger, 1996). State anger is a temporary negative emotion occurring in response to a particular event, whereas trait anger is a person's stable tendency to experience state anger over time and in different situations. Individuals with high levels of trait anger are likely to feel state anger more frequently than are those with low levels of trait anger (Douglas & Martinko, 2001). In other words, those with high levels of trait anger become angry more easily and more often than do those with low levels of trait anger.

Research by Douglas and Martinko (2001) showed that high trait anger is related to aggressive behavior. This is most likely because trait anger causes people to perceive a wider range of events as anger provoking (Douglas & Martinko, 2001) and to attribute the events to external causes such as disrespectful treatment (Gibson & Barsade, 1999).

Attributions

Attribution processes are at the heart of our model. These theories are based on the idea that all people are "naive psychologists" who seek to understand and control the causes of outcomes that occur in their lives (Heider, 1958). The key idea underlying this is that people are motivated to avoid psychological discomfort. When this discomfort is felt, an attribution is made for the cause of the discomfort and behavioral responses are made with the goal of eliminating it (Martinko & Zellars, 1998).

Martinko (2002) described the attribution process as follows. A negative outcome occurs, and an initial emotional reaction is made (e.g., feeling frustrated, angry, or sad). A causal search process then begins, resulting in an attribution (i.e., a causal explanation) for the negative outcome. Examples of causal explanations for negative outcomes include ability, effort, an inflexible organizational policy, and a poor economy. Martinko (2002) postulated that all of these explanations can be classified according to two underlying cognitive dimensions: locus of causality and stability. Locus of causality is concerned with whether the cause is internal (e.g., lack of ability) or external (e.g., insufficient resources) to the person. Stability is concerned with whether the cause is expected to remain the same over time or change over time. In addition, several other dimensions have been proposed, including controllability and intentionality (Kent & Martinko, 1995). Controllability has to do with whether or not the individual has control over the cause. Causes that can be changed are controllable, whereas those that cannot be changed are uncontrollable. Finally, intentionality is concerned with whether someone deliberately caused the negative outcome to occur (Betancourt & Blair, 1992).

As Kent and Martinko (1995) noted, the dimensions that are relevant depend on the behavioral domain of interest. Thus, intentionality is usually not relevant when describing the reason why an individual fails because virtually no one intends to fail. On the other hand, when describing external causes for an individual's failure, intentionality can be relevant. We believe that within the domain of aggressive behavior, all four of the dimensions mentioned previously are relevant. More specifically, we propose—and our model indicates—that individuals are most likely to be aggressive when they attribute their negative outcomes to external, stable, and intentional causes that are controllable by others. Conversely, we predict that individuals will respond in passive nonaggressive ways when negative outcomes are attributed to internal and stable causes.

Some comment regarding the effects of dimensions on behavior is in order here. The locus of causality dimension affects emotions. When internal attributions are made for negative outcomes, they result in negative affect that is directed inward such as depression and feelings of helplessness (Martinko & Gardner, 1982). On the other hand, external attributions result in externally directed emotions and, when accompanied by negative outcomes, can result in anger (Gundlach, Douglas, & Martinko, 2003).

The stability dimension affects expectancies. When outcomes are believed to be unstable, the same outcomes are not expected in the future. On the other hand, when outcomes are perceived to be stable, they create the belief that the same thing will happen again in the future. Thus, as our model predicts, the belief that a negative outcome is stable and was intentionally caused by an external source (i.e., a punitive administration) will result in a person who feels trapped and angry and may result in aggressive behavior.

Emotions

As shown in Figure 10.1, three main types of emotions are expected to result from attributions based on negative outcomes. As noted earlier, the first two, shame and guilt, are the result of internal and stable attributions for the negative outcomes (Martinko, 2002). Put simply, these emotions result because there is no action that can be taken to remedy a flaw that is perceived to be both internal and stable. There is no external person at whom to direct one's anger, and the flaw cannot be changed due to its stability.

The third emotion, anger, is thought to result from hostile attributions. Because anger does not always relate to violence, it is important to know when anger is likely to lead to violent outcomes. A study by Douglas and Martinko (2001) found that a primary factor in the anger–violence relationship was the frequency of anger felt by a person. Specifically, people who have high levels of trait anger, and thus feel this emotion on a regular or constant basis, were found to be more prone to aggressive responses. Therefore, this trait, along with other individual factors mentioned previously such as impulsivity and gender, are assumed to explain why some people are more prone to hostile aggression than are others given the same stimulus.

Aggressive Behaviors

The final stage of this model concerns the aggressive behaviors that may result in response to negative outcomes. We can place these behaviors on a continuum ranging from the mundane but common occurrence of low-level aggression, such as gossip and antisocial behavior, to less frequent and extreme forms of aggression, such as violence in the form of physical assault and murder. Although it is not entirely clear why individuals choose a specific form of aggression, we believe that the factors described in the model are capable of at least partially explaining aggressive behavioral choices.

Thus, we expect that more (rather than less) aggressive forms of aggression are displayed when the perpetrator (a) attributes a negative outcome to a specific individual (rather than to an impersonal entity such as the organization), (b) perceives that the outcome of a negative event is extremely serious and was caused intentionally, (c) is in a culture where aggression is common, (d) feels trapped with no way out as a result of perceiving the cause as extremely stable, and (e) exhibits high levels of the individual differences associated with aggression (e.g., negative affectivity, male, hostile attributions, impulsivity, trait anger). Clearly, more research and theory are needed to address these issues more fully. Nevertheless, although our model does not provide a complete explanation of all the factors associated with aggression, we believe that it does point us in the right direction so that managers can begin to anticipate and manage aggressive acts.

Prevention Strategies for Managing Aggression

Our model illustrates a number of individual and situational variables that influence workplace aggression and violence. Furthermore, it shows that attributions and emotions play significant roles in this process. Therefore, it is not surprising that academics and practitioners alike make numerous recommendations and put forth broad-based programs to address these factors and, thus, to reduce the potential for aggression and violence in the workplace. It is to these preventive and reactive strategies that we now turn.

Policy-Level Interventions

At the societal level, the criminal law is the principal mechanism with which to address and reduce acts of aggression and violence. If those who have violated these laws are caught and convicted, they are sanctioned by the criminal justice system (Chappell & Di Martino, 1998). At the organizational level, however, the Health and Safety Work Act of 1974 indicates that employers must make concerted efforts to ensure their employees' health, safety, and welfare at work. Moreover, it requires that employers develop and implement policies and systems for carrying out these responsibilities (Chappell & Di Martino, 1998).

Although cases of spontaneous workplace violence are rare, Nicoletti (1994) and Kennish (1994) argued that disruptive behaviors will continue, or will escalate, if the individuals are not confronted. Moreover, some professionals believe that belligerent, intimidating, and threatening verbal behavior is a precursor to committing physical assault (Kinney, 1996). Therefore, early intervention by employers is of the utmost importance. One method for achieving early intervention is the development of, adoption of, and strict adherence to "zero-tolerance" policies (Neuman & Baron, 1998). For example, the U.S. Postal Service (1992), in conjunction with its unions and management associations, developed and issued a zero-tolerance policy for violence or threats of violence by any employee at any level. It further stated that there would be no tolerance of harassment, intimidation, threats, or bullying by anyone.

Although the development and adoption of zero-tolerance policies are often uncomplicated, strict adherence to their mandates is more problematic. At the very least, all employees should be given written statements clearly detailing these policies and related consequences. In addition, employees should be required to sign a statement indicating that they read and understand the policies (Nicoletti & Spooner, 1996). Furthermore, managers must "walk the talk" by modeling constructive and positive behaviors that reinforce zero-tolerance expectations. Abusive managers who correct subordinates by pounding their fists, swearing, or humiliating them should assess how their behaviors can manifest workplace incivility (Andersson & Pearson, 1999; Tepper, 2000; Tepper, Duffy, & Shaw, 2001), aggression, and violence. When giving negative feedback, it is important for managers to treat employees with dignity and respect. Finally, managers are encouraged to allow more employee participation in decision making given that exclusionary decision practices can increase acts of employee deviance (Aquino, Lewis, & Bradfield, 1999).

Selection Procedures

Screening and selection of employees is perhaps the first line of defense for organizations. The ability to identify individuals who are better aligned with their jobs and the goals of the company decreases the potential for employee failure

(Chappell & Di Martino, 1998). The higher the probability that employees will encounter success, the more likely it is that they will experience eustress, which often leads to positive emotions and outcomes (Selye, 1974). On the other hand, the higher the probability that employees will encounter failure due to seemingly difficult tasks, the more likely it is that they will experience negative emotions and engage in workplace aggression or violence (Martinko et al., 2002).

Before hiring applicants, employers should conduct multiple interviews (Andersson & Pearson, 1999) and attain written permission to conduct background and reference checks. When practical, tests for drug and alcohol abuse are also recommended. In addition, employers should inquire about any gaps in applicants' employment histories (Martucci & Clemow, 1995) because such gaps might indicate a period of incarceration rather than merely unemployment or hospitalization (Bush & O'Shea, 1996). Other checks might include confirmation of reported education, experience, and training; inquiries about military service, general character, and reputation (Nicoletti & Spooner, 1996); and reviews of driving records as an indicator of applicants' impulsivity.

Psychological testing (e.g., State–Trait Anger Inventory [Speilberger, 1996]; International Personality Item Protocol [Goldberg, 1999]; Organizational Hostile Attributional Style Questionnaire [Douglas & Martinko, 2001]) can aid in screening out applicants who exhibit traits associated with workplace aggression and violence. However, because the reliability and validity of these tests are often circumspect, major restrictions have been placed on their use (Chappell & Di Martino, 1998). Furthermore, background checks and psychological tests to identify suitable employees may lead to disability discrimination under the Americans with Disabilities Act or to racial discrimination under Title VII of the Civil Rights Act (Chappell & Di Martino, 1998). Hence, practitioners are faced with a significant dilemma: (a) risk violating the laws on equal opportunity employment by implementing a multifaceted screening and selection process that includes psychological and physiological testing and background and reference checks or (b) risk violating the Health and Safety at Work Act and being held liable for negligent hiring or retention.

Community-Based Interventions

Dietz, Robinson, Folger, Baron, and Shulz (2003) recently suggested an intervention that might alleviate the need for extensive testing and background and reference checks. Because the level of community violence in which organizations exist is positively related to the level of aggression experienced in the workplace, organizational leaders should promote and support community efforts to reduce violence in the community (Dietz et al., 2003). The rationale for this recommendation is that, because the majority of employees for most organizations are recruited from the local community, reducing the level of exposure to violence in the larger labor pool will reduce the likelihood of hiring people who will engage in aggressive workplace behavior. To this recommendation, we would add that conducting local outreach programs by providing internships for people from surrounding communities may be another mechanism for enhancing the local labor pool while giving supervisors a low-risk opportunity to assess the fit between their organizations and prospective interns.

Cultural and Environmental Interventions

At the macro level, organizations should establish cultures that discourage workplace aggression and violence (Dietz et al., 2003). Several types of organizational culture have been identified and are typically described as aggressive, passive, or constructive. In general, aggressive and passive cultures exhibit characteristics associated with heightened levels of aggression and violence, whereas constructive cultures exhibit characteristics that discourage these behaviors. Aggressive–defensive cultures that support oppositional norms of confrontation and negativism stimulate overt expressions of anger (Aquino, Douglas, & Martinko, 2004), which often precede acts of workplace aggression and violence. Aggressive–defensive and passive–defensive cultures that support existing power structures and conventional norms, however, encourage subordinates to conform to authority and, thus, increase the potential for employees to overlook abusive supervisory practices. Constructive cultures, on the other hand, support norms that encourage enthusiasm, intrinsic satisfaction, helping behaviors, and constructive interpersonal relations (Cooke & Szumal, 1993). Hence, practitioners are encouraged to establish constructive organizational cultures.

There are several ways in which to embed a constructive culture in organizations (Schein, 1983). Mission and vision statements that promote constructive interpersonal relations, slogans, and sayings indicating the pursuit of individual growth and intrinsic satisfaction for employees, the communication of stories where employees have exhibited positive behaviors, selection and recruiting materials that clearly illustrate a desire to hire people who support constructive values, and the deliberate modeling of appropriate behaviors by managers are mechanisms for instilling a constructive organizational culture. The design of the workspace and work environment can also be used to communicate a culture where the organization cares about its employees' health, safety, and welfare. Designing the workplace so that there is proper ventilation and thermal control, reduced noise levels, and adequate lighting and restroom facilities communicates a concern for employee well-being, as does the presence of security guards, alarms, protective barriers, and surveillance cameras (Chappell & Di Martino, 1998).

The systems and procedures that organizations employ to monitor, reward, and promote employees are yet another mechanism for instilling a culture that discourages workplace aggression and violence. In short, systems that are perceived as fair and just are more likely to stimulate enthusiasm and promote helping and constructive interpersonal behaviors than are systems that are perceived as unfair and unjust.

Managing Perceptions of Justice

Because individuals distinguish among distributive, procedural, and interactional justice (Bies, 2001; Tepper, 2000), managers should consider how their actions are likely to be perceived along these three dimensions. Recognizing this three-dimensional approach, Folger and Baron (1996) made several suggestions concerning perceptions of justice during performance appraisals, layoffs, and firings. In the performance appraisal context, they recommended that managers use job analyses to develop relevant criteria to determine reward allocations, clearly explain these criteria to their employees, solicit employee self-appraisals using these criteria, and discuss any discrepancies between self-ratings and managerial ratings.

Folger and Baron (1996) recommended that when organizations are laying off employees, they should notify their members in a timely manner and should not increase the pay of upper management shortly before, during, or shortly after this process. They further suggested that managers clearly explain their rationales for layoffs and make it apparent that they considered other financial alternatives. Moreover, employers should seek employee participation in the layoff process (e.g., asking employees for suggestions on how to avoid biased decisions about whom to lay off) and provide relevant details on severance options. When firing employees, managers should first determine the validity of the criteria on which the firing decisions are made (e.g., performance ratings) and be sure that the criteria are adequately explained and consistently applied (Folger & Baron, 1996). In addition, organizations should provide and support a grievance process that is well understood, transparent, and trusted by employees.

Obviously, managers should treat employees with dignity and respect in all areas of the workplace. However, we would add that managers can further enhance perceptions of interactional justice by placing special emphasis on being sincere when firing or laying off employees. Therefore, managers should avoid making insincere platitudes such as "I know how you feel" and "I wish there was some way we could help." It is important that managers respect employees' need for privacy and desire to avoid additional humiliation (e.g., allow them to save face by gathering their personal belongings after work). Sincerity can also be undermined if managers do not stop all calls or other forms of interruptions while informing employees of layoff or firing decisions.

Hughes Electronics Corporation demonstrated its sincere interest in respecting and protecting its employees' well-being. When faced with the downsizing of its operations in Fullerton, California, the corporation developed an on-site career resource center, an internal placement program, and a highly flexible benefit package to help laid-off employees with their transitions (Root & Ziska, 1996). The career resource center was available to both existing and laid-off employees. It provided traditional outplacement services such as workshops on vocational selection, résumé writing, and job searching and interviewing. Employees were also helped with applying for unemployment benefits (Root & Ziska, 1996). To complement these services, Hughes Electronics also gave displaced employees first choice of other job opportunities within the organization. Still, the company's transition benefit package was perhaps the most impressive of all. It provided 3 months of continued health coverage, up to 12 weeks of severance pay, and educational reimbursement. Moreover, on receipt of the 60-day notice of layoff, the transition package allowed employees to take advantage of release time to conduct job searches, interview with other employers, and attend transition training

(Root & Ziska, 1996). In short, rather than just abruptly laying off its employees and leaving them to their own devices, Hughes Electronics conveyed a sense of justice to its members through its sincere consideration and implementation of alternatives strategies.

The work of Martinko, Douglas, Ford, and Gundlach (2004) suggested additional strategies for developing justice perceptions. Given their arguments that perceptions of justice and dues paying reflect underlying attributions for performance outcomes, interventions that address these attributions may be useful. Immunization strategies (Martinko & Gardner, 1982), which pair new employees with existing employees who are particularly competent, increase the likelihood that new employees will attribute their outcomes to internal causes, which in turn manifest positive affective reactions (Martinko et al., 2004). In addition, because justice and dues-paying perceptions are enhanced when employees attribute their coworkers' rewards to internal, stable, and global causes, managers should make concerted efforts to communicate information indicating that recipients are responsible for the rewards (internal), are likely to continue their exemplary behaviors (stable), and exhibit these behaviors in domains outside of the immediate workplace (global). For example, managers might attribute rewards to the recipients' superior work ethics (Martinko et al., 2004).

Attributional Training

Techniques such as attributional training and cueing can be used to address individuals who demonstrate hostile attribution styles (Martinko & Douglas, 1999), which can be readily assessed with attributional style measures (e.g., Organizational Attributional Style Questionnaire [Kent & Martinko, 1995]; Hostile Attributional Style Questionnaire [Douglas & Martinko, 2001]). Attributional training (Albert, 1983; Martinko & Gardner, 1982) involves making people aware of their biases and how they affect people's interpersonal relations. Attributional cueing (Lee, Hallahan, & Herzog, 1996), on the other hand, is a technique to motivate people to increase their level of cognitive processing when making success and failure attributions, thereby alleviating the effects of underlying attribution styles on subsequent behavior. Given that people who exhibit hostile attribution styles are likely to see themselves as victims in multiple workplace situations, and research indicates that a history of perceived victimization leads to heightened aggression (McGue, Bacon, & Lykken, 1993), intervention strategies that focus on people's attribution styles seem particularly relevant.

Attributional training may be an effective strategy when addressing people who tend to be emotionally charged, suffer from low self-esteem, and/or exhibit low generalized self-efficacy. People who exhibit a heightened tendency to become angry or frustrated also tend to make external and stable attributions for their negative outcomes (Aquino et al., 2004). Thus, attributional training that is focused on raising employee awareness of how these causal tendencies stimulate negative emotions and behaviors directed toward others should be considered. People with low self-esteem and low generalized self-efficacy are likely to exhibit a pattern of making external/unstable attributions for their successes and internal/stable attributions for their failures (Martinko et al., 2002). Hence, in these cases, attributional training would emphasize the importance of acknowledging how one's ability contributes to his or her successes (i.e., internal/stable) while recognizing that, on occasion, situational and contextual factors (i.e., external/unstable) can contribute to one's failures.

Attributional cueing and stimulating emotional intelligence capacities are other viable interventions for addressing employee emotions, efficacy, and esteem. Attributional cueing and stimulating emotional intelligence capacities encourage employees to engage in objective causal reasoning, which can help them to overcome attributional patterns that result in negative emotions and underestimations of their workplace capabilities (Gundlach, Martinko, & Douglas, 2003). Underestimation of one's capabilities in the workplace erodes self-efficacy perceptions and, over time and performance domains, is likely to undermine perceptions of self-esteem as well.

Other forms of training that organizations frequently use to prevent workplace aggression and violence include developing employees' communication and customer service skills, improving their abilities to recognize and defuse potentially aggressive or violent situations before they occur, and enhancing the interviewing skills of managers and recruiters (Chappell & Di Martino, 1998). Additional examples include programs that focus on recognizing and defusing potentially aggressive or violent situations, on educating employees about precursors or cues to aggressive behavior and the motivations of aggressors, and on how to respond to emotionally charged persons. In addition to overt cues of pending aggression, such as a tendency to blame others for negative outcomes, elevated voice, clenched fists, and tight jaws, employees should be advised to watch for more subtle cues such as social withdrawal and/or isolation, increased expressions of discontent and psychosomatic complaints, and decreased productivity. Teaching employees to recognize their limits is an important element of defusing programs. Employees need to be skilled at knowing when to discontinue contact with potentially aggressive or violent individuals (Chappell & Di Martino, 1998). To enhance the willingness of employees to disengage, however, organizations should provide outlets that are likely to be viewed as superior resources for addressing these situations.

Employee Assistance Programs

Many organizations have established employee assistance programs (EAPs) to help employees with a wide range of problems that can affect their performance at work (Wexley & Latham, 1991). These programs are often staffed by social workers or trained clinicians who provide confidential counseling services to employees and, in some cases, members of employees' families. Typically, employees contact EAPs due to drug or alcohol abuse and/or emotional, financial, or marital problems (Wexley & Latham, 1991).

However, organizations often use these professionals to aid in the development of programs to address workplace aggression and violence as well. For instance, the U.S Postal Service often works with its EAP during the employee selection process, in developing a positive corporate culture, and in creating early identification and intervention strategies for potentially aggressive or violent situations. Furthermore, its EAP is actively involved in cases where terminated employees require assistance or are deemed as a threat to themselves or other parties (U.S. Postal Service, 1992).

Organizations can also turn to the Occupational Safety and Health Administration (OSHA) for guidance. OSHA (2003) prepared comprehensive guidelines to address workplace aggression and violence. In addition, OSHA offers a sample workplace violence prevention program. This program discusses and provides templates for developing and managing threat assessment teams, which are responsible for assessing an organization's vulnerability to workplace violence. In so doing, the program provides guidance on conducting a workplace security analysis, including the inspection of physical facilities (e.g., surveillance equipment, building access, lighting in parking lots), reviews of work tasks and procedures (e.g., level of crime in the area where tasks are being conducted, staffing level relative to task requirements, procedures for employee dismissal), and the administration of workplace surveys to identify issues not indicated in the other stages of the security analysis (e.g., level of exposure to threats of violence).

The program also addresses the threat assessment team's responsibility to recommend measures to reduce the risk of workplace violence (e.g., enhanced security systems, policy changes concerning staffing levels and employee dismissal, additional training on how to report all incidents of violence or threats of violence) that are derived from the security analysis. OSHA provides templates for making policy statements regarding workplace violence, for incident reporting, and for keeping records of any meetings held by the threat assessment team.

Dealing With the Media

The media often take an interest in some of the more extreme cases of workplace violence. Consequently, it is important to have systems in place for dealing with reporters. Typically, the highest level official on the premises is responsible for handling the situation. However, if possible, a spokesperson should be trained to deal with the media because statements and actions on behalf of the company can be reviewed in the event of litigation (Baughn, 1998). Hence, this person should be trained to not accept blame or responsibility, to avoid giving his or her personal opinions, and to refrain from engaging in discussions on liability or other legal issues (which should be deferred to the company attorney). In addition, the spokesperson should inform the media as to the positive steps that the company is taking (Baughn, 1998).

Conclusion

As we emphasized at the beginning of the chapter, managers have both the moral and legal responsibility to assess potential aggression and then to provide appropriate responses to these situations, protecting the individual rights of potential perpetrators but taking preemptive actions whenever possible. Although many of the strategies suggested in this chapter appear to be simple common sense, they also reflect the realities of the complex interactions illustrated by our model. As the model indicates, aggressive actions are often triggered by negative organizational outcomes that occur in the context of specific environments and are reacted to by unique individuals. To the extent that managers understand the dynamics of these interacting forces, they will be able to apply and fine-tune the strategies we have suggested. We are hopeful that by sensitizing managers to the individual differences and attributional patterns that are likely to be associated with aggression, they will be better able to screen and select productive employees and also better able to identify and respond to potential threats. Similarly, by understanding the types of environmental factors that often cue aggression, we hope that managers will be better equipped to manage their environments so that the frequency of aggressive actions can be reduced.

In closing, we once again emphasize that the process by which aggression is generated is extremely complex and dynamic. Although our model and recommendations are limited, we are compelled to note that many of the components of the model have empirical support and that many of the practices we recommend have become established practices in many organizations. Thus, we are hopeful that the model and strategies are a step in the right direction and reflect a proactive approach to managers' responsibilities to manage and, whenever possible, to reduce the incidence of aggression in organizations.

References

A record of workplace shootings in United States since mid-1980s. (2003, August 27). *Associated Press.* Retrieved September 7, 2003, from LexisNexis database

Albert, R. (1983). The intercultural sensitizer or cultural assimilator: A cognitive approach. In D. Landis & R. Brislin (Eds.), *Handbook of intercultural training* (Vol. 2, pp. 186–217). New York: Pergamon.

Andersson, L., & Pearson, C. M. (1999). Tit for tat? The spiraling effect of incivility in the workplace. *Academy of Management Review, 24,* 452–471.

Aquino, K., Douglas, S. C., & Martinko, M. J. (2004). Overt anger in response to victimization: Attributional style and organizational norms as moderators. *Journal of Occupational Health Psychology, 9,* 152–164.

Aquino, K., Lewis, M. U., & Bradfield, M. (1999). Justice constructs, negative affectivity, and employee deviance: A proposed model and empirical test. *Journal of Organizational Behavior, 20,* 1073–1091.

Bandura, A. (1978). Learning theories of aggression. In I. L. Kutash, S. B. Kutash, & L. B. Schlesinger (Eds.), *Violence: Perspectives on murder and aggression* (pp. 29–57). San Francisco: Jossey–Bass.

Baron, R. A., & Neuman, J. L. (1996). Workplace violence and workplace aggression: Evidence on their relative frequency and potential causes. *Aggressive Behavior, 22,* 161–173.

Baughn, B. (1998). *Controlling a crisis: Preparing for the media.* [Online]. Retrieved September 21, 2001, from http://my.shrm.org/whitepapers/documents/default. asp?page= 61586.asp

Bennett, R. J. (1998). Perceived powerlessness as a cause of employee deviance. In R. W. Griffin, A. O'Leary-Kelly, & J. M. Collins (Eds.), *Dysfunctional behavior in organizations: Violent and deviant behavior* (Vol. 23, Part A, pp. 221–239). Stamford, CT: JAI.

Bensimon, H. F. (1994). Violence in the workplace. *Training and Development Journal, 1,* 27–32.

Betancourt, H., & Blair, I. (1992). A cognition (attribution)–emotion model of violence in conflict situations. *Personality and Social Psychology Bulletin, 18,* 343–350.

Bies, R. J. (2001). Interactional (in)justice: The sacred and the profane. In J. Greenberg & R. Cropanzano (Eds.), *Advances in organizational behavior* (pp. 89–118). Stanford, CA: Stanford University Press.

Bush, D. F., & O'Shea, P. G. (1996). Workplace violence: Comparative use of prevention practices and policies. In G. R. VandenBos & E. Q. Bulatao (Eds.), *Violence on the job* (pp. 283–297). Washington, DC: American Psychological Association.

Chappell, D., & Di Martino, V. (1998). *Violence at work.* Geneva, Switzerland: International Labour Office.

Collins, J. M., & Griffin, R. W. (1998). The psychology of counterproductive job performance. In R. W. Griffin, A. O'Leary-Kelly, & J. M. Collins (Eds.), *Dysfunctional behavior in organizations: Non-violent dysfunctional behavior* (Vol. 23, Part B, pp. 219–242). Stamford, CT: JAI.

Cooke, R. A., & Szumal, J. L. (1993). Measuring normative beliefs and shared behavioral expectations in organizations: The reliability and validity of the Organizational Culture Inventory. *Psychological Reports, 72,* 1299–1330.

Dietz, J., Robinson, S. L., Folger, R., Baron, R. A., & Schulz, M. (2003). The impact of community violence and an organization's procedural justice climate on workplace aggression. *Academy of Management Journal, 46,* 317–326.

Douglas, S. C., & Martinko, M. J. (2001). Exploring the role of individual differences in the prediction of workplace aggression. *Journal of Applied Psychology, 86,* 547–559.

Feshbach, S. (1964). The function of aggression and the regulation of aggressive drive. *Psychological Review, 71,* 257–272.

Folger, R., & Baron, R. A. (1996). Violence and hostility at work: A model of reactions to perceived injustice. In G. R. VandenBos & E. Q. Bulatao (Eds.), *Violence on the job* (pp. 51–85). Washington, DC: American Psychological Association.

Folger, R., & Skarlicki, D. P. (1998) A popcorn metaphor for employee aggression. In R. W. Griffin, A. O'Leary-Kelly, & J. M. Collins (Eds.), *Dysfunctional behavior in organizations: Violent and deviant behavior* (Vol. 23, Part A, pp. 43–81). Stamford, CT: JAI.

Fox, S., & Spector, P. E. (1999). A model of work frustration–aggression. *Journal of Organizational Behavior, 20,* 915–933.

Gibson, D. E., & Barsade, S. G. (1999, August). *The experience of anger at work: Lessons from the chronically angry.* Paper presented at the meeting of the Academy of Management, Chicago.

Goldberg, L. R. (1999). A broad-bandwidth, public-domain, personality inventory measuring the lower-level facets of several five-factor models. In I. Mervielde, I. Deary, F. De Fruyt, & F. Ostendorf (Eds.), *Personality psychology in Europe* (Vol. 7, pp. 7–28). Tilburg, Netherlands: Tilburg University Press.

Gundlach, M. J., Douglas, S. C., & Martinko, M. J. (2003). The decision to blow the whistle: A social information processing framework. *Academy of Management Review, 128,* 107–123.

Gundlach, M. J., Martinko, M. J., & Douglas, S. C. (2003). Emotional intelligence, causal reasoning, and the self-efficacy development process. *International Journal of Organizational Analysis, 11,* 231–248.

Heider, F. (1958). *The psychology of interpersonal relations.* New York: John Wiley.

Hotel worker kills five in shooting spree, police say. (1999, December 30). www.cnn.com/1999/US/12/30/hotel.shooting.02/

Judge, T. A., Erez, A., & Bono, J. E. (1998). The power of being positive: The relation between positive self-concept and job performance. *Human Performance, 11,* 167–187.

Judge, T., Locke, E., Durham, C., & Kluger, A. N. (1998). Dispositional effects on job and life satisfaction: The role of core self-evaluations. *Journal of Applied Psychology, 83,* 17–34.

Kennish, J. W. (1994). Violence in the workplace: Stemming the tide. *Professional Safety, 40*(6), 34–36.

Kent, R., & Martinko, M. J. (1995). The development and evaluation of a scale to measure organizational attribution style. In M. J. Martinko (Ed.), *Attribution theory: An organizational perspective* (pp. 53–75). Delray Beach, FL: St. Lucie Press.

Kinney, J. A. (1996). The dynamics of threat management. In G. R. VandenBos & E. Q. Bulatao (Eds.), *Violence on the job* (pp. 299–313). Washington, DC: American Psychological Association.

Lee, F., Hallahan, M., & Herzog, T. (1996). Explaining real-life events: How culture and domain shape attributions. *Personality and Social Psychology Bulletin, 22,* 732–741.

Martinko, M. J. (2002). *Thinking like a winner: A guide to high performance leadership.* Tallahassee, FL: Gulf Coast.

Martinko, M. J., & Douglas, S. C. (1999). Culture and expatriate failure: An attributional explanation. *International Journal of Organizational Analysis, 7,* 265–293.

Martinko, M. J., Douglas, S. C., Ford, R., & Gundlach, M. J. (2004). Dues paying: A theoretical explication and conceptual model. *Journal of Management, 30,* 49–69.

Martinko, M. J., & Gardner, W. L. (1982). Learned helplessness: An alternative explanation for performance deficits. *Academy of Management Review, 7,* 195–204.

Martinko, M. J., Gundlach, M. J., & Douglas, S. C. (2002). Toward an integrative theory of counterproductive workplace behavior: A causal reasoning perspective. *International Journal of Selection and Assessment, 10,* 36–50.

Martinko, M. J., & Zellars, K. (1998). Toward a theory of workplace violence: A cognitive appraisal perspective. In R. W. Griffin, A. O'Leary-Kelly, & J. M. Collins (Eds.), *Dysfunctional behavior in organizations: Violent and deviant behavior* (Vol. 23, Part A, pp. 1–42). Stamford, CT: JAI.

Martucci, W. M., & Clemow, D. D. (1995). Workplace violence: Incidents and liability on the rise. *Employment Relations Today, 21,* 463–470.

McGue, M., Bacon, S., & Lykken, D. T. (1993). Personality stability and change in early adulthood: A behavioral genetic analysis. *Developmental Psychology, 29,* 96–109.

Neuman, J. H., & Baron, R. A. (1997). Aggression in the workplace. In R. Giacalone & J. Greenberg (Eds.), *Antisocial behavior in organizations* (pp. 37–67). Thousand Oaks, CA: Sage.

Neuman, J. H., & Baron, R. A. (1998). Workplace violence and workplace aggression: Evidence concerning specific forms, potential causes, and preferred targets. *Journal of Management, 24,* 391–420.

Nicoletti, J. (1994). *Violence goes to work.* Englewood, CO: Mountain States Employers Council.

Nicoletti, J., & Spooner, K. (1996). Violence in the workplace: Response and intervention strategies. In G. R. VandenBos & E. Q. Bulatao (Eds.), *Violence on the job* (pp. 267–282). Washington, DC: American Psychological Association.

Occupational Health and Safety Administration. (2003). *Workplace Violence Prevention Program: Part III.* Retrieved December 15, 2003, from www.osha.gov/workplace_violence/wrkplaceViolence.partIII.html

O'Leary-Kelly, A. M., Griffin, R. W., & Glew, D. J. (1996). Organization-motivated aggression: A research framework. *Academy of Management Review, 21,* 225–253.

Ones, D. S., & Viswesvaran, C. (1998). Integrity testing in organizations. In R. W. Griffin, A. O'Leary-Kelly, & J. M. Collins (Eds.), *Dysfunctional behavior in organizations: Nonviolent dysfunctional behavior* (Vol. 23, Part B, pp. 243–276). Stamford, CT: JAI.

Ones, D. S., Viswesvaran, C., & Schmidt, F. L. (1993). Comprehensive meta-analysis of integrity validities: Findings and implications for personnel selection and theories of job performance. *Journal of Applied Psychology, 78,* 679–703.

Robinson, S. L., & Bennett, R. J. (1997). Workplace deviance: Its definition, its nature, and its causes. In R. J. Lewicki, B. H. Sheppard, & R. J. Bies (Eds.), *Research on negotiations in organizations* (Vol. 6, pp. 3–28). Greenwich, CT: JAI.

Root, D. A., & Ziska, M. D. (1996). Violence prevention during corporate downsizing: The use of a people team as context for the critical incident team. In G. R. VandenBos & E. Q. Bulatao (Eds.), *Violence on the job* (pp. 353–365). Washington, DC: American Psychological Association.

Schein, E. (1983). The role of the founder in creating organizational culture. *Organizational Dynamics, 11,* 13–28.

Selye, H. (1974). *Stress without distress.* Philadelphia: J. B. Lippincott.

Seven die in Chicago warehouse shooting. (2003, August 28). www.cnn.com/2003/US/Midwest/08/28/chicago.shooting/

Shavit, H., & Shouval, R. (1977). Repression–sensitization and processing of favorable and adverse information. *Journal of Clinical Psychology, 33,* 1041–1044.

Shooting suspect pleads not guilty to office killings. (2000, December 27). www.cnn.com/2000/LAW/12/27/office.shooting.04.crim/

Speilberger, C. D. (1996). *State–Trait Anger Expression Inventory, research edition: Professional manual.* Odessa, FL: Psychological Assessment Resources.

Tepper, B. J. (2000). Consequences of abusive supervision. *Academy of Management Journal, 43,* 178–190.

Tepper, B. J., Duffy, M. K., & Shaw, J. D. (2001). Personality moderators of the relationship between abusive supervision and subordinates' resistance. *Journal of Applied Psychology, 86,* 974–983.

U.S. Postal Service. (1992, February 14). *Joint statement on violence and behavior in the workplace.* Washington, DC: Author.

Wexley, K., & Latham, G. (1991). *Developing and training human resources in organizations* (2nd ed.). New York: HarperCollins.

Disney or Bust

John Davis and 10 family members had been sitting in Newark International Airport in New Jersey for hours when they began boarding their flight for a vacation trip to Disney World in Orlando, Florida.

Tempers were getting heated on that summer evening at the airport. A windowless terminal, frequently termed "the dungeon," was packed with hundreds of frustrated passengers who had been waiting for hours for delayed planes and who had been provided with little information as to when their planes would depart. Continental gate agent Angelo Sottile was among the airline employees who were attempting to respond to passengers' concerns.

The Davis family had arrived from Virginia at 3 pm for a 6:45 pm flight to Orlando. When the flight was already more than 2 hours late, airline personnel began to allow the boarding of the aircraft. Davis and his family members, taking advantage of an invitation to preboard because they had small children, were stopped in the process when Sottile told them that they did not have enough boarding passes for everyone.

At that point, Davis's 2-year-old daughter wandered into the Jetway toward the airplane. Davis's wife, Victoria, who had been pushing her mother in a wheelchair, tried to chase after the little girl. Davis, a 29-year-old assistant plant manager, attempted to follow but Sottile stopped him, according to witnesses.

That is where the stories of the two men and witnesses to the incident seriously conflict. Sottile, 52 years of age, said that Davis lifted him in a bear hug and threw him headfirst to the ground when he attempted to block Davis's way. Davis said that Sottile pushed his wife, backed into his daughter, and

AUTHOR'S NOTE: This case was prepared by Roland Kidwell (Niagara University) as the basis for classroom discussion. It was developed from information included in accounts listed in the bibliography at the end of the case. All names of individuals and the organization are real.

then began strangling him before Davis lifted him off the ground and they both fell to the floor of the terminal.

Sottile, a post office employee who worked part-time for Continental, suffered neck and head injuries in the July 1999 incident. He told a criminal court jury in March 2001 that the incident had cost him 80% of the range of movement in his neck.

A fellow gate agent for Continental testified that during the struggle, she saw Davis pick up Sottile and throw him several feet. "I thought he [Sottile] was dead," she said. "I thought he had choked him. He was bleeding from his mouth and nose. His eyes were completely white."

Victoria Davis testified that Sottile had pushed her when she tried to get to her daughter but that she went around him anyway. She said that she saw Sottile grab her husband by the neck and begin to choke him before both of them fell to the floor.

Davis, a much larger man than Sottile, was arrested and charged with second-degree assault, which carries a maximum sentence of 10 years in prison. Nearly 2 years later, the "air rage" case—as it was dubbed by the media— came to trial in Newark. Witnesses gave conflicting testimony about how the incident started and about whether Davis was to blame for the injuries or they were the result of an accident.

Leslie Mann, the prosecutor, told the jury that Davis and his family's claims of self-defense conflicted with the testimony of several witnesses and Davis's own statement to police the night of the incident. He accused the defense of trying to sway the jury by playing up the jurors' possible hatred of the airline industry and emphasizing the wholesome image of Davis and his wife, who was often in court holding one of their children.

In his closing argument, Davis's defense attorney, Anthony Pope, told the jury that Sottile had already worked a full day at the post office when he came to work that evening with Continental at a terminal where he had to handle hundreds of people whose flights had been delayed. Other passengers described Sottile as angry and aggravated, Pope said, whereas Davis was "a happy man going on vacation." Sottile brought on the injuries himself by using ineffective customer service skills, Pope said.

After several days of hearing testimony, the eight-woman, four-man jury deliberated for several hours before acquitting Davis of assault. Jurors later reported that they initially believed the prosecution's witnesses but that when they attempted to simulate the story that Sottile and others related, they could not succeed in the jury room.

In addition, jurors interviewed by the *New Jersey Law Journal* said that they thought the gate agent had been the aggressor even though they were sympathetic about his injuries. Jurors said that the evidence indicated that Sottile had displayed a belligerent personality. When Sottile arrived at the hospital, he was so upset that he had to be given a sedative so that he could undergo treatment, according to a hospital report highlighted in Pope's closing argument. Apparently, the jurors were also swayed by testimony that Sottile had raised his voice to passengers during the long wait to board.

The criminal matter ended, but the legal action continued. Sottile filed a civil suit against Davis as well as the airport's operator and a security firm. He accused the airport operator and the security firm of failing to take actions to prevent passenger violence. Davis filed a suit against Continental charging that its insufficient training led to employees acting in a violent and hostile way toward their customers.

Eventually, Davis and his family drove to Disney World the following year. Continental had banned him from future flights.

"It's a sad day when somebody can break a person's neck in anger and walk away without being punished," a Continental public relations manager said after the verdict. "We carry 40 million people a year. If one of them wants to turn a public airline terminal into the WWF [World Wrestling Federation], we have to believe that that's an isolated incident."

Discussion Questions

1. Is this a case of deviant workplace behavior? Why or why not?

2. What triggers and their environmental and individual sources discussed in Chapter 10 relate to incidences of aggression and violence that occurred in the airport?

3. Now that John Davis has been acquitted by a jury, what action, if any, should the airline take regarding its employee, Angelo Sottile?

4. According to the model in Chapter 10, what outcomes and reactions might be expected if disciplinary action is directed at an employee in a case such as this?

5. Based on Chapter 10's suggested prevention strategies, what might the company have done to stop an incident such as this from occurring? In your answer, examine how employees should be trained to react to irate customers before situations escalate into violence, the company's human resources management responsibilities, and its ethical responsibilities.

Bibliography

Lima, P. (2001, March 28). Defendant's wife says gate agent pushed her. *The Record,* p. A6 (Bergen County, NJ). Retrieved December 12, 2003, from LexisNexis database

Newman, M. (2001a, March 20). Trial opens over scuffle at airport. *The New York Times,* p. 5. Retrieved December 12, 2003, from LexisNexis database

Newman, M. (2001b, March 28). Witnesses say airline agent at Newark attacked first. *The New York Times,* p. 7. Retrieved December 12, 2003, from LexisNexis database

Newman, M. (2001c, March 30). Man in scuffle at airport says agent was instigator. *The New York Times,* p. 5. Retrieved December 12, 2003, from LexisNexis database

Newman, M. (2001d, March 31). Passenger cited self-defense, officers testify. *The New York Times,* p. 5. Retrieved December 12, 2003, from LexisNexis database

Newman, M. (2001e, April 3). Jury deliberates in trial over fight at airport boarding point. *The New York Times,* p. 2. Retrieved December 12, 2003, from LexisNexis database

Newman, M. (2001f, April 4). Man found not guilty of attack on airline worker. *The New York Times,* p. 1. Retrieved December 12, 2003, from LexisNexis database

Peach, R. J. (2001, April 9). Agent's demeanor led to acquittal, not "air rage" empathy, jurors say: Hospital report, almost redacted, described agent as combative. *New Jersey Law Journal.* Retrieved November 17, 2003, from LexisNexis database

CHAPTER 11

Addictive Behavior in the Workplace

Paul M. Roman

ddictive behaviors affect many employed Americans and their dependents. Contrary to widespread imagery of homelessness, despair, and lack of social affiliations, the vast majority of those with alcohol or drug problems are "respectable" people who either are employed or are dependents of employed people. The significant presence of alcohol problems in the workforce was documented in a 1997 national survey indicating that approximately 7.6% of people in the full-time employed workforce are heavy drinkers and that approximately 7.7% are users of illegal drugs (Zhang, Huang, & Brittingham, 1999). According to the study, about one third of the heavy drinkers are also illegal drug users. For these prevalence reasons alone, these behaviors should be important concerns for employers as well as for unions and other organizations representing interests of employees.

Beyond the impressive data about problematic behavior relative to alcohol and drugs, concerns with addictive behaviors have been extended to many other areas such as gambling (Moreyra, Ibanez, Liebowitz, Saiz-Ruiz, & Blanco, 2002), deviant eating patterns (Rogers & Smit, 2000), sex addiction (Irvine, 1995), and excessive use of the Internet (Soule, Shell, & Kleen, 2003). As a concept, addiction might seem simple and straightforward, but it is part of a long historical record in the United States. Over time and space, concern about addictive behaviors has ebbed and flowed, both in the attitudes held by the general population and in those found among employers. This chapter addresses the "why" of this attention.

First, however, it is important to place in context what is meant by "addictive behaviors." Understanding its application in the workplace is aided by a critical examination of this concept. Unfortunately, addictive behaviors are viewed very glibly, particularly in the mass media but also in general public discourse, including that in which workplace leaders participate. This broad application of the addiction concept is particularly marked during these early years of the new millennium. The term is applied loosely and to a myriad of behaviors. Interests range from genetic inheritance of addictive tendencies to litigation against restaurateurs who have supposedly played some causal role in people's addiction to high-fat "junk" foods that are consumed in mass quantities across Western societies. In fact, the addiction concept is fairly complex, with a rich cultural history, and also is the subject of a wide range of carefully designed scientific investigations.

We note only briefly a particular application of the addiction concept in the workplace that demonstrates its arbitrary features, its relationship to cultural norms, and its ambiguity. This is the phenomenon of "workaholism," which is variously defined as intense love of work, irrational commitment to work, or a syndrome of compulsion, perfectionism, and achievement (Harpaz & Snir, 2003). The manifestations of workaholism are readily observable in most workplaces, frequently among employees regarded as the most "heroic" of those protecting the organization's well-being as well as among employees who are intensely centered on their own achievements and mobility but who offer advantages to the organization through their obsessive-like behaviors. Although we discuss interventions later in this chapter, it is clear that employers rarely move quickly (and probably rarely do anything) to curb this particular pathology. In fact, if we look at employers' practices to promote commitment and loyalty, it is clear that obsession and total involvement of one's life energies in work is not that far down the continuum from "normality." Nonetheless, the behaviors of those we call workaholics bear many resemblances to addictive behaviors.

Key Features of the Addiction Concept

Turning back to those behaviors that are viewed as more or less pathological, we ask this question: Why has addictive behavior become such a prominent concept in contemporary American culture? Although at best it is a loosely defined paradigm when characterizing behavioral excesses in eating, gambling, or viewing the Internet, the core of most people's conception of addiction centers on psychoactive drugs, including alcohol but with particular fascination linked to addictions to cocaine and the opiates. Here, through florid imagery of progressions of social and psychological loss and physical deterioration, the embedded notions of "compulsion" and "loss of control" and overall chaos in addicts' pattern of living hold dramatic cultural potency.

Over the past three decades or so, the model of addictive "progression" has spread to eating, sexual activity, shopping, using the Internet, gambling, and viewing pornography. A key issue, although a rarely addressed one, is whether this extension of the addiction concept contributes to the enhancement or muddling of understanding. A closely accompanying question is whether this imagery enhances the effectiveness of prevention or intervention. Nonetheless, addiction is an idea that captures and grasps popular attention. Furthermore, there currently seems to be no end to the extension of "addiction" as a means of categorizing certain patterns of repeated behavior as well as to the application of the term to new behavioral forms.

Attention paid to addictive behaviors in American culture during the early 21st century far exceeds the attention that was paid to addictive behaviors at any point during the 20th century or earlier. An obvious explanation is that this increased attention is simply a reflection of the increased prevalence of these behaviors. Although increased attention certainly suggests increased occurrence, this is an argument that is difficult to either defend or refute. Where baselines are available, such as in the cases of alcohol and certain drug dependencies, there is no compelling evidence of increased prevalence (Faupel, Horowitz, & Weaver, 2003) but no doubt of an increase in societal attention. In the cases of deviant patterns of eating, pathological gambling, compulsive shopping, and sexual obsessions, there are no baseline measurements for comparison even though many of these behaviors have apparently persisted for eons. Internet addiction stands out as a behavior that is newly prevalent and, thus, possibly adding to the overall prevalence of addictive behaviors because it does not clearly represent the transformation or reinvention of an earlier behavioral pattern.

Noting this exception but assuming that the overall pattern of societal attention is not due to new epidemic waves of aberrant behavior, the diffusion, adoption, and extension of the addiction concept may reflect two cultural structures that are subtle and rarely discussed. First are the implications of the addiction concept for the normalization or abnormalization of an entire class of behaviors. The concept of addiction tends to avoid labeling as problematic essential behaviors such as eating, drinking alcohol, gambling, and having sex, allowing the vast majority of these behaviors to be classified as "normal." Instead, the concept draws attention to certain people who, for various reasons, are prone to uncontrolled and/or compulsive patterns that are defined as destructive to the self and others. However, these so-called addictions are not unique, bizarre, or "discontinuous" behavior patterns but rather are exaggerations of what are otherwise regarded as normal (and sometimes essential) behaviors. The implication of this reasoning is that most people can engage in these behaviors without significant harm and without jeopardizing their own or others' physical or psychological well-being. From this perspective, the normalizing effects of the use of the addiction concept are evident.

Two other consequences of this perspective are worth noting. First, by characterizing the addictions as continuous extensions of normal behavior, this allows the possibility of the deviant actors being moved down the continuum such that their behavior comes to parallel that of the "normals." This further allows the possibility of the deviants "returning to the fold" if they modify, moderate, or even abandon their aberrant behavior patterns. A second and more problematic implication is that when a continuum between normal and abnormal is assumed, "cutting points" are necessary to distinguish between where normality ends and deviance begins. There are clearly challenges in generating cutting points that can be scientifically defended and around which popular consensus can be generated.

The second cultural structure, an alternative to using the continuum model (which focuses on addictive patterns of normal behaviors), is to "abnormalize" an entire set of behaviors such that the whole class of behaviors is forbidden, that is, defined and dealt with as illegal acts. This eliminates the need to establish cutting points but appears to offer the opportunity for deviants to change their behaviors and return to the fold. This paradigm is well known in various forms of prohibition of certain behaviors, including the use of certain psychoactive substances, most notably marijuana, cocaine, and many of the opiates.

To demonstrate an earlier point about the complexity of thinking associated with addictive behaviors, current society includes versions of the continuum conception, the abnormalization conception, and combinations of both. The presence of these multiple paradigms is illustrated in everyday life in the workplace. When what appear to be addictive behaviors become evident among employees, managers wring their hands and shake their heads in bewilderment over the "right thing to do" while supervisors and coworkers become frozen into inaction due to ambivalence and doubt about "getting involved."

The dynamics of both of these paradigms are best described with behaviors that, over time and cultural space, have shifted back and forth between these two perspectives. To illustrate these points, we look briefly at the societal histories of alcohol, drugs, and gambling.

Alcohol and Drugs:
From Normal to Evil and Back

American history, as well as the history of many other countries, is marked by a period of national prohibition of the production and distribution of alcoholic beverages. The 13 years of prohibition, from 1920 to 1933, were preceded by nearly a century of cultural conflict and struggle over the apparent social, psychological, and physiological menaces presented by the consumption of ethyl alcohol or ethanol. This experience had its own context, namely the previous centuries and eons during which the vast majority of the ancestors of those who had come to populate the United States had used alcoholic beverages as part and parcel of everyday life. It is of some interest to note that the social institution where prohibition was (and still is) successfully implemented was the American workplace (Rumbarger, 1989).

During the late 19th century, while social concerns over alcohol and pressure to enact some form of prohibition of its manufacture and distribution were major preoccupations of the American people, substances containing cocaine, morphine, and other opiates were widely available as over-the-counter medications for a wide range of discomforts (Musto, 1999). These remedies were not limited to adult administration; some were recommended for infants' discomfort during teething and children's experience of nausea. Although there was clear evidence of social concern about morphine dependence among Civil War veterans, the widespread availability of opiates and cocaine through legal channels elicited little reaction. To the extent that documentation exists, employers were ambivalent and confused about these drugs but generally appeared to want to keep users off their payrolls (Morgan, 1974).

These contrasting patterns of societal management of alcohol and of cocaine and the opiates did, of course, reverse themselves during the 20th century. Alcohol prohibition was enacted but then repealed, and alcohol was allowed to reenter society in a context of modest controls. Not only did drug concerns envelope opiates and cocaine, but they also extended to marijuana with the enactment of a form of prohibition considerably more intense than that designed to eliminate traffic in alcoholic beverages.

The fit of addiction concepts into these two historical cycles seems to be full of contradictions. During the 19th century, alcohol came to be viewed as extremely potent and dangerous, easily seducing its regular users into a described behavior pattern that appeared to be similar to addiction (but was rarely labeled as such) and, more significant, destroying these drinkers' ability to work and support their families. After the repeal of prohibition, this vision changed and a disease concept of addiction was slowly adopted (Roman, 1988; Schneider, 1978). It is clear that repeal of prohibition could not be justified if it was accompanied by the notion that anyone who tried alcohol could readily become addicted to its use. Instead, the aforementioned normalization notion spread, with scientists asserting that a small portion of the population was vulnerable to alcohol addiction but that the majority of responsible adults could use the substance safely. This redirected societal efforts away from controlling the availability of alcohol to developing means for identifying and rehabilitating addicts. Addicts could safely reenter social roles only as abstainers from alcohol. In this sense, prohibition was continued but was limited to a tiny proportion of the population.

The vision of danger associated with illegal drugs shifted in a reverse direction, namely from an assumption that opiates and cocaine could be used safely by nearly anyone, including infants, to the idea that even a single "taste" of these substances could produce addiction. Although opiates continue to be used in medicine for the treatment of pain (but not without controversy that has escalated during recent decades [e.g., Meier, 2003]), prohibition of drugs, including marijuana, became the norm of the land. This social and cultural achievement is complex but very important in providing insights into American culture, particularly the diffusion of stigma associated with minority and immigrant groups (Musto, 1999).

Thus, today the "War on Drugs" continues, primarily concerned with ceasing the manufacture and distribution of illegal opiates, cocaine, and marijuana. Drug addicts are socially real and are viewed by many to exist in far larger numbers than is socially tolerable. However, rather than being viewed as physiologically different from the rest of the population (as is the case with alcohol addicts), drug addicts are viewed as people who deliberately, inadvertently, and/or stupidly "tasted" drugs and became victims to powerful forces of chemical seduction far beyond their control. Drugs are a menace to all of us, and all of us have the potential to become addicts if we dare to "taste" these potent chemicals.

An extreme of this vision has, in fact, permeated a great many American workplaces through the adoption of preemployment drug screening. Applicants whose urine or other physiological samples indicate any use of marijuana, cocaine, or opiates are typically denied employment. Thus, an addiction criterion is far from that required for rejection from employment on the basis of alleged illegal drug use. The fact that these tests indicate nothing about the ability to perform the job is seen as irrelevant (Normand, Lempert, & O'Brien, 1994). Evidence that individuals have engaged in criminally linked behaviors is enough for many employers to deny employment. Thus, in comparison with other items typically included in employee selection batteries, preemployment drug testing has more features of a moral screen than of a performance screen.

Gambling: From Prohibition to Normality

Gambling has a long history in human societies but has not been a significant social issue in American culture until the recent past. From the founding of the United States until the last quarter of the 20th century, most gambling was defined as illegal. Gambling that occurred was limited to localized small venues, and to some extent, gambling in association with drinking in saloons was one of the ignominious activities that helped to fuel the anti-saloon movement that preceded the national prohibition of alcohol manufacture and distribution (Clark, 1976).

During the early 20th century, organized casino gambling was legalized in most parts of the state of Nevada as a means of generating public revenue and attracting visitors and settlers to an otherwise undeveloped locale. Small pockets of highly regulated legalized gambling were found in numerous locations across the country by way of pari-mutuel betting on horse and dog races. Individuals also had the opportunity to engage in legalized gambling by way of investments in the various public stock markets, although there remains a strong cultural norm to restrict this behavior from inclusion in most definitions of gambling.

During the last quarter of the 20th century, large-scale gambling opportunities emerged very rapidly at multiple venues across the United States. One particular opportunity that had been previously unknown for many decades was the large-scale public lottery. Because of the perception that publicly controlled gambling offers important opportunities for revenue for state and local governments, lotteries and casino opportunities have spread in nearly "boom" fashion across the nation. The emergence of the Internet has added nearly infinite opportunities to these other venues for gambling, although nearly all Internet gambling is currently beyond the reach of governmental authorities that might seek their share of revenue from these activities.

Legislation that provides special opportunities for casino development to American Indian tribes may assuage a long-term national guilt. Reservation-based casinos have spread gambling opportunities into areas that otherwise would be viewed as strongly opposed to such activity, specifically the Deep South. A related vehicle of moral justification for gambling is the assignment of state lottery revenues to the funding of public education, including college and university scholarships in states such as Georgia.

Viewed from a broad perspective, the transformation of gambling from a prohibited marginal activity to one that is now accessible to practically any American who seeks such opportunities is truly astonishing. Within the addiction treatment community, there has been a small movement toward using the continuum paradigm in which "pathological" gambling is distinguished from "normal" gambling. Curiously, there is nothing approaching a national social movement in opposition to organized gambling, and currently the public mood appears to view these activities as a legitimate, reasonable, and noncompulsory source of public revenue. So far, there is no evidence of a movement within the community of employers to address the many facets of gambling that might manifest themselves in the workplace.

"Cures" as Support for Addiction Concepts

One of the ways in which the normalization model attracts societal support is through the successful cultural assignment of an addiction-related problem to the health care delivery system. In early postrevolutionary America, there were carefully argued published tracts, notably those of Benjamin Rush, centering on the idea that excessive use of alcohol and other psychoactive substances represented a disease that might best be handled through the expertise of medical care rather than through the single-minded punishment approach of the criminal justice system.

These ideas were further developed during the 19th century, and during the 1890s a physician, Leslie Keeley, founded a system of treatment programs that provided care to hundreds of thousands of clients (White, 1998). The complex of centers grew to a substantial magnitude in the form of the "Keeley Cures," where individuals who could not control their use of alcohol or drugs were placed in residential care. While in residential care, these individuals were lectured extensively about the importance of abstinence while, at the same time, they received doses of a secretly formulated "bichloride of gold," which was believed to aid in motivating these individuals to reform their behaviors. This massive and financially successful treatment system collapsed with the death of Keeley, a typical charismatic leader of great energy who was also highly secretive and provided no plan of organizational succession.

The 20th century saw the slow but substantial medicalization of treatment for both alcohol and drug problems through the distinctive presence of physicians at the core of early treatment programs and as the advocates of research to develop more efficacious treatments. These efforts are distinctively present today as extensive research programs across the country work to find new biological interventions for substance abuse as well as refinements of psychosocial treatments, all of which are delivered under the aegis of medical and paramedical specialists.

This process of medicalization is intertwined with a second cultural force that may be seen as supportive of the addiction concept. This is the widespread application of a common structure for controlling addictive behaviors, namely a variety of self-help programs that are more or less based on the "Twelve Steps" of Alcoholics Anonymous

(AA). Since AA was founded in 1935, there has clearly been a lag in the application of these principles to other behavior patterns. People who have reached various stages of "recovery" from their various addictive behaviors often present their affliction with the disease and their recovery achievements with pride, tapping into American values of achievement and self-control (Trice & Roman, 1970; Williams, 1970). This reasoning reflects an apocryphal statement that cures are primary forces in the invention of diseases. These self-help programs clearly describe the route by which people whose behavior was once addictive can be returned to the fold.

A consequence of major implications for both the workplace and other venues where addictive behaviors become evident may be posited to capture the outcomes of both of these meso-processes. Both the addiction concept and its avoidance of prohibition and the self-help recovery concept and its routes to control over addiction serve to atomize social problems of addictions. In other words, both the definition of the disorder and the definition of the cure focus attention on the afflicted individual rather than on a class of individuals who are characterized by common patterns of etiology and/or who have experienced shared interactions.

In fact, the imagery of these disordered individuals casts them as moving about bars, liquor stores, casinos, strip joints, and/or cyberspace in the company of a multitude of normal others; the deviants generally do not move together in groups. This circumvents social conflict that could arise if the definition of disordered behavior challenged the lives and lifestyles of classes of people, as once was the case with homosexual behavior in American culture until the American Psychiatric Association and related organizations actually "voted out" their earlier definition of homosexuality as a problem of mental disorder that needed treatment (Kirk & Kutchins, 1992).

Addictive behaviors have been variously characterized as diseases, compulsions, and bad habits. Common across such behaviors are repetitive actions that apparently become independent of structures of punishment and reward, at least as these structures are viewed by outside observers. Key to viewing and thinking about these behaviors is the idea that their sources lie somewhere within the individuals, their family backgrounds, and the kinds of choices they have learned to make during the socialization process.

Particularly crucial is the manner in which this paradigm draws attention nearly completely away from the manner in which social institutions, such as the workplace, schools, colleges, systems of medical care, and even churches or other religious establishments, embed within themselves behavioral and social generators of anxiety and depression and also provide, supplement, and/or enable the kinds of behaviors that ultimately come to be labeled as addictive. Thus, from employers' perspectives, enthusiastic and committed adoption of the normalization approach and its accompanying addiction concept might ultimately serve as a protection against litigation that something in the nature of work "caused" the problem.

The Workplace Response

Within the written and unwritten strategic human resources plans in workplaces, attention paid to addictive behaviors is highly variable. Approximately 60% of

American workplaces have in place some form of employee assistance program (EAP) (Roman & Blum, 2004), a mechanism that is supposed to address problems of addiction as well as a range of other issues that employees bring from the home and community to the workplace. Despite their widespread presence, EAPs vary greatly in the extent to which they are distinctively integrated into the managerial and human resources structures of organizations. Furthermore, although these programs were originally designed to address addiction-related issues, particularly alcohol problems, there is substantial evidence that they have shifted from these foci to dealing with employees' self-defined problems, particularly in the arena of marriage and family issues—problems that are much more "user-friendly" than stigmatized behaviors such as the addictions.

At the same time, the concept of addiction is largely associated with illegal drugs, and for some time this has been a "hot button" issue of major importance to many workplaces. Central to the issue of addiction in the workplace is how and when the focus should be on exclusion or inclusion within the workforce of employees whose behaviors might be called addictive. However, as described earlier, there is only ambiguous evidence that employers who use drug screening are attempting to target potential addicts.

Adding to the confusion is the fact that most American adults use alcohol, a legal psychoactive drug that is vaguely accepted as a "social lubricant" and only rarely is viewed as a medication. Distinguishing among alcohol use, alcohol abuse, and alcoholism is arbitrary at best, usually residing in the eye of the beholder. Behaviors that are often objectively very similar may be viewed by some as criminal deviance and by others as manifestation of illness (Roman & Blum, 1991). An indisputable conclusion, however, is that a significant proportion of those with alcohol or drug problems are stigmatized by their significant others, leading to a variety of avoidance behaviors along with other indicators of ambivalence.

If a majority attitude can be distilled from America's workplace leaders during the 21st century, it is that job applicants who use drugs should be denied employment but that current employees with drug or alcohol problems should be given a chance to deal with their problems before being excluded from the workplace (Knudsen, Roman, & Johnson, 2004). When viewed in combination, these strategies have a contradictory element. One policy embeds a notion of primary prevention whereby illegal drug users are precluded from being hired and contaminating the workplace with their disrespect for legal authority, questionable job performance, and/or inducement of coworkers to also become users of illegal drugs. The second policy acknowledges that drug and alcohol problems are reversible or correctable. Thus, when these problems emerge among people who are already employed, they are the targets of what can be called a human resources conservation policy. Viewing these human resources policies in this way, rather than as corporate humanitarianism, it is clear that they may be based on avoiding loss of the organizational investments made in employees who may have "messed up" in one or more areas of their lives (Roman & Blum, 1999).

The foregoing discussion offers an important context for understanding how employers implement this strategy and the extent to which they invest resources in it. The medicalized rhetoric of intervention and recovery is definitely affected by the "just say no" principle that implies individual control over the decision of whether to use psychoactive substances. The commitment of employers to saving the employment of substance-abusing employees is limited and may be accompanied by multiple contingencies. We currently know little about addictive behaviors beyond those involving alcohol and drugs, and it is likely that ambivalence and mixed messages will extend to these other addictive behaviors as well.

Historical Development of Intervention Strategies

Effective means to deal with employed persons with alcohol problems have existed for more than 60 years (Trice & Schonbrunn, 1981). However, diffusion of these techniques was very slow because employers did not perceive large-scale problems with alcohol abuse in their workforces or because public relations concerns made them reluctant to admit such problems (Roman, 1981). The turning point occurred during the 1970s with the invention of the EAP (Roman & Blum, 1985; Trice & Roman, 1972; Wrich, 1973).

This strategy has much more of a human resources management flavor than did the earlier programs, which were heavily oriented toward outreach and recovery by way of the ideology of AA. It shifted the focus from employees with alcohol problems to employees with any kind of personal problems that affected their work. Few employers would argue that they had no employees who brought personal troubles to the workplace.

The rapid diffusion of EAPs suggested that they would be used in a variety of ways by their organizational sponsors. Because adoption has been voluntary, there are only suggested program standards for the structure and content of EAPs. These emanate from occupational associations of EAP specialists, which do not cover the entire field and within which there is little consensus about any issue. Consequently, there is no reason to assume that an extant EAP includes an emphasis on, or even sensitivity to, addictive behavior issues among the workforce or that it is equipped to deal appropriately with these problems when they occur. Some EAPs consist only of telephone contact points that are unlikely to provide the necessary mechanisms to manage cases of employees with addictive behavior problems. But in many settings, EAP structures can incorporate adequate supports for addictive problem intervention.

Making an EAP Effective in Dealing With Addictive Behaviors

The vast majority of EAPs suggest that employees access services by self-referral (sometimes they suggest *only* this possibility). Thus, the culture of a given workplace will affect the types of behavior that lead peers and/or supervisors to "nudge" employees toward sources of help. These norms often have a considerable effect on what employees themselves perceive as their own personal problems for which they should seek help.

Five components are essential for an EAP to address addictive behavior problems effectively:

1. The program policy and program philosophy are clearly based on job performance.

2. The program is appropriately staffed to provide services for employees with addictive behavior problems.

3. The program is directly and readily accessible to supervisors and employees.

4. Supervisors, employees, and union representatives all are aware and supportive of use of constructive confrontation (described later).

5. Staff specialists are equipped and supported to link employees with appropriate resources for assistance, engage in case management throughout the treatment period, and implement long-term follow-up based in the workplace.

Supervisors should be fully trained regarding the organization's intervention policy for employees with addictive behavior problems. The pivotal issue is whether the suspected problem has generated a job performance problem that can be documented. It is only under these circumstances that an intervention is legitimate unless employees refer themselves for assistance without supervisory involvement. Such self-referral often occurs due to nudges from coworkers or supervisors.

The performance emphasis is key. For example, it may be counterintuitive to suggest that the most effective way in which to identify and motivate an employee with an alcohol problem is to ignore the alcohol problem and focus on documented evidence of job performance problems. This reflects the first policy fundamental, namely that the employer's scope of legitimate interest is in work performance rather than in personal lifestyles or off-the-job behavior. This does not mean, of course, that an EAP policy suggests that the employer must tolerate on-the-job drinking, drugging, gambling, or sexually inappropriate behavior. It does mean that the scope of the EAP is limited to job performance issues. If a behavior that is proscribed by company policy occurs on the job, it is dealt with as a disciplinary issue under the rules that are set down in the proscriptive policy. This underlines the importance of a distinctive and well-diffused written policy about the parameters of the EAP and its interface with other organizational policies.

Help seeking by either supervisors or employees requires minimal social distance between those who need help and those who are equipped to provide it. Especially in dealing with ambiguous conditions such as addictive behaviors, there must be a reasonable level of trust and confidence in the person who is expected to be the source of assistance. Thus, it is important for the workplace-based intervention service to have competent personnel actually based in the workplace. Familiarity with such an individual and confidence in that person's skills are likely prerequisites to many, if not most, supervisory referrals.

Such visibility and confidence will be enhanced by the active participation of EAP staff members in supervisory training as well as by their ongoing "presence" in the workplace. Such participation includes integrating EAP staff members with the medical or human resources function in the organization and ensuring that they are knowledgeable about all aspects of workplace culture, regulations, and personnel policies. Many EAPs are staffed outside the host organization, with EAP personnel located elsewhere and coming on-site only occasionally if at all. Although such an arrangement may work well for self-referrals, especially where confidentiality is the primary concern, it is not ideal for supervisory access.

Access to a trusted expert usually precedes a successful referral of a subordinate with an addictive behavior problem. Workplace management should encourage such consultation before attempting a supervisory referral and should discourage the attitude that the policy expects the supervisor to "go it alone." Consultation allows the EAP staff members to encourage the supervisor to proceed with the referral and review the appropriate steps to ensure conformity with policy. At the same time, such consultation can be of great value in precluding inappropriate referrals.

Constructive Confrontation

A strategy with proven effectiveness in dealing with employees with substance abuse problems and that likely extends effectively to intervention with other addictive behavior problems is constructive confrontation. This strategy is not used frequently but is vital for approaching employees who deny that anything needs to be done about either their behavior or their performance or who repeatedly insist they can deal with things on their own. Constructive confrontation involves a meeting between the supervisor and the problem subordinate, with a representative of the union or employee association present if specified in the organizational policy. The meeting proceeds with presentation to the employee of documented evidence of performance decrements coupled closely with assurances of the employer's willingness to suspend disciplinary steps and to support help seeking if the employee will follow prescribed steps to deal with the problem.

It is critical to underline that the responsibility for change rests completely with the employee and that statements made during a constructive confrontation do not constitute a contractual agreement implying that employment will be maintained regardless of help seeking or the possible outcomes of help seeking. The alternatives of progressive discipline and possible dismissal on the grounds of the poor performance record are also outlined in this meeting. The combination of positive and negative elements in this meeting is critical, and it is essential that the supervisor and/or manager be carefully coached by the EAP staff professional before attempting a constructive confrontation. By offering assistance as an immediate part of the process, the constructive element is emphasized. But at the same time, job jeopardy is suggested, indicating a distinctive confrontation. It is absolutely critical for the discussion to underline that the singular concern of the employer is the employee's job performance.

For obvious practical reasons, the use of constructive confrontation typically occurs as a "last resort," and it is clear that most supervisors would prefer not to become involved in such a meeting. A classic research study indicated that constructive confrontation was most effective for those employees who were heavily invested in their jobs (Trice & Beyer, 1984).

The EAP's Role in Follow-up

There is substantial importance attached to the participation of the EAP in follow-up. Recovery from alcohol or drug problems, as well as from other long-term and ingrained addictive behaviors, is a gradual learning process with substantial risks of relapse. Enlightened employers with a commitment to dealing with addictive behaviors will recognize that relapse is not the ultimate disaster or failure but rather is often part of the recovery process. However, employers cannot tolerate endless relapses. Policy on job performance expectations should govern the management of relapses.

Experience has demonstrated the efficacy of posttreatment follow-up by the EAP (Foote & Erfurt, 1991). Follow-up should be systematic and frequent, and it should occur for a relatively lengthy period. The "captive" nature of the workplace and of work roles helps to ensure that this can happen and that it can be carried out in a cost-efficient manner. Such ease of access between the professional and the client within the work setting contrasts sharply with community-based attempts at follow-up. The integration of follow-up into the expectations of the EAP staff role is also a much better fit than are attempts to assign this role to treatment functionaries.

Conclusion

Addictive behaviors offer a number of challenges to employers, beginning with how they are defined and conceptualized. Many workplaces have in place EAPs that have the potential to effectively address employees' addictive behavior problems, but it is not safe to assume that the EAPs always do so automatically and without explicit monitoring and attention.

EAPs were launched with primary attention to substance abuse problems, the intervention technology for which is easily extended to other addictive behaviors. Since government support for this programming effort was withdrawn during the 1980s, it appears that this attention has been steadily declining. Employers found EAPs to be useful for other problematic issues, and this interest went hand in hand with the marketing efforts of those purveying EAP services. Changes in EAP design and emphasis made them responsive to a variety of other workplace issues that seem to have captured the majority of EAP resource investment in many settings.

EAPs have the potential to effectively address employees' addictive behaviors through specific mechanisms of identification, referral, treatment, and follow-up. This will not happen, however, unless EAPs are especially equipped with specialist knowledge and orientation through their staffing and program operations. Addictive behaviors present many potential costs to employers, and it is foolhardy to ignore them. At the same time, employers should look closely at concepts of addiction, normality, and abnormality as they design and implement new policies or revisit and redesign existing policies.

Finally, our current knowledge of EAP activity points to the potential fallacy of workplace decision makers' inadequate level of information and the possible faulty assumption that addictive behavior problems are being dealt with through their EAPs, which are in fact unequipped to deal with them.

References

Clark, N. S. (1976). *Deliver us from evil: An interpretation of American prohibition.* New York: Norton.

Faupel, C. E., Horowitz, A. M., & Weaver, G. (2003). *The sociology of American drug use.* New York: McGraw–Hill.

Foote, A., & Erfurt, J. C. (1991). Effects of EAP follow-up on prevention of relapse among substance abuse clients. *Journal of Studies on Alcohol, 52,* 241–248.

Harpaz, I., & Snir, R. (2003). Workaholism: Its definition and nature. *Human Relations, 56,* 291–319.

Irvine, J. M. (1995). Reinventing perversion: Sex addiction and cultural anxieties. *Journal of the History of Sexuality, 5,* 429–450.

Kirk, S. A., & Kutchins, H. (1992). *The selling of DSM: The rhetoric of science in psychiatry.* New York: Aldine de Gruyter.

Knudsen, H. K., Roman, P. M., & Johnson, J. A. (2004). The management of workplace deviance: Organizational responses to employee drug use. *Journal of Drug Issues, 34,* 121–134.

Meier, B. (2003). *Pain killer: A "wonder" drug's trail of addiction and death.* New York: Rodale.

Moreyra, P., Ibanez, A., Liebowitz, M. R., Saiz-Ruiz, J., & Blanco, C. (2002). Pathological gambling: Addiction or obsession? *Psychiatric Annals, 32,* 161–166.

Morgan, H. W. (1974). *Yesterday's addicts: American society and drug abuse, 1865–1920.* Norman: University of Oklahoma Press.

Musto, D. F. (1999). *The American disease: Origins of narcotic control* (3rd ed.). New York: Oxford University Press.

Normand, J., Lempert, R. O., & O'Brien, C. P. (1994). *Under the influence: Drugs and the American work force.* Washington, DC: National Academy Press.

Rogers, P. J., & Smit, H. J. (2000). Food craving and food "addiction": A critical review of the evidence from a biopsychosocial perspective. *Pharmacology, Biochemistry, and Behavior, 66,* 3–14.

Roman, P. M. (1981). From employee alcoholism to employee assistance: An analysis of the de-emphasis on prevention and on alcoholism problems in work-based programs. *Journal of Studies on Alcohol, 42,* 244–272.

Roman, P. M. (1988). The disease concept of alcoholism: Sociocultural and organizational bases of support. *Drugs & Society, 2,* 5–32.

Roman, P. M., & Blum, T. C. (1985). The core technology of employee assistance programs. *ALMACAN: Magazine of the Association of Labor and Management Administrators and Consultants on Alcoholism, 15*(3), 8–19.

Roman, P. M., & Blum, T. C. (1991). The medicalized concept of alcoholism: Contemporary social sources of ambiguity and confusion. In D. Pittman & H. White (Eds.), *Society, culture, and drinking patterns revisited* (pp. 753–774). New Brunswick, NJ: Rutgers University, Center of Alcohol Studies.

Roman, P. M., & Blum, T. C. (1999). Internalization and externalization as frames for understanding workplace deviance. In I. H. Simpson & R. L. Simpson (Eds.), *Research in the sociology of work: Deviance in the workplace* (pp. 139–164). Greenwich, CT: JAI.

Roman, P. M., & Blum, T. C. (2004). Employee assistance programs and other workplace preventive strategies. In M. Galanter & H. D. Kleber (Eds.), *The textbook of substance abuse treatment* (3rd ed., pp. 527–546). Washington, DC: American Psychiatric Press.

Rumbarger, J. J. (1989). *Profits, power, and prohibition: Alcohol reform and the industrializing of America, 1800–1930.* Albany: State University of New York Press.

Schneider, J. (1978). Deviant drinking as disease: Alcoholism as a social accomplishment. *Social Problems, 25,* 361–372.

Soule, L. C., Shell, L. W., & Kleen, B. A. (2003). Exploring Internet addiction: Demographic characteristics and stereotypes of heavy Internet users. *Journal of Computer Information Systems, 44,* 64–73.

Trice, H. M., & Beyer, J. M. (1984). Work related outcomes of constructive confrontation in a job-based alcoholism program. *Journal of Studies on Alcohol, 45,* 393–404.

Trice, H. M., & Roman, P. M. (1970). Delabeling, relabeling, and Alcoholics Anonymous. *Social Problems, 17,* 468–480.

Trice, H. M., & Roman, P. M. (1972). *Spirits and demons at work: Alcohol and other drugs on the job.* Ithaca: Cornell University, New York State School of Industrial and Labor Relations.

Trice, H. M., & Schonbrunn, M. (1981). A history of job-based alcoholism programs, 1900–1955. *Journal of Drug Issues, 11,* 171–198.

White, W. L. (1998). *Slaying the dragon: The history of addiction treatment and recovery in America.* Bloomington, IL: Chestnut Health Systems.

Williams, R. M. (1970). *American society: A sociological interpretation* (3rd ed.). New York: Knopf.

Wrich, J. M. (1973). *The employee assistance program.* Center City, MN: Hazelden Foundation.

Zhang, Z., Huang, L. X., & Brittingham, A. M. (1999). *Worker drug use and workplace policies and programs: Results from the 1994 and 1997 National Household Survey on Drug Abuse.* Rockville, MD: U.S. Department of Health and Human Services, Substance Abuse and Mental Health Services Administration.

Gambling at Amyfixe: Reality and Fantasy

M arcia Trent, vice president of finance, told the three other Amyfixe executives who had joined her in the conference room of the management consulting firm, "I've called this meeting to deal with some difficulties we seem to be having with gambling in the workplace."

Trent had called Jean Baker, the human resources (HR) director, Leon Flowers, the accounting manager, and Sam Cjeka, the information technology (IT) manager, to an emergency meeting after Flowers had contacted her about an employee with a known gambling problem who apparently had been using the company's Internet access to engage in his habit.

"Marcy Smoot called me earlier this week," Flowers told the group. "It seems that Bart has had a relapse with his gambling demon. When she looked through his credit card bill the other day and saw some unusual charges totaling several hundred dollars, she confronted him. He told her he had been placing bets on baseball games through our Internet server with an outfit down in Costa Rica. And he'd been losing big time." Bart Smoot was a long-time company accountant whose performance was of high quality despite his periodic bouts with gambling.

"We can limit his access to certain Internet sites," said Cjeka, the IT manager. "That should help resist the temptation."

AUTHOR'S NOTE: This case was prepared by Roland Kidwell (Niagara University) as the basis for classroom discussion. Although Amyfixe and its managers are fictional, the problems faced by the company and the solutions proposed in this case are based on the experiences of actual organizations. The author thanks Brian O'Neill, a fantasy baseball league team "owner," for providing insights about fantasy sports. Additional sources about the topics in this case are listed in the bibliography at the end of the case.

"We can get him into some counseling through the employee assistance program," said Baker, the HR director. "When he had this problem a few years ago, we did that and it really helped. I'm glad his wife called you because last time they almost lost their house."

"Thankfully, we've caught this before it got out of hand," said Flowers, the accounting manager. "Once we restrict access and make sure everyone understands that Internet gambling is against the rules, the problem is solved."

"I don't think so," Trent said. "We've dealt with a symptom, but there's a larger problem in the company."

Baker and Flowers looked at Trent quizzically, seeking the elaboration that she quickly provided.

"Last week, I walked by Francis Gregory's cubicle over in client marketing," Trent said. "I didn't mean to snoop, but I saw stacks of paper listing the upcoming football games for the first week of the NFL season and a dozen phone messages from clients scattered all over the desk. The messages had to do with getting a pool sheet over to them by fax or e-mail before the Friday deadline."

"The office pool," Baker said.

"Yes," Trent said. "Then I passed by another group down the hall, and they were having an animated discussion about their fantasy baseball league. These are the same guys who have fantasy teams in a basketball league and a football league, too. This place is turning into Atlantic City. Based on what I saw and overheard, I've asked Sam to check into some other Internet surfing that has gone on around the office in the past few weeks."

Flowers shifted uncomfortably in his chair. He was a regular player in the National Football League (NFL) and National Collegiate Athletic Association (NCAA) basketball tournament pools and knew that several of his employees had teams in fantasy sports leagues.

The office NFL pool charged $5 to enter each week along with a $1-per-season fee to cover copying the entry sheets. With as many as 120 employees and clients participating, the payout for the person who picked the most games correctly was potentially $600. The NCAA basketball pool was even more lucrative. With a $20 entry fee and 200 people playing, the winner could receive $4,000.

Fantasy sports leagues worked a bit differently. To become a team owner in a fantasy baseball league, each person contributed $150. That money was used partly to cover the cost of a computer service (e.g., www.allstarstats.com) that tabulates league standings and provides periodic statistical reports, but mainly it was used to provide money for the prize pool. Before the season started, owners were allocated $300 in fictional money, which was used to bid for the rights to 2 catchers, 10 pitchers, 5 outfielders, 6 infielders, and 2 utility players.

At the end of the real baseball season, the team owner whose players displayed the best statistics in terms of batting averages, home runs, wins, earned run averages, and so on won half the prize pot. Second place received 25%, third place received 15%, and fourth place received 10%. The latter two places were pretty much "break-even" for participants because transaction fees are assessed if owners make player trades with other owners during the season. One participant described fantasy baseball not as gambling but rather as more of "a crazed intellectual exercise." Part of this crazed nature occurs because during the season the participants obsessively check the major league box scores every day to see how well their players performed.

"Now, I know we allow the pools and this fantasy stuff to take place in the office," Trent said. "But I'm curious about whether our employees are taking company time to use the Internet to prepare for the office pool. And what about those fantasy league people checking the statistics? We have poor Bart Smoot, a gambling addict, using the Net to place bets. They can't be a good example for him. Do we have employees wasting time getting stats for their own gaming activity? And are they getting addicted to the Web on our dime?"

"I know it gets bad during March when the employees are in this very room checking out the early NCAA games on TV or on the Net," Baker said. "But that's only 2 days of the year. I know these pools and what-not may distract from work, but they also help relieve stress in the office."

"Yeah," Flowers said. "I think the pool is good for business. I'm told by Gregory that it keeps up client contact on an unofficial basis. And it helps morale. It gets people talking and excited, from top management to the janitors. People talk more face-to-face about the sports pool than just about anything else. It's an experience they can share no matter who they are. And when they talk personally rather than sending a bunch of e-mail to each other, they develop a better working relationship."

"Did you read that in a management book?" Sam asked.

"Sure did," Flowers responded. "And the same is true for the fantasy leagues, I think. The people who are participating seem to be doing their jobs all right. I don't think they're wasting much time surfing the Net. At least I don't think it takes place on an addictive basis. And speaking of obsessions, what about shopping on the Web? I think a lot of that goes on as well from our office computers."

On this point, Trent was a bit more lenient. "Well, we ask a great deal from our people, and sometimes working 50 or 60 hours a week and travel-ing to meetings and engagements, they can't get to the stores as much as they'd like."

"That's certainly true," Baker said.

"At any rate," Trent said, "we can discuss that issue in the context of some information I've asked Sam to collect for this meeting. Sam?"

The IT manager passed out a spreadsheet to the others. They studied it a bit before he elaborated.

"Based on your request, Marcia, I checked website access for the 10 par-ticipants in the company's fantasy baseball league over the last 2 weeks. I also looked at the time spent on each site. As you can see on the spreadsheet, this indicates that half of the participants spend more than an hour each day looking at these sites. One of them, Michael Fontaine, is logged into espn.com, nfl.com, and ncaa.org for more than 4 hours each day on average."

"Wow," Flowers said. "That seems excessive."

"Let's not forget that Fontaine is part of the sports management consulting team," Baker said. "He could be spending much of that time doing his job rather than collecting statistics and so on."

There were murmurs of agreement around the table.

Trent was the next to speak. "I think we've only scratched the surface here, Sam. The next questions involve the effect on company productivity. And what about Bart? The temptation of surfing the Net for scores and statistics may have put him back in touch with his gambling problem. And these other fellows—does this seem like obsessive behavior to you?"

"It seems a bit much," Sam agreed.

"Well, it's not covered under our Internet and e-mail policies," Baker said. "While we have some general comments on using the computers only for work purposes, we only specifically outlaw downloading pornography and accessing sexually oriented sites. That doesn't apply to sports sites and even gambling sites. The latter was an oversight that we can fix. Also, as we discussed, there's a connection between the use of the Internet to get stats and to do other things such as collect job-related information for our sports management consultants."

"I really don't think the use of Internet sites seems to have an effect on the productivity of my staff," Flowers commented. "But these guys who are surfing the Net are obsessed with this fantasy league and the stats. Should we look into Internet shopping now?"

"I don't have any data on that," the IT director said. "I could do another search, but one thing I have received are complaints from some departments that our Internet connection has been slowing in recent months. It could be due to surfing, shopping, or legitimate use. What I've read about this issue indicates that companies that monitor their employees say Web shopping is the most addictive activity on the Internet, and looking at news and sports sites is a close second."

"Other than writing in a ban on accessing gambling sites to our policy, what options do we have to deal with this situation?" Trent asked Cjeka.

The IT director listed a few alternatives. All of them involved increasing monitoring of computer use or changing company policies.

The first alternative involved implementing a more strict policy on Internet surfing and e-mail use from work, banning inappropriate e-mails and participation in e-mail chain letters as well as banning visits to retailer sites, auction sites, and other non-job-related sites. The company could purchase software that analyzes words that are typed into company computers, including Web addresses and e-mail, and company managers would be able to log in to check the way in which company computers were being used. The software could also block all employee access to certain prohibited websites. This software offered the least expensive option (other than doing nothing), not including costs associated with managers' time watching their employees' computer use.

A second alternative would be to install software that allowed workers to regulate their own Web use. An icon on each computer screen would show Internet use divided into business and nonbusiness groupings based on how Amyfixe viewed what was a business-related site versus a non-business-related site. The program would also show the employees how much time they spent on business-related sites versus non-business-related sites. This was the most expensive option.

Finally, to limit recreational Internet use, the company could allow only certain employees to access sites related to sports and/or shopping. Some employees' computers would be blocked, whereas others' computers would be allowed expanded access based on job needs.

"Except for these office pools, we have a ban on gambling in the workplace," Trent said. "At least I thought we did until I heard about these Internet sites. Now I'd like to hear your thoughts on the extent of our problems and whether Sam has offered us any feasible solutions to deal with what I believe is fast becoming addictive behavior."

Discussion Questions

1. List and examine the various examples of employee behaviors that were discussed at the meeting. Which of these behaviors, if any, should be viewed as deviant? Reflecting on Chapter 11's approach to the addiction concept, are the employees participating in the office pools and/or fantasy leagues engaging in addictive behavior? Why or why not?

2. Discuss Chapter 11's description of the changing societal views toward gambling. How might those changing views have had an impact on what is going on at Amyfixe?

3. Based on Chapter 11, is the use of an employee assistance program appropriate in the case of Bart Smoot? Why or why not? Would another type of intervention be more appropriate?

4. Identify the ethical issues regarding the use of company resources for office pools and fantasy leagues. Can an organization effectively use an office pool or a fantasy sports program to help manage potentially addictive gambling behavior? If so, how might this occur?

5. a. What are the pros and cons associated with the three monitoring options discussed by the IT manager, Sam Cjeka? Which of them would be most effective in dealing with the behavior that takes place in this case? Why?

   b. What would your reaction be to the three monitoring options if they were adopted in your workplace? Do any of them invade employee privacy? Do any of them interfere with legitimate work use of the Internet? Explain.

Bibliography

Abueva, J. E. (2000, March 15). How big a part of G.D.P. are office pools? Make a bet? *The New York Times,* p. G1. Retrieved August 20, 2003, from http://proquest.umi.com/pqdweb

Berentson, B. (2000, September 11). Steinbrenner wannabes. *Forbes,* pp. 38–42. Retrieved August 20, 2003, from http://proquest.umi.com/pqdweb

Davies, P. (2002, November 4). Problem gamblers in the workplace. *Canadian HR Reporter,* p. 17. Retrieved August 20, 2003, from http://proquest.umi.com/pqdweb

Fatsis, S. (1995, December 8). Major corporations see huge potential in on-line fantasy sports. *The Wall Street Journal,* p. B8. Retrieved August 20, 2003, from http://proquest.umi.com/pqdweb

Web surfing at work? Just the news, honest! (2002, September 22). *The New York Times,* p. 9 (Personal Business Diary). Retrieved August 20, 2003, from http://proquest.umi.com/pqdweb

Wingfield, N. (2002, September 27). The rise and fall of Web shopping at work. *The Wall Street Journal,* p. B1. Retrieved August 27, 2003, from http://proquest.umi.com/pqdweb

CHAPTER 12

"I Deserve More Because My Name Is on the Door"

Entitlement, Embeddedness, and Employee Deviance in the Family Business

Rebecca J. Bennett

Stefan Thau

Jay Scouten

> *The image is nearly a cliché. The boss's son, no older than my favorite sneakers, squeals into the parking lot in a little red sports car with the name of the business on the license plate. The thumping bass stops just before the front door opens, and the 8 gallons of cologne on the kid hit me and make my eyes water. He issues a perfunctory greeting and reaches past me to do what he does every time he's here—hit the "no sale" button, open the cash register, and take $20. He says it's an advance on his commission, but I'm sure it's never deducted from his paycheck. This twerp is my future boss.*

Fully 85% of family-run companies do not survive to the third generation. To be sure, running a family business is a risky endeavor ("Who'll Take Over," 2002). But why do so many family businesses fail? Case examples, such as the one discussed in Case 12, suggest that family members sometimes opportunistically exploit the business for their own immediate gain. How could this be? A family business filled with interrelated people with a common long-term goal might be expected to always act in the family's (and business's) best interest. Moreover, shouldn't family members be *more* committed to the business than we would expect nonfamily employees to be?

This chapter unravels the puzzle of why some family members might be more prone to deviant behaviors than are nonfamily employees. We explore theories that suggest why family members should be more loyal and committed to their family's business. In addition, we propose conditions under which family bonds might lead to greater deviance and, in so doing, might result in harm against the family's own collective good, for example, doing things such as squashing employee morale and committing outright thievery against the business.

Before tackling the relative deviance of family members versus nonfamily members, we first explore theories that emphasize the social bonds, or social embeddedness, of employees and the relation of this social context to the employees' behavior. We predict, based on these theories, that family members should, in general, be more loyal (and less deviant) to the family business than are nonfamily members. In so doing, we draw on insights of various theories proposed in biology, sociology, and economics.

Theoretical Perspectives on Deviance and Connections to Family Business

Sociobiology

What are the ties that bind family members? A womb and a cash register? Why are individuals more likely to sacrifice for a family member than for a nonfamily member? Sociobiology predicts that family members should be more inclined to help their relatives than to help strangers. The central idea behind this theory is that family members do not act on the basis of simple reciprocity rules. That is, family members are unlikely to cooperate with each other merely because they expect a quid pro quo exchange for their services (Gouldner, 1960). Family members do not always expect their kids to work for their food merely because they are offspring. Rather, family members exhibit "nepotistic solidarity"; that is, an individual's willingness to behave "altruistically" increases with the degree of genetic relatedness. One should be more willing to sacrifice himself or herself to save his or her own child than to save a stranger because saving one's own child helps to increase the survival rate of one's own genes (Burnstein, Crandall, & Kitayama, 1994; Dawkins, 1976).

What can we learn from this perspective about cooperation within a family business? First, family members should be inclined to behave benevolently when working in the family business. Not only does the family business provide financial gains and social status, but it also provides the chance for family members to ensure the fitness of their close relatives and, hence indirectly, their own genes' survival.[1] Nonfamily members of the business (those who have no relationship ties to the business) will be less inclined to act altruistically to help the business.

Social Relations and Employee Deviance

Sociologists generally predict that the bonds an individual has within a social system affect the likelihood of that person violating the norms of the community (Hirschi, 1969). The main idea comes down to the following: Employees deviate from societal rules (e.g., one should not take organizational property for one's private use) because their bond to the rest of the organization is broken. Such a broken bond might be caused by an employee's belief that the supervisor does not support him or her or that the employee's relations with coworkers are poor. If organizational relations are good, however, social approval works like an informal control mechanism that governs employees in a desirable fashion (Homans, 1961). Feeling as though one is treated fairly by his or her boss and is respected by his or her coworkers causes an employee to feel more connected to the organization and less likely to attempt to rob it blind.

Durkheim (1961) suggested that people are moral beings to the extent that they are social beings. In other words, to the extent that an employee has relationships with other employees or supervisors in the organization, the employee will be less likely to engage in behaviors that violate their shared norms.[2] However, if an employee is isolated or alienated from coworkers, he or she is more likely to behave in ways that may harm them or their shared welfare.

Hirschi's (1969) social bonding theory suggests specifically that certain elements of the bond are critical in determining one's likelihood of behaving deviantly. The relevant elements to family business, as shown in Table 12.1, include (a) the quality and quantity of bonds, (b) investment in the organization, (c) involvement with tasks within the organization, and (d) identification with the organization's values/beliefs. In the next few paragraphs, we elaborate on the likely elements of each of these facets in explaining lapses in social bonds and the resulting propensity to engage in employee deviance.

First, the number and quality of one's relationships is clearly an indication of his or her connections within the organization. The number of bonds is looked on by the person as predictive of (or related to) his or her loyalty and commitment to the firm. Qualitatively, attractiveness of these bonds is essential to assessing the importance of a relationship's influences.

For example, in a family business, it may be the case that a person is related to most of the other employees, and regardless of the amount of time spent with those family members (e.g., at home, at family gatherings), the person may still feel only a weak bond with the organization because he or she feels little affection for those family members. So, perhaps even a womb and a cash register are insufficient; effective family ties also require affection. Without this affection, we would expect those family members to have lower incentives to stick to the rules. After all, togetherness is not necessarily a good thing if one does not like those with whom he or she is in close frequent contact. Hence, the effect of the quantity of family-related relationships depends on the way in which employees evaluate these relations, and we expect that a higher number of family relations will be less likely to result in deviant behaviors when the value of these relationships is also high. Conversely, a higher number of *negative* family relations is likely to lead to *more* deviance.

Table 12.1   Social Context and Employee Deviance

	Relation to Deviance	Relation to Deviance When Entitlement Beliefs Are High
Social Relations and Employee Deviance		
Family ties	Less deviant	More deviant
Quantity of organizational relations (high)[a]		
Evaluation of relations (positive)		
Commitment (high)	Less deviant	More deviant
Involvement (high)	Less deviant	More deviant
Value integration (high)	Less deviant	More deviant
Social Embeddedness (social context)		
Temporal embeddedness		
Organizational Tenure (high)		
×	Less deviant	More deviant
Intention to Stay (high)		
Network embeddedness		
Attractive Alternatives (high)		
×	Less deviant	More deviant
Accessible Alternatives (high)		
Institutional embeddedness		
Control (high)		
×	Less deviant[b]	More deviant
Fair Treatment (high)		

a. Assuming nondeviant norms.

b. Deviance is lessened when fair treatment is high but is possibly increased when fair treatment is low.

The second element of the social bond is based on the contributions that one has made to the organization. This part of social bonding is captured by a concept that organizational researchers call "task commitment" (Porter & Lilly, 1996); that is, a person has invested his or her time, talents, efforts, and so forth in the organization. Traditional commitment theory would predict that a person will lose these investments when he or she behaves deviantly. Thus, if a person has invested something in an organization, it would be in his or her best interest to conform to the organization's rules so that he or she does not become separated and lose the investment.

The third element of the bond is involvement. Hirschi (1969) proposed that, to the degree that one is involved in many tasks, he or she would have less opportunity to engage in deviance. Some moralistic platitudes, such as "idle hands are the devil's workshop" and "virtue is just a lack of opportunities," illustrate this idea. Because we presume that family members are more inclined to pick up the slack in undone tasks within the business (Fleming, 2000), they should have less opportunity to engage in deviant behaviors such as gossiping, harassment, taking extended breaks, and sabotaging equipment.

Fourth, belief in and commitment to shared norms affect one's likelihood of engaging in employee deviance. The more an employee is committed to the organization's values, mission, and purpose, the less likely he or she should be to engage in behaviors that violate those norms. Identification of and involvement with the work role are important components of organizational commitment (Hirschfeld & Field, 2000). We expect family members to be more committed to the organization's values because presumably they are the same values that are important to their family of origin (Paisner, 1999; Schein, 1983).

Social Bonds Reconsidered

Social embeddedness is based on the idea that any transaction is embedded within a social context (Buskens, Raub, & Snijders, 2003). According to this perspective, employees are "embedded" in at least three different realms: temporal factors, social structure factors, and factors regarding the rules and expectations of the organization (network factors). The theory assumes that employees are rational egoists and, as such, are less likely to give in to the temptation to behave deviantly in the short term due to their embeddedness in a social construct with its own expectations and penalties.

Temporal embeddedness refers to both the history of past transactions and the anticipated span of future transactions. For example, consider a nonfamily employee who has recently been hired and intends to leave soon. Because previous transactions with the organization are rare and potential future sanctions while misbehaving are unlikely, a self-interested employee should have higher incentives to exploit his or her employment relationship than would an employee with a longer organizational past and a bigger shadow of the future. For instance, employees with little intention to leave (a bigger shadow of the future) should be more cooperative because they might fear being sanctioned for their misbehavior (including loss of their employment), and they also realize that their futures with the organization will be brighter if they abide by its norms and are perceived as "team players." In addition, family members could be expected to be more aware of the shadow of the future because their misdeeds are more likely to haunt them for the duration of their communications with the family. That is, a deviant family member might never be allowed to "live down" his or her transgressions in the eyes of the family. Therefore, family members in a family business may be expected to be on "better behavior" than are their nonfamily counterparts.

Network embeddedness refers to the fact that employees are part of, or have access to, a social net of other alternatives, and they take these into account when making decisions regarding their current employment relationship. These alternatives encompass not only their current employment situation but also potential alternative employers. Having attractive and easily accessible alternative employers creates a situation in which cooperation in employment relationships becomes less likely (Thau, Bennett, Stahlberg, & Werner, 2004). For instance, family members who have training and experience only within that business may have few chances to find alternative employers. Theory and past empirical research suggest that misbehavior in such a situation should be less likely for these "wallflowers" (employees with few alternatives) than for those who have already "mentally checked out" (are already choosing their office décor with their next employers). Those with few alternatives have little choice but to cooperate with their current employer and to obey the rules. Those who have many alternatives are less likely to concern themselves with burned bridges resulting from misbehavior.

Institutional embeddedness refers to rules and policies. These might be designed to prevent misbehavior that has not yet occurred (ex ante preventions) or to sanction deviant behavior that has occurred (ex post sanctions). That is, holding all employees accountable with both informal and formal control mechanisms might prevent deviance because the costs of engaging in deviance are higher than when control is low (Riker & Ordeshook, 1973; Robinson & Bennett, 1997). However, these control systems might not always have their desired effects. A formal control system might also communicate to employees that the organization considers them to be not trustworthy (Baron & Kreps, 1999) and creates a self-fulfilling prophecy effect where the employees then behave in an untrustworthy manner, for example, by engaging in employee deviance (Deutsch-Salamon, 2003). Thus, control systems are expected to reduce the amount of deviance in which employees engage, but only when employees and managers have high-trust relationships. From a management perspective, then, it is necessary that supervisors treat employees fairly and supportively to make the employees trust them. If the degree of mistrust is high, control systems might have adverse effects.

Entitlement as Related to Employee Deviance

In this section, we turn our interest to entitlement belief. This individual belief is understood to be an expectation that one deserves to get a larger share of organizational outcomes relative to other members of the organization. Entitlement is understood to be a multifaceted outcome expectation rooted in the belief that one (a) has invested more than others have invested, (b) has a higher status than others have, and/or (c) is in need of greater resources than he or she is currently allocated. Because of these perceptions of deservingness, employees who have a strong sense of entitlement are more likely to take what they want even when rules dictate that this behavior is inappropriate. Put differently, employees with a strong sense of entitlement believe that they have their own rules. Moreover, they believe that they *deserve* to have these special privileged exceptions to everyone else's rules. A relevant metaphor might be a bottomless piggy bank reserved just for them.

We believe that this entitlement belief might influence workplace deviance above and beyond the effects of social embeddedness and might also be influenced by organizational policies. We discuss these issues later in this section. First, we briefly review the treatment of entitlement in previous research and describe potential factors making up this construct. Then, we relate these factors to the family business.

In crime research, entitlement attitudes represent the belief that one has the right to take whatever he or she wants (Mills, Kroner, & Hemmati, 2003). This "criminal thinking style" (Walters & White, 1989) results in criminals differing from noncriminals in their ways of interpreting situations. In short, criminals' expectations about what is personally seen as legitimate are different from those of noncriminals (Lewis & Smithson, 2001). Heath, Knez, and Camerer (1993) extended this societal view of criminal behavior to organizations in defining entitlement as the benefits that employees believe they deserve in the employment relationship.

Our conceptualization of entitlement builds on these earlier definitions by suggesting that individuals with entitlement beliefs perceive that they deserve more from the employment relationship and legitimize this perception because, in their view, they have contributed more to the exchange relationship than have other employees and/or are entitled to a larger share of the outcomes than are other organizational members.

In the context of family business, family members with entitlement beliefs are presumed to add weight to the input side of the equation because they are family or because of past injustices and struggles they experienced on behalf of the family business. As a result, they believe that they are entitled to more of the outcomes of the business than are nonfamily members or even other family members who experienced no such injustices and struggles. Hence, our conceptualization of entitlement beliefs considers the weighting of a family member's contribution and also considers whether the balance between input and outflow (norms) applies to him or her. In the latter condition, employees might believe that they *need* more of a certain resource or outcome than they have received, and they believe that they *deserve* to receive more than their "fair share" (as defined objectively).

Contribution-based entitlement is rooted in the belief that one has made greater investments in the organization than have others and, hence, is entitled to get more out of the organization than are others. This belief may or may not be objectively true. However, for our purposes, what is important is that the person *thinks* that his or her investments were bigger than those of others. Family employees might believe that they have a greater indirect investment in the firm because their name is on the door. Perhaps because of their parents' or grandparents' investment in the firm, they feel some entitlement to a larger share of the firm's resources. Some family members may have worked for the firm since they were young enough to push a broom and so may *perceive* that they have made greater contributions to the firm overall than have nonfamily members or even family members who started working at the firm later. Second-generation family members may also believe that they deserve more because they suffered the loss of a parent's time to the entrepreneur's dedication to getting the business off the ground. Now that the business is successful, the child believes that he or she is entitled to a share of the wealth due to his or her poor or neglected childhood (Fleming, 2000).

Need-based entitlement refers to the belief that resources should be allocated within an organization based on need rather than on contribution. In general, resources can be allocated equally, based on needs, or based on merit. That is, equality-based allocation systems divide resources based on the number of members, need-based systems give greater shares to those who need them most, and merit-based systems allocate their resources based on performance. People differ in what allocation system they believe is appropriate for the circumstances. We believe that some family members who have entitlement beliefs share a belief that they have greater needs than do others.

Because family systems tend to allocate resources based on need rather than on merit (Lansberg, 1983), family members have an expectation that the family business system works in the same manner (Jaffe, 1990). In other words, if family members have a need for some resource that the company owns, such as a vehicle, they feel entitled to just take it. Consequently, there is a mismatch between these two normative standards for allocating resources.

Status-based entitlement refers to the perceived position of one person relative to others in an organization. These relative social positions might be connected to rights, that is, what one is allowed to do in comparison with others (for an overview, see Ridgeway & Walker, 1995). If people believe that they are higher in status than are others, they might also believe that they have more rights than do others. Because family members are presumed to hold higher status positions in their family-owned organization, they will also possess greater power and, hence, a greater sense of entitlement (e.g., "I'm entitled to five-martini lunches because *I'm* a vice president").

Managing Employee Deviance Within the Family Business

Recently, scholars have emphasized that organizational behavior should put its emphasis on the question of how organizations organize behavior (Heath & Sitkin, 2001; Rousseau & House, 1994). Previously, when discussing social embeddedness, we introduced the notion that employees are institutionally embedded; that is, they make their decisions within a social context of social norms and control systems that might influence the way in which those decisions are made. In the following subsections, we discuss organizational policies within the family business that might either prevent or hamper deviant behavior. The discussion is organized around the recommendations shown in Table 12.2, which also presents the advantages and disadvantages of each proposed policy.

Table 12.2   Organizational Policies to Prevent Deviance in Family Business

Internal Controls		
Policy	*Advantage*	*Disadvantage*
Consistent performance assessment of family and nonfamily members	Increases procedural justice beliefs of nonfamily members	Family members with strong entitlement beliefs might believe that they do not need to be treated like nonfamily members
Internal controls (requiring work double-checking)	Helps to prevent fraud directly	Time-consuming
Leading generation demonstrably ethical	Role model	Larger than life, hard to live up to
Uniform hiring standards	Better quality employees	Makes salient alternatives
Careful mentoring	Better developed employees	Perception of favoritism
Follow-through on consequences	Better discipline	Requires energy and time to follow through
External Controls		
Policy	*Advantage*	*Disadvantage*
Outside training of family members	Might reduce entitlement beliefs through confrontation with merit-based systems	Increases exit options and lowers dependence
Frequent auditing of policies and financial statements	Engenders open and professional culture	Potentially costly to hire auditor; assumes that management is not trustworthy
Zero tolerance for drugs or addiction	Lower insurance premiums due to drug-free workplace policy	Family members may feel as though they are being spied on

Internal Controls

Strong internal controls are another means to control deviant behavior—in the form of fraud—in the family business. Because family member employees often are highly trusted and may have little supervision, the situation is ripe for abuse. Improving management's workplace presence, such as requiring managers to follow control procedures and address employee issues, is one way in which to reduce fraud. Having well-defined procedures is another way ("Strong Internal Controls," 2003). Policies and procedures should be developed concerning several areas of employee management: proper recording and deposit of cash receipts, a partner system for work involving cash handling, validation of payroll hours, proper depreciation and monitoring of assets such as inventory, security devices such as cameras and bar coding of inventory, and clear and consistent consequences for misbehavior of all employees. Such internal controls make it more difficult for anyone to engage in deviant behavior.

Honest Assessments of Performance

Family business owners need to set clear expectations for their offspring working in the family business regarding acceptable performance standards. Family members should be held to the same standards as are other employees. There should be no "free" vacation days, midday golf games, or helping themselves to inventory or cash unless all employees are allowed those same privileges (and if that is the case, the business is almost certainly in trouble).

Some authors (e.g., Hollander, 1987; Jaffe, 1990) have claimed that founders may overcompensate for spending little time with their children while they were growing up by letting them "nose around" in the business and by hesitating to correct them when they underperform or make mistakes. This is sometimes referred to as the "silver spoon syndrome" (Hollander, 1987), that is, the seeming inability of the founder to take a stand when the offspring undermine the intent and morale of the business. The refusal of the typically hard-driving, competitive founder to give honest feedback to his or her children about their poor job performance, unacceptable absenteeism, and/or outright fraud/theft is remarkable, but perhaps it is not surprising when considered from a social bonds perspective where the founding parent does not want to take the chance of adversely affecting his or her already tenuous contact with the children. Nonetheless, these employees are not getting an accurate assessment of their performance.

Modeling of Appropriate Behavior

Perhaps one of the most effective ways in which to curb deviance in the family business that results from entitlement beliefs is the modeling of appropriate behavior by company leaders. Individuals tend to model the behavior of those in higher status positions (Bennett, Aquino, Reed, & Thau, in press), and the culture of the organization comes from the top (Schein, 1983). So, if corporate leaders want to stop deviant behavior fueled by entitlement beliefs, they should take a close look at their own actions and what sorts of norms and expectations they are implying to those who are observing their actions. For example, the child might know he will not be punished for doing something wrong because his dad just bought a condo in Fort Lauderdale, Florida, by trading inventory.

Leaders are called on to reward appropriate behaviors in organizations and to hold accountable those who engage in deviance. If leaders do not penalize their children when the offspring take advantage of their familial bonds by abusing rules of the organization, resentment and employee deviance may run rampant.

Uniform Hiring Standards

The family business should develop consistent policies regarding family employment. Family members should be required to have the same skills and abilities as are outside applicants when applying for positions within the family firm. By effectively raising the barriers to entry into the family business, the owner can emphasize the equality of the employees rather than emphasizing his or her own favoritism.

Careful Mentoring

Family members should be mentored, preferably by a trusted nonfamily manager. This individual should feel secure enough to give critical and constructive feedback to the son or daughter of the boss. Typically, a child does not work effectively when he or she has a parent mentor, although the parent can be effective at encouraging the development and understanding of family values. Heirs to the family business need to be shown clearly that their contributions are no greater than those of other employees. Perpetuating a status difference that they are "better than" the nonfamily members only encourages the heirs to overestimate their contributions to the firm (and hence what they deserve to get back out of the firm).

Follow-Through on Consequences

The road to organizational anarchy is paved with empty threats. Proprietors must be certain to carry out punishments of both family and nonfamily members. If they do not, proprietors will hurt their own credibility and moral standing with the other employees.

External Controls

Managers and owners should also set the expectation that no one's work is above question by establishing the policy that *everyone* must have his or her work checked and that detailed records are expected and kept. By employing external agencies to educate, drug test, and financially audit the firm, no one will be able to violate these minimal standards of conduct, regardless of lineage. Although auditing of financial records and organizational policies is perhaps best conducted by external agencies to promote objectivity, useful development can result from internal auditing as well.

Required Outside Training

One such organizational policy is that family businesses sometimes require training (education) and work experience outside the family business as a precondition to enter the family business (Bork, 1992). A "family employment policy" will create more realistic expectations of what one is entitled to receive when working for the family business. Family members' sense of entitlement will decline as they are confronted with a policy that sets clear expectations about merit-based promotional systems.

On the other hand, outside experience and training also allows family members to realize their exit options (Hirschman, 1972). They will no longer perceive themselves as dependent on the firm. Rather, those with attractive and available alternatives are likely to withdraw extra-role "helping" behaviors and to engage in employee deviance (Thau et al., 2004). Mentally, they are already working for the new employer and have less motivation to be perceived as team players at their current jobs.

Frequent Auditing of Policies and Financial Statements

Although recently questioned in the wake of the myriad accounting scandals the United States has witnessed during recent years, the value of an external objective auditor is even greater when considered in the context of the family business. Because opportunism is the redheaded stepchild of free reign in a business, accountability should be enforced by qualified professionals. Unfortunately, these auditors can be costly and may offend upper level managers by assuming that they are untrustworthy.

Zero Tolerance

Managers in the family business should have zero tolerance for addiction of any kind or for theft/fraud from the business. Addiction and the corresponding need for quick cash is a primary cause for theft and violence in the business. Organizational leaders need to take a firm hand so that they are not viewed as condoning these destructive behaviors through their reluctance to react to such challenges to their authority. Here again, the leading generation has the responsibility to set a good example of "clean and righteous living."

Conclusion

Given the opportunity to implement these changes, one would hope that the 85% of family-run companies that do not survive to the third generation might be successful instead of falling victim to the unchecked feeling of entitlement in the younger generations. This situation seems to be a paradox, however, as the chapter has built on biology, sociology, and economics to argue just the opposite—that family members should be *more likely* to sacrifice for the family business. The common perception, and that of the theories presented in this chapter, suggests that a family business full of related people with a common long-term goal might be expected to always act in the family's (and business's) best interest. By implementing the fair and universal practices listed in the final section, the family business might overcome the wanton desires of the offspring and realize the long-term success of the firm.

Notes

1. As the family business grows, however, later generations may perceive greater genetic distances from other family members involved in the business. As such, sacrificing for the business is seen as having limited opportunity to affect their indirect fitness.

2. We are assuming, of course, that the norms themselves are not deviant to overall performance-enhancing norms (for the theoretical analysis of such a situation, see Bennett, Aquino, Reed, & Thau, in press).

References

Baron, J. N., & Kreps, D. M. (1999). *Strategic human resources: Frameworks for general managers.* New York: John Wiley.

Bennett, R. J., Aquino, K., Reed, A., & Thau, S. (in press). The normative nature of employee deviance and the impact of moral identity. In S. Fox & P. E. Spector (Eds.), *Counterproductive work behavior: Investigations of actors and targets.* Washington, DC: American Psychological Association.

Bork, D. (1992, April). If family members ask for a job. *Nation's Business.*

Burnstein, E., Crandall, C., & Kitayama, S. (1994). Some neo-Darwinian decision rules for altruism: Weighing cues for inclusive fitness as a function of the biological importance of the decision. *Journal of Personality and Social Psychology, 67,* 773–789.

Buskens, V., Raub, W., & Snijders, C. (2003). Theoretical and empirical perspectives on the governance of relations in markets and organizations. In V. Buskens, W. Raub, & C. Snijders (Eds.), *Research in the sociology of organizations,* Vol. 20: *The governance of relations in markets and organizations* (pp. 1–18). Amsterdam, Netherlands: JAI/Elsevier.

Dawkins, R. (1976). *The selfish gene.* Oxford, UK: Oxford University Press.

Deutsch-Salamon, S. (2003). *Trust that binds: The influence of collective felt trust on responsibility norms and organizational outcomes.* Unpublished doctoral dissertation, University of British Columbia.

Durkheim, E. (1961). *Moral education.* New York: Free Press.

Fleming, Q. J. (2000). *Keep the family baggage out of the family business: Avoiding the seven deadly sins that destroy family businesses.* New York: Fireside.

Gouldner, A. W. (1960). The norm of reciprocity: A preliminary statement. *American Sociological Review, 25,* 161–178.

Heath, C., Knez, M., & Camerer, C. (1993). The strategic management of the entitlement process in the employment relationship. *Strategic Management Journal, 14,* 75–93.

Heath, C., & Sitkin, S. (2001). Big-B versus Big-O: An examination into what is distinctly organizational about organizational behavior. *Journal of Organizational Behavior, 22,* 1–16.

Hirschfeld, R. R., & Field, H. S. (2000). Work centrality and work alienation: Distinct aspects of general commitment to work. *Journal of Organizational Behavior, 21,* 789–800.

Hirschi, T. (1969). *Causes of delinquency.* Berkeley: University of California Press.

Hirschman, A. O. (1972). *Exit, voice, loyalty: Responses to decline of firms, organizations, and states.* Cambridge, MA: Harvard University Press.

Hollander, B. S. (1987). Silver spoon syndrome. In C. E. Aronoff, J. H. Astrachan, & J. L. Ward (Eds.), *Family business sourcebook II* (pp. 499–500). Marietta, GA: Business Owner Resources.

Homans, G. C. (1961). *Social behavior: Its elementary forms.* New York: Harcourt Brace.

Jaffe, D. T. (1990). *Working with the ones you love: Strategies for a successful family business.* Berkeley, CA. Conari Press.

Lansberg, I. S. (1983). Managing human resources in family firms: Problem of institutional overlap. *Organizational Dynamics, 12*(1), 39–46.

Lewis, S., & Smithson, J. (2001). Sense of entitlement to support for the reconciliation of employment and family life. *Human Relations, 54,* 1455–1481.

Mills, J. F., Kroner, D. G., & Hemmati, T. (2003). Predicting violent behavior through a static–stable lens. *Journal of Interpersonal Violence, 18,* 891–904.

Paisner, M. B. (1999). *Sustaining the family business: An insider's guide to managing across generations.* Reading, MA: Perseus Books.

Porter, T., & Lilly, B. (1996). The effects of conflict, trust, and task commitment on project team performance. *International Journal of Conflict Management, 7,* 361–376.

Ridgeway, C. L., & Walker, H. (1995). Status structures. In K. Cook, G. Fine, & J. House (Eds.), *Sociological perspectives on social psychology* (pp. 281–310). New York: Allyn & Bacon.

Riker, W. H., & Ordeshook, P. C. (1973). *An introduction to positive political theory.* Englewood Cliffs, NJ: Prentice Hall.

Robinson, S. L., & Bennett, R. J. (1997). Workplace deviance: Its definition, its manifestations, and its causes. In R. J. Lewicki & R. J. Bies (Eds.), *Research on negotiation in organizations* (Vol. 6, pp. 3–27). Greenwich, CT: JAI.

Rousseau, D. M., & House, R. (1994). MESO organization behavior: Avoiding three fundamental errors. In C. Cooper & D. M. Rousseau (Eds.), *Trends in organizational behavior* (pp. 13–30). New York: John Wiley.

Schein, E. H. (1983). The role of the founder in creating organizational culture. *Organizational Dynamics, 12*(1), 13–28.

Strong internal controls help prevent fraud. (2003, March 4). *Business Journal of Youngstown, Ohio.* Retrieved November 24, 2003, from www.business-journal.com/articles/startrun/preventfraud.html

Thau, S., Bennett, R. J., Stahlberg, D., & Werner, J. M. (2004). *Why should I be generous when I have valued and accessible alternatives? Alternative exchange partners and OCB.* Unpublished manuscript, University of Groningen, The Netherlands.

Walters, G. D., & White, T. W. (1989). Heredity and crime: Bad genes or bad research. *Criminology, 27,* 455–485.

Who'll take over is big question for family firms. (2002, December 9). *Orange County Register.*

Adelphia Communications and the Rigas Family

The year was 1952. War raged in Korea. Dwight Eisenhower was elected president of the United States. The word game Scrabble gained nationwide popularity. *I Love Lucy* was a television hit. And in a small town in Pennsylvania, John J. Rigas, the son of Greek immigrants, paid $100 for a cable-TV franchise.

By 2002, Rigas's investment would grow from 25 customers in one town to millions of people across the United States. The family business eventually became Adelphia Communications Inc., a multibillion-dollar company named for the Greek word for brother, *adelphos*.

During the 1920s, Rigas's father, Demetrius "James" Rigas, had opened a restaurant in Wellsville, New York, after arriving in America from a small Greek village. A year after he started the business, James was joined by Eleni Brazas, a young woman from the same village who became his bride, and eventually by John in 1924. The first of four children, John began cleaning tables in the family hot dog stand when he was 9 years old and went on to become a successful student and high school athlete.

Later, as a U.S. Army veteran of World War II, John Rigas was the first in his family to go to college. After graduating from Rensselaer Polytechnic Institute on the G.I. Bill, he returned to his hometown to again work in the

AUTHOR'S NOTE: This case was prepared by Roland Kidwell (Niagara University) as the basis for classroom discussion. It was developed from accounts listed in the bibliography at the end of the case as well as from the author's personal observations. All names of individuals and organizations are real.

family restaurant. He spent only a few months there before he sought bigger things. His ambitions were first realized in 1951 when he scraped together several thousand dollars to purchase a movie theater in Coudersport, Pennsylvania, roughly 25 miles from Wellsville.

Soon after, Rigas entered the cable business. Television was growing in popularity throughout the nation, and cable was needed to bring it to remote locations that could not be effectively reached by a strong over-the-air signal. Rigas and his associates, including his brother Gus, began to build other cable networks near Coudersport. In a speech many years later, he recounted the early challenges. When a partner became insolvent during the building of Rigas's third cable network in Punxsutawney, Pennsylvania, the sheriff prepared to foreclose. "I really thought that was the end of John Rigas's enterprises in cable," Rigas said, because all of his holdings served to back the company's loan. He was saved by an employee who came up with $50,000 of her own savings to pay it off.

As the business grew during the 1950s, Rigas and his wife, Doris, started a family. Within 6 years, they had four children: Michael, Timothy, James, and Ellen. Gus Rigas continued to operate the family's Wellsville restaurant while working with John in the cable business. In 1972, the cable company was formally incorporated as Adelphia. At that time, it served more than 6,000 subscribers in small Pennsylvania towns. As cable-TV grew rapidly during the 1980s and 1990s, Rigas's three sons moved up in the company, which became a publicly traded corporation in 1986.

During the 1990s, the company expanded into Internet access, paging services, and business telecommunications. It operated a sports network that telecast Buffalo Sabres ice hockey games, and within a few years the Rigas family took control of the team. This created excitement in western New York because it ended speculation that the team might move to a bigger city and seemed to indicate that more money would be available to bring in talented players to pursue a championship.

Meanwhile, cable deregulation led Adelphia to use a combination of cash, stock, and debt to make several major acquisitions across the United States. By the late 1990s, Adelphia had become the sixth largest cable operator in the country, but some analysts expressed concern that the Rigas family still ran it like a small private business.

"The Most Popular Person in Buffalo"

In 1998, John Rigas was identified by *Buffalo News* sports columnist Jerry Sullivan as the city's most popular individual due to his work with the Sabres and the growth of Adelphia. Sullivan quoted Rigas recalling his days playing tackle football in high school and likened it to his business success: "Every once in a while, you'd take the ball and see an opening in the line. You had to determine if it was the right opening because it closes very fast. That's the way it is in life. You take the ball. There's no gain. It hurts. But you keep looking for that opening."

Rigas spoke at a business dinner sponsored by a western New York university in 1999. At first, he expressed uncertainty about why he had been invited to speak and what he was expected to discuss. In what appeared to be an unscripted talk, Rigas recounted stories of working at the hot dog stand, starting his business in Coudersport, and stringing cable lines in several Pennsylvania communities. He also discussed the risks and opportunities of recent Adelphia cable acquisitions.

Rigas came across as a charming and unassuming individual. He privately offered the university's business school dean use of his personal box for faculty and staff members to attend an upcoming Sabres game. At the dinner, he was honored with the university's annual corporate leadership award.

Within 2 weeks of the speech, Rigas underwent coronary bypass surgery at the Mayo Clinic in Minnesota. It was his second heart procedure in 4 months. Although he was said to be back to work in 2 months with enough on his plate to keep six secretaries busy, Rigas's health and age led to industry speculation as to who would succeed him as the head of Adelphia.

A New Generation of Leadership

The three Rigas sons played key roles in Adelphia's development into a large nationwide cable company that diversified into related areas of telecommunications, including telephone service, Internet services, and cable sports programming.

Michael Rigas, the eldest, served as Adelphia's vice president for operations. Timothy Rigas, educated at the University of Pennsylvania's Wharton School, served as Adelphia's chief financial officer and was a leader in the company's growth spurt during the late 1990s. Finally, James Rigas served as Adelphia's executive vice president for strategic planning.

Even though Adelphia became a publicly traded corporation during the mid-1980s, the family retained private partnerships and a family-owned cable operation that assisted the Rigases in maintaining control of Adelphia. Over the years, the Rigas family members sold some of their cable holdings but retained several family businesses, including a real estate leasing group.

"When we went public, I wasn't comfortable that we should be public," John Rigas told *Broadcasting & Cable* magazine in 1999. "We'd been private all these years, and I wasn't comfortable with the exposure to the public. I felt comfortable keeping some properties outside so we could move in and out. We've leveraged those companies, too, and that gave us the ability to keep control in Adelphia by buying up Adelphia stock."

The Rigas family held voting control and a substantial portion of the corporation's equity into the 21st century. Of the 11 members of the corporate board of directors, 4 were family members, including John, the chairman. The family was said to make slow and deliberate decisions by consensus of all key players. A successor to Rigas among his three sons was not immediately identified. The family stressed that a team approach worked best.

Rigas told *Broadcasting & Cable,*

> Over the past few years, when I talk to investors or employees, I tell them that one of the strengths of Adelphia—and it's a big strength—is the passing of leadership from one generation to the second generation, which has in fact occurred. Now it's more of a partnership. Sometimes people ask me which son would take over. I would never want to make that decision.

Big Expectations and Results

The late 1990s represented a heady time for Adelphia. From 1997 to 1999, the corporation grew into an $8 billion-plus company, acquiring a variety of cable companies and operations across the country. Riding a nationwide stock market boom, the share price went from $5.00 in April 1997 to as high as $86.56 in May 1999.

Adelphia had reached a customer base of 2 million in 1998, 46 years after Rigas had started the business. During a 4-month period in 1999, Adelphia moved beyond its traditional western Pennsylvania and New York operations, announcing deals that more than doubled its number of customers and expanded its operations into Philadelphia and Los Angeles.

Rigas had invested $22 million in the Sabres in 1994 and became the major owner of the financially ailing hockey team within 5 years. In 1999, the Sabres reached the Stanley Cup Finals, and after their defeat in the finals, Rigas promised to find the tools "to finish the job." That did not happen. The team lost several key players during the next couple of years, continued to be a money loser, and did not repeat its on-ice success.

Other than the Sabres, Adelphia had big plans in western New York. With the assistance of federal and state funds and tax breaks negotiated over several years, the company planned to build a 15-story, $125 million operations center that would bring more than 1,000 jobs to downtown Buffalo near the hockey arena. In early 2002, the company hired an architect to design the center and boasted that many of the employees it had promised to hire as part of its efforts to obtain government aid were already working at other locations in the Buffalo area.

Adelphia also meant a great deal to Coudersport, Pennsylvania, which had remained its headquarters during the rapid expansion. The company finished a $30 million headquarters building on Main Street across from the Rigas movie theater in early 2002. At the time, it employed several hundred people in the small town of 3,000 approximately 100 miles from Buffalo. For years, Rigas refused suggestions to move the headquarters to a large city. He was the town's major benefactor. When a resident had a problem or a local organization needed a donation, Rigas was extremely generous in providing assistance.

"John Rigas . . . has been committed to this town for all of his life, and each of the Rigas sons has also been committed to the town for all of their professional lives," a Rigas family attorney told the *Wall Street Journal*. "There is a bond between the company and the town that was important to both and remains important to both."

A Conference Call Changes Everything

During the spring of 2002, it was obvious that Adelphia was heavily in debt, and even a Coudersport financial adviser suggested that his clients stay away from the stock. The problems apparently began toward the end of 1999 when three cable systems, worth approximately $10 billion, were purchased. These acquisitions greatly increased Adelphia's debt load and put more pressure on the company to reduce debt and continue meeting projected earnings.

Something else had been going on behind the scenes, and it would drive Adelphia to ruin. On March 27, 2002, in a conference call with Wall Street analysts to discuss 2001 results, Tim Rigas revealed that the company had cosigned $2.3 billion in off-the-books loans that had been tapped by partnerships run by Rigas family members. This accompanied the bad news that the company's telephone spin-off, Adelphia Business Solutions, had filed for Chapter 11 bankruptcy protection and that Adelphia had lost more money in the fourth quarter of 2001 than had been stated previously.

The Adelphia stock took a severe hit. And at a time when corporate financial scandals dominated the headlines, it was not long before the revelation caused Adelphia to unravel. By June, the stock was delisted after it had plummeted to 79 cents per share, the federal government started a criminal investigation, the company was in bankruptcy, and the Rigas family members had been forced out of the company they had built.

Making an Example for Corporate America

The Securities and Exchange Commission accused Adelphia of hiding more than $2.3 billion in debt from its financial statements and misleading the public about those liabilities, issuing more than $1.3 billion in stock and notes to benefit the Rigas family, paying off $241 million of family members' personal debt, paying $26.5 million for timber rights on a Rigas property, spending $12.8 million of company money to build a golf course and clubhouse controlled by the Rigases, and giving the family exclusive use of Adelphia-paid properties in Colorado, Mexico, and New York City.

Adelphia declared Chapter 11 bankruptcy on June 25, 2002, so that it could continue to operate while a reorganization occurred. New company officials, brought in to turn Adelphia around, sought civil damages from the Rigases. The new management team replaced the Rigas-appointed board of directors and moved the headquarters from Coudersport to Denver, Colorado.

A month after the bankruptcy filing, the Rigases were charged with violating federal laws in connection with the off-the-books loans. Refusing an offer by the family's lawyers to surrender their clients, the federal government raided the family's New York City apartment, handcuffed the elderly Rigas and two of his sons, Tim and Michael, and paraded them in front of television cameras. The father and all three sons were named in a Securities and Exchange Commission civil suit, but James Rigas was not criminally charged.

Indictments of John, Timothy, and Michael Rigas, as well as of other company executives, came 2 months after the public humiliation. The charges included conspiracy, securities fraud, wire fraud, and bank fraud. The U.S. attorney in New York City called the case "one of the most elaborate and extensive corporate frauds in United States history."

The indictment said the Rigases had set up a system of buying stock in Adelphia whenever the company issued new shares so that their holdings would not be diluted. To make sure that they had money to buy the stock, they set up a credit line that allowed the family to borrow it, with the loans being guaranteed by Adelphia, whenever the company issued new shares. If convicted, the defendants faced lengthy prison sentences and millions of dollars in fines.

John Rigas's lawyer, Peter Fleming, gave the following statement: "Starting with nothing, John Rigas built a major American corporation, which now has suffered serious damage through these accusations and charges. When the prosecution fails to prove its case, which is my expectation, who will take responsibility?"

"We Did Nothing Illegal"

The media predictably labeled the rise and apparent fall of the Rigas family as a Greek tragedy. Two Adelphia officials quickly pleaded guilty, but the case against the family culminated in a 4-month trial in 2004.

Several months after the indictments, John Rigas spoke to the press. As his three sons looked on, the company founder blamed his family's woes on the company's outside directors. "We did nothing illegal; my conscience is clear about that," he told the *New York Times*. Criminal and civil actions against the Rigases were a "misrepresentation, a big P.R. [public relations] effort on the part of the outside directors and their lawyers to shift the responsibility," Rigas said. "They made up this thing that we had borrowed, that we had taken this money from Adelphia, when in fact we had borrowed the money from the banks."

And, Rigas pointed out, the board minutes showed that each of the co-borrowing agreements was approved by the company's board of directors.

The agreements were designed to allow the company and the Rigas family to get a larger loan on better terms by leveraging the assets of both the company and the family.

Although Rigas likened the arrangement to a joint checking account, in which either side could draw from a credit line and both were liable for ensuring the loan repayment, prosecutors called it the Rigas family's personal piggy bank.

On July 8, 2004, a federal jury convicted John Rigas and Timothy Rigas of bank and securities fraud and conspiracy, finding the two men guilty on 18 of 23 counts. But the jury acquitted Michael Rigas on some charges and could not reach a verdict on others, meaning that he might have to face a retrial in the case.

After the jury's decision, John Rigas, the 79-year-old family patriarch, told the *Buffalo News,* "After building the company and starting from scratch, it hasn't been easy. It's certainly the biggest challenge I've ever faced in my life."

Discussion Questions

1. Identify and discuss examples of social bonds that existed in this case.

2. Was an entitlement mentality operating within the Rigas family and Adelphia Communications? Explain. How could the family members justify a sense of entitlement?

3. How did Adelphia's history, culture, and policies contribute to the downfall of the Rigas family?

4. Based on Chapter 12 and your own research, suggest some ways in which the Rigas family members might have avoided the disastrous consequences they suffered.

Bibliography

Cauley, L. (1999, March 8). Adelphia will buy Century in $3.6 billion deal. *The Wall Street Journal,* p. A3. Retrieved August 12, 2003, from LexisNexis database.

Colman, P. (1999, June 14). Family ties. *Broadcasting & Cable,* pp. 24, 34.

Fabrikant, G. (2002, September 24). Indictments for founder of Adelphia and two sons. *The New York Times,* p. C1. Retrieved August 12, 2003, from LexisNexis database.

Farrell, M. (2002, July 29). No surrender: Rigases arrested. *Multichannel News,* pp. 1, 42. Retrieved August 12, 2003, from LexisNexis database.

Frank, R. (2002, May 28). In Coudersport, Pa., Adelphia chief is a hometown hero: Locals stand by John Rigas as inquiries proliferate—A line at the coffee shop. *The Wall Street Journal,* p. A1. Retrieved August 12, 2003, from LexisNexis database.

Gallagher, L. (2003, May 26). What did they know? *Forbes,* pp. 53–54. Retrieved August 12, 2003, from LexisNexis database.

Gleason, B. (1999, March 17). Sabres owner to undergo heart surgery at Mayo Clinic. *Buffalo News,* p. F5. Retrieved October 22, 2003, from LexisNexis database.

Linstedt, S., & Williams, F. O. (2002, January 16). Adelphia ready to take big step: Amid skepticism about its operations center, the company has brought jobs to the area and is hiring an architect. *Buffalo News,* p. A1. Retrieved October 22, 2003, from LexisNexis database.

Moules, J., & Larsen, P. T. (2002, July 25). Family's private affairs hit public domain; Rigas allegations: Adelphia boss charged with orchestrating one of the most extensive frauds at a U.S. public company. *Financial Times,* p. 2. Retrieved August 12, 2003, from LexisNexis database.

Personal piggy bank. (2002, August 5). *MacLean's,* p. 12. Retrieved August 12, 2003, from LexisNexis database.

Sorkin, A. R. (2003, April 7). Fallen founder of Adelphia tries to explain. *The New York Times,* p. C1. Retrieved August 12, 2003, from LexisNexis database.

Sullivan. J. (1998, November 1). The most popular person in Buffalo: With courage and a touch of magic, Sabres owner John Rigas reminds us how to dream. *Buffalo News First Sunday Magazine,* p. M6. Retrieved October 22, 2003, from LexisNexis database.

Williams, F. O. (1999a, March 9). Adelphia chief says acquisitions risky but rewarding, *Buffalo News,* p. E3. Retrieved October 22, 2003, from LexisNexis database.

Williams, F. O. (1999b, May 2). Small-town roots anchor ever-widening branches of cable TV empire. *Buffalo News,* p. A1. Retrieved October 22, 2003, from LexisNexis database.

Williams, F. O. (2002a, March 28). Adelphia reveals $2.3 billion in off-books debt. *Buffalo News,* p. F1. Retrieved October 22, 2003, from LexisNexis database.

Williams, F. O. (2002b, April 7). Here are answers to a few questions about the Adelphia situation. *Buffalo News,* p. B13. Retrieved October 22, 2003, from LexisNexis database.

Williams, F. O. (2002c, March 31). Rigas has some explaining to do: Wall Street wants to know the precise details of Adelphia Communication's loans. *Buffalo News,* p. B6. Retrieved October 22, 2003, from LexisNexis database.

Williams, F. O. (2003, June 30). Adelphia takes it slow: A year after filing bankruptcy, cable giant's case is moving slowly. *Buffalo News,* p. C1. Retrieved October 22, 2003, from LexisNexis database.

Zremski, J. (2004a, July 10). Justice—but no joy—in verdicts: A mixed bag of emotions as the former heroes of Coudersport are convicted. *Buffalo News,* p. A1. Retrieved July 21, 2004, from LexisNexis database.

Zremski, J. (2004b, July 9). Jury convicts John Rigas, son Timothy; Second son acquitted of some counts; others pending: Panel finds Mulcahey not guilty on all charges. *Buffalo News,* p. A1. Retrieved July 21, 2004, from LexisNexis database.

CHAPTER 13

Organizational Deviance and Culture

Oversights and Intentions

Linda Thorne

Joanne Jones

onsider the seemingly simple concept of punctuality, which may be seen by some to be trivial but also is critical to the way in which numerous organizations function. In many countries (e.g., England, Australia, Canada, the United States), when a person is significantly late, it is expected that he or she apologize (Brislin & Kim, 2003). However, what is considered to be "significantly" late may vary between organizations and across cultures. For example, punctuality is a very precise concept in England, whereas punctuality is fluid in Peru, where being 10 minutes tardy might not be considered to be significantly late (Brislin & Kim, 2003).

Imagine that the American leader of a transnational team is having the first meeting with fellow cross-national team members. They arrive over a period of time and make no comment. Other team members from North American cultures who arrived precisely "on time" are upset. From a North American perspective, the actions of the "late" team members could be interpreted as lack of respect for the American's leadership or as a lack of commitment to the team or organization. However, on confronting the "latecomers" from Latin cultures and asking why they are late, imagine hearing their response: "But . . . we were not late." To add insult to injury, not only are these individuals late, but they also respond in a way that the team leader considers to be inappropriate. What should the leader do?

Although this may appear to be a trivial example, issues around time and how it is handled are the root cause of many cross-cultural misunderstandings in the workplace (Cushner & Brislin, 1996). As the lateness example illustrates, our cultural perspective provides the categories with which we understand the world, which we use to guide judgments and behavior (Mezias, Chen, & Murphy, 1999). From the perspective of the American team leader, punctuality means arriving precisely on time or, perhaps at the very latest, within 5 minutes of the appointed time. Furthermore, the team leader considers time to be a valuable and limited resource; therefore, not following the punctuality script is judged to be rude and disrespectful. However, it is quite possible that these team members are unaware that they have breached some sort of norm (i.e., acted in a deviant manner) or have offended anyone. From the perspective of the latecomers, they might not consider themselves to be late and might be unaware of the team leader's definition of punctuality. Furthermore, they might not consider that their response may be perceived by others to be deviant and an attempt to undermine the team leader and the team.

As has been discussed throughout this volume, deviant behavior is considered to be intentional behavior that threatens the well-being of an organization and/or its members. However, deviant behavior may be perceived in different ways by the individual acting (e.g., arriving late) and by the manager (team leader) and/or team members. Accordingly, the perception of deviant behavior is significantly affected by the norms of the individual, the organization, and the society in which the organization operates (Vardi & Wiener, 1996).

As the world becomes more and more global, managers are increasingly in contact with people—other managers, team members, subordinates, superiors, and so forth—who have different norms reflecting the various cultural diversities from which they originated. For instance, consider an executive's description of Eastman Kodak's workplace: "We have people of many nationalities who lead multicultural teams, work on multicountry projects, and travel monthly outside their home countries; in any year, they may work in Paris, Shanghai, Istanbul, Moscow, or Buenos Aires with colleagues from a different set of countries" (Delano, 2000, p. 77).

To understand how cultural norms affect perceptions of deviant behavior, this chapter investigates several key dimensions of culture and describes how cultural dimensions might affect the perceptions and motivations behind deviant behavior across cultures. An understanding of how the dimensions of culture affect individuals' perceptions of deviant behavior in different ways can help to bridge perceptual gaps, improve interpersonal communication, reduce conflicts and misunderstandings, raise work productivity, and possibly reduce the likelihood of deviant behavior in the workplace (Gopalan & Thomson, 2003).

Deviant Decision Making: Oversights or Intentions

Deviant decision making results in the identification of actions that possess an element of choice and that are perceived to potentially cause harm (Jones, 1991; Robinson & Bennett, 1997). The outcome of a deviant decision-making process, deviant behavior, can be the result of either individual oversight or individual intention. *Oversight* represents a failure by an individual to perceive that his or her behavior may potentially cause harm. This is essentially due to a lack of awareness of how the individual's actions will affect other people or to a lack of sufficient thought given to the issue (Rest, 1986, 1994).

On the other hand, individual *intention* captures the situation where an individual is aware that his or her behavior will be perceived to be deviant, but the individual chooses to go ahead with the decision anyway. For instance, if the team leader in the lateness example perceives that the team members were late on purpose, they may evoke "retaliation" against the team leader (Bies & Tripp, 1996; see also Bies & Tripp, this volume). Accordingly, the team leader, in the role of the "wronged" victim, may turn a culturally ambiguous situation of lateness into a justification for punishment of the team members who are late (Seabright & Schminke, 2002).

Although deviant decision making occurs in all cultures, the circumstances that may activate and affect the deviant decision process may differ across cultures (McDonald, 2000). Going back to the lateness example, we can use the model of deviant decision making to evaluate judgments and decisions. The team leader interprets the latecomers' behavior as the result of a purposeful and active reasoning process and assesses the latecomers' behavior accordingly. The latecomers, on the other hand, are not sensitive to the Western norms regarding punctuality and, therefore, were unaware of the potential harm they could cause by arriving late. The team leader's and latecomers' cultural backgrounds activated and affected the reasoning process in different ways.

Integrated Dimensions of Culture

Every culture has developed its own set of basic assumptions, that is, the rules and methods for thinking and acting (Trompenaars & Hampden-Turner, 1998). Cultural *dimensions* capture these basic assumptions. Many of these dimensions are difficult for someone within a particular culture to identify, but they may be noticeable when a person encounters others from a different culture or when a person is outside his or her own culture. Just as it is difficult for the individual to identify his or her culture's dimensions, it is difficult for an outsider to recognize these basic assumptions.

Table 13.1 summarizes 10 key dimensions of culture that may influence deviant decision making: individualism/collectivism, power distance, uncertainty avoidance, masculinity/femininity, short-term versus long-term orientation, universalism/particularism, neutral/affective, specific/diffuse, achievement/ascription, and internal/external. Each dimension is discussed in turn.

Individualism/Collectivism

The first dimension of culture, *individualism/collectivism*, is the degree of integration between members of society and the relative emphasis on individual needs

Table 13.1   Integrated Framework of the Dimensions of National Culture

Dimension and Source(s)	Definition	Illustrative Example
Individualism/Collectivism (Hofstede, 2001; Trompenaars & Hampden-Turner, 1998)	The degree of integration between members of society and the relative value of the individual over collective needs	Individualists tend to believe that personal interests are more important than group interests, whereas collectivists value reciprocation of favors, a sense of belonging, and respect for tradition
Power distance (Hofstede, 2001)	The degree to which an unequal distribution of power is accepted in society	Individuals with high power distance perceive superiors as being entitled to privileges, whereas individuals with low power distance are more likely to prefer democratic participation
Uncertainty avoidance (Hofstede, 2001)	The degree to which a society's members tolerate ambiguity or uncertainty	Individuals with high uncertainty avoidance feel a need for written rules and procedures and are intolerant of deviations from these rules, whereas individuals with low uncertainty avoidance are less concerned with codified rules
Masculinity/Femininity (Hofstede, 2001)	The relative emphasis in society on achievement and accomplishment versus overall quality of life	Masculine individuals are interested in material success, whereas feminine individuals are more concerned with human relationships
Short-term versus long-term orientation (Hofstede, 2001; Trompenaars & Hampden-Turner, 1998)	The relative emphasis in society on others' perceptions and viewing events along a time continuum	Individuals with a high long-term orientation are more concerned with the future and emphasize perseverance and thrift, whereas individuals with a high short-term orientation are more concerned with the past and present and emphasize tradition and social obligations
Universalism/Particularism (Trompenaars & Hampden-Turner, 1998)	The relative emphasis in society on the degree to which the same rules apply to all people across all situations	Universalists see morality as a matter of standard rules that apply to all situations, whereas particularists see morality as variable and depending on the nature of the relationship and the circumstances

Dimension and Source(s)	Definition	Illustrative Example
Neutral/Affective (Trompenaars & Hampden-Turner, 1998)	The relative emphasis of society's members on the acceptability of showing emotions	Affective individuals openly show their emotions, whereas neutral individuals rarely show their emotions
Specific/Diffuse (Trompenaars & Hampden-Turner, 1998)	The relative emphasis of society's members to consider organizations or events in terms of separable parts versus consideration of the whole	Diffuse individuals tend to consider factors and implications beyond a specific domain, whereas specific individuals tend to focus on a specific domain or realm
	The degree to which roles and relationships are interrelated versus compartmentalized	In specific-oriented cultures, people tend to compartmentalize their personal and professional lives; in diffuse cultures, all relationships are considered to be interrelated and personal and professional lives are intertwined
Achievement/Ascription (Trompenaars & Hampden-Turner, 1998)	The relative emphasis in society on achieved status versus ascribed status	In an achievement culture, one's status is based on what he or she has accomplished; in an ascription culture, one's status is a function of his or her position in society and at birth
Internal/External (Trompenaars & Hampden-Turner, 1998)	The relative emphasis of society's members on sources of motivation and values stemming from the individual versus the environment	When the source of motivation/values is external, individuals strive to remain in harmony with their environment; when the source of motivation/values is internal, individuals attempt to control their environment

SOURCE: Adapted from Thorne and Bartholomew-Saunders (2002).

over the needs of the community. In individualistic cultures, the ties between the individual and collectives are loose and "everyone is expected to look after himself or herself and his immediate family" (Hofstede, 2001, p. 227). In contrast, in collectivistic cultures, the focus is on the interconnectedness between individuals and the groups to which people belong.

Evaluating the lateness example in light of individualism/collectivism can help us to understand the team leader's initial interpretations of the latecomers. Because the leader is from North America, he made his evaluation based on his individualistic perspective. His assumption that their lateness demonstrated lack of commitment to the team leads to his evaluation that they made a *choice* to arrive late based on their own self-interests and goals. Although the team leader is not entirely clear on their motivation, he assumes that the latecomers have made a purposeful attempt to undermine the legitimacy of the project and, therefore, that they acted in a deviant manner. If the team leader had made his evaluation from a collectivistic perspective, the outcome may have been different. Because collectivists tend to demonstrate more loyalty to their organizations and groups, the team leader might not assume that their lateness was motivated by self-interest. Rather, he might question what other circumstances may have caused their lateness. Were there traffic problems? Was there a misunderstanding about the set time? Because his initial evaluation does not attribute the cause of their lateness to be purposeful, he does not decide that they were deviant.

Collectivism implies loyalty to one's organization and work group (Hamilton & Sanders, 1988). Gundling (1991) provided an interesting example of a well-known Hitachi–IBM spy incident that occurred during the late 1980s. William Palyn, the American consultant for Hitachi who tipped off the Federal Bureau of Investigation, was seen in a positive light by Americans for upholding ethical principles at his personal expense. However, the Japanese press portrayed him as dishonest and selfish in that he betrayed those who trusted him. Thus, depending on the cultural norms of collectivism/individualism, the individual's behavior was considered either deviant or altruistic.

Furthermore, what is interpreted to be deviant behavior may vary from culture to culture. For instance, collectivistic societies place a high emphasis on fulfilling interpersonal obligations or "duty." In contrast, individualistic societies consider the rights of the individual to be paramount. Given these contextual factors, interpretations of *deviant* can be quite different. For example, the North American emphasis on individual achievement may be interpreted by individuals from collectivistic cultures as deviant behavior (Moon & Woolliams, 2000).

A study by Mezias and colleagues (1999) on the goal-setting process at AmBankCo provides some insight into the differences in perceptions of deviance. When comparing the various national sites, the researchers discovered that the Asian site, rather than following the company's norm of setting sales goals for individuals, set goals for the position. When they explained to the AmBankCo person who had arranged their visit that other sites set goals for individuals, her immediate response was that it was "unfair." In other words, by following the company's norm, the Asians would be engaging in deviant behavior when viewed from their cultural perspective.

In an individualistic culture, the freedom of the individual comes first. In a collectivistic culture, society comes first—even at the cost of the individual's freedom. These norms define what ought to be done in any particular situation. For instance, consider the case of helping others. In their studies of Americans and Hindu Indians, Miller and colleagues (Miller & Bersoff, 1992; Miller, Bersoff, & Harwood, 1990) found that the Indian participants believed that all requests for help, regardless of the individual or the degree of urgency, are an objective and moral obligation. However, Americans tend to see such responsibilities in conflict with individual freedom of choice. Responses to requests depend on the closeness of the individual (e.g., a child) and the degree of urgency in the request. Findings such as these have important implications for understanding deviance. In an individualistic culture, deviant behavior may be perceived to be a function of the association between the individual and the other person in need.

In collectivistic cultures, maintaining social order and meeting the obligations of one's role is paramount. In contrast, in individualistic societies, the focus is on the individual and his or her rights; the "every man for himself" attitude prevails and supports the notion of retaliation (Bennett & Robinson, 2003). Interestingly, Robinson and Bennett (1997) attributed one of the causes of workplace deviance to the need to "vent, release, or express one's feelings of outrage, anger, or frustration" (p. 16). However, depending on the collectivistic versus individualistic nature of the culture, emotional responses may be different (Mesquita, 2001). Emotions such as anger and shame, which tend to precede deviant acts of violence and aggression, may be triggered by different circumstances (Glomb, 2002). A study by Mesquita (2001) found that the emotional responses of Turkish participants (collectivistic), in comparison with those of Dutch participants (individualistic), to situations where they were treated in an offensive, inconsiderate, or deviant manner were more related to concerns about loss of respect from in-group members and loss of social position.

Power Distance

The second dimension of culture, *power distance,* describes the degree to which unequal distribution of power is accepted in society. High-power distance cultures place more emphasis on hierarchical order, in-group loyalty, and respect for position (Kim, 1999; Marsland & Beer, 1983). Low-power distance cultures place more emphasis on autonomy and equity (Kim, 1999). Power distance also has important implications for interpretations of injustice and how acts of deviance can become ethically justified. Several studies found that American managers, in comparison with Chinese managers, were more willing to judge critical remarks and actions from a higher status manager (but not from a lower status manager or an equal-status manager) to be deviant (Bond, Wan, Leung, & Giacalone, 1985; Leung, Su, & Morris, 1996). Because this type of behavior by a superior is deemed to be appropriate in Chinese culture, the Chinese participants did not feel as though they were being treating unfairly.

Building on the lateness example, imagine that the team members did have problems with the team leader and wanted to undermine the leader's authority through "small" acts of deviance such as disrupting meetings by arriving late. Because the team leader is from a low-power distance culture, his initial assessment that the latecomers were behaving in a rude and disrespectful manner may be correct. Furthermore, his evaluation that their behavior was intentional and deviant appears to be accurate. However, if the team leader were from a high-power distance culture, he would assume that the team members would comply with his request to arrive at a particular time. Furthermore, he would not expect employees to challenge his authority, and it is unlikely that he would interpret their lateness as a challenge to his authority.

Power distance appears to have significant implications for the acceptability of performing deviant behavior. For instance, many studies of Indian and Chinese organizations[1] have found that superiors expect loyalty, compliance, and total submission, whereas subordinates expect protection, assistance, and patronage (Farh & Cheng, 2000; Law, Wong, Wang, & Wang, 2000; Sinha & Sinha, 1990). In high-power distance cultures, deviant behavior would include superiors failing to bestow appropriate protection and patronage as well as subordinates failing to comply with their superiors' requests.

Thus, power distance appears to influence the tendency of individuals to question superiors' deviant behavior. Individuals in high-power distance cultures tend to comply more with their superiors' requests, whereas individuals in low-power distance cultures tend to put greater weight on their own judgments (Vitell, Nwachukwu, & Barnes, 1993). High power distance implies a hierarchical order where individuals are expected to act according to their duties and the wishes of their superiors (Su et al., 1999). For instance, in Hispanic cultures, there is a cultural script of *respeto* that prescribes deference to positions of higher prestige, recognition, and power (Marin & Triandis, 1985), suggesting that individuals may more likely be deviant when requested to by superiors. In high-power distance cultures, subordinates would be rewarded for their unquestioning loyalty rather than for their abilities (Khatri & Tsang, 2003; Redding, 1990). In low-power distance cultures, subordinates may be more prepared to stand up to their superiors.

Deviant behavior in the form of retaliation against one's superior may also be less likely in high-power distance cultures because deference to one's superior is the expected relationship between low-status employees and superiors. Challenges to authority would more likely be considered deviant in high-power distance cultures than in low-power distance cultures. However, a recent study demonstrated that collectivism and power distance together may influence what an employee perceives to be deviant behavior and how he or she responds to "unfair" treatment by a supervisor (Jackson, 2001).

Uncertainty Avoidance

The third dimension of culture, *uncertainty avoidance,* characterizes the degree to which individuals tolerate ambiguity and uncertainty. This dimension is concerned with the level of rules and regulations that are needed to manage the potential ambiguity of a situation. Jackson (2001) suggested that in high-uncertainty avoidance cultures, determination of deviant behavior is likely based on the implicit adherence to rules. In low-uncertainty avoidance cultures, it is more likely based on the interpretation of rules and a consideration of possible outcomes. For example, Nakano (1997) found that Japanese employees (high uncertainty avoidance) were more likely to act in accordance with their company's code of conduct than were their American counterparts (low uncertainty avoidance) because Americans are more tolerant regarding deviations from the code of conduct. Nevertheless, although it would appear that high uncertainty implies less deviance from the rules, it may lead to situations where individuals may follow the letter of the rules but ignore the spirit of the rules. In contrast, low uncertainty implies that individuals are more likely to consider the spirit of the rules.

Again, referring back to the lateness example, when the team members arrived late, the team leader remembered reading somewhere that misunderstandings regarding punctuality can cause difficulties in intercultural encounters. The team leader, being from a low-uncertainty avoidance culture, likely would be comfortable with the concept that different cultures have different interpretations of punctuality. Given this perspective, he may realize that the team members' tardiness is due to their lack of awareness of his cultural script regarding punctuality. However, an individual from a high-uncertainty avoidance culture may have more difficulty in understanding that more than one interpretation exists. After all, the rule dictates that team members arrive on time; therefore, anything else is considered to be deviant behavior.

Masculinity/Femininity

The fourth dimension of culture, *masculinity/femininity,* captures the relative emphasis that a culture places on achievement versus overall quality of life. Masculine cultures tend to value assertiveness, material success, and occupational status. Feminine cultures tend to value cooperation and relationships and tend to place less importance on work being a central aspect of a person's life space. A deviant act may also be influenced by the relative orientation of a person's society on the masculinity/femininity dimension. Masculine cultures encourage individuals to achieve and accomplish material concrete objectives and tend to have distinct categories of male/female roles (Hofstede, 2001). In masculine cultures, time off for family duties (for both men and women) may be considered to be deviant. In comparison, feminine cultures place a greater emphasis on the overall quality of life and tend to have a blurring of the male/female roles. The implications for organizations in more feminine societies, such as Scandinavian countries, are a greater awareness and acceptance of the demands of family responsibilities on both men and women. Therefore, employees taking time off for parental and family duties would be less likely to be considered to be deviant in feminine cultures than in masculine ones.

Again, consider the lateness example. Imagine that the latecomers provided a reason for being late to the team leader. Each of these team members has children who attend the same school. Early this morning, the school announced that it would be closed due to a suspected gas leak. Each team member had to rush to make alternative child care arrangements and, as a result, was late for the meeting. Because the team leader is from a masculine culture, his reaction may be that the team members' child care problems are not an acceptable reason for being late. The team members need to be 100% committed to the team. On the other hand, if the team leader were from a feminine culture, he would be more accepting of the latecomers' circumstances and not judge their late arrival as anything but an unfortunate incident.

Short-Term Versus Long-Term Orientation

The fifth dimension of culture, *short-term versus long-term orientation,* refers to the degree to which the past, present, and future are the foci of people's efforts in life. A long-term orientation to life is focused on the future and emphasizes virtues such as perseverance and thrift. In contrast, a short-term orientation is focused on the present and the past, with an emphasis on virtues such as tradition, preservation of "face," and fulfillment of social obligations. The time dimension also captures how time is structured, encompassing the degree to which time is considered to be a fluid or rigid concept. The cross-cultural impact of this dimension for deviant behavior is illustrated in the following example. Two former high-level NEC Electronics Inc. executives filed a lawsuit against their employer for violation of assurances that they would receive rapid promotional advancement with the company. The response from the Japanese company was that the American executives had an unrealistic time frame for advancement in the Japanese system (Gundling, 1991).

Differences in the ways in which cultures view the structure of time are fundamental to understanding the lateness example of the employees arriving late to a team meeting. Imagine that the team leader steps outside the meeting room to ask the receptionist whether the latecomers have arrived, and he notices that they have indeed arrived and are standing around looking at pictures of the receptionist's new baby. The team members are laughing and joking and seem to be in no hurry to get to the meeting. Because the American culture has a short-term orientation, the team leader considers time to be a fixed and inflexible concept. The team leader concludes that the team members are wasting a valuable resource—time—and are acting in a deviant manner. However, cultures with a long-term orientation consider time to be a fluid concept. The first-time viewing of pictures of a new baby is an event. The team members attend that event until it has run its course and then move on to the next event—the meeting. The team members do not consider their lateness to be deviant.

Universalism/Particularism

The sixth dimension, *universalism/particularism,* is the degree to which cultures apply the same rules to all people across all situations. Universalistic cultures share the belief that general rules, codes, and standards are applied equally to everyone. Particularistic cultures place a great emphasis on relationships and their interrelatedness. In particularistic cultures, exceptions to the rules can be made so as to maintain the social order.

With respect to deviant behavior, particularistic individuals tend to consider special relationships and circumstances in their deliberations. They may first consider special relationships, with adherence to organizational rules and norms having a secondary influence. In contrast, universalistic individuals consider it paramount to treat everyone equally. The lateness example and the receptionist's baby pictures can highlight the cultural dimension of universalism/particularism. The team leader believes that the punctuality script—arrive on time—applies to all situations, particularly business situations. In his eyes, the team members have breached the norm and are deviant. However, the team members feel an obligation to the receptionist. She is a friend, and it would not be appropriate to ignore her request to look at the baby pictures. In their minds, their behavior was appropriate and in no way deviant.

The following example provided by Gopalan and Thomson (2003) is very useful in explaining these concepts:

> An American professor (a universalist) has found that an international student from a particularistic culture has plagiarized his paper. The course syllabus clearly stated that the punishment for plagiarism is an "F"—no exceptions. The professor, following the plagiarism rule, gave the student an F in the course. The student went to visit the professor to discuss his grade. During the meeting, the student raised several issues related to his family and his past relationship with the professor (he had taken several courses and never plagiarized previously). He also mentioned that he was under a lot of pressure, that an F in the course would mean he could not go home for the summer, and that he would have to delay future educational plans. The professor explained that none of these circumstances was relevant to the situation. He then went on to explain the purpose of the rule and that it would be unfair to other students not to apply it equally. As the example demonstrates, the primary emphasis for the universalist is upholding the rule and enforcing penalties for any violations. In contrast, the particularist considers the importance of relationships to be paramount. (p. 323)

As part of their cultural awareness training exercises, Trompenaars and Woolliams (2000) presented the following dilemma[2]:

> You are riding in a car driven by a close friend. He hits a pedestrian. You know he was going at least 35 miles per hour in an area of the city where the maximum allowed speed is 20 miles per hour. There are no witnesses. His lawyer says if you testify under oath that he was only driving 20 miles per hour, it may save him from serious consequences. What right has your friend to expect you to protect him?
>
> My friend has a DEFINITE right as a friend to expect me to testify to the lower figure.
>
> He has SOME right as a friend to expect me to testify to the lower figure.
>
> He has NO right as a friend to expect me to testify to the lower figure.
>
> Would you help your friend in view of the obligations you feel you have to society? (p. 5)

Responses from 55,000 managers show that the Swiss, Americans, and Canadians are nearly totally universalistic in their approach to the problem

(Trompenaars & Woolliams, 2000), meaning that these cultures accept that the same rules apply to everyone. Thus, it would be considered deviant behavior to lie for a friend. Latinos, Africans, Asians, and Russians, on the other hand, tend to be more particularistic in their approach. Thus, it would not be considered to be deviant to lie for a friend. The English and French fall somewhere in between in that they would reserve judgment until they know the degree of harm to the pedestrian (Kleiner, 2001).

Interestingly, when the respondents were told how their responses differed from those of other cultures, Trompenaars and Hampden-Turner (1998) invariably heard comments from Americans such as "You can't trust them—they won't even tell the truth" (Kleiner, 2001), showing that departures from their position is considered to be deviant behavior. Similarly, individuals from collectivistic societies made comments such as "This proves you can't trust Americans—they won't even help their friends" (Kleiner, 2001), again illustrating that departures from expected cultural positions are construed as deviant behavior by other cultures.

Neutral/Affective

The seventh dimension, *neutral/affective,* describes the degree to which it is acceptable to display emotions. Affective cultures accept open displays of emotion, whereas neutral cultures consider open displays of emotion to be inappropriate. Neutral/Affective refers to the degree to which the culture openly displays emotion. Many studies have shown that deviance is very much an emotionally charged issue (Lee & Allen, 2002; Robinson & Bennett, 1997). Misunderstandings regarding displays of emotions can easily be interpreted as deviant responses. Trompenaars and Hampden-Turner (1998) found that Americans and Europeans display emotions rather openly. In other societies, such as Indonesia, public displays of emotion may be considered childish, harmful, and possibly rude. Moon and Woolliams (2000) provided this example:

> You accidentally insulted a group of Indonesians. . . . They may feel insulted but probably would not show it. You might not even be aware that you had insulted them, but their trust in you would be damaged. You might feel your project failing and never understand why—and the more you express your frustration and disappointment, the more rapidly the project fails! (p. 110)

As Moon and Woolliams (2000) highlighted, depending on the cultural backgrounds, misunderstanding over emotions can lead to deviant acts such as project sabotage, noncompliance, and withdrawal of effort. We can easily visualize the lateness example spiraling into a web of misunderstandings of emotions. After the team meeting, the leader decides to have a private conversation with the team members. He tells them, "I am very unhappy that you are late." In the leader's mind, his behavior is appropriate. He is being up front and open. However, the team members are upset because they have been humiliated. Yet because they are from a neutral culture, they do not express their feelings. The team leader leaves the meeting thinking, "That went well." Little does he know.

Specific/Diffuse

The eighth dimension, *specific/diffuse*, is the relative emphasis that a culture places on specific elements as part of a whole. Specific/Diffuse refers to the relative orientation of a culture's members to the consideration of a larger integrated perspective versus a specific and often reductive consideration of separable parts. This is similar to Nisbett, Peng, Choi, and Norenzayan's (2001) description of the East Asian holistic (diffuse) approach to problem solving versus the North American analytic (specific) approach. Individuals in specific cultures tend to lead highly compartmentalized lives where business and social relationships are kept separate. Individuals in diffuse cultures consider all relationships to be related; therefore, many aspects of professional and personal lives are interrelated.

Again, we turn to the lateness example. Because the team leader is from the United States, we assume that he has a specific perspective. Therefore, he tends to focus on the individuals and their personal attributes when evaluating the outcome. The team members were late and, therefore, not committed to the team. A holistic thinker would consider the outcome and the individuals in relationship to one another. In addition to looking to other causes for the behavior, the team leader would consider the outcome in the context of the entire team. Will one event really have such a big impact on the whole team? He may consider their lateness inappropriate but not consider it to be of a serious nature.

A specific/diffuse perspective has very important implications for attributing cause in social situations. Many studies have found that holistic (diffuse) thinkers tend to focus on many factors in the environment when evaluating the outcome of an event. Analytic (specific) thinkers, on the other hand, consider the few variables that are closely related when considering the cause and outcome of the event. For example, Trompenaars and Hampden-Turner (1998) found that North Americans, who score the highest of any group on this specific dimension, have a strong tendency to compartmentalize their work relationships. As a result, when they are at work, they tend to focus on the task at hand and treat their peers impersonally. As Hampden-Turner and Trompenaars (1993) put it, "No intimacy, affection, brotherhood, or rootedness is supposed to sully the world of work" (p. 133).

In comparison, Latin Americans are more holistic (diffuse) in their information processing and see their work relationships as encompassing both personal and business. Latin American culture stresses that it is important to be a *buena gente* (nice person) and to develop personal relationships (Stone-Romero, Stone, & Salas, 2003). It is easy to imagine how these two views can collide. A North American manager responsible for Latin American operations could easily view the ongoing workplace socialization a waste of time and unproductive. Such misunderstandings can lead to "unfair" performance appraisals, strained relationships, and conflict (Sanchez-Burks, Nisbett, & Ybarra, 2000).

Achievement/Ascription

The ninth dimension of culture, *achievement/ascription,* is the relative emphasis that a culture places on achieved status (based on the individual's actions and accomplishments) versus ascribed status (based on age, gender, class, and/or wealth). As applied to deviant behavior, achievement/ascription captures the degree to which legitimacy is accorded to individuals in positions of status. For example, in achievement cultures such as the United States, managers who are parachuted into positions due to their connections and are "incapable" of performing their particular roles would be granted little legitimacy by subordinates; therefore, it might not be considered deviant to question their authority. On the other hand, in ascription cultures such as India, managers' legitimacy comes from their roles. Furthermore, individuals from ascription cultures would accept managers being promoted due to their connections. Therefore, it would be considered deviant to question their legitimacy regardless of their capability in fulfilling their roles.

In the lateness example, imagine that the team leader speaks to one of his peers after the meeting and expresses his concern over some team members' apparent lack of commitment to, and enthusiasm about, the project. He is then warned by his fellow leader to be careful how he handles those team members because they have powerful connections. In fact, the peer goes as far as to suggest that the leader should give them preferential treatment. The leader, in response, says that would be unfair and that everyone should be treated equally and rewarded based on their accomplishments. Because he is from an achievement culture, he believes that employees should be rewarded for their efforts. Conversely, because the team leader was given his position based on past accomplishments, he might not be given the same amount of respect as would a manager who is promoted based on his status within a particular relevant group or groups.

Internal/External

The final dimension of culture, *internal/external,* captures the degree to which individuals believe that they can control their own fate. Internalistic cultures have a mechanistic view of nature; it can be controlled and dominated. Individuals in internalistic cultures believe in control of their own destiny and do not believe in luck or fate. Externalistic cultures are in harmony with nature; they cannot dominate it. Individuals in externalistic cultures do not believe they can shape their own destinies but instead believe that destiny is beyond their control and is determined by fate. Our final take on the lateness example can help us to understand why North Americans and other internalistic cultures consider time to be fixed. Because they believe that they can control the environment, they believe that they can control and own time. That helps us to understand why the team leader considers time to be a valuable resource. Conversely, if the team members are from an external culture, they see time as more of a fluid concept over which they have little control. It is not their fault that the receptionist asked them to view the baby pictures.

We can also reconsider the professor and student example. The professor, being from the United States, is socialized to believe people have control over their destinies; therefore, an act of plagiarism is a personal choice. The student, on the other hand, believed that he had plagiarized due to a combination of external events over which he had little control; therefore, plagiarism would not be considered to be deviant behavior on his part (Gopalan & Thomson, 2003).

What Do Cultural Differences Mean to Managers?

Understanding that cultural differences in perceptions of deviant behavior exist is only a first step for managers and organizations. The question remains as to whether the individual, the manager, and/or the organization should change and adapt to the cultural variation. Lack of an organizational position may, in fact, be avoiding the problem or imposing an ethnocentric culture on the workforce. Although this may appear to be the easiest solution, deviant behavior that may be engaged in unconsciously (from an employee's perspective) may follow, and ineffective organizational performance may result. Therefore, managers not only must understand the culture in which they are operating but also must understand their own cultural background and the cultural meaning of their organizational practices. All parties should be sensitized to, and should engage in identification and resolution of, the variation in cultural norms, as they affect organizational norms, to diminish the dysfunctional effects of deviant behavior in the workplace. Only by sharing perceptions and explicitly identifying norms can deviant behavior be mitigated.

Keeping in mind that managers and organizations need to recognize that the cross-cultural view of deviance involves the consideration of perceptions, we highlight the following key points. First, when attempting to understand the underlying cause of deviance, both the culture of the individual and the culture of the organization must be examined. What may appear to be deviance from the manager's point of view might not from the employees' point of view. In the same vein, employees may perceive managerial behavior to be deviant (unfair or unjust) when in fact the manager is merely behaving in accordance with his or her cultural scripts. We emphasize that this observation may be true even when individual cultural differences are not apparent. However, people often fail to consider this when they are evaluating deviance.

Second, an understanding of the employees' cultural background may allow both individuals and the organization to prevent acts of deviance from occurring. This cultural understanding can lead to insights into how individuals define morality and how they interpret the underlying tensions in various ethical dilemmas. It may lead to a better understanding of how seemingly "unethical" values can motivate employees to decide to act in a certain manner. As the cross-cultural research by Trompenaars and Hampden-Turner (1998) illustrated, responses to an ethical dilemma involving a friend vary according to a number of cultural dimensions.

Third, the development of effective deterrents to, and controls on, deviant behavior should consider the impact of culture. In collectivistic societies, whistle-blowing may be interpreted as a deviant act. For instance, a cross-cultural study of Australian, Indian, and Malaysian Chinese professional accountants found that the Australian participants (individualistic) were more likely to engage in and accept the practice of whistle-blowing than were the other two groups (collectivistic) (Patel, 2003). This is not to say that individuals from collectivistic societies would not blow the whistle, but the act of whistle-blowing by individuals in these cultures is considered to be deviant by others in the collective. Therefore, incentives to encourage whistle-blowing must take steps to counter or address the collective as well as the individual. In comparison, individualistic societies might not interpret whistle-blowing by individuals as a deviant act,[3] although individual-based protections and incentives must be used to encourage whistle-blowers to step forward (Jensen & Hodson, 1999).

Examining the cross-cultural aspects of deviant behavior provides insight into how to effectively control or mitigate this behavior in organizations. Academics have found that the most effective controls are sanctions that tend to reflect dominant features of the society (Grasmick & Kobayashi, 2002). For instance, threats from others in one's group, in the form of shame and embarrassment, are an effective method of control in collectivistic societies, whereas guilt, a personal sense of failure, and responsibility are more effective in individualistic societies (Hofstede, 2001). For example, Chinese law (Yuan Zuo) has always stressed that the offender's in-group has an obligation to monitor the individual's behavior and, therefore, should have been able to prevent the deviant act (Su et al., 1999). Culturally appropriate sanctions are also effective at the organizational level. Hirokawa and Miyahara (1986) found that Japanese managers considered socially imposed embarrassment as an important source of compliance to organizational rules more so than did their American counterparts.

Fourth, we stress that managers should recognize that the North American view on deviance is not necessarily the "best" or "most accurate" view. We highlight this because most studies and theories are grounded in North American perspectives of deviance. As our various examples highlight, in many instances, a North American viewpoint may cause misunderstandings to occur. However, managers' cultural perceptions and views, North American or otherwise, do not need to continue to cause misunderstandings. Many researchers and practitioners suggest that managers' cultural awareness and understanding can be improved through cross-cultural training. Many cross-cultural trainers consider role-playing, evaluations of ethical dilemmas, and other activities that encourage perspective taking and reflection to be very effective tools for developing cultural awareness and understanding.

Concluding Comment

The purpose of this chapter was to consider how one's cultural perspective affects the perceptions and motivations behind deviant behavior. One's cultural perspective is shaped by the basic assumptions of each culture regarding the rules for acting and thinking. As the lateness example illustrates, interpretations of oversights and intentions can vary according to one's cultural perspective. A seemingly trivial act, such as arriving late to a team meeting, can be interpreted as an intentional act that conveys a lack of commitment to the team or as a lack of respect for the team leader. However, the latecomers may have a different cultural understanding of lateness, whereby the act merely demonstrates a lack of awareness, or an oversight, of the team leader's understanding of punctuality. As the lateness example demonstrates, initial misunderstandings can easily spiral into webs of misunderstandings. Subsequent events, such as a confrontation with the team members, can further exacerbate the situation if the team leader is not culturally aware. To avoid these situations, it is necessary to understand the culture of the individuals, the organization, and the society in which the organization operates.

Notes

1. Chinese and Indian cultures are typified by high power distance (Hofstede, 2001).
2. The story was originally created by Stouffer and Toby (1951). The movie *The Sweet Hereafter* and Russell Banks's novel on which the film is based present a similar problem.
3. *Time* magazine's 2002 Women of the Year were two famous whistle-blowers: Sherron Watkins (Enron) and Cynthia Cooper (WorldCom).

References

Bennett, R. J., & Robinson, S. L. (2003). The past, present, and future of workplace deviance research. In J. Greenberg (Ed.), *Organizational behavior: The state of the science* (2nd ed., pp. 247–281). Mahwah, NJ: Lawrence Erlbaum.

Bies, R. J., & Tripp, T. M. (1996). Beyond distrust: "Getting even" and the need for revenge. In R. M. Kramer & T. Tyler (Eds.), *Trust in organizations* (pp. 246–260). Thousand Oaks, CA: Sage.

Bies, R. J., & Tripp, T. M. (2005). Badmouthing the company: Bitter employee or concerned corporate citizen. In R. E. Kidwell, Jr., & C. L. Martin (Eds.), *Managing organizational deviance* (pp. 97–108). Thousand Oaks, CA: Sage.

Bond, M., Wan, K., Leung, K., & Giacalone, R. (1985). How are responses to verbal insults related to cultural collectivism and power distance? *Journal of Cross-Cultural Psychology, 16,* 111–127.

Brislin, R., & Kim, E. (2003). Cultural diversity in people's understanding and uses of time. *Applied Psychology: An International Review, 52,* 363–382.

Cushner, K., & Brislin, R. (1996). *Intercultural interactions: A practical guide.* Thousand Oaks, CA: Sage.

Delano, J. (2000). Commentary on "Beyond Sophisticated Stereotyping: Cultural Sensemaking in Context." *Academy of Management Executive, 14*(1), 77–78.

Farh, J. L., & Cheng, B. S. (2000). A cultural analysis of paternalistic leadership in Chinese organizations. In J. T. Li, A. S. Tsui, & E. Weldon (Eds.), *Management and organizations in the Chinese context.* New York: St. Martin's.

Glomb, T. (2002). Workplace anger and aggression: Informing conceptual models with data from specific encounters. *Journal of Occupational Health Psychology, 7,* 20–36.

Gopalan, S., & Thomson, N. (2003). National cultures, information search behaviors, and attribution process of cross-national managers: A conceptual framework. *Teaching Business Ethics, 7,* 313–328.

Grasmick, H., & Kobayashi, E. (2002). Workplace deviance in Japan: Applying an extended model of deterrence. *Deviant Behavior: An Interdisciplinary Journal, 23,* 21–43.

Gundling, E. (1991). Ethics and working with the Japanese: The entrepreneur and the "elite course." *California Management Review, 33*(3), 25–39.

Hamilton, V. L., & Sanders, J. (1988). Punishment and the individual in the United States and Japan. *Law and Society Review, 22,* 301–328.

Hampden-Turner, C., & Trompenaars, F. (1993). *The seven cultures of capitalism.* New York: Doubleday.

Hirokawa, R., & Miyahara, A. (1986). A comparison of influence strategies used by managers in American and Japanese organizations. *Communication Quarterly, 36,* 157–168.

Hofstede, G. (2001). *Culture's consequences* (2nd ed.). Thousand Oaks, CA: Sage.

Jackson, T. (2001). Cultural values and management ethics: A 10-nation study. *Human Relations, 54,* 1267–1302.

Jensen, G., & Hodson, R. (1999). Synergies in the study of crime and the workplace: An editorial introduction. *Work and Occupations, 26,* 6–22.

Jones, T. (1991). Ethical decision making by individuals in organizations: An issue-contingent model. *Academy of Management Review, 16,* 366–395.

Khatri, N., & Tsang, E. (2003). Antecedents and consequences of cronyism in organizations. *Journal of Business Ethics, 43,* 289–303.

Kim, S. U. (1999). Determinants and characteristics of corporate culture of Korean enterprises. In H. Kao, D. Sinaha, & B. Wilpert (Eds.), *Management and cultural values: The indigenization of organizations in Asia* (pp. 86–101). New Delhi, India: Sage.

Kleiner, A. (2001, March). The dilemma doctors. *Strategy & Business, 23.* (New York: Booz Allen Hamilton)

Law, K. S., Wong, C. S., Wang, D., & Wang, L. (2000). Effect of supervisor–subordinate *guanxi* on supervisory decisions in China: An empirical investigation. *International Journal of Human Resource Management, 11,* 751–765.

Lee, K., & Allen, N. (2002). Organizational citizenship behavior and workplace deviance: The role of affect and cognitions. *Journal of Applied Psychology, 87,* 131–142.

Leung, K., Su, S., & Morris, M. (1996, August). *Reactions to negative feedback: A cross-cultural investigation of the effects of interactional justice, feedback privacy, and relative status.* Paper presented at the annual meeting of the Academy of Management, Cincinnati, OH.

Marin, G., & Triandis, H. (1985). Allocentrism is an important characteristic of the behavior of Latin Americans and Hispanics. In R. Diaz-Guerro (Ed.), *Cross-cultural and national studies in social psychology* (pp. 85–104). Amsterdam, Netherlands: Elsevier.

Marsland, S., & Beer, M. (1983). The evolution of Japanese management: Lessons from U.S. managers. *Organizational Dynamics, 11*(3), 49–68.

McDonald, G. (2000). Cross-cultural methodological issues in ethical research. *Journal of Business Ethics, 27,* 89–104.

Mesquita, B. (2001). Emotions in collectivist and individualist contexts. *Journal of Personality and Social Psychology, 80,* 68–74.

Mezias, S., Chen, Y-R., & Murphy, P. (1999). Toto, I don't think we're in Kansas anymore: Some footnotes to cross-cultural research. *Journal of Management Inquiry, 8,* 323–333.

Miller, J., & Bersoff, D. (1992). Culture and moral judgment: How are conflicts between justice and friendship resolved? *Journal of Personality and Social Psychology, 62,* 541–554.

Miller, J., Bersoff, D., & Harwood, R. (1990). Perceptions of social responsibilities in India and United States: Moral imperatives or personal decisions? *Journal of Personality and Social Psychology, 58,* 33–47.

Moon, C., & Woolliams, P. (2000). Managing cross-cultural business ethics. *Journal of Business Ethics, 27,* 105–115.

Nakano, C. (1997). A survey study on Japanese managers' views of business ethics. *Journal of Business Ethics, 16,* 1737–1751.

Nisbett, R., Peng, K., Choi, I., & Norenzayan, A. (2001). Culture and systems of thought: Holistic vs. analytic cognition. *Psychological Review, 108,* 291–310.

Patel, C. (2003). Some cross-cultural evidence on whistle-blowing as an internal control mechanism. *Journal of International Accounting Research, 2,* 69–96.

Redding, S. G. (1990). *The spirit of Chinese capitalism.* Berlin, Germany: Walter de Gruyter.

Rest, J. (1986). *Moral development: Advances in research and theory.* New York: Praeger.

Rest, J. (1994). Background theory and research. In J. Rest & D. Narvaez (Eds.), *Moral development in the professions* (pp. 1–26). Hillsdale, NJ: Lawrence Erlbaum.

Robinson, S., & Bennett, R. (1997). Workplace deviance: Its definition, its manifestations, and its causes. In R. J. Lewicki, B. Sheppard, & R. Bies (Eds.), *Research on negotiation in organizations* (Vol. 7, pp. 3–27). Greenwich, CT: JAI.

Sanchez-Burks, J., Nisbett, R., & Ybarra, O. (2000). Cultural styles, relational schemas, and prejudice against out-groups. *Journal of Personality and Social Psychology, 79,* 174–189.

Seabright, M. A., & Schminke, M. (2002). Immoral imagination and revenge in organizations. *Journal of Business Ethics, 38,* 19–31.

Sinha, J. B., & Sinha, D. (1990). Role of social values in Indian organizations. *International Journal of Psychology, 25,* 705–714.

Stone-Romero, E., Stone, D., & Salas, E.(2003). The influence of culture on role conceptions and role behavior in organizations. *Applied Psychology: An International Review, 52,* 328–362.

Stouffer, S., & Toby, J. (1951). Role conflict and personality. *American Journal of Sociology, 5,* 395–406.

Su, S., Chiu, C-Y., Hong, Y-Y., Leung, K., Peng, K., & Morris, M. (1999). Self-organization and social organization: U.S. and Chinese constructions. In T. Tyler, R. Kramer, & J. Oliver (Eds.), *The psychology of social self* (pp. 193–222). Mahwah, NJ: Lawrence Erlbaum.

Thorne, L., & Bartholomew-Saunders, S. (2002). The socio-embeddedness of individuals' ethical reasoning in organizations (cross-cultural ethics). *Journal of Business Ethics, 35,* 1–14.

Trompenaars, F., & Hampden-Turner, C. (1998). *Riding the waves of culture: Understanding diversity in global business* (2nd ed.). New York: McGraw–Hill.

Trompenaars, F., & Woolliams, P. (2000). *When two worlds collide.* Amsterdam, Netherlands: Trompenaars Hampden-Turner Intercultural Management Consulting. Available: www.7d-culture.nl/downloads/whentwoworldscollide.pdf

Vardi, Y., & Wiener, Y. (1996). Misbehavior in organizations: A motivational framework. *Organizational Science, 7,* 151–165.

Vitell, S., Nwachukwu, S., & Barnes, J. (1993). The effects of culture on ethical decision-making: An application of Hofstede's typology. *Journal of Business Ethics, 12,* 753–760.

The Bob Smith Affair

Skye Susans

Alan J. Fish

Bob Smith was an ambitious, bright, and aggressive manager working for a well-known U.S. bank in Australia. Management had previously told him that he was part of the company's succession plan for a regional role in Malaysia. He was also told that if he was successful in Malaysia, there would be an opportunity to work in Shanghai, China, with a further promotion promised. He was extremely excited about the notion of being the company's youngest regional director, which would be his status if he eventually made the move to China.

Bob was married to Shirley, another Australian. They had been brought up in the same country town in regional New South Wales and had known each other since their school days. When they married, Bob was already established with a major Australian bank in its regional operations in a medium-sized city not far from their hometown. Within a few years, the couple had three children. Shirley was happy in her role as a mother and housewife and, with the help of her own mother, cared for their three little boys. In her spare time, Shirley undertook volunteer work for her church.

Approximately 10 years ago, the couple and their young children moved to Sydney to enable Bob to progress in his career. He was recruited to take a job with a U.S. bank operating in Australia. Moving to Sydney created new

---

AUTHOR'S NOTE: This case is based on an actual incident investigated by the authors. The names of all characters are fictitious, as are some details, to protect the identities of the individuals and the organization involved.

difficulties for Shirley because she was no longer able to rely on her mother for daily assistance.

Bob's career progressed quickly. Within 5 years of joining the U.S. bank, he had been promoted several times and was earmarked for an overseas appointment. He had been loath to discuss this possibility with Shirley. But when the human resources director discussed with Bob a definite career move to Kuala Lumpur in Malaysia, with the distinct possibility of the subsequent move to Shanghai, Bob realized that it was time to bring Shirley into the picture, even though a move in the immediate future appeared unlikely. That evening, he raised the issue with Shirley, who had never traveled outside Australia before and, being very close to her family, her church, and her social network, was somewhat naive on matters like these. Bob told Shirley that the current regional manager was not planning to leave his job in Malaysia anyway and that it could be a long time before any move occurred. This would allow them plenty of time to explore all of the possibilities associated with a move to Malaysia.

As fate would have it, and sooner than later, the manager in Malaysia was offered a more senior role with a competing bank, and he duly accepted the job offer. Before Bob knew it, he was offered the new manager's role in Malaysia, based in Kuala Lumpur. Bob was excited and saw career success laid out before him. He had only one problem—how to tell his wife that the family was moving to Malaysia (with a possibility of moving on to China within 3 years) and had only 1 month to prepare. Bob thought that the one thing that would swing her over was the very generous housing package he had been able to negotiate.

Bob had told the human resources director that he might not be able to accept the promotion due to his wife's feelings about moving overseas and her close family and church involvement in Australia and that the large housing allowance would be needed to ensure that Shirley would agree to go. Bob also had significant concerns about Shirley agreeing to move on to China, but he did not advise the bank about that because he was certain that there would be eventual problems at the family level.

Finally, after much discussion and debate, Shirley and Bob packed up their house and moved to Malaysia with their children. On agreeing to go, Shirley consoled herself with the thoughts that she would have a fabulous house and that Kuala Lumpur (and Malaysia more generally) was not too far from Australia. In addition, thoughts of having a maid to help look after the children and of taking an occasional trip home were very enticing.

On arrival, Shirley was awestruck by the size and grandeur of the house, and she quickly realized that one maid working alone would not be adequate to clean it as well as to cook and look after the children. Bob was not happy about employing two maids, but at that point he was willing to do anything to keep his wife happy. He had still not told her about the subsequent career move to China that would occur if everything went well in Malaysia. Shirley employed two Indonesian maids who had been close friends for a number of years. They were not well educated, and their English was not the best, but after a few months they fit into the family, the boys loved them both, and they cleaned and cooked well.

The next 2 years flew by, and Shirley slipped into what seemed to her to be expatriate paradise. She felt as though she was living in the lap of luxury. However, for reasons unknown to her, Shirley had become very unpopular with the other corporate wives. She could not understand why. At first, they all appeared very eager to meet her, and it seemed that they had lined up to visit her new home when she arrived. They had also invited her back to their respective homes. At first, it had struck Shirley that she was very lucky indeed to have a house far grander than that of any of the other expatriate families, even that of Bob's boss.

Although Shirley had adjusted fairly well in Malaysia, it soon became clear that life was not exactly the utopia she first thought it to be. Despite the high standard of living, life could be quite distressing and frustrating at times. She missed her mother, friends, and church community terribly. It had been great to learn activities such as bridge, mah-jongg, golf, and tennis, but the weather was so constantly hot and humid that Shirley had finally given up sports. Anyway, just how much bridge and mah-jongg could one stand to play week after week?

As with most "trailing spouses" in Malaysia, shopping had become a regular pastime for Shirley, and it was not unusual for her to be out shopping in Kuala Lumpur or even to take a short trip to Singapore for an occasional shopping venture. As a consequence, the house was crammed to the rafters with expensive Chinese antiques, artworks, and rugs. So, shopping was not much fun anymore either. The amount of money that Shirley spent seemed to infuriate Bob (even though they could afford it). The current Islamic unrest had also become a bit nerve-racking, and she worried about the children's safety. The worst thing, however, was the constant erosion of her expatriate friends as their husbands were inevitably assigned to the next frontier.

During the third year in Malaysia, Bob was offered the new position in China coupled with a promotion to regional director—Asia. He was as happy as he could be, and he accepted the post before he had even discussed the situation and circumstances with his wife.

That evening, Bob shared the news with Shirley, and following a very heated discussion, he informed her that he had already accepted the offer and had agreed to commute to Shanghai and return back to Kuala Lumpur every weekend. He explained that because the new role was a regional one, he would be responsible for all Asian countries but would complete all of his travel requirements during the week, so it would not affect her at all. Shirley would stay in the house with the children and the two maids.

But Shirley had discovered that the maids came with many frustrations. Two recent incidents had contributed to Shirley's strong desire to return to Australia. First, one of the maids had trimmed the fringe on a new Persian rug that had been purchased the previous week at the significant cost of $18,000. "To even up the ends, ma'am" was the explanation offered by the maid, who apparently did not realize that the uneven fringes were part of the originality of the rug and added to its value. In Shirley's view, cutting that fringe had completely destroyed the value of the rug.

The other incident occurred about a month before a return trip to Australia to see Shirley's mother. Shirley had offered to purchase some gifts for the maids. When she asked them what they would like, one of them said, "I want some false teeth like yours." When Shirley explained that you couldn't buy false teeth in a shop, and that they had to be fitted and made specially, the maid retorted, "But I tried yours on, ma'am, and they fitted perfectly."

Initially, as planned, Bob was diligent about his return trips from Shanghai to Malaysia, but over time it became a hassle. Besides, for a number of months before accepting the China appointment, he and Shirley had not been getting along so well. From Bob's perspective, it seemed that he had worked long and hard to earn his substantial package and keep her in her fabulous house. All she did was go on expensive shopping jaunts. From Shirley's perspective, it seemed that when Bob was home all he did was work, and his phone always rang at the most inappropriate hours.

On one visit home, shortly after his assignment to China, Bob told Shirley that he was having more and more trouble with the office in Thailand and, as a result, would need to spend much more time there. These problems continued for several months, and on one of his rare weekends at home from China while he and Shirley were catching up with an old friend, Bob's mobile phone rang very late at night.

Bob quickly left the room to take the call, saying that it was a business colleague from China named Peter. Afterward, when his friend gibed him about the call and accused him of having a girlfriend, Bob's face became a deep red and he became very angry before charging off to bed, saying that he was exhausted. The friend commented to Shirley that even allowing for his important position, it was unusual that he should be disturbed with a business call so late at night.

After their visitor left, Shirley sat brewing and started to feel very suspicious, wondering whether Bob, like many other expatriates and local senior businessmen, was having an affair. It was not unusual for senior businessmen from both Asian and Western countries to have "girlfriends" on the side, particularly Asian girlfriends, to spend time with and possibly even to discreetly accompany them on occasional business trips. But surely not Bob.

After checking that Bob was asleep, Shirley picked up the mobile phone from beside his bed and took it into the lounge room, where she pressed the recall function. The last number came up, and she pressed call. To her surprise, the voice of a young woman came on the phone exclaiming what a lovely surprise it was to hear Bob's voice again so soon. Shirley confronted the woman, who admitted that she was a very close friend of Bob's and was living in Thailand. Beside herself with anger, Shirley terminated the call and quietly retrieved Bob's briefcase from the bedroom while he slept peacefully.

Shirley went through Bob's briefcase, discovering letters from someone who was apparently his Thai mistress along with several unpaid bills. One was his mobile telephone bill, which was full of calls to the same number she had just dialed, and another was a credit card account for quite substantial sums owed to the Banyan Tree Resort in Thailand. This resort was one of the most expensive chains in Asia. She quickly photocopied the accounts in their home office and returned the phone and briefcase to the bedroom.

The following morning, Shirley confronted Bob with the fact that he was having an affair. Bob freely admitted that he was having a relationship with a Thai woman and said he had no intention of giving her up. A huge argument raged for days. Bob said that he would agree to keep Shirley in the Kuala Lumpur house with the two maids so long as his company did not hear of their problems. If Shirley mentioned it to anyone in the company, he would divorce her and see to it that she got as little financially as possible. Shirley suddenly realized that she did not even know how much her husband was earning, and because he was paid through the United States, she would have a hard time finding out.

Shirley was feeling very vulnerable, but as the days and weeks went on with Bob hardly returning to Malaysia at all, even to see the boys as they were entering their teenage years, she became even more angry. Bob had also reduced her access to money, and as a consequence, her lifestyle became more and more curtailed. One day, Shirley was looking at the accounts she had photocopied from Bob's briefcase, and a realization hit her like a thunderbolt: The credit card bill was a company account, not their personal account. Shirley suddenly realized why Bob had been so adamant that she not mention their marital problems and his frequent trips to Thailand to anyone in the company.

The organization for which Bob worked was conservative in many ways, and although it frowned on its senior people getting into "relationships" with locals, there were no explicit rules against such relationships. In fact, company officials accepted these sorts of liaisons as an element of the local expatriate culture. More important, however, the company had been picking up the bill for Bob's weekends at the Banyon Tree Resort with his mistress, and that was definitely prohibited by policy as well as by law.

For approximately 6 months after discovering the affair, Shirley thought of nothing but revenge. At that point, she decided to visit the wife of the financial controller in Malaysia, intending to confide in her about her woes and showing her the photocopied bills. The financial controller's wife, having suffered years of jealousy about Shirley's fabulous house, could not wait to inform her husband of Shirley's accusations, saying that Bob had been involved in corporate fraud.

Subsequently, the financial controller went through all of Bob's expense claims and company credit card bills and reported the findings to his senior vice president. As a result, Bob was fired and charged accordingly by the police.

Shirley lost her residency status and was required to leave Malaysia. She returned to her old country town in Australia, where she and her children moved into a small cottage with her mother.

Discussion Questions

1. Identify the instances of deviant behavior that occurred in this case. Was Bob Smith's affair an example of deviance? Explain.

2. Did the organization's practices contribute to Bob's situation? If so, how?

3. Use the framework presented in Table 13.1 to analyze how Bob, Shirley, and others behaved in this case?

4. How might a perception of different cultural norms have led Bob to act the way in which he did? To what extent can Bob's behavior be justified on the basis of a claim that "I am now in a different culture that has and accepts different values and behaviors"?

5. What recommendations would you make to the organization to prevent such situations from occurring in the future?

Name Index

Ackroyd, S., 3, 5
Adams, A., 188
Adams, J. S., 219, 224
Addis, K., 225
Adler, P., 214
Adler, P. A., 214
Ajzen, I., 41, 42, 44
Albanese, R., 114, 118
Albert, R., 253
Alge, B., 219, 222
Alge, B. J., 15
Allred, G., 98, 99
Altheide, D. L., 214, 216, 217, 220
Ambrose, M. I., 75
Ammons, J. L., 118
Anderson, Gerard, 25
Anderson, L., 249, 250
Aquino, K., 164, 165, 166, 169,
        249, 251, 253
Archer, D., 191, 199
Armour, S., 3
Aroney, Constantine, 3
Arthur, M. B., 77
Arvey, R. D., 72
Ash, P., 213
Avolio, B., 78
Avolio, B. J., 72, 74, 77

Bachrach, D. G., 75
Bacon, S., 253
Badaracco, J., 57
Ball, G. A., 73
Banaji, M. R., 51
Bandura, A., 72, 244
Bardi, Y. E., 5
Barker, M., 193, 195
Barling, J., 70
Baron, D. P., 18
Baron, R. A., 99, 100, 146,
        219, 239, 249, 250, 252

Barry, D., 4
Barsade, S. G., 246
Barstow, D., 4
Bass, B. M., 72, 74, 77, 78
Baughn, B., 255
Bazerman, M., 50
Bazerman, M. H., 49, 51
Beadles, N. A., 50
Bebeau, M. J., 71
Becker, H. S., 141
Becker, T. E., 164, 165
Behr, D., 98
Beis, R., xiii
Bennett, N., xi, 114, 117,
        118, 121, 122
Bennett, Nathan, 113
Bennett, R., xi, 2, 5, 17, 19, 139
Bennett, R. E., 116
Bennett, R. J., ix, 2, 3, 5, 6, 8,
        14, 15, 69, 75, 76, 114, 219
Bensimon, H. F., 243
Bernardi, L. M., 187
Berstein, Carl, 178
Bertels, T., 11
Beyer, J. M., 277
Bies, R. J., xi, 8, 15, 75, 98, 99,
        100, 101, 102, 103, 104,
        105, 106, 220, 251
Bies, Robert, 97
Bing, S., 123
Black, D. W., 214
Blair, Jayson, 4
Blair, E., 211
Blakely, G. L., 74
Blanco, C., 265
Blau, P. M., 74
Blum, T. C., 273, 274
Bodsky, C. M., 188
Boettger, R., 142
Boettger, R. D., 12

Bok, S., 158, 169
Boles, T. L., 164
Bolino, M. C., 167
Bommer, W. H., 75
Bono, J. E., 245
Bottom, W. P., 166
Bovender, Jack O., 28
Boye, M. W., 15
Bradfield, M., 249
Bradlee, Ben, 178, 179, 180
Bratton, V., 167
Breinin, E., 78
Brennan, Edward, 65
Breslin, David, 185
Bretz, R. D., Jr., 167
Brinkman, J., 50
Brinkman, R. J., 15
Brittingham, A. M., 265
Brockner, J., 222
Brodt, S. E., 74
Brooks, C. M., 118
Brooks, P., 12
Brown, M., xi, 70, 73
Brown, M. A., 50
Brown, M. E., 216
Brown, Michael E., 69
Bruun, S., 117
Buckley, M. R., 113
Bullard, P. D., 211
Burns, J. M., 77
Burt, R. S., 165
Bush, D. F., 250
Buss, A. H., 99
Butcher, V., 70
Butterfield, B., 81
Buttram, R. T., 142
Byrne, Z. S., 75

Cahn, E., 100
Caldwell, D. F., 50
Camerer, C., 165
Cappelli, P., 115
Capps, M. H., 213
Carlson, D. M., 167
Carrns, A., 155
Carroll, A., 50
Carter, M., 224
Cashman, J. F., 76
Castro, S. L., 76
Chalykoff, J., 120
Chan, A. Y. L., 78
Chandler, T. D., 114, 115, 120
Chang, M., 41
Chapman, D. F., 50
Chappell, D., 249, 250, 254
Chappell, D. V., 251
Chatman, J. A., 50

Chauvin, K., 115
Chen, G., 77
Cherrington, D. J., 216
Cherrington, J. O., 216
Chetoff, Michael, 26
Child, J., 16
Christie, R., 163
Chugh, D., 51
Ciulla, J., 70
Clark, J. P., 213, 219
Clark, N. S., 270
Clemow, D. D., 250
Cobbin, D. M., 224
Cochran, P. L., 52, 134
Cogliser, C. C., 76
Collins, J. M., 5, 6, 240
Colquitt, J. A., 222
Comer, D., xii
Comer, Debra, 183
Conger, J., 77
Connell, D. W., 50
Cooke, Janet, 173, 179, 180, 181
Cooke, R. A., 251
Cooper, C. I., 187, 189, 190
Cooper, W. H., 116
Costigan, L., 187
Coughlan, D., 198
Coyne, I., 189, 193, 194, 195
Crane, D. B., 139
Crawford, N., 189, 192, 196
Cressey, D., 215, 219
Crom, S., 11
Cropanzano, R., 75, 100
Croson, R. T. A., 164
Cullen, J. B., 81, 83
Culp, E. Ronald, 67

Dabney, D., 218
Dafoe, R., 227
Daley, H., 197
Dalton, D. R., 213
Dalton, M., 216, 218
Daniels, S. E., 166
Daniels, D., 214
Dansereau, F., 76
Darer, Michael, 39
Davey, M., 186, 191
Davis, J. H., 117, 165
Davis, J. L., 211
Davis, John, 261, 263
Day, Diana, 93
De George, R. T., 133
Decker, H., 214
Delaney, J., 211
Delaney, J. T, 52
Demore, S. W., 219
DePaulo, B. M., 170

Deshpande, S. P., 50
Devine, Dan, 173
Di Martino, V., 249, 250, 251, 254
Dickinson, Becton, 137
Dienesch, R. M., 142
Dietz, J., 250, 251
Dineen, B. R., 216
Dirks, T., 16, 17, 75, 76
Ditton, J., 216, 218, 224
Donaldson, T., 40, 57,
    70, 137, 138
Douglas, S., xii
Douglas, S. C., 146, 238, 239,
    246, 248, 251, 253, 254
Douglas, Scott C., 237
Douma, B., 45, 161
Duffy, M., 69, 118, 249
Dukerich, J. M., 71, 142
Dulebohn, J. H., 167
Dumaine, B., 14, 191
Dunfee, T. W., 138
Dunn, J., x
Dunn, Jennifer, 39
Durand, Douglas, 81
Durham, C., 245
Dutka, E., 181
Dvir, T., 77

Ebbers, Bernie, xiii, 70, 89,
    90, 91, 92, 93, 95
Eden, D., 77
Einarsen, S., 186, 187, 188, 190
Einarsen, S. E., 193, 194
Ekman, P., 158
Ellen, P. S., 41
Elm, D. R., 71
Elmes, M., 8, 11
Elvin, J., 181
Emler, N. P., 73, 102
Emshwiller, J. R., 211
Enrich, D., 142
Enz, C. A., 163, 166
Epitropaki, O., 70
Erfurt, J. C., 277

Fairhurst, G. T., 76
Fallenius, S., 196
Farrell, B. J., 224
Farrell, D., 116
Farrell, H. M., 224
Faupel, C. E., 267
Feldman, D. C., 226
Felsenthal, C., 181
Ferrell, O. C., 71
Ferrin, D. L., 75, 76
Ferris, G. R., 113, 167, 214
Feshbach, S., 239

Finkelstein, L., 12
Fishbein, M., 41
Fisher, J. D., 219
Fitgerald, L. F., 186
Flannery, B. L., 45, 46
Folger, R., 98, 99, 100, 101, 225,
    239, 240, 250, 252
Foote, A., 277
Ford, R., 253
Fox, S., 106, 240
Freeman, R. E., 70
Frink, D. D., 113
Fuller, J. B., 77
Fuller, R. W., 190
Futa, T., 15

Gagne, M., 118
Galbraith, J. R., 158, 165
Gardner, W. L., 247, 253
Gartner, R., 135
Gecas, V., 77
Geis, F. L., 163
George, J. D., 118
George-Flavy, J., 214
Giacalone, R. A., 5, 6
Gibson, A. M., 41
Gibson, D., 47
Gibson, D. E., 246
Gibson, D. G., 70, 135
Gibson, K., 166
Gicalone, R. A., 69
Gilbert, D. R., 70
Gilder, George, 90
Gini, A., 70, 73
Ginnett, R. C., 226
Glater, J. D., 4
Glendinning, P. M., 187, 191,
    192, 193, 195, 198
Glew, D. J., 146, 239
Glickman, Elyse, 3
Goffman, E., 160
Goldman, B. M., 75
Gouldner, A. W, 74, 215
Graen, G., 76
Graham, J., 142
Graham, J. W., x, 11, 141
Greenberg, J. xii, 2, 5, 6, 7, 15, 48,
    69, 71, 75, 139, 161, 211, 213, 214,
    215, 216, 217, 218, 219, 220, 221,
    222, 224, 225, 226, 227
Griffin, R. W., ix, 5, 6, 9, 69, 146, 239, 240
Gross-Schaefer, A., 225
Grover, S., xii
Grover, S. L., 158, 160, 161, 162,
    163, 164, 166, 169
Grover, Steven L., 157
Guerrero, Lena, 167

Gundlach, M. J., 239, 253, 254
Gutman, A., 214

Hackman, J. R., 134, 137
Haft, Herbert, 191
Haga, W. J., 76
Hallahan, M., 253
Hare, R. D., 214
Harkins, S., 117
Harrell-Cook, G., 113, 167
Hart, J. W., 118
Hartman, E., 70
Hartman, L. P., 73
Hartshorne, H., 159
Harvey, P., xii, 146, 237
Haugh, D., 4, 177
Hegarty, W. H., 45, 46, 139, 140
Heider, F., 246
Herzog, T., 253
Hester, K., 77
Hill, Anita, 184
Ho, T., 55
Hochwarter, W. A., 113
Hodges, T. D., 78
Hoel, H., 187, 189, 190
Hofstede, G., 106
Hogan, R., 73, 102
Hogg, M. A., 218
Holinger, R. C., 211, 213, 217, 218, 219, 224
Hollis, J., 177
Holstrom, A., 224
Holtz, Lou, 173
Homans, G. C., 219
Hopper, H., 214
Horning, D. N. M., 216, 217, 218, 224
Hornstein, H. A., 100
Horowitz, A. M., 267
House, R., 77
House, R. J., 72, 77, 160
Hoyvald, Neils, 39
Hsee, C., 40
Huang, L. X., 265
Hubert, A. B., 197, 198
Hui, C., 161
Hyti, J., 190

Ibanez, A., 265
Ireland, Timothy O., 31
Irvine, J. M., 265

Jackson, J. M., 117
Jackson, Jesse, 91
Jagatic, K., 188
Janis, I. L., x, 16

Janoff-Bluman, R., 194
Jaworski, R. A., 118
Jensen, M. C., 46
Johnson, J. A., 273
Johnson, J. J., 50
Jones, A. P., 72
Jones, E. E., 106
Jones, G. R., 114
Jones, J., xii
Jones, J. W., 15
Jones, T. M., 158
Joseph, C., xii, 146
Joseph, Charles, 237
Joseph, J., 79, 81
Judge, T., 114, 115, 120
Judge, T. A, 167, 245
Jung, D. I., 72

Kacmar, M., 167
Kakabadse, A., 220
Kamp, J., 12
Kanfer, R., 72
Kanungo, R., 77
Kanungo, R. N., 76, 77, 80
Karau, S., 118
Karau, S. J., 114, 117, 118
Kark, R., 77
Keashly, L., 188
Kelly, T., 181
Kelly, Tom, 178
Kelman, H. C., 72
Kemper, T. D., 72, 216, 219
Kennish, J. W., 249
Kent, R., 247, 253
Kerr, N. L., 117
Kerr, S., 47
Kidd, David, 174
Kidwell, R., 116, 233
Kidwell, R. E. Jr., 1, 9, 122
Kidwell, R. E., 8, 114, 117, 121
Kidwell, Roland, xvii, 23, 61, 89, 127, 151, 173, 178, 281
Kiggundu, M. N., 121
Kim, H., xii
Kirk, S. A., 272
Kleen, B. A., 265
Klein, H. J., 114, 118, 123
Kluger, A. N., 245
Knippenberg, D. V., 121
Knudsen, H., 273
Kochan, T. A., 120
Kochanowski, S. M., 8, 9, 233
Kohlberg, L., 70, 71, 77, 162
Konovsky, M. A., 74, 75, 76
Korppoo, L., 196
Korsgaard, M. A., 74

Kouzes, J. M., 72, 169
Kramer, R. M., 75, 98
Kroeck, G., 77
Krueger, A. B., 115
Kruglanski, A., 56
Krum, Peter, 110, 111
Kurland, N. B., 41
Kutchins, H., 272

LaFrentz, Jake, 1
Lam, L. W., 137
Landry, Kimberly, 110, 111
Larson, C. L., 214
Lassiter, G. D., 17
Latane, B., 117
Latham, G., 254
Latham, G. P., 45, 226, 227
Lazear, E. P., 115
Leahy, Frank, 173
Leck, J. D., 116
Lee, D., 188
Lee, R., 253
Leeson, Nick, 131
Leeuwen, E. V., 121
Leibowitz, A., 114
Leighton, P., 188
Lempert, R. O., 270
Leonard, B., 3
LePine, J. A., 11, 142
Leung, C., 15
Leventhal, G., 222
Lewicki, R. J., 41, 215, 216, 219
Lewis, M. V., 249
Lewis-McClear, K., 75
Leymann, H., 188, 190, 193
Leyva, Silvio Izquierdo, 237
Liden, R. C., 76, 116, 118
Liebowitz, M. R., 265
Liefooghe, A. P. D., 186, 191
Lim, V. G., 115, 116, 117
Lima, P., 263
Lipman, M., 211
Liptak, A., 4
Lirtzman, S. I., 160
Locke, E., 245
Locke, E. A., 7, 17, 45
Lowe, B., 77
Lowery, C. M., 50
Lykken, D. T., 214, 253

Mack, D. A., 15
MacKenzie, S. B., 75
Madden, T. J., 41
Maggio, Barbara, 1
Mainouse, A. G., 116
Malatesta, R. M., 75

Malhotra, D., 55
Mancuso, Anita, 31
Mangione, T. W., 218
Mann, Leslie, 262
Mannix, E. A., 50
Maraniss, David, 180
Marietta, Martin, 144
Markus, H. R., xii
Mars, G., 216, 217, 218
Martin, C. L., 1
Martinko, M., xii, 239, 243
Martinko, M. J., 146, 238, 239, 240, 244,
    245, 246, 247, 248, 251, 253, 254
Martinko, Mark J., 237
Martinko, S. C., 254
Martucci, N. M., 250
Masarech, M. A., 123
Maslow, A., 77
Masterson, S. S., 75
Matano, R. A., 15
Mathiessen, S. B., 193, 194
Matsueda, R. L., 135
Matthews, C., 104
Mattila, M. L., 196
Matza, D., 218
May, D. R., 45, 46, 78
May, M. A., 159
Mayer, R. C., 165
Mayo, E., 16
McCabe, D. L., 81
McCarthy, D., 53
McDermott, Michael, 237
McGraw, W. R., 211
McGue, M., 253
McGurn, S., 211
McIlduff, E., 198
McIntye, C. L., 50
McLean Parks, J., 16, 17
McLean Parks, J. M., 98, 101
Meier, B., 269
Melin, K., 224
Mendonca, M., 76, 77, 80
Messick, D., 46, 47, 50
Messick, D. M., 49, 51, 135
Metzger, M. B., 213
Meyers, J. W., 52
Meyerson, D., 11, 142, 143
Miceli, M. P., 11, 142
Mikulay, S., 12
Miles, D., 106
Miles, J. A., 114, 118, 123
Miller, G., 155
Miller, M., 142
Milliken, F. J., x
Milner, C., 70
Miner, J. B., 213

Minton, J. W., 215
Mitchell, T. R., 214, 215
Moag, J. S., 75, 220
Moberg, P. J., 17
Moorman, R. H., 74, 75
Moran, M., 177
Moreyra, P., 265
Morgan, H. W., 269
Morrill, C., 100, 101
Morrison, E. W., x, 142
Mueller, Robert, 98
Mullen, B., 117
Murnighan, J., 55, 164, 166
Murphy, R., 213, 215
Mussman, L. M., 15
Musto, D. F., 268, 269

Namie, G., 187, 189,
    190, 193, 194
Namie, R., 193, 194
Naumann, S., xi
Naumann, Stefanie E., 113
Navaez, D., 71
Neale, M. A., 50
Near, J. P., 11, 142
Negus, J., 225
Nelson, A., 70, 224
Neuman, G., 12
Neuman, J. H., 18, 99, 146, 239, 240, 249
Newman, M., 263, 264
Nicoletti, J., 249
Nicols, M. L., 71
Niehoff, B. P., 74, 75, 224
Nisbett, R. E., 106
Nixon, Richard, 178
Normand, J., 270
Northcraft, G. B., 50

O'Connor, S., 187
O'Brien, C. P., 270
Olafson, S., 155
O'Leary, George, 4, 173, 174, 175, 176
O'Leary-Kelly, A. M., ix, 5, 6, 69,
    146, 239, 240
Olson, M., 118
O'Malley, B., 4
Ones, D. S., 213, 240, 246
Ordonez, L., 45, 161
O'Reilly, C. A., 50
O'Shea, P. G., 250

Paine, J. B., 75
Paine, L. S., 134, 135, 137,
    140, 144, 146
Parry, K., 78
Parry, W., 169

Parseghian, Ara, 173
Parsons, T., 16
Patterson, C. E., 77
Payne, S. L., 217, 218
Peach, R. J., 264
Pearson, C. M., 249, 250
Pemberton, P. S., 187
Perlstein, R., 181
Peters, Alex, 94
Petty, M. M., 50
Peyrefitte, J., 71
Pfeffer, J., 168
Pffafenbach, W. L., 185
Phelps, C. C., 142
Piliavin, I., 135
Pillai, R., 74
Podsakoff, P. M., 75
Poland, T., 215
Pope, Anthony, 262
Popper, M., 78
Posner, B., 50
Posner, B. Z., 72, 169
Pratt, M. G., 77
Proctor-Thomas, S. B., 78, 169
Pryor, J. B., 186
Puffer, S., 53
Pugh, S. D., 74, 76
Putsey, L., 227

Quick, J. C., 15
Quick, J. D., 15
Quinn, R. P., 219

Rahim, M. A., 16, 17
Randall, D. M., 41
Randall, P., 189
Ratnesart, R., 98
Rayner, C., 187, 189, 190,
    191, 192, 193, 194
Resnick, A. J., 211
Rest, J. R., 71
Richard, J., 197
Richards, D., 155
Rigas, J., 4
Rizzo, J. R., 160
Ro, C., 225
Roan, Amanda, xvii
Robie, C., 114
Robin, G. D., 213
Robinson, S., xi, 2, 5, 17, 19, 69, 139
Robinson, S. L., ix, 2, 3, 5, 6, 7, 8, 14,
    69, 75, 76, 114, 219, 250
Rodgers, T. J., 191
Rogers, G., 116
Rokeach, M., 77
Roman, P., xii

Roman, P. M., 269, 272, 273, 274
Roman, Paul M., 265
Root, D. A., 252, 253
Rosen, S., 115
Rosentahl, J., 123
Rosenzweig, D., 139
Rost, J. C., 70
Rousseau, D., 165
Rowan, B., 52
Rowley, Colleen, 98
Rumbarger, J. J., 268
Rupp, D. E., 75
Rusbult, C. E., 116
Rush, Benjamin, 271

Sackett, P. R., 5, 6, 213
Sager, M., 179, 181
Saiz-Ruiz, J., 265
Sandberg, J., 211
Santoro, M., 140
Saunders, D. M., 116
Schein, E., 15, 251
Schein, E. H., 49, 51, 123
Schmidt, F. L., 213, 240
Schmidt, W., 50
Schminke, M., 7, 71, 75, 225
Schnake, M. E., 117
Schneider, J., 269
Schonbrunn, M., 274
Schoorman, F. D., 165
Schriesheim, C. A., 74, 76
Schweitzer, M., 55, 161
Schweitzer, M. E., 40, 45, 46, 164
Schweitzer, Maurice, x
Schweitzer, Maurice E., 39
Schwenk, C., 11
Scott, S., 213, 214, 215
Scott, L. R., 216
Scott, Richard, 24
Scrushy, Richard, 109, 110, 112
Scully, M., 11, 142, 143
Seabright, M. A., 7, 75
Sebora, T. C., 71
Seigne, E., 189
Seiye, H., 250
Shamir, B., 77, 78
Shannon, C., 15
Shapiro, D. L., 223, 225, 226
Shavit, H., 244
Shaw, J. D., 118, 249
Sheehan, M., 193, 195
Shell, L. W., 265
Shepard, J., 50
Sheppard, B. H., 215
Shore, L. M., 75
Shouval, R., 244

Shulz, M., 250
Sidgmore, John, 94
Sieh, E. W., 216, 217, 224
Simpanen, M., 224
Sims, H. P., 45, 46, 139, 140
Sims, R., 15
Sims, R. R., 16, 50
Singletary, Charlie, 153
Sitkin, S. B., 165
Sivasubramanian, N., 77
Sjoblom, Thomas, 112
Skarlicki, D. P., 98, 99, 101,
    226, 227, 239, 240
Smith, G., 4, 177
Snyder, N. H., 211
Sockell, D., 52
Soule, L. C., 265
Sparrowe, R. T, 76, 116
Spector, P. E., 106, 240
Speilberger, C. D., 246, 250
Spencer, J., 120
Spooner, K., 249
Staw, B. M., 12, 142
Steidlmeier, P., 78
Steinberg, J., 4
Stone, J. I., 170
Stringer, D. Y., 77
Strudleer, A., 136
Sullivan, Scott, 93
Swanson, S., 155
Sykes, G. M., 218
Szumal, J. L., 251

Taft, W. F., 226
Tapia, Salvador, 238
Tatham, R. L., 217, 218
Taylor, M. S., 75
Tehrani, N., 198
Tenbrunsel, A., 45, 46, 47, 50
Tenbrunsel, A. E., 135
Tepper, B. J., 244, 249, 251
Terry, D. J., 218
Tetrick, L. E., 75
Thibaut, J., 222
Thoma, S. J., 71
Thomas, C. W., 123
Thomas, Clarence, 184, 185
Thompson, J. D., 121
Thompson, P., 3, 5
Thorne, L., xii
Thornton, C., 135
Thornton, E., 139
Tilley, B., 227
Toffler, B., 47
Toffler, B. L., 70, 135
Tollison, R., 114

Tomlinson, E., xii
Tomlinson, E. C., 215, 216
Treviño, L., xi, 47, 48, 50, 52, 70, 71,
    72, 73, 75, 78, 79, 81, 82, 83,
    134, 135, 136, 139, 141, 146,
    214, 216, 223, 224, 225
Treviño, Linda Klebe, 69
Trice, H. M., 272, 274, 277
Trigilio, J., 225
Tripp, T., xi, xiii
Tripp, T. M., 8, 15, 98, 99, 100,
    101, 102, 103, 104, 105, 106
Tripp, Thomas M., 97
Turner, N., 70, 78
Turnley, W. H., 167

Unterberg, M. A., 198

Valachik, J. S., 11
Van Dyne, L., 11, 141, 142
Van Fleet, D. D., 114, 118
Vandenberghe, C., 50
Vandivier, K., 132
Vardi, Y., ix, xi, 2, 14, 5, 6, 8, 14, 139, 219
Vartia, M., 190, 196
Vaughn, D., 133
Vega, Gina, xii, 183
Verton, D., 115
Victor, B., 81, 83, 223
Viswevaran, C., 213, 240, 246
Vollrath, D. A., 71
VonHentig, H., 215
Vroom, V. H., 115, 122

Wachner, Linda, 191
Wade-Benzoni, K., 50
Waldron, Murray, 90
Walker, L., 222
Walker, LeRoy, 91
Wanat, S. F., 15
Warren, D. E., x, 8, 9,
    136, 139, 142
Warren, Danielle E., 131
Watkins, Sherron, 98
Wayne, L., 167
Wayne, S. J., 75, 76, 118
Weaver, G., 267
Weaver, G. R., 47, 48, 52, 70,
    134, 135, 225

Weaver, M., 71
Webb, A., 57
Weiner, A. N., 227
Weisskopf, M., 98
Weitz, E., ix, xi, 2, 5, 6, 219
Weitz, Y., 14
Wells, D., 71, 225
Wener, J. M., 74
Wexley, 254
White, Kevin, 173
White, L. P., 137
White, W. L., 271
Whitener, E. M., 74
Wiener, Y., 5, 6, 8, 139
Weinstein, Bob, 191
Weinstein, Harvey, 191
Wiesenfeld, B. M., 222
Williams, E. S., 74
Williams, K. D., 114, 117, 118
Williams, M. W., 139
Williams, R. M., 272
Wimbush, J. C., 213
Wimbush, J., 50
Wimbush, J. C., 216
Withey, M. J., 116
Witt, A., 98
Wolf, G., 76
Woman, B. B., 214
Wong, E., 177
Woodward, Robert, 178, 179
Wray, Christopher A., 111
Wrich, J. M., 274

Yamada, D., 189, 196
Youngblood, S., 214
Youngblood, S. A., 52, 139
Yuspeh, Alan, 26

Zahn, G. L., 76
Zakay, E., 78
Zapf, D., 187, 189, 190, 193
Zeitlin, L. R., 218
Zellars, K., 140, 239, 243, 245
Zey, M., 71
Zey-Ferrell, M., 71
Zhang, Z., 265
Zimmerman, Celia, 186
Ziska, M. D., 252, 253
Zuckerman, M., 118

Subject Index

AA. *See* Alcoholics Anonymous (AA)
Abusive supervision, 244
Addiction concept, key
    features of, 266-268
Addictive behavior, 7, 265-279
    cures as support for, 271-272
    defined, 265-266
    gambling case, 281-282
    intervention strategies, 274
    making EAPs to deal with, 274-276
    workplace response to, 272-274
Adelphia Communications, 4
Affective traits, 106
Age discrimination Employment
    Act of 1967, 187
Aggression, 10
    cultures of, 244
    personal, 5-6
    See also Organizational aggression
Aggressive-defensive culture, 251
Agreeableness, 189
Alcohol, 265, 268-274.
    See also Addictive behavior
Alcoholics Anonymous (AA), 271-272
Alcohol prohibition, 269
Altruistic behavior, 117
American Indian tribes, 270
American Medical Association, 25
Americans with Disabilities
    Act of 1990, 187
Anger, 240, 246, 248
Antisocial behavior, 5-6
Artifact, 51
Assumptions, 51
AT&T, 90-91
Attendance, poor, 7
Attitudes, 41-44
Attributional training, 253-254
Attribution process, 246-247
Attributions, 246-247

Attribution styles, 244-245
Authentic leadership, 78
Autocratic leadership styles, 243
Avenger, 102-104

B. F. Goodrich, 131-132, 145
"Bad apples" approach, 213
Badmouthing, 97-112
    constructive, 102-104
    destructive, 102-105
    motivations for, 98
    understanding individuals, 105-106
    Web revenge case, 109-112
Bankruptcy, 94-95
Bargaining. *See* Negotiation
Barings Bank, 131-132
Beech-Nut, 39-40
Behavior. *See* Deviance
Behavior. *See individual*
    deviant behaviors
Behavioral beliefs, 41-44
Bell regional operating companies, 91
Biased punctuation of conflict, 101
Blair, Jayson, 4
"Boiler room," 49
British Telecom, 91-93
Brown & Williamson, 142
Bullies, group, 192-193
Bullying, 13-14, 183-209
    across different societies, 195
    benefits of, 198-199
    case of, 205-209
    controlling, 196-198
    costs due to, 193, 196
    ethics of, 199-201
    harassment *vs.*, 184-185
    impact of, 193-196
    increased interest in, 188-189
    power, organizational structure
        and, 190-193

targets, perpetrators,
    and effects of, 189-190
why people submit to, 192
See also Harassment
Burlington Industries v. *Ellerth*, 187

Campaign Against Bullying at Work, 194
Celia Zimmerman v. *Direct
    Federal Credit Union*, 185-186
Charismatic leadership, 76-78, 80
"Churning," 53
Civil Rights Act, 186-188, 250
Codes of ethical conduct, 224-225
Cognitive moral development,
    70-71, 80, 162
Columbia/HCA, 23-30
    compliance and ethics, 26-27
    ethics and compliance, 26-29
    settlement, 27-28
    strategies for rapid
        growth, 24-26
Communication, 57
Compliance, 26-29. *See also*
    Noncompliance
Concealment, 158
Conflict, 10, 16-18, 101
Confrontational (integrative)
    approach, 17
Conscientiousness, 189
Constructive:
    for avenger, 102-103
    for organization, 103-104
    for perpetrator, 103
Constructive confrontation, 275-277
Constructive culture, 251
Constructive deviance, 7-9, 11-13, 142
Continental Airlines, 261-263
Continuous quality improvement
    (CQI) program, 127
Control beliefs, 41-44
Controllability, 247
Conventional individuals, 71
Conventional level of moral
    development, 162-163
Cooke, Janet, 178-181
Corporate hotline, 225-226
Costs:
    due to bullying, 19, 196
    of deviance to organization, 3
    of managerial oversight, 54-55
Counterproductive behavior, 5-6
Counterproductive work behaviors
    (CWBs), 106
Counter-role behavior, 142
CQI. *See* Continuous quality
    improvement (CQI) program
Cross-cultural concerns, 53

Cultural intervention, 251
Cultural tendencies, national, 195-196
Culture, 189
CWBs. *See* Counterproductive work
    behaviors (CWBs)
"Cyberloafing," 115-116.
    See also Job neglect

Death, from deviant behavior, 3
Deception, 158. *See also* Lying
Decisions. *See* Ethical decision making
Defense Criminal
    Investigative Service, 23
Destructive, 102
    for avenger, 104
    for organization, 105
    for perpetrator, 104
Destructive deviance, 7-9, 11-13
Deterrence theory, 135
Deviance:
    antecedents of, 14-15
    constructive *vs.* destructive,
        7-9, 11-13
    deadly manifestations of, 3
    defined, 2
    definitions and terms related to, 4-7
    ethical ambiguity of, 7-13
    health care fraud case, 23-30
    pervasive nature of, 2-4
    prevalence and ambiguity of, 1-30
    publicity of, 2-3
    research of, 4-5
    traditional definition of, 8
    types of, 5-6
    See also individual deviant behaviors
Deviance process, five steps in, 5, 7
Dignity at Work Bill, 189, 195
Discipline, 73, 80
Discrimination, 5-6, 185-187
Disney World, 261, 263
Distributive justice, 219-220
Dow Chemical, noncompliance
    at, 151-155
"Drive-reducing" behavior, 117
Drugs, 268-274. *See also* Addictive
    behavior; Undercover operations
Drug screening, 269-270
Dysfunctional behavior, 5-6

EAPs. *See* Employee assistance
    programs (EAPs)
Eating, excess in, 266.
    See also Addictive behavior
Ebbers, Bernard, 89-96
Education:
    classes and tests, 140
    online, 134, 143

role-playing, 134, 143
video, 137, 140
EEOC. *See* Equal Employment
    Opportunity Commission (EEOC)
E-mail abuse, 151-154
Emotional stability, 189
Emotions, 100, 247-248
Employee as malcontent approach, 105
Employee assistance programs (EAPs),
    254-255, 273-278
    components of, 275
    making, in dealing with addictive
        behavior, 274-276
Employee selection, 120, 122-123
Employee theft. *See* Theft
Enron, 4, 72, 99
Environmental intervention, 251
Equal Employment Opportunity
    Commission (EEOC), 187
Equity theory, 115
Ethical ambiguity of deviance, 7-13
Ethical behavior, leadership
    styles and, 76-80
Ethical codes of conduct, 224-225
Ethical decision making:
    applications to, 43-44
    change reward system to improve, 48
    guiding, 40-41
    managerial oversight, 53-56
    model of, 41-44
    organizational culture, 48-53
    reward systems, 44-48
    theory of planned behavior, 41-42
    See also Unethical behavior
Ethical issues, in withholding effort, 123
Ethical leader, 78-80, 82
Ethically neutral leader, 82
Ethics, 26-29
Evaluations, self-, 245-246
Expectancy theory, 115, 122
Expression of voice, 10
Extraversion, 189

Fairness perception, 219-223
Farugher v. *City of Boca Raton*, 187
Federal Bureau of Investigation (FBI), 23
Foreign Corrupt Practices Act, 137
Fraud, 94. *See also* Medicare fraud
Free riding, 113, 118.
    See also Withholding effort
Functional disobedience, 142

Gambling:
    case, 281-282
    excess in, 266
    from prohibition to
        normality, 270-271

"pathological," 271
    See also Addictive behavior
Gender, 245
"Generic harassment," 486
Goal setting, 45-46
Group bullies, 192-193
Group membership, work, 226
Group norms, 216-218
GTE Communications, 91
Guilt, 248

Harassment, 5-6, 183-209
    Anita Hill and Clarence Thomas, 184
    bullying *vs.,* 184-185
    "generic," 186
    impact of, 193-196
Harris v. *Forklift Systems*, 187
Health care, 23-30
HealthSouth Corporation, 4, 109-112
Hill, Anita, 184-186
HJ Meyers, 49-50
Honesty:
    how much, 169-170
    what organizations do about, 166
    See also Lying
Hostile Attributional Style
    Questionnaire, 253
Hostile organizational aggression, 239
Hughes Electronics Corporation, 252-253
Hypocritical leader, 82

Ignorance about rule application, 132,
    145-146
    education, 137-138
    examples, 136-137
    sanctions, 138
    strategy for managing, 137-138
Ignorance about rules, 132-136, 145-146
    codes of conduct, 133-134
    education, 133-134
    examples of, 133
    sanctions, 135-136
    strategy for managing, 133-136
IJT. *See* Interpersonal justice training (IJT)
Impression management, 167-168
Impulsivity, 240, 246
Incentive system, 64-65,
    120, 122. *See also* Sears
        Automotive; Reward system
Individual differences, 162-163,
    240, 244-246
Individual differences
    orientation, 213-214
Individual leadership, 81
Informal social processes, 215-218
Information:
    misuse of, 7

providing misleading, 10
withholding, 10
Injustice, theft as response to, 219-223
Innovative thinking, 8
Instrumental organizational
    aggression, 239
Insubordination, 7
Integrative approach. *See* Confrontational
    (integrative) approach
Integrity, 240, 246
Intel, 109
Interactional justice, 219-223
Interjuice Trading Corporation, 40
International Personality
    Item Protocol, 250
International Union of Operating
    Engineers Local 546, 153
Internet:
    excess use of, 266
    revenge on, 109-112
    used in deviant behavior, 3
    See also Addictive behavior
Internet gripe site, 109
Interpersonal justice training (IJT), 227
Interpersonal violence, 5-6
Intervention:
    community-based, 250-251
    cultural and environmental, 251
    policy-level, 249
    strategies for, 274

Job design, 120-121
Job neglect, 113
    altruistic behavior, 117
    defined, 114
    extrinsic motivator, 116
    intrinsic motivator, 116
    noneconomic motivations, 117
    See also Withholding effort
Job stressors, 106
Justice:
    distributive, 219-220
    interactional, 219-223
    managing perceptions of, 251-253
    perceived interactional, 75
    procedural, 219, 222-223
    train managers to promotion
        organizational, 226-227
"Just say no" principle, 274

LDDS, 90-91
Leadership, 13-15
    authentic, 78
    autocratic, 243
    case of Bernard Ebbers, 89-96
    charismatic, 76-78, 80
    ethical, 78-80, 82

ethically neutral, 82
hypocritical, 82
individual, 81
insights from cognitive moral
    development theory, 70-71
levels of, 82-83
potential limitations on role of, 80-82
principled, 27
role of, in influencing unethical
    behavior, 69-96
styles, 76-80
supervisory, 81
transformational, 76-78, 80
    unethical, 82
L&H Korea, 44-46
Listening, 57
Litigation, 102
Locus of causality and stability, 247
Locus of control and self-efficacy, 240
Lying, 5-6, 9-13, 157-182
    and negotiation, 163-166
    consequences of, 165-166
    defined, 158
    George O'Leary case, 173-176
    individual differences, 162-163
    morality of, 158-159
    natural or unnatural, 168-169
    nonverbal cues associated with, 170
    pupil constriction associated with, 170
    reasons for, 159-163
    situational factors, 159-162
    who is, 163-165

Machiavellian individuals, 166
Machiavelli's Renaissance
    prescriptions, 163
Malpractice approach, 105
Management, 16-19. *See also* Leadership
Management impression, 167-168
Managerial oversight, 53-56
    costs of, 54-55
    prescriptions for, 55-56
Managers, influence of, 215-216
Manufacturing, Science, and Finance
    (MSF) Union, 194
Massachusetts Commission Against
    Discrimination (MCAD), 185
Material benefits, 102-103
MCAD. See Massachusetts Commission
    Against Discrimination (MCAD), 185
MCI, 91-95
Measurement, 47
Media, dealing with, 255
Medicare fraud, 23-30, 82
Merck, 152
Message board, 109-112
Misbehavior, 9-13

Misleading information, 10
Misuse of information, 7
"Mobbing," 188. *See also* Bullying
Monitoring systems, 44, 53-56
  customizing, 56
  forms of, 53
  for noncompliance, 146
  who should conduct, 56
Moral development, 70-71, 162-163
Morality of lying, 158-159
Moral person. *See* Ethical leader
Moral reasoning, 71
Morgan Stanley, 109
MSF. *See* Manufacturing, Science, and
  Finance (MSF) Union

National Collegiate Athletic Association
  (NCAA), 173-174
NCAA. *See* National Collegiate Athletic
  Association (NCAA)
Negative affectivity, 240, 244
Negative publicity, 97-112
Negotiation, lying and, 163-166
Neutralization, 116
New York Times, The, 152
Noncompliance, 9-10
  benefits of, 131-132
  Dow Chemical, 151-155
  education systems, 146
  managing, 131-155
  monitoring systems, 146
  types of, 132-136, 145-146
Noneconomic motivations, 117
Nonverbal cues, associated with lying, 170
Normative beliefs, 41-44
Notoriety, of deviant behavior, 2-3
Notre Dame, 173-176

Obsession. *See* Rumination and obsession
Occupational Safety and Health
  Administration (OSHA), 255
  case, 261-263
  dealing with media, 255
O'Leary, George, 173-177
Online training, 134, 143
Opportunistic noncompliance,
  132, 145-146
  education, 140
  examples, 138-139
  sanctions, 141
  strategy for managing, 139-141
  See also Noncompliance
Organization, 102-105
Organizational aggression, 9-13
  abusive supervision, 244
  aggressive behaviors, 248
  attributional training, 253-254

attributions, 246-247
attribution styles, 244-245
autocratic leadership styles, 243
community-based
  interventions, 250-251
controllability, 247
core self-evaluations, 245-246
cultures of aggression, 244
defining, 239
emotions, 247-248
employee assistance
  programs (EAPS), 254-255
environment, 243-244
examples of, 237-238
gender, 245
impulsivity, 246
individual differences, 244-246
integrity, 246
locus of causality and stability, 247
managing, 237-259
managing perceptions
  of justice, 251-253
model of, 240-248
negative affectivity, 244
policy-level interventions, 249
prevention strategies for
  managing, 248-255
rigid policies and procedures, 243
selection procedures, 249-250
shame and guilt, 247-248
stressful working and economic
  conditions, 243
task difficulty, 243-244
theories of, 239-241
trait anger, 246
triggers of, 242-243
Organizational Attributional Style
  Questionnaire, 253
Organizational change, 9-14
"Organizational charlatans," 7
Organizational culture, 48-53
  and ethics, 49-51
  cross-cultural concerns, 53
  prescriptions for creating, 51-52
Organizational deviance.
  See Deviance
Organizational dissent, 8
Organizational Hostile Attributional
  Style Questionnaire, 250
Organizational misbehavior, 5-6
Organizational structure,
  and bullying, 190-193
Organization culture, 44
OSHA. *See* Occupational Safety and
  Health Administration (OSHA)
Overly personalistic attribution, 101
Oversight. *See* Managerial oversight

Passive-defensive culture, 251
"Pathological" gambling, 271
PDI. *See* Power distance index (PDI)
PDSD. *See* Prolonged duress
    stress disorder (PDSD)
"Peer listening scheme," 197
Pep Boys, 64-65
Perceived control, 41-44
Perceived fairness, 74-75
Perceived interactional justice, 75
Perpetrator, 102-104
Personality traits, 189
Planned behavior, theory of, 41-42
Political activity, 9
Political (badmouthing or
    spreading rumors), 5-6
Popcorn model, 240
Positive deviance, 142
Posttraumatic stress
    disorder (PTSD), 193-194
Power distance index (PDI), 196
Preconventional individual, 71, 81
Preconventional level of moral
    development, 162
Pregnancy Discrimination Act of 1978, 187
Principled individuals, 71
Principled leadership, 27
Principled level of moral
    development, 162-163
Principled noncompliance, 132
    consulting with upper
        management, 143-144
    education, 143
    examples, 141-143
    sanctions, 144-146
    strategy for managing, 143-143
    See also Noncompliance
Principled organizational dissent, 142
Procedural justice, 219, 222-223
Production (damaging quantity
    and quality of work), 5-6
Production deviance.
    See Withholding effort
Prolonged duress stress
    disorder (PDSD), 193
Property, abusing or stealing, 5-6
Provoked behavior, 99-100
Prudential, 53
PSTD. *See* Posttraumatic
    stress disorder (PTSD)
Psychological benefits, 103
Psychological reactance, 54-55
Psychological testing, 250
Psychopathology orientation, 214
Publicity:
    dealing with media, 255
    negative, 97-112

of deviant behavior, 2-3
    See also Badmouthing
Pupil constriction,
    associated with lying, 170

Quid pro quo harassment, 187

Reservation-based casinos, 270
Revenge, 5-6, 98
    as provoked act, 99-100
    consequences of, 102-105
    emotions as figural
        elements in act of, 100
    HealthSouth Corporation, 109-112
    including rationality
        and morality, 100-101
Reward system, 44-48, 80
    change in, to improve
        ethical decision making, 48
    goal setting and unethical
        behavior, 45-46
    managing incentives, 46-48
    measurement, 47
    sanctions, 46
Risk-taking, 10
Role conflict, 160-162
Role modeling, 72
Role-playing, 134, 137, 143
Royal Caribbean, 139-140
Rules:
    noncompliance to, 9
    organizing, 134
    teaching, 134
Rumination and obsession, 101

Sabotage, 5-6, 9-13
Sanctions:
    defined, 46
    ignorance about rule
        application, 138
    ignorance about rules, 135-136
    opportunistic noncompliance, 141
    principled noncompliance, 144-146
Scandal:
    corporate, 69-70
    Sears Automotive, 65-66
Screening. *See* Selection procedures
Sears Automotive, 48, 61-68, 140
    commissions at Pep Boys, 64-65
    incentive plan, 63-64
    response to scandal, 65-66
    undercover investigation, 62
    years following scandal at, 66-67
Selection procedures, 249-250
Self-efficacy, 43, 240
Self-evaluations, core, 245-246
Self-interest, 161-162

Sexual harassment, 3-4,
   184-188. *See also* Harassment
Shame, 247-248
Shirking, 113-117
   and job neglect, 117
   defined, 114
   equity theory, 115
   expectancy theory, 115
Social cognitive dynamics, 101
Social exchange, 74-76
   liking and affection
      for supervisor, 76
   perceived fairness, 74-75
   relationships of, 80
   trust in supervisor, 75-76
Social impact theory, 117
Social learning, 71-73, 80
Social loafing, 113, 117-118
   defined, 117
   "drive-reducing" behavior, 117
   social impact theory, 117
   See also Withholding effort
Social processes, informal, 215-218
Status and power derogation, 99
Stealing. *See* Theft
Stress. *See* Organizational aggression
Subjective norms, 41-44
Supervision, style of, 120-121
Supervisor:
   liking and affection for, 76
   trust in, 75-76
   See also Leadership; Managers
Supervisory leader, 81
Supreme Court, sexual
   harassment and, 187

TAP Pharmaceuticals, 82
Tempered radicalism, 142-143
Texas Instruments (TI), 52
Theft, 3, 5-6, 9-13
   case of, 233-235
   create awareness of, 223-224
   create corporate hotlines, 225-226
   discouraging, by managing
      social norms and promoting
      organizational justice, 211-232
   individual differences
      orientation, 213-214
   influence group norms on, 216-218
   influence of managers, 215-216
   institute codes of
      ethical conduct, 224-225
   limitations of traditional nonsocial
      approach to, 214-215
   psychopathology orientation, 214
   rates of, 221
   response to injustice, 219-223

result of informal
   social processes, 215-218
rotate work group
   membership, 226
social-based strategies for
   managing, 223-227
train managers to promote
   organizational justice, 226-227
Theory of planned behavior, 46-47
Thomas, Clarence, 184
TI. *See* Texas Instruments (TI)
Title VII, Civil Rights Act, 186-188
Tobacco industry, 142
Training:
   attributional, 253-254
   online, 134
   to promote organization
      justice, 226-227
   See also Education; Employee
      assistance programs (EAPs)
Trait anger, 240, 246
Transactional exchange, 74
Transformational leadership, 76-78, 80
Trust, defined, 165-166. *See also* Lying
Trust in supervisor, 75-76
Truthfulness. *See* Honesty; Lying
2000 KPMG Organizational
   Integrity Survey, 40
*2002 Report of the Queensland Government
   Workplace Bullying Taskforce*, 195
Tyco International, 4

UMIST. *See* University of Manchester
   Institute of Science and Technology
   (UMIST)
Undercover operations, 31-37
   defined, 31-32
   drug case, 32-36
   Sears Automotive, 62
Unethical behavior, 39-60
   goal setting and, 45-46
   leadership styles and, 76-80
   role of leaders in influencing, 69-96
   See also Ethical behavior
Unethical leader, 82
Union, 153, 194
Universal Juice Company, 39
University of Manchester
   Institute of Science and
   Technology (UMIST), 190
U.S. Department of Defense, 134
U.S. Office of Government Ethics, 134

Values, 51
Video training, 134, 137, 140, 143
Violation of rules, norms,
   and promises, 99

"War on Drugs," 269
Washington Post, 178-181
Web-based interactive ethics, 134
Web revenge, 109-112
Whistle-blowing, 5-6, 8-9, 143
    and litigation, 102
    defined, 142
    positive aspect of, 11
Withholding effort, 113-129
    challenges for managers, 119-123
    employee selection, 122-123
    ethical issues in, 123
    explanations for low
            performance, 119-120
    incentive systems, 120, 122
    job design, 120-121

low-quality loafers case, 127-129
    style of supervision, 120-122
Withholding information, 10
"Workaholism," 266
Workplace Bullying & Trauma
        Institute, 190
WorldCom, 4, 69-70, 72, 89-95

Xerox, 152

Yahoo!, 109-110

Zimmerman, Celia, 185-186
"Zero-tolerance"
        policies, for organizational
        aggression, 249

About the Editors

Roland E. Kidwell, Jr., is Associate Professor of Management in the College of Business Administration at Niagara University. He has a Ph.D. in business administration from Louisiana State University. His research interests include withholding effort in work groups and other collectives, business ethics, and human resources issues in small businesses. His research has appeared in various academic journals, including the *Academy of Management Review, Journal of Management, Journal of Accounting and Public Policy, Small Group Research, and Journal of Business Ethics*. He coauthored (with Christopher L. Martin) the text, *HRM from A to Z: Critical Questions Asked and Answered* (McGraw–Hill Irwin, 2001).

Christopher L. Martin is Professor and Dean of the Frost School of Business at Centenary College of Louisiana, where he holds the Rudy and Jeannie Linco Eminent Scholar Chair of Business Administration. He received his Ph.D. in organizational behavior and human resources management from the Georgia Institute of Technology. His writings have addressed organizational fairness, anger and disruptive workplace behavior, technologically driven change, organizational downsizing, human resources management strategy, leadership, and the theoretical underpinnings of trust. His research has been published in numerous journals, including the *Journal of Applied Psychology, Academy of Management Journal, Journal of Management, OBHDP,* and *Administrative Science Quarterly*. He coauthored (with Roland E. Kidwell) the text, *HRM from A to Z: Critical Questions Asked and Answered* (McGraw–Hill Irwin, 2001).

About the Contributors

Nathan Bennett is Senior Associate Dean and Professor of Management in the DuPree College of Management at the Georgia Institute of Technology. His research interests include withholding effort in organizations, work group performance, and hierarchical modeling of behavior in organizations. His research has appeared in the *Journal of Applied Psychology, Academy of Management Journal, Academy of Management Review*, and *Journal of Management.*

Rebecca J. Bennett is Associate Professor in the College of Administration and Business at Louisiana Tech University. She was formerly a member of the management faculty at the University of Toledo, where she was associate director of the Family Business Center. She holds an M.S. and a Ph.D. in organizational behavior from Northwestern University. Her primary research interests include employee deviance and revenge and forgiveness in the workplace.

Robert J. Bies is Professor of Management in the McDonough School of Business at Georgetown University. He received his M.B.A. from the University of Washington and his Ph.D. in organizational behavior from Stanford University. His primary research interests are organizational justice, workplace revenge and forgiveness, and the delivery of bad news.

Michael E. Brown is Assistant Professor of Management in the Sam and Irene Black School of Business at Pennsylvania State University–Erie. He holds an M.B.A. from the University of Texas at Austin and a Ph.D. in management from the Pennsylvania State University. His primary research interests include ethics and leadership.

Julie Ann Cogin is Lecturer in the M.B.A. and M.B.A. Executive programs at the Australian Graduate School of Management, where she teaches the core subject, organizational behavior, in addition to managing people and organizations, managerial skills, and change management. She holds a Ph.D. from Charles Sturt University in Australia. Prior to her academic life, she was a human resources manager at Qantas Airways, working in recruitment and selection, performance management, culture adjustment, process improvement, equal employment opportunity, and occupational safety and health.

Debra R. Comer is Professor of Management in the Zarb School of Business at Hofstra University. She earned her M.A., M.Phil., and Ph.D. in organizational behavior from Yale University. She has published articles on organizational socialization, social loafing, workplace diversity programs, and employees' attitudes toward drug and fitness-for-duty testing. Many of her publications and current projects involve the use of literature and experiential exercises to teach management and ethics.

Scott C. Douglas is Assistant Professor of Management in the School of Management at Binghamton University. He received his Ph.D. from Florida State University. His current research interests are in the areas of attributional processes, decision making, and antisocial behavior.

Jennifer Dunn is a doctoral candidate in operations and information management in the Wharton School at the University of Pennsylvania. She holds an M.S. in industrial engineering from the University of Michigan. Her research interests involve the role of emotion in social judgments and behavior, including trust, reputation, negotiation, and ethical decision making.

Alan J. Fish is Associate Professor in Human Resources Management at Charles Sturt University in Australia. He holds a Ph.D. in international human resources management from the University of Sydney. His research interests are in cross-border management, international human resources management, and the more strategic use of cross-border assignments to enhance business growth and development and management careers. His current research project is titled "Behavioural Fit: Identifying, Selecting, and Deploying Cross-Border Managers."

Jerald Greenberg is Abramowitz Professor of Business Ethics and Professor of Organizational Behavior in the Fisher College of Business at the Ohio State University. He has published extensively in the fields of organizational justice and employee deviance, and he has won numerous awards for his research. He also has authored or edited numerous books, including *The Quest for Justice on the Job, Advances in Organizational Justice,* and *Behavior in Organizations.* He holds fellow status in the Academy of Management, the American Psychological Association, and the Society for Industrial and Organizational Psychology.

Steven L. Grover is Professor of Management at the University of Otago in New Zealand. He has published widely in the leading management journals, and his research specialty examines the conditions under which people lie or tell the truth. He has recently embarked on a program to investigate leadership integrity, that is, the honesty and consistency exhibited by leaders. Before permanently joining the University of Otago in 2002, he held appointments at Indiana University and Georgia State University. He earned his Ph.D. from Columbia University.

Paul Harvey is a doctoral candidate at Florida State University. He holds an M.B.A. from the State University of New York at Binghamton. His research interests include the influence of cultural factors on cognitive processes such as attributions and other perceptions. He teaches in the area of organizational behavior and has private sector experience working in manufacturing finance.

Timothy O. Ireland is Associate Professor and Chair of the Department of Criminal Justice at Niagara University. He holds a Ph.D. in criminal justice from the University at Albany. He conducts research in the areas of child maltreatment, violence in public housing, and theory development in criminology as well as drug treatment as an alternative to prison. He has published in journals on criminology, psychology, and drug/alcohol use.

Joanne Jones is a doctoral candidate in accounting in the Schulich School of Business at York University. Her research interests include professional ethics, cross-national ethics, and trust. She is currently involved in dissertation research on trust in the auditor–client relationship and its implications for professional skepticism. She has published in the *Journal of Accounting Literature* and *Business Ethics Quarterly* (2004).

Charles Joseph is a research assistant and doctoral candidate in the School of Management at Binghamton University. His current research interests are in the areas of conflict management, attribution theory, and antisocial behavior.

Anita Mancuso is a detective constable with the Toronto Police Service, where she has been employed since 1988. She holds an M.S. in criminal justice from Niagara University. Her work experience and academic studies have focused on undercover operations and the operatives on which they depend.

Mark J. Martinko is the Bank of America Professor of Management in the College of Business at Florida State University. His research focuses on attribution theory and leadership. He has authored or coauthored 7 books and more than 80 articles and book chapters. He is a past president and fellow of the Southern Management Association. His most recent book is *Thinking Like a Winner: A Guide to High Performance Leadership* (2002).

Stefanie E. Naumann is Assistant Professor of Management and Organizational Behavior in the Eberhardt School of Business at the University of the Pacific. Her research interests include employee fairness perceptions, helping behaviors, and work group climates. Her research has appeared in the *Academy of Management Journal, Journal of Organizational Behavior*, and *Journal of Applied Psychology*.

Paul M. Roman is Director of the Center for Research on Behavioral Health and Human Services Delivery in the Institute for Behavioral Research at the University of Georgia, where he is a tenured professor in the Department of Sociology and the Graduate School. He received his Ph.D. from Cornell University. He has been awarded three consecutive 5-year terms as Distinguished Research Professor. His research focuses on organization and management of treatment systems, design of intervention efforts to deal with employees with substance abuse problems, and the sociological analysis of substance abuse problems and policies. His recent publications include four edited volumes of original articles and chapters: *Encyclopedia of Criminology and Deviant Behavior* (Vol. 4), *Self-Destructive Behavior and Disvalued Identity, Drug Testing in the Workplace,* and *Alcohol Problem Intervention in the Workplace: Employee Assistance Programs and Strategic Alternatives.*

Maurice E. Schweitzer is Assistant Professor of Operations and Information Management in the Wharton School at the University of Pennsylvania. He is interested in the negotiation process, and much of his work focuses on deception and trust. His work has appeared in journals such as the *Journal of Risk and Uncertainty, Organizational Behavior and Human Decision Processes, Management Science, Journal of Applied Social Psychology,* and *Academy of Management Journal.* He serves on the editorial boards of the *International Journal of Conflict Management* and *Organizational Behavior and Human Decision Processes.*

Jay Scouten is pursuing his medical degree at the Medical College of Ohio. He received his M.B.A. from University of Toledo. He belongs to the second generation of his family's business and drives a red sports car.

Skye Susans is a doctoral candidate in the Faculty of Commerce at Charles Sturt University in Australia. She is a registered nurse with postgraduate qualification in intensive care. She also holds an M.S. in management from the University of Technology in Australia. She has a background in health care management and is currently a "trailing spouse" with research interests in the preparation and adjustment of the trailing spouse.

Stefan Thau is a doctoral candidate in the Interuniversity Centre of Social Science Theory and Methodology (ICS) at the University of Groningen in The Netherlands. He holds an M.A. in social psychology from the University of Mannheim in Germany. His main research interest is the impact of social networks on employee cooperation.

Linda Thorne is Associate Professor of Accounting in the Schulich School of Business at York University. She received her Ph.D. in 1997 from McGill University. Her research interests include professional ethics, emotion and ethics, and cross-national ethics. She has published numerous articles in various journals, including the *Journal of Business Ethics, Contemporary Accounting Research, Behavioral Research in Accounting, Journal of Accounting Education, Research on Accounting Ethics,* and *Audit: A Journal of Practice and Theory.*

Edward C. Tomlinson is a member of the Management Faculty in the Boler School of Business at John Carroll University. He holds an M.B.A. from Lynchburg College as well as a masters in labor and human resources and a Ph.D. in organizational behavior from the Ohio State University. His primary research interests include the role of trust in professional relationships, negotiation and dispute resolution, and employee deviance.

Linda Klebe Treviño is Professor of Organizational Behavior, Franklin H. Cook Fellow in Business Ethics, and Director of the Shoemaker Program in Business Ethics in the Smeal College of Business Administration at the Pennsylvania State University. She holds a Ph.D. in management from Texas A&M University. Her research focuses on the management of ethics in organizations and has received multiple awards. She has published numerous articles in top journals. She has also coauthored a textbook titled *Managing Business Ethics: Straight Talk About How to*

Do It Right (now in its third edition) and an academic book titled *Managing Ethics in Business Organizations: Social Scientific Perspectives.*

Thomas M. Tripp is a member of the Management and Decision Sciences faculty at Washington State University and Director of Business Programs at its Vancouver campus. He holds a Ph.D. in organization behavior from Northwestern University. His primary research interests are organizational justice, workplace revenge, and forgiveness.

Gina Vega is Associate Professor of Management at the Francis E. Girard School of Business and International Commerce at Merrimack College. She holds a Ph.D. in organizational behavior and entrepreneurship from the Union Institute. She has written extensively in the areas of business ethics, small business management, and the management of telework. She has authored numerous scholarly articles and two books: *A Passion for Planning* and *Managing Teleworkers and Telecommuting Strategies.*

Danielle E. Warren is Assistant Professor at Rutgers University. She received her Ph.D. from the Wharton School at the University of Pennsylvania. Her research is in the areas of organizational behavior and business ethics. Her specific research interests include norms, sanctions, and constructive and destructive deviance in the workplace.